Media and Sovereignty

Media and Sovereignty

The Global Information Revolution and Its Challenge to State Power

Monroe E. Price

The MIT Press
Cambridge, Massachusetts
London, England

This book was set in Sabon by SNP Best-set Typesetter Ltd., Hong Kong

Printed and bound in the United States of America.

Library of Congress Cataloging-in-Publication Data

Price, Monroe Edwin, 1938–
    Media and sovereignty : the global information revolution and its challenge to state power / Monroe E. Price.
        p. cm.
    Includes bibliographical references and index.
    ISBN 0-262-16211-3 (alk. paper)
    1. Mass media—Law and legislation. 2. Government information. 3. Freedom of information. 4. Sovereignty. 5. Globalization. I. Title.

K4240 .P75   2002
343.09′0—dc21   2002024616

Contents

Acknowledgments

In writing this book, I have had support from a variety of institutions and many friends around the world. During the recent past, this support has rested on backing at my principal academic homes: the Benjamin N. Cardozo School of Law of Yeshiva University in New York and the Programme in Comparative Media Law and Policy (PCMLP) at Oxford University's Centre for Socio-Legal Studies. At Cardozo, I was a beneficiary of the Jacob Burns Institute for Advanced Legal Studies and the Howard M. Squadron Program in Law, Media, and Society. Since the second half of the 1990s, I had the good fortune to be a Communications Fellow of The Markle Foundation, a Fellow of the Media Studies Center of the Freedom Forum, a resident at the Rockefeller Foundation's Bellagio Conference Center, and a Member of the School of Social Science at the Institute for Advanced Study in Princeton, New Jersey. The hospitality of each was vital to the outcome of the book. I want to acknowledge especially the support, over an extended period of time, of The Markle Foundation. It was Lloyd Morrisset and Zoë Baird, Presidents of the Foundation, and Edith Bjornson, then Senior Program Officer there, whose loyalty and vision allowed the Oxford Programme to begin and to serve as a platform for this work.

Stefaan Verhulst, who founded the Oxford Programme and was its leader for four very fruitful years, was a constant friend, a never-ending source of information, partner in writing, and an able and resourceful ally throughout. At Cardozo, the administration of the Law School, including the support of Professor Michael Herz, Senior Associate Dean, and Dean Paul Verkuil, was especially important. Cardozo's Howard M. Squadron Program in Media, Law, and Society also provided necessary support.

A number of other readers commented and contributed to the manuscript. Bethany Davis Noll, as thoughtful editor, composer of charts, and brilliant manager, was indispensable in bringing the manuscript to final publication (juggling it with many other significant projects for the Oxford Programme). She was a trusted reader, an extraordinary researcher, and a reliable force to assure completion. Stacy Sullivan, my research assistant at the Media Studies Center, is owed a great debt for her excellent journalistic work in piecing together the story of the seizure of transmitters in Republika Srpska. Eric Blinderman, who wrote an important thesis in information intervention at Oxford, also worked on this material. Dr. Beata Rozumilowicz, as a researcher at the PCMLP, allowed me to draw from our collaborative work on media in transition societies. Roxanna Nazari, then a student at Cornell Law School, wrote a research paper on the history of illegal and harmful content statutes that was an important source for chapter 5. Melissa Mathis, as an officer of The Cardozo Law Review, edited a version of chapter 6. Two particularly helpful students at the Yale Law School, where I taught a course in the spring of 2000, were Barton Beebe and Daphne H. T. P. Keller. Michael Likosky contributed significantly to the research on Radio Free Asia in chapter 8. Lillian Choi, Joseph Perkovich, Milan Milenkovic, and Jessica Stalnaker, all, at times at the Oxford Programme, made contributions. Kenneth Donow, Research Analyst at the International Broadcasting Bureau, was a thoughtful, generous and critical interlocutor on questions of satellite policy and international broadcasting. Alan Heil, a retired executive at the Voice of America also was instrumental in shaping my views on the subject. A lecture tour of India in 1999, on the subject of media globalization, sponsored by the United States Information Agency (USIA), also helped to shape my ideas.

I gave part of chapter 1 as the annual Socio-Legal Lecture at the Centre for Socio-Legal Studies, at Oxford, thanks to Professor Denis Galligan, its director. That talk helped lead to the development of the PCMLP at the Centre and to this book. Part of chapter 4 appeared, in another version, in an essay in *Public Culture* and benefited from comments by Gerry Oberst and Philip Spector. Chapter 7, in an early form, was the John D. Evans Lecture on the Social Consequences of New Media Technology at the University of Michigan, delivered at the kind invitation of Michael Traugott, Chair of Communications Studies at the College of Literature, Science, and the Arts. My initial thinking on privatization was formed in a lecture given in Mexico City at a Conference on the Future of Broadcasting at the IberoAmerican University. The research on self-regulation, done in collaboration with Stefaan Verhulst, was at the behest of the Bertelsmann Foundation. Work on an "enabling environment" for free media in transition societies was supported by funds from USAID, and evolved from conversations with Ann Hudock, then a Democracy Fellow at the Agency. Gary Hansen and David Black were also encouraging of research and writing in this area. Peter Krug and I collaborated in writing a study on the enabling environment that was distributed by USAID to its officers and to nongovernment organizations. Students at Cornell Law School, including editors at the *Cornell Journal of International Law*, assisted in editing a portion of chapter 7. I gave a version of chapter 9 at the Institute for Advanced Study's closing conference on Information Technology and Society. It was my good fortune to have, as a commentator for the work, Professor Clifford Geertz.

In addition to those mentioned above, a few people made overarching contributions to the book. Professors Larry Lessig and C. Edwin Baker and Marc Raboy, through their own scholarship, have been extremely helpful. Other scholars, including Joshua M. Price, Vivian Price, Julie Mertus, Neil Netanel, and Jamie Frederic Metzl, were also influential through their work and their useful comments. I have profited from ongoing conversations with Eric Johnson of Internews and Andrei Richter, the director of the Media Law and Policy Center at Moscow State University. Asa Briggs, the great broadcast historian, has been, since my early days as a member of the International Broadcasting Institute, an inspiration. Aimée Brown Price not only set an estimable scholarly standard but accompanied me through much of the global trajectory that made writing this book possible. I want to single out as an immense resource, critical to my research, the work of BBC Monitoring in Cavesham Park, Reading, in gathering information on broadcasting developments throughout the world and making the material accessible to scholars in a useful form. Studying the output of these dedicated BBC analysts over the last decade has been one of the best tutorials imaginable.

I

Remapping Media Space

1

New Role of the State

New technologies, political upheavals, changed concepts of human rights—all these conspire to make this an important moment for rethinking and reformulating speech freedom and regulation in a global environment. The ability of any state fully to control the images that permeate its territory is questioned everywhere.[1] During the 1990s, destiny seemed to lie with the freedom to receive and impart ideas regardless of national boundaries. But it would be naïve to see the world as a place where information moves without various forms of restriction. Redefined state power and changes in modes and practices of authority are more likely than what is often characterized as state decline. States have undergone a frenzied testing of new and modified techniques aimed at regulating, if not mastering, the market for speech in response to the forces that seem to undercut their autonomy. Many elements are at work in this experimentation and redefinition by the state, and elaboration of them forms the substance of this book. In particular, there is a shift away from the singularly inward forms of state control to outward-looking, regional, or multilateral approaches, and away from law and regulation toward negotiation and agreement. The tentacles of influence by one state over the media of another are hardly new, but the process of interaction, through treaty or agreement on the flow of ideas, information, and sheer data, is every day, intensifying.

Globalization of media encompasses more than the pervasive activities of big conglomerates and the extent to which messages they produce dominate the world's consciousness. The global media market is far more enveloping than a forum for trade in films and television programs. It is also an increasingly interdependent site for the development and application of formal and informal rules that shape common narratives, a space in which ideologies compete and forge allegiances that ultimately determine the persistence of governments and nations themselves, and an arena where imagery becomes a supplement or substitute for force. Pressure to affect policy formulation and public opinion abroad has always been a preoccupation of those holding or seeking power as governments attempt to influence populations through propaganda, both inside and beyond their boundaries.[2] With the stakes greatly raised since September 11, 2001, governments, more explicit, now, about the interplay between conflict, instability, and ideology, recognize their need to affect hearts and minds abroad.

It suddenly became obvious, in the "war against terrorism," as in many preceding wars, that public opinion was a significant front and space for engagement. In the early days of US flights over Afghanistan, bombers destroyed local radio transmitters and replaced Radio Shari'ah with US programming. Reflecting a preoccupation with hostile attitudes across the world, Congress hastened to confirm Charlotte Beers, a veteran of the advertising industry, as under secretary for public diplomacy hoping to achieve more aggressively favorable US images abroad. In a moment of exasperation, Congressman Henry Hyde summarized the feeling of many: "How is it that the country that invented Hollywood and Madison Avenue has such trouble promoting a positive image of itself overseas?"[3]

In this interdependent environment, the definition of speech practices within states and how information technologies evolve within their boundaries is no longer left wholly to the states themselves. Evolution of local systems is an essential part of the global infrastructure. Decisions involving a state's information space have external ramifications for trade and global security.

International attention is sharpened as governments become obsessed with the power of information, both as an attribute of domination and wealth creation in times of peace and as a weapon in times of war. Thus, though states still legislate individually to maintain their cultural identity, the significance of what they do is increasingly becoming subject to international incentives, pressures, and obligations.

The world is engaged in a vast remapping of the relationship of the state to images, messages, and information within its boundaries. National governments, public international agencies, multinational corporations, human rights organizations, and individuals are involved in this process. All is under construction, yielding a thorough shaking and remodeling of communications systems.

Thirty years ago, cable television sparked transformations; twenty years ago the communications satellite did the same. In the last ten years the Internet and the convergence of new technologies have invited wholesale restructuring. In this teeming experiment, the various players and observers are seeking a vocabulary of change and a set of laws and institutions that provide them with legitimacy, continued power, or the opportunity to profit from technological advantage. There is a need to examine this process of remapping from different perspectives and provide a framework for understanding its background, mechanisms, and prospects. Only with a grasp of the massive changes taking place can implications for cultural and political change, for human rights debates, and for the shape and functioning of governments be understood in a sophisticated and detailed way. In the chapters that follow, I set the groundwork for a systematic approach to issues of media regulation in a world of changing technology, altered corporate arrangements, and shifting ideologies.

In this chapter, I describe tones of global media reorientation, the constellations of change that occur as geopolitical, ideological, and technological transformations interact. In chapter 2, I set forth several analytic theories that might be used to explain shifts in state strategies.

In part II, chapters 3 to 6, I analyze tropes of restructuring in this global framework: not only the use of models and metaphors, but the significance of specific themes and influences such as privatization, self-regulation, national security and control of offensive content. I explore new categories of thinking about the relationship of the state to its media, in the face of the inevitable persistence of older modes of description and analysis. I deal with the language of change, the exterior housing in which state and non-state actors articulate and reformulate doctrine with respect to wildly varied contexts for the adaptation of information technologies.

In part III, I try to piece together what elements exist of a more or less coherent foreign policy, especially at a time of heightened security concerns, toward media globalization. Finally, I bring these various influences and actions together by redefining and categorizing national responses to new information technologies. The task is to pull explanatory factors apart and, by doing so, see their interconnectedness.

Interactions and Influence

It is helpful to turn to the anecdotal: epiphenomena of the complex contemporary formation of information policy and law by the extension of government interest outside its boundaries. Examples of such actions or efforts to act, in the day-to-day life of the world, are extraordinarily rich and varied. Those concerning the United States are legion.

I take only one of many examples from post–September 11 events. In the opening days of the war in Afghanistan, Secretary of State Colin Powell called the Emir of Qatar seeking his cooperation in moderating the views of Al Jazeera, the now-famous satellite service with an important demographic of Arab viewers. Prior to the events of September 11, 2001, Al Jazeera had been proclaimed a beacon of diversity and openness in a sea of state-dominated Middle Eastern Media. After September 11, its programming, reach, and effectiveness were viewed by many in the US government as inimical to its campaign against terrorism. Its service as a platform for Osama bin Laden videotapes was a cause for enormous concern in the United States. After persistent efforts to persuade the satellite service to refrain from airing the videotapes, a second approach was tried, one that offered US officials for interviews on Al Jazeera. The State Department then studied the possibility of purchasing air time on Al Jazeera for advertisements that would help in the redefinition of the United States in the minds of the satellite channel's broad-ranging and critical audience.[4] Finally there were efforts to consider supporting competitors to Al Jazeera, either by providing modes of financial support for other, possibly blander, satellite services that might draw audiences away from Al Jazeera or by establishing, through the US international broadcasting structures, a service that itself would compete for attention and viewership among those the United States sought to influence. The Al Jazeera story serves as a case study for the ways governments attempt to modify infrastructure and the market in order to influence message.

Throughout time, the instances of US interest in foreign media structures has been frequent. Among other the examples, in the 1990s the US ambassador to India attempted, on behalf of US business interests, to discourage Indian broadcast reform legislation that would severely restrict US foreign investment or ownership in the sector. The Office of Trade Representative wrote the chair of the Federal Communications Commission to further a policy preventing the use of Canadian satellites to deliver signals to US audiences so long as Canada prevented the use of US satellites for Canadian audiences within its borders. When Liberia forbade local radio stations to retransmit Voice of America programming, US officials protested.

In the late 1990s the US Ambassador in the Czech Republic intervened with Czech authorities in a legal struggle between US investors in a private station and their former Czech partners. Also in Prague, American officials encouraged the Czech government to seek postponement of European program quota requirements (because of their potential impact on US exports) that would otherwise be imposed as a condition for Czech accession to the European Union.

Striving to isolate the then–Serbian leader, Slobodan Milosevic, the United States urged Israel to eliminate a Yugoslav channel from a transponder on an Israeli satellite system. In 1997 the United States petitioned Australia to lease an Australian transmitter for sending Radio Free Asia signals to Vietnam; however, Australia refused due to "foreign policy and technical considerations."[5]

These are almost random examples of US efforts to affect media structures outside its borders. A similar list can easily be compiled for other countries. When the government of Angola determined that it was not obligated, under the Lusaka Protocol (which provisionally resolved aspects of its civil war), to allow the United Nations to set up a shortwave radio station designed to increase pluralism in Angola, foreign policy issues came into play.[6] Greek state radio established a nine-language program for foreign workers in Greece, partly to compete with messages sent to the same workers from their countries of origin.[7] When Turkey acted to keep what its government called "reactionary broadcasts" off the air, a head of its Supreme Radio and Television Board recognized that "silencing" a station meant that the affected parties would "complain to Europe."[8] The Organization of Security and Cooperation in Europe (OSCE) sent delegations to Slovakia to help ensure that Slovakia's media law did not contain language provisions that discriminated against native Hungarian speakers. One goal was to lessen or prevent tension in the region and another was to ensure that European standards were approximated.[9]

The consequences of the change in governance in Hong Kong in 1997 is a useful instance of media decisions that were once purely domestic, but now have international implications.[10] The new authorities announced that Radio Television Hong Kong (RTHK) should not retransmit BBC programs critical of the Special Administrative Region government. "The handover has brought an end to Britain's power," the statement argued. "Why does the BBC still have a 'colony' in the radio, to give expression to Britain's political intention, making irresponsible remarks on and flagrantly interfering in Hong Kong's political affairs?" Officials stated:

Hong Kong has returned to Chinese sovereignty, but radio and departmental-level officials still want to maintain the BBC's relaying slot and interpret the practice as 'editorial independence.' This runs counter to autonomy and legal principles. ... Which government-operated radio in the world has provided a slot for a state-owned radio of a foreign country and relayed its political programmes as they were, while these programmes attacked the elections prescribed by the constitution of the country concerned?

Regulation of Russian media in their attempts to reach ethnic Russians in the now-independent states of the former Soviet Union also carries foreign policy implications. Many decisions concerning Russia's television networks are of continued interest for the "near abroad," and government decisions in other newly independent states which appear "local" or domestic in impact can be construed to have strategic implications for the relationship with Russia. A 1998 article in *Nezavisimaya Gazeta*, about moves against Russian media in the former Soviet Union, reported:

With the creation of the Commonwealth of Independent States . . . it was contemplated that the information relations and cultural cooperation that had taken shape over decades would remain and develop successfully. But unfortunately, . . . following the sovereignty parade . . . relations in the sphere of the exchange of information are weakening from year to year.[11]

In the 1990s Ukraine demonstrated a marked dislike for Russian media within its borders. Officials were reported to desire a ban on Russian newspapers and to have protested a Russian television report on weather conditions in Ukraine as "interference in Ukrainian affairs."[12] In Kazakhstan, the national leadership decided to switch its own television channel distribution to the Intelsat satellite system instead of Gorizont, partly to impede reception of Russian programs. Kazakhstan, like other post-Soviet states, adopted language laws that favored non-Russian speakers, furthering an exodus of the Russian language population. Decisions in Kazakhstan, Ukraine, and elsewhere that reduced or cut off transmission of Russian television led to street demonstrations by Russian nationals who argued that they were the subject of cultural and language discrimination. In Uzbekistan, relay of Russian stations to domestic radio-receiving stations was terminated. In Georgia, a ban on advertising on foreign TV channels was perceived as directly antagonistic to Russian channels.[13] The Discovery Channel replaced one such starved-out Russian channel, NTV, on cable systems. Throughout the zone, domestic decisions for restructuring the media were closely tied to implications for relations with Russia.

During the Serbian conflict over Kosovo in 1999, Serbia banned the rebroadcasting of foreign services like RFE/RL or the Voice of America. According to then–Information Minister Aleksandar Vucic, the services "aim[ed] to spread fear, panic, or defeatism" within the former Republic of Yugoslavia. Vucic saw the ban as "a way to prevent the psychological propaganda war which foreign countries have waged against us by broadcasting their programmes on domestic radio and TV stations or by directly or indirectly influencing the editorial concepts of media companies." Vucic said that if any station or other medium acted contrary to the preservation of the territorial integrity, sovereignty, and independence of Serbia, it would be warned and then seized by the Information Ministry. "This has nothing to do with the freedom of the press because they are not spreading information, but conducting a propaganda war against our country on behalf of their governments."[14]

An example from the Koreas, prior to rapprochement, provides an additional perspective.[15] North and South Korea, long engaged in image-related maneuvers designed to shape attitudes toward an adversary and each other, sought to maintain control of their own information space. In October 1999 the South Korean Ministry of Unification issued a communiqué about North Korean Television occasioned by the greater availability of its signals.

The document is an exemplar in the legal history of transnational satellite regulation, though it is of minor political significance. The communiqué illustrates the measured use of public regulation as a response to messages from abroad and the subtle workings of government in a contested market for loyalties. The Ministry of Unification favored exposure of the North Korean signal, on the reasoning that opening South Korea to broadcasts from Pyongyang would "promote the South Korean people's understanding of the true conditions in North Korea, enhance their capacity to assess the falsehood of the North Korean system," and contribute to restoring national homogeneity through "knowing North Korea properly."

In a way, the inevitable accessibility of South Korean information space meant that fashioning a guarded opening was a better strategy than pretending that the South Korean public could not observe North Korean television. The document could be interpreted as evidence that few states are capable of screening out powerful and desirable satellite signals and that it was better to take credit for promoting speech than to appear overly restrictive. On the other hand, one could interpret the communiqué as evidence that states believe that they can decide, spoonful by spoonful, how information will be introduced into the society. In the case of South Korea's action, the opening was an aspiration of control. It occurred four months after a North Korean satellite signal had been launched capable of transmitting signals that could be picked up by anyone in South Korea and redistributed by cable or other means. Under the newly enunciated approach, South Korean broadcasting stations would be permitted to receive the satellite signal and use excerpts in their news and other programs. Such uses were a dispensation. Until the communiqué, video clips from North Korean television were only available through specific distribution by the South Korean government and were to be shown only in government-determined "unification-related" programs.

Now, "self-regulation," undergirded by state policy would determine when South Korean broadcasters could show such excerpts. Broadcasters were exhorted to limit the use of the signals to those contexts that "endeavour to provide grounds for restoring a sense of national homogeneity, national reconciliation, and a proper understanding of the actual situation in North Korea." Stations were also advised "to provide sufficient commentary" so that the contents of the North Korean broadcasts would not "create confusion in the public's awareness about North Korea." These were rules for broadcasters, not for citizens. For individuals, an even narrower kind of peephole liberalization was provided. South Korean citizens could watch the satellite signal (when not mediated through stations), only at specially approved sites, typically called Unification Training Centers. Limitations on direct viewing by citizens were justified as part of a gradual, step-by-step opening to North Korean broadcasts.

Neither the United States nor other developed countries put pressure on the South Korean government at the time to allow greater access to information from the North. To the extent that the West and South Korea were, together, part of a cartel of the imaginary, they had an interest, prior to the active process of normalization, in limiting access by North Korea to a potentially sensitive citizenry in the South. Access would be increased as part of the process of unification, with each droplet of received information considered a bargaining chip for altering the mix of information in the North. Geopolitical factors, not the competition of the private against the public, decide these questions, while technology, in the form of satellite signals, triggers the tepid opening. Technology seems capable of causing a redefinition in the law, a rechanneling of information, and a redefinition of who is the gatekeeper and what standards that gatekeeper should follow.

Canada is a well-examined case where national media policy has had a consistent dimension of international concern (primarily an understandable preoccupation with images coming from the United States). In the early 1960s Graham Spry wrote of the evolution of the Canadian system into one where the Canadian Broadcasting Corporation (CBC), the national public service broadcaster, was "outflanked, surrounded, and hemmed in to a subordinate place in the structure of Canadian broadcasting."[16] As private broadcasting established its strength, Spry could describe the combination of messages as a "predominantly commercial system used to sell goods, most of them American."[17] In its 1971 policy statement on cable television, the Canadian Radio and Telecommunications Commission (CRTC) recognized the need for a stronger program production industry in order to keep Canadian broadcasting from being reduced to "a technically sophisticated distribution system for imported programs." One noted Canadian communications scholar, Marc Raboy, underscored the need for an industrial policy. "The creative development and perpetuation of a Canadian program production industry is mandatory if Canada is to survive as a culturally autonomous nation."[18]

Throughout the period of technological transformation from broadcasting to cable television, the principal task of the CRTC was to improve the ratio of Canadian to US programs. One technique was to reduce the incentives to cable operators for carrying US stations by requiring that Canadian commercials be substituted for those that had been placed by the originating US broadcasters. The CRTC suggested amendments to the Income Tax Act to favor Canadian advertisers using Canadian stations and attempted to require cable systems to carry all local Canadian stations, all regional Canadian stations, distant Canadian stations, and other Canadian options before carrying those from the United States.

The CRTC also established rules that limited importing US cable channels into Canada where there was a Canadian alternative. A famous application of this policy occurred when a Canadian entrepreneur, recognizing the opportunity presented by the preference, approached US-based Country Music Television and demanded a share of the channel against the threat to establish a local preemptive competitor. Upon their refusal, he established a competing Canadian country music channel, though one that performed mainly US music. The CRTC ordered the US channel removed even though it had been in the market for a decade.[19]

The Canadian regulatory regime, like those in many other states, used ownership rules presumably to affect content. Canadian policies established in 1988 prohibited foreign takeovers of Canadian-owned film distribution firms unless the investor undertook to reinvest a portion of its Canadian earnings, usually up to 10 percent of gross revenues. Foreign investors were permitted to establish new distribution firms for their proprietary products only. The 1994 decision of Investment Canada to allow Viacom to acquire indirectly all of the Canadian interests of Paramount Communications, Inc as part of its general acquisition of the parent was an example of negotiation for cultural enhancement. Viacom, as a condition for the approval, agreed to provide international distribution of at least four Canadian feature films of suitable commercial quality within the following five years.[20]

The effort that Malaysia has put into the process of establishing "technologies of boundary" is also an important example of national response. Direct-to-home satellite broadcasting was, prior to the Internet era, always thought the greatest threat. As late as 1994, only the prime minister, the minister of information, and Malaysia's nine hereditary rulers were allowed to receive satellite television. In a further liberalization, hotels with ratings of three star and above could gain satellite television delivery of CNN.[21] When Malaysia finally authorized more general availability for satellite broadcasting, delivery was vested in a favored private monopoly provider, Malaysia-EastAsia Satellite (MEASAT). The population could only use parabolic dishes with a diameter of less than two feet, dishes designed only for the reception of signals from MEASAT's satellite. Under Malaysian legislation, adopted in October 1996, larger dishes, or dishes that were not licensed, became illegal and would have to be dismantled. As the information minister at the time, Mohamed Rahmat, said, "We will open our sky, but just a little with the use of the specific satellite dish. . . . We can ill-afford the influx of foreign elements which could be detrimental to our efforts in nation-building."[22] MEASAT allowed "the authorities to better manage the new services . . . preventing the influx of negative elements into the country."

Malaysia required that all programming distributed by the MEASAT satellite to its population be uplinked from Malaysia. The physical custody of a point of origin provides an opportunity to review signals for content-related violations. There has been, apparently, a great viewing center, with 1,000 workers, watching every program as it is dispatched from earth to one of MEASAT's transponders.[23] India, too, in its 1997 draft-broadcasting bill, had an uplinking requirement. For international channels with central headquarters in important production centers, this might mean sending a program stream by satellite from Taiwan or Hong Kong to India or Malaysia, downlinking it there, and uplinking it again to the satellite that will distribute the programming to the ultimate consumer.

Constellations of Change

Media structures, laws, and policies are scarcely ever modified to find a more beautiful form, or even to develop a more efficient way to achieve commonly agreed-upon goals. Changes in structure, including changes in law, occur because of pressure from within industry, the society, and the government, from within or without the state. As the twenty-first century opened, the global struggle against terrorism seemed to lead to new forms of dependence between media and government, and as a consequence, toleration of even greater tendencies to monopoly. Even before the implications of national security had set in, mergers of extraordinary size caused many to wonder what new form of competition would develop in the zone of media and communications and whether residual ideas of social responsibilities for media could be realistically maintained.[24] In Europe and elsewhere, the long-standing tradition and privileged status of public service broadcasters was in decline.[25] Across the former Soviet Union, in India, Indonesia, and elsewhere, communications laws and policies were developed with new purposes and a new rhetoric to accompany them.[26] As the very structure of the communications industry worldwide was being reformulated, agencies, national and international, charged with management and regulation of the sector, were under pressure to review and alter policies in accord with deemed global transformations.

In each national case there were local reasons for change and local differences in implementation of changes. But from the whole, themes emerge, possibilities for identifying large causes and patterns in this reordering of the relationship between the means of communication and the state. A great global communications system is being built (or rebuilt). Because its contours are important for the fundamentals of national identity, for trade, and the world political order, the shaping of it is a matter not only of domestic preference but also of international debate and foreign policy.

There are those who see the process as technologically determined, inevitable, and inexorable, the product of innovation fueled by the energy of capitalism.[27] A geopolitical perspective sees media reform as an instrument that follows and affects shifting balances of power.[28] Altered relationships between United States and Iran, between India and Pakistan, or between Russia and any of its former affiliated republics, or rapprochement between South and North Korea—each has its media policy consequences.[29] A modified version of the school of cultural imperialism may attribute legal transformations to the engulfing nature of international trade in imagery. Change can be understood as an adjustment to or reaction against an outside wave of programs and information. Still another perspective might attribute transformations in selected media structures to altered ideologies of freedom of speech, human rights, and the democratization of authoritarian and totalitarian regimes. None of these perspectives—of technological or geopolitical determinism or the influence of trade and ideology—is alone sufficient to explain the global reshaping of media structures. Together, in varying ratios and various settings, they explain a great deal.

Looking across the dark, initially undifferentiated sky of media transformations, various distinct constellations begin to emerge. Think of the post-Soviet transitions. A rhythm developed between the ideological and the actual, the motivation and the realization.[30] The impetus for change in media laws and structures in these states followed a stated shift in ideology, but almost from the outset, ideological motivations gave way to the intensely political. In virtually every of the post-Soviet polities, from Latvia and Lithuania, south to the Balkans, and across to Central Asia, remapping began with the old monopoly state broadcaster.[31] Almost everywhere new governments sought succor in the old monopoly, though their hold on the ancient ways had to be cushioned in a new rhetoric. In many of these societies, there were questions about whether the media, rising from the shards of history, could contribute to the enhancement of democratic processes. It was a puzzle how a stable set of young media institutions could develop without an effective rule of law and absent the economic underpinning for independence. Corruption too was endemic, especially as those who received valuable licenses during privatization and those in power became closely intertwined.

Another constellation of change, as stark in distinction as can be imagined, has been the transformation of information space in Western Europe. There, it is not ideology but technology, not the dissolution of the state but adjustments between the European Union and its members and issues like concentration and ownership that have sparked change.[32] Mutation there initially concerned itself only indirectly with media as a force that underwrites or alters modes of democratic practice. As the commitment to public service broadcasting flagged, there were rhetorical flourishes of support but unenthusiastic budgets to achieve them.[33] In these highly developed societies, transformations occur with the industrial expansion of information flows. The transformations are dramatic, with a new generation of corporate scale far transcending the pace of change of ten years earlier. While the collapse of the Soviet Union brought about, in essence, the sundering of its vast information space, in Europe the project has been to create a newly unified field of imagery, even if it was largely commercial in nature. The adoption of the Television without Frontiers Directive of 1989 was the beginning of a rigorous effort to create transnational broadcasting regulation.[34]

What had been a political and economic aim in the European Union, namely to remove restrictions to the delivery of services, including information services, was facilitated by the onrush of technology that made such delivery cheaper and virtually unblockable. Change and remapping information space is, in this context, an overwhelming and expansive undertaking. It is an enterprise of financial institutions, technical experts, and powerful industries, together enlarging their economic sway. In the states of Europe and the United States, convergence is the hallmark—convergence not only of varying technologies but also of public service broadcaster with the private, and of information with consumption.[35] The remapping of media is supposed to transform politics to e-democracy, government to e-government, business to e-commerce and beyond. In the United States, in Europe, in the First World in general, this era seems like the industrial revolution or the coming of the railroad in transformative significance. Vast changes in information would mean the dismantling of the old scaffolding for regulation and the substitution of the new.

There are many other constellations of change: one exists in the steady effort to extend access to media (and telephony) to areas where the basic infrastructure of modernity is not yet in place but there is a rising and potentially large middle class. India is an example where the relentless search for new markets by indigenous and transnational entrepreneurs put pressure on the legal and regulatory system.[36] There, as well, concern was rampant about the relationship among the discordant narratives arising from imagery from abroad and the consequences for local power, local culture, and local concepts of good and right.[37] Remapping in China is tied to hopes or fears of porousness, predictions of challenge to central control or new techniques for asserting government dominance.[38] Technologies widely thought to be inherently democratic are often programmed, designed, and built (whether successfully or not) to maintain lines of strong authority.[39]

A major constellation of change—one with vast implications for the remapping of media laws and policies—has emerged from the war in Afghanistan, the campaign against terrorism, and the heightened preoccupation with global stability and threats to national security. An altered set of information policies emerged with new forms of words and differently accentuated principles. Readjusted balances had the capacity of challenging hard-won speech commitments, seeking to harmonize them with more clearly emphasized public order concerns. Within the new constellation of change were such fundamental matters as the relationship between government and Internet service providers, the relationship between government and Internet users (surveillance), and the relationship between the freedom to receive and impart information and the needs of national security. Greater attention may be paid to exceptions to the freedom to receive and impart information in the jurisprudence of Article 10 of the European Convention on Human Rights and similar instruments during times of crisis. Speech-related restrictions could result from a rise in the incidence of national emergencies. In a constellation of change driven by national security considerations, there would be changes in freedom of information policies, changes in content regulation in broadcasting and press, including changes in regulation of hate speech.[40]

These constellations are composed of various combinations of ideology, technology, demography, and history. They reflect the cycles in domestic and international moods toward regulation and interference in the operations of private entrepreneurs. The last two decades have been a time when, in many states, forms of regulation were severely scrutinized as their contribution to some larger public or national objective was questioned.[41] International trade agreements brought even greater market-oriented constraints to bear on the capacity of individual states to shape regulatory policy. The idea that broadcasting should be private, not public, became surprisingly dominant. Attitudes have shifted toward greater acceptance of multinational corporations operating in the global sphere. Indeed, laws designed to avoid concentration at home are revised, in many countries, on the ground that large multinational corporations are necessary for competition in a global market. Thus governments engage in industrial policy so that their media companies can gain influence and traction in a new global environment.[42] The formation of trading blocs and the liberalization of trade has dramatic implications for media and telecommunications law. As the US Federal Communications Commission announced, it would "pursue an aggressive agenda aimed at increasing competition in communications markets around the world," so as "to benefit American consumers and "open new market opportunities for American companies.""[43]

In a fragile world where new routes of information can tear at sensitive existing arrangements, religiously divisive speech, encouragement of violence, violation of cultural norms, and terrorism become the subjects of accelerated regulatory demands.[44] These are areas where domestic laws are constantly revisited in light of new circumstances, new technologies, greater jurisprudential complexity owing to crossborder data flow, and the abundance of modes and pathways of distribution. Protection of intellectual property has its place here as well; coalitions of publishers and other related parties use international agreements to compel modifications in domestic laws in order to protect copyrighted property.

Geopolitics, as a motivation for change, exists in another form, the use of force. After World War II successful military campaigns followed by occupation triggered wholesale modification of the domestic media laws of the reconceived state.

At the end of the century, massive revisions of the media structures in Bosnia-Hercegovina and Kosovo were the consequence of a militarily similar but legally different use of force and intervention. The resulting more frequent use of "peace-keeping forces" is accompanied by a greater dependence on the shaping of media as a component of their success.[45]

In the era of change, the United States initiated, among others, Radio Free Asia, Radio Democracy in Africa, and Radio Free Afghanistan and overhauled the governance of Voice of America and Radio Free Europe/Radio Liberty to establish post–cold war roles for them.[46] The restructuring of such services across the world, actions to preclude transborder satellite transmission of disfavored parties, the development of new engineering techniques for clandestine transmissions are part of this new mode of propaganda to affect the mix of information within another nation's boundaries.

There are many ways to describe the importance of new technologies to thoroughgoing transformations in national media and telecommunications law and to the international organizations that are active in the area. New technology contributes to the robust process of global media law revision because existing patterns of law and regulation are perceived as outmoded to the extent that those laws and regulations are technology specific.[47] New technologies have led to a widespread discounting of the capacity of the state to maintain control over the flow of images within its borders; States, as a consequence, react.[48] The Internet caps a progression of powerful improvements in media technology that have transformed boundaries and political realities. The inevitability of crossborder data flow makes the task of controlling information almost impossible or, at the least, very costly. For those societies—and there are many—where control of information is critical to maintaining power, steps are taken to deflect the dangers of too many channels, too many diverse sources of information, and national boundaries that are too permeable.

As states interested in taking such steps have discovered, new technologies can enhance as well as diminish forms of control. Some states have sought an Internet architecture that will allow historic patterns of state power to continue and in some ways be enhanced.[49] Restrained by little other than the limits of acquiescence by the international community, states like China, Iran, and Iraq have responded to the consequences of technological innovation with dramatic measures, including the imposition of severe restrictions on the availability of satellite dishes and the intensified application of customary and informal pressures to conform. It is, however, too easy to attribute these responses to more authoritarian societies alone. Almost all countries, including Western democracies, articulate a need to shape information technologies to permit monitoring for security purposes, or tracking and intervention where child pornography, terror, fraud, or other crimes may be involved.[50]

Technological innovation almost always creates the problem of parallel mechanisms of information distribution with asymmetrical relations to government.[51] One form of distribution is regulated and the other not, while the players complain that the playing field is not level. Such was the argument when cable television began to compete with terrestrial broadcasting or satellite began to compete with cable. Technologies of abundance undermine traditional bases for broadcasting regulation, the most familiar of which is scarcity, and in societies where courts take doctrine seriously, these new technologies can have dramatic effects on the nature of law and policy.

On the other hand, new technologies also create new bottlenecks and enhance the capabilities of dominant players to thwart competition. Since technology presents both an opportunity and a threat, new modes of communication can remake the composition and power of messages sent out by various speakers with disturbing implications for the status quo. It is almost a cliché that the new technologies of satellite and the Internet disrupt or enable the reinforcement of new national identities. Certain diasporic groups can consolidate with more effective means of internal communication at their disposal, and by so doing, may bolster or endanger political alignments. Media structures are placed under challenge either to embrace or resist these new capacities. China, Saudi Arabia, and India, reaching out to their own populations abroad through satellite and the Internet, gain strength in political and national identity arenas.[52]

An Altered Bubble of Identity

These examples, these constellations, begin the process of illustrating how international and domestic media decisions are inextricably intertwined with global communications realities. They help demonstrate how, in a time of global media interconnections, it is almost impossible to reach decisions or adopt practices about broadcasting or the Internet in one state that are not the consequence of or do not affect the political and legal climate of other states. They inaugurate an inquiry into why states act as they do.

I begin this inquiry by suggesting the division of national responses to the complexity of information inflows into two categories or types. The first is the state's efforts to protect its own information space—its own bubble of identity—against unwanted incursions.[53] This is often an act of defensiveness, for the protection of domestic producers, sometimes creative and supportive of valuable aspects of national identity, territorial integrity, national security, and the strengthening of citizenship. The second category is less often recognized and documented, but it is central to the development of theory. This is the effort by a state (or states) to influence or alter media space and media structures outside its own borders. I use this distinction—between state efforts directed inward and state efforts directed to other states—to underscore my departure from a more or less standard or static conception of the shaping of media structures in which it is the domestic media space that is the exclusive target of attention.

To make things more complicated, each of these two categories of state activity can be divided into two further segments. When a state seeks to protect its information space from the influence of external imagery, it can, on the one hand, do so unilaterally by using technology, internal force, or the power of law. On the other hand, it can do so by negotiating with other states (or with media conglomerates) and seeking their cooperation in the distribution or regulation of distribution of information across borders. Whether it does so one way or another has significant legal and policy implications.[54] Conversely, states that aggressively seek to influence the information space of other countries can do so unilaterally (that is, without negotiation or consent), or they can do so in a mediated or negotiated manner. Understanding these various contexts helps to explain a wide array of state responses and provides an opportunity to evaluate them as well.

The most familiar category, one most associated with the debate over national sovereignty, includes states' *unilateral* efforts to control their own information space from undesired external influences. There are myriad examples. An historic archetype of this state approach is the Soviet Union's jamming of shortwave RFE/RL broadcasts.[55] A current manifestation is the (increasingly difficult) outlawing of satellite receiving dishes in some countries in order to deter the reception of CNN, Disney, or other undesired signals from various parts of the globe.[56] A softer version, more negotiation than unilateral action, is the legendary telephone conference call initiated by Condoleezza Rice, the US National Security Advisor, during which she urged television network news executives to refrain from playing videotapes of Osama bin Laden.

The most complex aspect of unilateral state action is efforts in some societies—like China—to design the Internet to facilitate the screening of unwanted information and provide a continued regulable gateway between information providers and citizenry.[57] A requirement, such as once proposed in India, for mandatory national uplinking of signals that will be downlinked within the territory, falls within this rubric. Such a rule provides the mechanical precedent for later control. A cousin, even if a distant one, is the Foreign Agents Registration Act (FARA), in the United States, first enacted in 1938 in response to a perceived flood of publications entering the United States from foreign governments. In its earliest form, FARA required "public disclosure by persons engaging in propaganda activities and other activities for or on behalf of foreign governments" and foreign principals "so that the Government and the people of the United States may be informed of the identity of such persons and may appraise their statements and actions in the light of their associations and activities."[58]

I have already referred to the case of newly independent states (like Ukraine and Kazakhstan) flexing their cultural muscles in the post-Soviet period by downgrading or excluding Russian broadcasters from the airwaves. These were usually unilateral decisions.

The move away from unilateral acts to negotiations or agreements characterizes many emerging state responses to the new technological environment. The realization that unilateral control over information space is weakening makes it more likely that there will be voluntary negotiations with states (or media conglomerates) from which undesirable information originates. This unwanted information, data, or images could be political in nature but could also disrupt local regulation on gambling, attitudes toward child pornography, or standards on the representation of women.

Historically international treaties or agreements embody such negotiation, though efforts in those areas traditionally have been quite unsuccessful. Examples of such agreements include the League of Nations' Convention Concerning the Use of Broadcasting in the Cause of Peace, which would have obligated its parties to prohibit broadcasting any transmission incompatible with the internal order of another party.[59] The UN resolution of 1982 concerning direct television broadcasting would have encouraged consultation between broadcasting states and receiving states.[60] The Television without Frontiers Directives, governing members of the European Union, is an example of a more successful operative effort to establish a regime that will mediate information crossing the relevant boundaries.

States have turned to almost invisible contacts and informal negotiations for controlling their information space. One example, discussed in chapter 3, is the story of MED-TV, the satellite service that broadcast to Kurdish populations, particularly in Turkey. Turkey failed unilaterally to suppress MED-TV by policing, within its borders, the purchase and mounting of satellite dishes; as a result it was required to employ a bilateral strategy to stifle the MED-TV channel. Turkish officials mounted a campaign to pressure the British government to withdraw MED-TV's license and sought, in other European capitals, to deny MED-TV leasing rights on government-controlled transponders on Eutelsat. Turkey contended that MED-TV was a "political organization" that supported the PKK, widely characterized as a terrorist organization. Undoubtedly other aspects of power relationships entered into its discussions with British and other counterparts.

I have referred to the effect of these unofficial negotiations among states and between states and global program services of distributors of channels. New global channel service competitors are much more dependent on agreements with states or with gatekeeper broadcast entities within states than is realized. Domestic structures are the pillars upon which global media systems are built. The television signals of CNN or BBC do not simply waft through the air, encountering no controllable gatekeeper before they invade the collective local consciousness. Today, to understand the actions of News Corporation or MTV and the competition between CNN and BBC World, we must look at the domestic pillars upon which they depend. We must see how shifts in those pillars are used to temper the entry of the global players. Indeed, "law," in the sense of officially developed norms that control behavior, may be more often the creature of negotiation than declared statute or regulation.

These negotiations take place in a double transition: the transformation of scope and scale among the producers of channel services and programming who seek to distribute signals transnationally, and the transformation of the structure of receiving mechanisms that exist as gatekeepers and filters within every country. For music video channels to gain entry into certain markets, to gain shelf space on cable or in a bouquet of channels carried by the favored direct-to-home provider, the channel must negotiate the program content with the provider, though there is usually no explicit legal standard at the base of such negotiations. Channels may promise that they will confine themselves to entertainment and not carry news, not as a result of formal law but as an informal condition for entry. I discuss, in chapter 8, negotiations between international broadcasters and local transmission facilities in the countries in which they are distributed. Formal or informal arrangements between states and large-scale international news organizations will become more frequent, implicating contractual ties with governments to operate terrestrial transmitters, to broadcast via the national system, or otherwise merely to gather information.

In addition to the negotiations between companies and states, there are other forms of negotiation, namely bilateral or multilateral efforts to limit or affect the impact of transborder data flow. Article 22 of the European Television without Frontiers Directive, requires bilateral consultations where a member state hosts programs that, arguably, significantly impair the moral development of children in a receiving member state, thus imposing a limit, though only an extremely narrow one, on the circumstances in which one member state can allow signals to flow, without objection, into the territory of another.[61]

There are an increasing number of such negotiations to protect information space. Some of the most known examples are between the receiving state and the large multinational private broadcasting firms. India agreed, in an arrangement that soon fell apart, to permit CNN to broadcast on a favored Doordarshan frequency if CNN agreed that the Indian broadcasting host would provide most of the news about its own domestic affairs. China agreed to more extensive entry for Star-TV, but in apparent exchange, Star-TV's parent, News Corporation, agreed that the BBC would not be carried.[62] It is extremely likely that MTV, the popular music television service, negotiates to ensure that it is cognizant of and, to the necessary extent, abides by local custom and preference in its choice of music, music videos, and hosts. More confident post-Soviet Republics negotiated with Russia to admit Russian language programming under approved circumstances. Similarly a meeting of information ministers of the Gulf Cooperation Council (GCC) served, even before the war in Afghanistan, as the arena to mediate disputes between Qatar, the home of Al Jazeera, the outspoken satellite broadcaster, and the government of Bahrain that considered its broadcasts deleterious and violative of the public order.[63]

But what of the second major category: decisions by countries to invade or affect the information space of other states without their consent? Chapter 8 is about how international broadcasting evolved from a classic cold war machine that made unilateral efforts to alter the nature of third-party information space into something more nuanced.[64] Black or clandestine radio, when secret financial support or actual physical invasion of a country is used to establish an unauthorized transmitter, is a quintessential example of such involuntary adjustment of voices in a state's information space.[65] In Afghanistan, from the outset, the wiping out of Taliban radio and the substitution of US-controlled and Western-originated broadcasts (from special Commander Solo aircraft) was an integral part of the military campaign. Radio and TV Marti, directed at Cuba, its legitimacy disputed in the target state, is another example of a unilateral effort by one state to affect the information space in another state.

The decision by European governments to support specific newspapers and radio stations in Slobodan Milosevic's Serbia can be characterized as an unmediated effort by one set of states to alter the information space of another country. Most dramatic, however, have been those events—approximating Occupation at the end of World War II—where a conquering army seizes both physical and media space and, invoking the rights and duties of Belligerent Occupation transforms that space so as to achieve particular political goals.[66]

The final subset of national responses involves affirmative efforts, consensually based, by one state to alter external media spaces. These responses sometimes mirror and sometimes overlap my earlier category described from the perspective of the receiving state. What distinguishes them is that governments enter and alter a third state's mix of information, but do so with the (often barely obtained) consent of the receiving state. Modern international broadcasting, where, for example, the Voice of America is carried on a state licensed FM station, with the state's consent, and frequently paying for the privilege, falls within this category. The Television without Frontiers Directive is a superb example, where multilateral negotiations have led to the development of a European information space in which the channels that are permitted within one member state must be, with few exceptions, accepted elsewhere in the Union. Chapter 7, dealing in part with Bosnia-Hercegovina, depicts an example of such an affirmative intervention where the question of the nature of consent will, in the future, be a subject of debate.

Place and Space: Globalization and Sovereignty Implications

Place and Space

The opposing notions of space and place are markers for a dual perspective on the impact of technology on governments and their responses. They mirror, to a large extent, the contrast between multilateral approaches to regulating information and the more traditional national expectation. Efforts to retain, reconfirm, and underscore traditional boundaries and established notions of community can be characterized as contributions to the idea of place. These efforts confront the challenge of the seemingly uncontrollable, alien, deconstructing, and erasing ideas of space.

Writing about South Asia and the arrival of satellites, Page and Crawley characterize the response of the state as far from peripheral. "It involved a re-thinking of a whole range of activities and policies at the heart of government and social organization."[67]

By space, I refer to a model of activity that assumes that transmission of images can occur in a manner impervious to imposed public parameters or sanctions. Here law is removed to a set of principles only, a virtual admission that the ordinary machinery of government is ineffective. In this new configuration of transmission there seems to be neither a fixed locus for enforcement or set of rules to be enforced. This idea of space captures a dream—or nightmare—where messages by individuals, groups, nongovernment organizations, and transnational corporations compete, unfettered by regulation, in the distribution of images throughout the globe.[68]

The idea of place is just the opposite. In my use of the term here, I refer to the capacity of government, linked to geography, to maintain control over identity-related media and to have some influence over the mixture of language and imagery that is a significant aspect of the binding nature of the nation-state. The history of broadcasting has been the struggle to domesticate frequency allocation to conform to those special ideas of place that are the state. International regulations and arrangements were designed, as the League of Nations–sponsored Convention Concerning the Use of Broadcasting in the Cause of Peace, put it, to "implement national service of good quality within the frontiers of the country concerned." Sometimes the issues surrounding place have been quite substantive; the never-realized Convention would have provided that:

The High Contracting Parties mutually undertake to prohibit and, if occasion arises, to stop without delay, the broadcasting within their respective territories of any transmission which to the detriment of good international understanding is of such a character as to incite the population of any territory to acts incompatible with the internal order or the security of a territory of a High Contracting Party.[69]

This is a remarkable use of an instrument of law to enshrine concepts of place. States would be sureties that their lands were not the source for information or imagery that would cause unrest elsewhere. It is worth asking what formal or informal understandings govern the same question today. Some governments establish clandestine radios precisely to encourage dissent and revolt within the territory of another. More complex is the relationship among allies, the extent to which a country can look to governments related by treaty of friendship to prohibit or discourage messages that are antagonistic to its own status quo.

In the early 1970s when concerns over satellite transmission were new, the term "spillover" was used to describe violations of the rule of place. It was the job of regulatory agencies to keep spillover to a minimum, and to regulate strictly or condemn intentional spillover. The United Nations discussed principles that would bar certain kinds of programs from direct broadcast satellites, require consultations with governments whose audiences were targeted and, in some instances, require national consent for direct broadcast signals that were specifically directed from one state into the territory of another.[70]

Opposition to radio pirates was applauded. Now, in the period of ascending globalism, the old ideal of signal transmissions that conform to national borders has changed. The efforts of countries to control their information space are questioned through the invocation of international norms. The excitement, the association with freedom, and the attraction to capital lie with the transnational, with the accumulation of audience and markets across borders. Space, both in terms of the locus for transmission and the absence of authority, can be said to be supplanting place. A resultant task is to understand which measures, administered in what way, represent an acceptable bridge between concepts of space and place.

Sovereignty

The ideas of space and place are affected by two other terms, "sovereignty" and "globalization." These terms are frequently used in discussions of media and new technologies. I use the term sovereignty to describe the power of a state (or other accumulation of power) to make and enforce laws and to seek to have a monopoly of the use of force. Though all may desire it, there are few states that have absolute sovereignty, and most sovereigns have recognized or bargained away limitations on their power, both domestically and internationally. Sovereignties are not fixed, even if, for reasons of stability, the world order often encourages the illusion that they are. It is a characteristic of many states that their very destiny, the heart of their sovereignty, has been historically contingent upon a variety of economic, military, and other factors, domestic and international.

Ultimately what is of concern for this book is not sovereignty in general, but the nature of sovereignty with regard to information or media space. Thus, for example, the expansion of the European Union would mean that the sovereignty of the Czech Republic and Hungary will be modified by their treaty obligation to install European-style quotas on programming by all broadcasters within their borders. In chapter 7, I explore how the Dayton Accords and their implementation affect the sovereignty of Bosnia over the structuring of media there. In chapter 7, I try, as well, to demonstrate how the foreign policy of the United States and other countries is implemented to induce change voluntarily or involuntarily in the media-related policies of other states. In the modern era it is also frequently the case that evolving ideas of national identity often themselves, cross-border, modify traditional notions of sovereignty. Under challenge, in particular, is the intense and long-standing idea that a convergence of sovereignty and identity is optimal.[71] Altered versions of self-determination spring from this challenge, with newer forms of autonomy related to the control of imagery (or access to imagery) rather than to older, boundary-configured ideas of sovereignty. The sustainability of a state depends in the long run on rational economic decisions of its citizens or on the use of force or on the pull of cultural bonds and historic loyalties. Media influence what constitutes the rational, the efficacy of power, and the strengthening or weakening of cultural bonds. To the extent the state depends on the bargained-for consent of the governed, media are effective for persuasion and consensus building. But media have a relationship with the other two modes of maintaining statehood as well. It is less expensive to assert sovereignty comfortably through an emphasis on imagery than through an emphasis on force, and it may be cheaper to build loyalties than to rely on terror. It stands to reason, then, that a state, unchecked, would prefer to have a monopoly over media imagery than to have such critical tools in the hands of others.

Globalization

Globalization is quite specifically related to sovereignty. Globalization means, at bottom, the increasing tendency toward the incapacity of the state to maintain control over the shape and mix of images. Globalization means that the potential of the media to buttress the identity of the state and its inhabitants is altered. Globalization means that the cultural bonds and loyalties that seemed once to be within the control of the state are now less so. Globalization could also be interpreted as the growing inability of a sovereign to keep out unwanted signals and information. It may mean the development of an international regime and international norms (e.g., "human rights") to prevent a sovereign from excluding information even when it is technically capable of doing so.

There are other definitions of globalization, such as the quite poetic description in *Space of Identity* by David Morley and Kevin Robins. Gobalization, they say, involves a shift from a world where "the notions of space as enclosure and time as duration are . . . redesigned as a field of infinitely experimental configurations of space-time."[72] Globalization could imply a positive aura: hands across the sea, development of a common vocabulary, and rendering the distribution of information and entertainment more equitable. On the other hand, globalization may be said to mean an overarching umbrella of sameness, at least cultural sameness in large regions. More specifically, globalization has been interpreted to mean the spread of a Western media culture, often a US culture of commercialization and consumerism. The scope of certain interpretations sometimes rises to suspicion of a United States imperialistic conspiracy: communications globalism as the nefarious construct of corporate investment, converting information into just another set of widgets, rather than a glorious basis for national identity. Satellites, surrealistically, extend invisible "footprints" that rechart and reimage areas of the world's surface. Globalization is said to imply the end of the nation-state, deprived of control over its information space. Most succinctly, globalization is the "radical increase in the technical, economic, and political costs of territorializing information."[73]

Conclusions

The widespread remapping of media laws is not new, though its current form, born out of the peculiar globalness of our era, is distinctive. Every new medium, every new technology for transmitting information, causes responses by those who feel threatened. A half-millennium ago, revolutions in print caused fears over dominion and sovereignty, and those in control responded. Even before print, when graven images held great sway, iconoclasts imposed a law of their own. The bonding of religion and state meant prohibitions too on symbols of those whose faiths were found discordant. Homing pigeons were an early technology for flying over boundaries with messages. Biblical stories of spies entering the Promised Land predate the present revolutionary technologies of boundary penetration and surveillance.

Each mode of gathering or transmitting information caused its own reaction. The introduction of radio broadcasting was no different. Almost from the beginning, radio was seen to be a threat to national sovereignty, much as the Internet is now. The very first broadcasts were ship to shore, a harbinger of pirate broadcasting. Radio, intrinsically, knew no political boundaries until it was tamed and domesticated. The 1920s and 1930s were chapters in regulatory history that confirmed state interests in maintaining control of information flows within their boundaries, though even then the growth of propaganda underscored other potentials for the radio medium. By the 1970s, satellite distribution of signals presented what seemed a decisive moment in the sundering of political lines. Now the Internet, with its silent, abundant ubiquity, seems to be the capstone of this tendency to obliterate borders.

Central to much of modern scholarship is the idea that modern technologies can be, in Ithiel de Sola Pool's memorable phrase, "technologies of freedom" precisely because of the capacity to overwhelm boundaries—whether physical or legislative—and as a result they become key to the spread of democracy.[74] Political transitions now taking place seem clear manifestations of this view. Technologies of freedom are the stuff of every morning's news: new generations of satellites, the promise of far more abundant telephony, and signals reverberating around the globe. It is a small jump from the profusion of these new technologies to the evanescence of national boundaries as gates or walls against the free flow of information. It is asserted almost everywhere that national borders are increasingly irrelevant, and that technology traverses boundaries so effectively that it continues to confound current modes of media and political organization.

Most of what is written and celebrated emphasizes this overwhelming and determined nature of technology to weaken national controls over information and cultural images within their borders. Seamlessness is tied to the promotion of human rights and democratic values. Information and its growth expand national economies and international trade. Enlarging the marketplace of ideas helps to reduce intense and troublesome separatist identities as well as the possibilities of genocide and war. The general benefits of the free flow of information are apparent. Still it is important to check enthusiasm, track popular resistance, and observe the efforts by states to continue control.

It is certainly inevitable, and often desirable, that states concern themselves with the sustenance of their language, enrichment of their history, and strengthening of their internal political and creative processes. Yet each of these has implications for the weight and impact of information across national borders. States have national security needs and these too, as we have seen in the wake of September 11, have radically transformative consequences for media policies. It is vital to examine the complexities and contradictions in Western attitudes toward unmediated distribution of information, the historic problem of oscillating between demands for freedom and concern over content. We do not yet know what constitutes an ideal global Republic of Information.

Given the active strategies of states responding to challenges to their authority in a post–global age, those who ring the death knell of the state may ring too soon.

There is a curious and present contradiction between the exaltations of theory and the less sublime practices of the everyday world. At the same time that the function of the state and its capacity to describe and enforce law is brought into doubt, law-making and invocation of the need and power to control imagery increase. It is not without precedent that these two phenomena, a disparagement of the capacity of law on the one hand, and a widespread turn to invoking law on the other, should coexist (perhaps one is a sign of the other), but there is something remarkable about it. The market is so powerful, technology so ubiquitous, that we are often reminded that the process of law making, especially in the field of media regulation, is like building castles in the sand where complex structures will be forcefully erased by an overwhelming cascade of waves. Yet simultaneously, there is a passion for moral controls, for regulation of indecency, and for restoring some sense of an order and security.

The relationship between media and borders is always in transition. However, that transition is not only what it is widely considered to be: technologies of freedom sweeping past traditional media monopolies designed to keep out new and dissenting cultural and political voices. That transition includes the efforts, not only in Malaysia, China, and India but also throughout the world to design new boundary technologies that will allow some continuing control over internal information space. The transition includes the use of new technologies to create diasporic boundaries: intense opportunities for the unification of physically dispersed populations. Political boundaries affect media boundaries, and the opposite is true as well: the radical changes in the media map will alter the physical map in ways yet unknown.

Military strategies, business planning, international diplomacy, the work of scholars and politicians, are all conducted in the shadow of this process of change. For all these actors and observers, precisely because so much turns on assumptions about the flow of information, the contours of transformations in the media and their relationship to the power of the state ought more closely to be examined. In the remainder of the book, I seek to focus on the way states refashion law and policy as methods of responding to the powerful, wide-ranging, and seemingly unregulable nature of modern communications.

2
Stability, Transitions, and the Market for Loyalties

It is hardly news that global information space is being transformed, media structures altered, and the role of the state, simultaneously, redefined.[1] Information, it is said to the point of cliché, is power, and in an information society, it is a considerable and increasing source of power.[2] While law has been used in the past to protect internal producers of national identity from external competition, the effectiveness of law to achieve that protective umbrella is now under question.

For most of the century, the international order assumed that radio transmissions should be contained primarily within the boundaries of each nation; the international function was to dispense frequencies so as to assure that these conditions of market division were met and enforced.[3] Over the twentieth century, international regulations and arrangements were built to reinforce the national impulse and to limit broadcasting to indigenous transmissions of good quality within the frontiers of the country concerned.[4] Now, however, the structure of information distribution within a state is so important that other states seek to affect it. That has always been true, to some extent, but expanded trade concerns and global security make it a priority. Economists, political scientists, scholars of cultural studies, and others have all made valuable contributions to a systematic understanding of this process.[5] My effort here is to adapt or suggest several approaches that have not been brought together in the literature of media globalization.

Market for Loyalties

I start with an approach I developed in an earlier book, *Television, the Public Sphere, and National Identity*.[6] There I identified a "market for loyalties," in which large-scale competitors for power, in a shuffle for allegiances, use the regulation of communications to organize a cartel of imagery and identity among themselves.

Government is usually the mechanism that allows the cartel to operate and is often part of the cartel itself. This market produces "national identity" or "community," to use the less discriminating Americanism. Management of the market yields the collection of ideas and narratives employed by a dominant group or coalition to maintain power. For that reason alone, control over participation in the market has been, for many countries, a condition of political stability. This market, I contended, has existed everywhere and at all times. What differs in today's market is the range of participants, the scope of its boundaries, and the nature of the regulatory bodies capable of establishing and enforcing rules for participation and exclusion.[7]

The "sellers" in this market are all those for whom myths and dreams and history can somehow be converted into power and wealth—classically states, governments, interest groups, businesses, and others. The "buyers" are the citizens, subjects, nationals, consumers—recipients of the packages of information, propaganda, advertisements, drama, and news propounded by the media. The consumer "pays" for one set of identities or another in several ways that, together, we call "loyalty" or "citizenship." Payment, however, is not expressed in the ordinary coin of the realm: It includes not only compliance with tax obligations, but also obedience to laws, readiness to fight in the armed services, or even continued residence within the country. The buyer also pays with his or her own sense of identity.[8]

It is easiest to understand the functioning of such a market for loyalties in the traditional context of a single state. One can make the general and expansive claim that much domestic broadcast regulation is an effort, within a society, to maintain or adjust the distribution of power among those who are dominant, with due recognition for subsidiary groups. While such legislation is often justified as a means of preserving or strengthening national identity, national identity can be reframed as essentially the set of political views and cultural attitudes that help maintain the existing power structure. Certainly that is often the operational goal (though hardly ever explicit) of those in control. I have suggested that while there were several ways to define "national identity," including a discovery of the "true" or "historic" national identity of a state, this slightly cynical definition (the construction of identity by the power structure so as to maintain its power) enhances our understanding of media legislation by providing an underlying analytic explanation. If familiar regulation of domestic media can be seen, at least in part, as the use of law to reinforce or adjust a political status quo, then much of contemporary national response to media globalization may have a similar explanation. Reregulation or the incentive to change media law and policy occurs, within a state, when the cartel of political allegiances can no longer maintain its position of civil dominance. In that sense the pressures of globalization lead to changes in domestic media laws and structures if either (1) existing domestic broadcasting laws are inadequate at protecting the cartel, or (2) national identity is changing or has changed and legislation is necessary to be more inclusive, to legitimate new players, and to protect them, in turn, against unregulated challenge.

Media globalization and new information technologies yield a crisis of domestic law and policy if barriers to entry are lowered for those excluded from the old political cartel, especially if the new entrants could be threats to the control of the *ancien regime*. In response, a government can either redefine the cartel and accommodate new entrants or take effective steps, through law or force, to try to raise the barriers to entry again. "Failed states" or states made to fail by force (Taliban-led Afghanistan, for example) lose control over their media space as force is exerted against them. External entities (corporations, states, and diasporic groups) also participate in the market for loyalties when they advocate the use of technology or international norms to force a state to enlarge the membership of a local cartel.

Media globalization also fosters the reinforcement of power across national lines and the development of international agreements to render new organizations of identity effective. A competition emerges among those who supply different ideologies for command of large-scale sectors.[9] For example, an international cartel could, as a means of shaping a transnational market for loyalties, establish a set of rules on a global level or encourage or impose a set of rules favoring its "products" in the bosom of a significant group of states. Tacit or explicit arrangements among states, or between states and multinational corporations or nongovernment organizations, may be designed to affect the nature of a global market in cultural and political attitudes and facilitate the predominance of one ideology over another. Thus, while the apparent determinant of the relationship between regulation and control remains the nation-state, communication avenues in any given state would increasingly be a matter of international action, justified under the aegis of stability, trade, and human rights.

International norms like Article 19 of the Universal Declaration of Human Rights, domestic constitutional rules like the First Amendment in the United States, and regional constraints, like the European Convention on Human Rights and the Television without Frontiers Directive in the European Union have a special role in limiting the cartelization of the market for loyalties. These provisions are usually considered curbs on the power of local political cartels to use law and regulation to screen out voices that seek to alter the current power structure, and especially those who seek to use broadcasting despite its power to force such change. Increasingly these norms are used swordlike by those external to the state, often NGOs and media corporations with existing global power, to encourage a more favorable legal regime within a state.[10] To be sure, such expansion often serves the honorable principle of the right to receive and impart information, but it is about the extension of power and influence as well. Less clear is the existence or role of international norms where, in times of conflict, external efforts seek to erase media power in a target state, such as in the Palestinian Authority, Milosevic-controlled former Yugoslavia, or in Afghanistan under the Taliban.

The structure of broadcasting is related to current views on federalism and relative autonomy. In Europe, where there is an effort to build stateless-nations like Catalonia and Scotland, broadcasting policy will, over time, reflect political adjustments.[11] Systems that have been tightly ordered from the center with state control of access to images, state-determined language of the media, and subsidization of emblems of unity will give way to more decentralized methods. In the United Kingdom, as Scottish and Welsh broadcasting become fully autonomous, political devolution is accompanied by devolution in communications structures; Spain and other countries have followed a similar pattern.

The 1989 European Television without Frontiers Directive illustrates the evolution from the long-standing approach of exclusion based on national borders to a more common union that encourages free competition for identity within the community of members while seeking to regulate competition, even if mildly, from without.[12] For reasons of trade and regional integration, the mix of information in each member state of the European Union became important to all other members. In the GATT negotiations of 1994, the European Union did not lower the trade barriers in the film and television industries as in other industries on the grounds that a European cultural space ought to be preserved, strengthened, and protected from the so-called Hollywood influx.[13] Canada, on the one hand, and Malaysia, on the other, are countries with very different traditions that seek to deploy law or utilize law in conjunction with structure of the industry to control the relationship between images from abroad and from within. Canada does so in a rather open society; Malaysia does so in a society in which televised images from abroad have, traditionally, been tightly controlled.

One can look to other contexts to understand the interaction between globalism and the market for loyalties. Let me turn to the example of India, about which there is a verdant media literature.[14] The effort to control media space domestically has, over the half century since Independence, been maintained through the state's monopoly on terrestrial broadcasting, more expansive a monopoly than in many other states that assert democratic traditions. The rise of foreign satellite channels, distributed by and large through relatively unregulated cable television systems, specifically threatened this enduring practice and possibly the political arrangements that depended on it. In 1997 a report of the Ministry of Information and Broadcasting summarized official views and decried the "adverse impact . . . on Indian values and culture" of the "large number of foreign satellite TV channels beaming their programmes over Indian sky."[15] Describing the early moments of the satellite invasion when he was minister of information, P. Unendra said, "A file was put up in the Ministry as to how to counter the satellite invasion. What steps should be taken to stop it? I wrote back saying you cannot stop the sun shining by holding an umbrella. The more you try, the more you encourage people to watch."[16]

Long preoccupied by concerns over the consequences of what might be called an "unbridled" press or a press controlled by entities not, in the historic view, sensitive to the complexities of local conditions, successive governments opposed Western broadcasting influences. India has seen itself as frequently subject to significant security threats from Pakistan (and vice versa). During the 1999 conflict with Pakistan over incursions in Kashmir, the minister of information issued a ban on broadcasting the signal of Pakistan-TV by cable television services on the grounds that India's opponent was spreading misinformation that might lead to disunity within the state. During the same period, Videsh Sanchar Nigam Limited (VSNL), then virtually a monopoly Internet service provider, removed *Dawn*, the Islamabad-based daily, from distribution probably at the behest of the government. Even after the ban on Pakistan-TV was lifted, the government's right to impose such a ban was generally accepted.

Section 10 of India's draft Broadcast Bill of 1997 embraced a list of concerns that reflected India's history and security consciousness. In a relatively standard list of prohibitions, the statute provided that any licensee, terrestrial or satellite, would be obliged to ensure that programming would not "offend against good taste or decency." There would be a prohibition on programs "likely to encourage or incite to crime or to lead to disorder or to be offensive to public feeling." Similarly the draft statute included standards requiring that programs reflect India's history and demography. Religious programs were to avoid "improper exploitation of religious susceptibilities" or offending "the religious views and beliefs of those belonging to a particular religion or religious denomination." Statutory standards would require that "due emphasis [be] given . . . to promote values of national integration, religious harmony, scientific temper and Indian culture." Officials were still smarting from fears that internal dissension and communal violence might become a significant problem if uncontrolled signals such as news coverage by the BBC not subject to national censorship, are allowed.[17]

These are a few fragments from a rich history in India. Restraint and restriction are based on the idea of maintaining a democratic state at a time of centripetal forces: national security needs, fears of internal violence because of religious strife, the need to protect morals from forces that endanger cultural traditions, and the need to use media for the balance between the notion of India as a whole and its several parts. The range of justifications for excluding certain entrants into the market is almost as broad as exists anywhere. The prior and existing regime structures reflect the regime's historic ties with Britain and India's period of neutrality and socialism. The centralized structure and belief in a nation-building purpose in Indian broadcasting demonstrate its British colonial origins. The ideas of control and belief in the instrumentality of the communications system emulate characteristics of socialist neutrality.

Now, internal norms are used by external players to change the mix of voices. A kind of "triumph of capitalism" element characterizes attitudes toward entry, competition, and growth. Human rights ideals have played a part in this trend, specifically in a significant Supreme Court decision that initiated a wholesale review of India's broadcasting laws.[18] Negotiations between Pakistan and India undoubtedly touch on information aspects of conflict and coexistence. Throughout, regulation reflects sensitivity to the relationship between power and the perceived threat of information and images to the maintenance of power. Restraints that control access from groups within the country give way to efforts to restrain, condition, and cushion images and information that come from Pakistan and abroad.

Turkey also provides a dramatic example of the effort to maintain control over competition in the market of loyalties explicitly in the name of national identity. Since the rise of Kemal Ataturk, the Turkish government, at least until the mid-1990s, considered aspects of Islamic fundamentalism a threat to the secular state. Advocates of secularism, and certainly those in control of the state, sought to limit the use of the mass media by competitors for loyalty. The Turkish Radio and Television Authority (TRT) was not only monopolistic, it was in essence the voice of the state, disseminating the unitary ideology and culture of Turkish republicanism. It found itself highly susceptible to government intervention.[19] Charged by statute with "promoting the values of country, unity, republic, public order, harmony, and welfare, and to strengthen the principles of Kemal Ataturk's reforms," TRT has been an instrument for cohesiveness in an environment riven by alternate national identities.[20] When TRT was attacked for broadcasting programs that legitimated Islamic fundamentalism, the government forced the agency's director general to resign.[21]

When threatening broadcasts of radical imams were transmitted by satellite from Germany to Turkey and potentially destabilizing Kurdish-oriented MED-TV broadcasts were transmitted from London and Belgium, the government responded with a variety of legal and political tools. The initial and strong responses included banning programs, regulating satellite dishes and intervening in the countries where the signals were uplinked. Then, however, Turkey took a rather different step. Largely informally and with a wink of the law, Turkey permitted the expansion of domestic commercial signals, program services that were not threatening politically and often provided by those close to the dominant party. This response was to open the skies, but with much greater influence over what would come into the country.

In the global or regional market for loyalties, Turkey, understanding the importance of a mix of signals entering a country, organized satellite services directed at Turkish-affinity communities in Central Asia. A similar set of circumstances occurred when Turkey succeeded in arranging Turkish-originated programing on cable services in Germany and The Netherlands and other states that housed large numbers of the Turkish diaspora. And we have seen in chapter 1 that Turkey appealed to domestic and international norms to persuade other countries not to host satellite services aimed at its Kurdish population. Finally the government bolstered its own favored channels to compete for Kurdish favor.

As a way of showing how this process of controlling information or using law works, we can consider the regulation of advertising. In a market for loyalties, advocates for disparate national identities will predictably have different attitudes toward the use of ordinary commercial advertising on television and the kind of Western programming that accompanies it.[22] The preoccupation that governments have long had with limiting advertising messages and excluding competition from commercial broadcasters suggests that the impact of programming on public allegiances yields a substitute for more traditional packages of identity. Advertising can persuade individuals to consume rather than to save and invest, with consequences for particular visions of the public good. In this sense marketers of pure national identities, ideologies that parade as such, compete with sellers of consumer goods, who are trying to impress the citizen with another identity. An individual must decide, at the margin, whether a higher or lower percentage of disposable income should go to the state (in taxes), for education or environmental protection (generosity), or, instead, for personal goods like food or television sets and automobiles.[23] In a poor society, particularly, the impact of an individual's choice may not be measurable in money alone but in his or her contribution to a purer form of sheer human loyalty to the state.

The effect of advertising and of modern Western-style programming in the market for loyalties may, thus, support certain groups and disfavor others. Proponents of some identities recognize the indirect supporting role that the barrage of traditional commercials, for everything from orange juice to computers, might play in connection with their own narrations of future happiness. Parties advocating a more rapid transition to a marketplace economy in states ambitious to increase their gross national product may see the political benefits of a citizenry exposed to a culture of advertising and consumerism because they contain indirect or secondary messages of political significance.

As such, there are assertions of national identity in the interstices of commercials, in their depiction of idealized home life, opportunities to travel, or of a certain idea of traditional family values.[24] "Free and independent media," because of their dependence on advertising, alter citizen priorities as between the state and consumerism. In transition societies, in developing societies, and in societies moving from reliance on public service broadcasting, the inclusion of advertising has cultural and political significance. The most avid proponents of free market television have, consistent with this position, argued that images of Western society, including Western advertising, are entitled to some of the credit for the fall of the Berlin Wall and the collapse of the Soviet Union.[25] The point here, of course, is not the truth of the claims about the impact of messages, but the perception of that impact and the rhetorical use of it in rendering markets more open or closed.

Advertising may be wholly laudable, it may be the underpinning of independence from state control, it may be liberating for the individual, but it has social and civic consequences. In an analysis that focuses on the state itself, one could say that if the images of consumer society are supportive of the party in power, that could be ground enough for their advocacy of an increase in advertiser-supported broadcasting. If a ruling coalition sees the images of advertising and the narratives of foreign programs as a threat to its continued hold on government, then the often-foreign images are characterized as subversive.[26]

In global environments of negotiated images, the question of whether or how much advertising should be permitted or encouraged is translated into new terms. Advertising is part of a logic of sustainability. If media must be independent of state support in order to be free, then (generally) advertising is necessary for continued existence. Global advocacy of this logic of sustainability is prevalent, yet it contains often unexplained implications for local and general markets for loyalties. Whether a society is closed or open, part of the World Trade Organization or not, interested in the development of human potential or not—these questions themselves have been globalized. Rules about who can speak, who can shape media structures, or what messages course within the society—in short the profile of the market for loyalties—is now a matter for an expanding cartel of state and private interests operating on a more global level.

This argument from the "market for loyalties" approach will reappear throughout this book. It suggests that countries that are in similar geopolitical contexts will take similar approaches to preserving (or modifying) the domestic cartel and employ tools similar to those used elsewhere. Those in charge of the cartel of loyalties would want to find devices to place the power of destabilizing images in what are deemed safe hands. Safe hands might be local hands, corporate hands, or transnational hands; the question would generally be whether those hands are as nonthreatening as possible. The rhetoric of broadcasting reform is, almost by definition and except in a few limited instances, different from the substance of broadcasting reform. Few modern and democratic governments or participants in policy making would articulate a policy of regulatory reform saying explicitly that it was designed to keep them in power. An authoritarian society with a monopoly on information that represents itself as an authoritarian society, might have little difficulty marrying rhetoric to reality. Threats to the monopoly must be defeated and making that explicit may be part of the ideology of control.

Related to these strategies is the domestication of the global broadcasting entities. More than that, as implied above, some states may prefer global suppliers of news and information because they may be less threatening than home grown opposition channels. The critical theorists, Adorno and Horkheimer, pointed to the political impact of assembly-line, standardized entertainment, the arts and education. Long before global television, they recognized that a vast industrialized culture industry could benefit a ruling class by separating the masses from critical perspectives and socialist ideas.[27] Blue jeans may be subversive, but they can be less subversive, at least at their introduction into public consciousness, than an indigenous, dissenting broadcasting regime clawing for increased influence in the society. A media space filled with commercials is thus often preferable, from the perspective of the status quo, to one crowded with opposing alternate identities (say, stations of Islamic fundamentalists in Egypt, Basque separatists in France, or Kurds in Turkey). Commercialization may, in the words of its critics, undermine historic cultures, but be seen as less subversive than destabilizing political messages. In this sense, at least in the short run, the gestation and entry of new and attractive commercial material provides powerful influences against which it may be difficult for competing national identities to emerge.

Exit, Voice, Stability

States (and various groups of states acting together) have an interest in the nature of political stability (or lack of stability) in sensitive areas of the world. Information flows can enhance stability or undermine it. To further a theoretical framework that helps with understanding how decisions become multilateral with respect to media space, I turn to the work of Albert O. Hirschman and his famous text, *Exit, Voice, and Loyalty*.[28] In the contemporary state, exit is a characteristic and familiar decision. Individuals leave en masse, avoiding genocidal violence, sometimes merely fleeing from countryside to city, sometimes as asylum seekers, or sometimes in search of a more economically and culturally satisfying life. "Leaving" can be more inward, more a matter of passive resistance or political anomie rather than actual flight.

   Voice, in my reading, may have a meaning slightly different from Hirschman's. For him, voice is defined as "any attempt at all to change, rather than to escape from, an objectionable state of affairs, whether through individual or collective petition to the management, ... through appeal to a higher authority, ... or through various types of actions and protests, including those that are meant to mobilize public opinion."[29] For the modern state, as I use it here, voice is constituted, in large part, in the more or less organized exercise of speech, through press and broadcasting, to affect public decisions.[30]

   The third characteristic in Hirschman's formula is *loyalty*. Loyalty for him, is "the set of conditions that makes exit somewhat more unlikely and voice a more important mechanism for feedback." ~~Loyalty~~ is the linchpin. It ~~is the expression of changes in the environment that determine stability.~~ Loyalty is furthered by a set of actions or strategies by the state to make remaining more attractive or to render exit less attractive or less possible. Loyalty is a key concept in the battle between exit and voice. Because members may be locked in to their organizations a little longer, they ~~seek to use the voice option "with greater determination and resourcefulness than would otherwise be the case.~~"[31] Hirschman pithily articulates the special meaning of loyalty: loyalty "helps to redress the balance by raising the cost of exit." Loyalty enhances pressure "into the alternative, creativity-requiring course of action from which they would normally recoil."[32]

I put something of a gloss on Hirschman's work, a gloss relevant to the remapping of media structures. Seeking the optimal mix between voice and exit in a state is no longer a question for one state alone.[33] There are external consequences of great importance to getting it "wrong." Too much exit for a state may lead to refugee crises or may take the form of "brain drain," hindering development. Duncan Campbell, writing in *The Guardian*, described a conversation with Roma groups in the Czech Republic where he tried to find the image of Britain that fueled asylum seeking. He asked a group of teenagers what they thought Britain would actually be like, and their very clear idea came from films and television: no racism, "a land of jocular men and compassionate princesses where Gypsy boys would be hugged on freshly cut lawns. Even if most immigrants have rather less rosy views of what awaits them, the images of comfort and ease which bombard the world only serve to encourage more people to cross borders, legally or otherwise."[34]

Suppression of certain elements of voice may mean systematic deprivation of human rights that bears within it the inevitability of conflict. On the other hand, in the interest of stability, certain voices are often suppressed, those characterized as "terrorist" being the prime example. During the post–September 11 era, those groups labeled as terrorist saw their funds frozen, not only to prevent them from arming, but to limit their capacity to influence the political environment in vulnerable polities. Conversely, assuring that programming opportunities are available to a particular ethnic or tribal group may be the price that a strong outside power exacts for benefits conferred or for peaceful cooperation. The particular mix of voices within a state is something that has potential international consequences. New technologies seem to permit, if not require, states to cooperate on how the mix of voices evolves transnationally and in any one context. Countries like the United States, increasingly, have particular views on what they consider an appropriate mix of voices in, say, Iran and Iraq or Central Asia or Kosovo. And some states use satellite transmissions to bring their perspectives to their diasporas abroad.

These are the strands that can be brought together as part of an emerging international policy. They are the playing out, in an international arena, of the Hirschman dynamic of exit, voice, and loyalty.

Let us look at some examples of the application of this approach to the reshaping of media policies. We have seen the great cost, regionally and globally, when states deteriorate and fail, as in Somalia, or when the form of stability they take closes out all dissent, as in Afghanistan. Neighboring states are affected when another state is in decline or recuperating. The mix of exit and voice is significant for each of these areas. How any state—Israel, Serbia, Russia, Turkey, or Rwanda— responds to its internal crises is of interest to other states. Other states may have to pay the price if decline takes a particular form (or they may benefit by certain forms of decline). These other states will therefore wish to affect the nature of voice, in the Hirschman sense. By intervening to alter notions of loyalty or to increase the potential of voice, these other states can induce citizens to stay and fight for another day rather than leave.

In 1999 the United States and other NATO powers helped encourage a Stability Pact for South Eastern Europe, drawing on the Royaumont Process for the elaboration of a Media Charter. It provided for a series of multilateral resolutions concerning the significance of open media. The document notes "the misuses of media in recent conflict situations," and asserts that "freedom of the press and unimpeded circulation of information, as well as open discussion" are "prerequisites for the establishment of mutual understanding and good relations among states and their peoples." According to this document, the proposed signatories "are convinced that cooperation among media professionals could contribute to enhancing mutual confidence and reduce the risk of tension in South Eastern Europe." The Stability Pact was established in the gulf between intention and implementation, but it provided the example of a multilateral umbrella for thinking about the relationship between media structure and regional peace. The parties would commit themselves to defend freedom of expression, to encourage the development of a plurality of viable and accessible electronic and printed media independent of government, and to establish impartial national independent media bodies for awarding broadcasting frequencies.

The Pact follows a particular form or idea of editorial professionalism, namely "objective, impartial, balanced, factual, fair, and free from political bias." In the evolving context of international standards, this form of objectivity and fairness has a specific meaning: programming should "be free from ethnic, racial, or religious hatred and should avoid language likely to incite xenophobia, civil unrest, or terrorist activities." Similarly diversity and independence are consistent with a rule that "programmes should not be subservient to any political, cultural, or religious group." As a matter of multilateral undertaking, "no individual convicted or indicted by the International War Crimes Tribunal for the former Yugoslavia should be allowed to serve" on the board of management of a public service broadcaster or of a private media company or to be employed by either in any other capacity. This idea of inclusion and exclusion reverberates both with the Hirschman formula and the idea of the "market for loyalties."

In chapter 7, I discuss particularly aggressive examples of stability-seeking efforts by the international community, dealing primarily with the seizure of broadcasting transmitters in Bosnia-Hercegovina. In Kosovo the focus was on the debilitating effect of hate speech on social and political stability. Thus, in February 2000, OSCE Head of Mission Daan Everts stated:

We cannot tolerate hate speech anywhere in society—whether it is on the radio, in the classroom, in a newspaper or at a political rally.[35]

In spring 2000 following the death of Petar Topoljski, a Serbian employee of the UN Mission in Kosovo who was murdered after an article in *Dita* stated he was guilty of crimes against ethnic Albanians and printed his name and address, the UN Special Representative in June 2000 signaled a shift toward a more aggressive approach. Officials of the international community abandoned media self-regulation in favor of a public safety rationale.[36] Crafted in a seemingly lawless Kosovo, this approach has a stability-oriented flavor: journalists have a responsibility, where a democratic state is not fully functioning and where violence is a regular means by which differences are resolved, not to write in such a way as to endanger the lives of individuals, or increase social tension. Where those duties are violated, the authority has the right to discipline. And it was the international community that would decide what mix of voices was "infringing."

There are many more examples. In the late twentieth century and the early twenty-first, armies forged war and then an uneasy peace partly through control of media and the space of information. Among other things demonstrated by the war in Afghanistan was that greater attention would be paid to the specific mix of voices in any society where harboring terrorists or undergoing destabilization could have global consequences. The very organization, content and influence of the press and broadcasting was a matter of combat for harshly divided ethnic groups, for civil authorities seeking their role in peacekeeping duties, for NGOs seeking to find their own voice in an area where old absolutes might not seem so applicable.

Stages of Transition

A third way of thinking about the internationalization of media space is to look at the process by which one state (directly or through proxy organizations) provides "assistance" to those in other societies to help alter its regime structure (usually, in recent times, to help nudge a society toward more democratic practices).[37] Of course, this notion overlaps with ideas of a market for loyalties or multilateral or regional efforts to stabilize or destabilize a particular government.

Here our examination must begin by considering the complex premises about the relationship between media assistance and shifting or changing governance in a society.[38] Political scientists, frequently with financial support from governments, build schema for classification of transition societies. These ask what we need to know about particular kinds of transitions so as to understand what forms of intervention will produce the desired outcome.[39] They have established modes of thinking about change: characterizing and categorizing states, as, for example, authoritarian, pre-transitional, transitional, or as a mature or a consolidated democratic society. The theory that "stages" or categories of social transformation exist underwrites many programs of technical aid in the reform of information space. These stages or categories serve, sometimes implicitly, as diagnostic tools to determine the nature of a particular society and the forms of intervention that would best move the target society from one point along a continuum to another (usually from authoritarian to more democratic).

The theology of the "stages" approach is dynamic and often fervently positive. Focusing on post-Communist societies, Zbigniew Brzezinski described three stages in language that imports the notion of upward directedness.

The first of Brzezinski's stages is the "breakthrough stage" of initial transformation from the authoritarian past. The breakthrough stage is defined by Brzezinski as the introduction of the basic architecture of democratic institutions, including many elements of a free press and an end to the one-party political system. The breakthrough stage is also characterized by the formation of a coalition oriented to promoting change. In addition to an effort at stabilizing the kind of economic crisis that accompanies any sudden transition, this "breakthrough" stage may include the beginning of a rule of law and the elimination of arbitrary state control over many areas of economic and political life.

The second Brzezinski stage is called, colloquially and optimistically, "change takes hold." In this period, which may begin and overlap with the "breakthrough," the actual institutions of transition gain traction and move from being formal ornaments of change to having real effects. Elections are held under a system of formal and fairly administered rules (often including rules concerning the use of the media by the state and candidates). Constitutionalism, usually with meaningful press guarantees, becomes a characteristic of political dialogue. A legal framework is put in place, in part to render the system itself more accountable. This development means that indendent media, among other businesses, can begin to depend on legally protected rights. Property rights also play a more substantial role.

Brzezinski's third stage is the "emergence of a stable democratic order." Stability involves competition among effective political parties and a political culture in which the processes of democratic elections are normalized. There is steady economic growth, a general move to privatize government assets, and the production of a private enterprise culture. The rule of law becomes solidified with an independent judiciary and a legal culture.[40]

There are many modes of intervention that relate to particular stages. These include training journalists, training publishers, subsidizing particular elements of the press, providing a stronger infrastructure for the media, and providing technical assistance with the legal framework in which media are enveloped. Intervention can take the form of extending the voice of an international broadcaster, like the Voice of America, or it can be far harsher, involving, in times of conflict, seizing or bombing the transmitters of disfavored broadcasters, or forcefully occupying the entire broadcast space. I deal in greater detail with the use of "stages" in the formation of a foreign policy toward media structures in chapter 7.

There is an appealing certainty to the idea of a political *science*, a way of looking at the world that allows the diagnostic enterprise of classification. In the model of stages of transition, identifying the category provides some clue as to the interventions that will facilitiate movement to another category. In the multilateral efforts to structure media in target societies, a vocabulary of categories at least provides some common language among the external agencies seeking to effect change. Unfortunately, the passage from one stage to another is hardly smooth or predictable and certainly is not inevitable. Not for nothing do some categorizations include the "failed state" and weak or unstable states. Nor is it always clear how external assistance (anything from student exchanges to a Marshall Plan) ensures or facilitates the maturation along this line of progress.

It is dangerous to rely too heavily on the idea of "stages" of transition as a prescription for policy initiatives.[41] There are too many factors exogenous to the menu of assistance to allow for a clear anatomy of transitions. Even in the last decade, transitions have been undone by ethnic and religious conflict, by economic failures in neighboring societies, by the death of key leaders, by the failure of political parties to develop, and by the change in strategies of the external states that advocate change.

The transition model may also work best where liberalism or democratic practices are restored—excavated from a not too distant past—rather than newly invented and implanted. In this respect, transitions in Central and Eastern Europe are different from those in Indonesia or Afghanistan.[42] The more finely drawn the categories, the more each one is a reflection of particular context. Then reality, not an abstract guide, provides the basis for interventions. The categories that have been described, and the dynamics that are suggested by them, fit a Western view of influencing targets that the West desires to transform. A very different kind of multilateralism would be in place if one were to establish categories of transition from the perspective of China, Russia, or the Conference of Ministers of Information of Islamic States. The location of the window determines what states see as they look out into the world and ask what exists, what changes should take place, and what pressures ought to be brought upon media institutions to facilitate those changes.

A final weakness of models of technical assistance in media reform is that they are based on a linked set of four important assumptions.[43] The first is key: the export of democracy is in the national interest of the donor states both for reasons of national security and to build a stronger global economy. The second assumption is that a strong civil society is a necessary condition to the building of a democratic society. There are those who believe, at this second level, that "electoral democracy" and its forms are important, rather than a focus on the underlying dynamics of the society.[44]

The third assumption holds that achieving either meaningful elections or a strong civil society requires what is generally called "free and independent media," media that are not dependent on the government (though it could also be served by a well-run public service broadcasting system). The fourth assumption justifies the diagnostic stages analysis I have just discussed and is the touchstone for the actual practice of media assistance. That assumption is that appropriate interventions (by or on behalf of the target society), including the reform of the legal and policy structure for the flow of information, will yield the kind of media that foster civil society and help to legitimate an election process. Understanding what interventions are appropriate and effective (rather than automatically imposed as part of a preexisting idea of free and independent media) is a function of both the nature of the target society and the ideological assumptions of the donor or intervening state.

There have been, historically and recently, critiques of each of these assumptions. The first assumption—the propagation of democratic states for reasons of national security—is enormously significant because that is a principal basis for the appropriateness of intervention to reform political systems.[45] Statements about the importance of the spread of democracy are legion. In "Exporting the First Amendment," Margaret Blanchard tells the story of journalists and press barons who, after WWII, thought, "if other nations adopted the American press system, the media of these countries would then be equipped to inform their audiences about their own government, in much the same way that the press in America did." These journalists and owners believed that their free-press system had prevented government leaders from propagandizing their country into war as Hitler and other WWII leaders had done. "If journalists only could manage to export the blessings that the American free-press brought to the US then, indeed, the world would be assured of democracy and peace."[46] In these cases there is a missionary zeal that augments national security considerations. The First Amendment embodies an approach to the human condition and the role of the individual in society that is fundamental and incapable of being universalized. As Napoleon considered that the Rights of Man should be everywhere recognized, there are those who believe passionately in the universality of free speech as it has come to be conceptualized in the United States.

Increasingly, however, while the rhetoric of the universal connection between national or global security and the increase in democratic practice is maintained, as well as a commitment to the human right to receive and impart information, there is a sense that these goals are contingent on other priorities. The objective of progress toward democracy and prosperity is deprecated on the claim, sometimes spurious, that achieving such goals is a function of a particular culture.[47] The realpolitik of priorities is marked by the fact that at times military assistance provided to sustain nondemocratic regimes towers over assistance to those struggling with a transition to democracy. The practice and the agenda of major powers often has more to do with strengthening a global order that is stable and not inimical than it has to do with furthering democracy.

The second and third assumptions relate to the question of the role of civil society in reinforcing democracy, and the role of media in reinforcing civil society. From the perspective of those providing technical assistance to foster transitions, the nature of this link is of critical importance. Much depends on the definition of a transition to democracy. Diamond, Linz, and Lipset emphasize structural conditions more than the extensiveness of the ballot.[48] For them, democracy is a system in which there is meaningful and extensive competition for power among individuals and organized groups, excluding the use of force. The selection of leaders and policy provides a sense of general inclusion, usually through regular and fair elections. Finally, civil and political liberties that ensure the integrity of political competition and participation are important. In terms of the operative aspects of media assistance, the definitions of the particular emblems of democracy are highly relevant. Each outcome summons a different ideal for civil society. And each also implies different emphasis in a constructed media system. Thus it is insufficient to say, from a pragmatic standpoint, simply that free and independent media, unrestrained by abusive government restrictions, are key components to building vibrant democracies. What constitutes "free and independent," what is within the context of the feasible, and what specific roles the press should play are all relevant questions in the process of designing an assistance strategy.

Problems of implementation, persistent, ubiquitous, and almost unavoidable, challenge the fourth assumption, namely the capacity surgically to intervene and help produce particular transition-related outcomes. This desire to find techniques of cause and effect motivates governments and nongovernmental organizations. It deals with the science of assistance, and the relationship between diagnosis and effective action. I discuss the state implementation of this idea as an element of a "foreign policy of media space" in chapter 7.

The Consitutive and the Instrumental

Theories of international communication are thick on the ground. Daya Kishan Thussu, in his analytic survey lists the following categories: theories of advancing free flow of information, modernization theory, dependency theory, structural imperialism, hegemony, critical theory, Habermasian public sphere, cultural studies perspectives, information society theories, and critical discourses of globalization.[49] Those who use theories not just to explain, but to advocate media reform do so for reasons that are instrumental or constitutive, or a combination of both. An instrumental approach asks what actual, measurable difference a media law makes, what kind of media law in what kind of society, at what stage in development, produces more newspapers or more radio and television stations independent of government or more users of the Internet within the target society. A different, and equally important question is the instrumental analysis of presumed benefit to the intervening or donor society. In many countries much of the reform process is the product of a belief in the instrumental aspect of free and independent media and the law that surrounds it.[50]

We can also look upon the development of media law with what is called a constitutive approach. Media laws are to be evaluated not merely in terms of a relatively simplistic notion of cause and effect. Laws and their adoption have a pervasive aspect, themselves, in structuring society that cannot be measured in terms of an occasional impact.[51] As Garth and Sarat have put it, "Law is seen as a way of organizing the world into categories and concepts."[52] Rather than asking what direct result a particular media law has accomplished (How many newspapers are there? What is the pattern of governance? How does a particular law affect readership?), a constitutive approach might ask a different set of questions about the effect of the law on patterns of thinking about the individual and the state. Do the citizens and officials of a society with one set of laws and institutions think differently about themselves and their relative power from those of a society that has a different set? By framing the issue of media organization in the language of "free speech" or "democratizing society," in terms of "ensuring equal access," or the development of "free and independent media," there are arguable consequences in addition to narrower legal outcomes. Here, too, there is a duality. For the advocacy of media reform may have a constitutive element not only in the target society but in the intervening society as well. Those who drive a policy, for example, of a particular kind of free and independent media in target societies may do so out of a deep belief in the existence of such practices at home.

Many elements of the global media law debate are framed in traditional instrumental terms. As to the Internet, for example, or other specific channel of distribution, one might ask what empirical effect will a particular structuring approach have on availability of information and the distribution of information in society.

Will regulation that provides Internet access in central locations, like cybercafes, disproportionately benefit individuals of higher status or income in the society? Will a law on rating systems actually reduce specific harms to minors? Will passing V-chip legislation for television actually and directly empower more parents to exercise measurable control over their children?

A constitutive approach, on the other hand, would focus on how the debate over the V-chip alters the way speech is perceived in the society. The very debate may shift attitudes and forms more than does the actual implementation of the law. The "squeegee" approach to crime prevention, one that pays attention to the details of everyday life so as to enhance the idea of order in the society, criminalizes the conduct of those who threaten to wash the windows of cars waiting at stoplights.[53] But it does so not to affect the lives of drivers, but to alter the environment and perception of law and its enforcement within the society. Free press and free speech laws may be constitutive in the way they set an aspirational climate. They may (or may not) encourage ethical arrangements among journalists or restraint of governmental censorial intervention.

This distinction illuminates foreign policy approaches as well: the United States or the Council of Europe can urge symbolic inclusion of particular free press principles in national constitutions as a required goal or aspiration. On the other hand, these governments can use instrumental measures of rights protection, charting, for example, the number of journalists harmed or killed as a result of particular government practices. It has been US foreign policy practice to insist, in the copyright sphere, not only on the adoption of law but the demonstration of bona fide efforts to see that international norm-based copyright policies are actually enforced.

The discussion here of media law and policy reform bridges the instrumental and constitutive dimensions within the target society. It assumes that law and changes in the structure of the relationship of the press to the state actually affect civil society, and that energy expended by states, NGOs, and international organizations can and does make a specific difference by influencing the environment in which media function. But the discussion qualifies that assumption in a more constitutive way by relating media law reform to the process of transition itself. An examination of the enabling environment looks at media reform not only for its direct impact on the supply and demand for media-related speech in a society, but for its influence on the nature of the society and its recognition of the importance of the press in constituting a public sphere.

The market for loyalties argument is instrumental in the largest sense: transitions are encouraged because they are a way to develop free and independent media as a mode of breaking the old cartel. But there are other consequences. Insisting on free and independent media early in the process may mean providing a building block for the future stable set of democratic institutions. Even if the press does not perform effective watchdog, information-providing, and value-transmitting functions in the early days, that may be because of lack of experience. Encouraging early steps toward a culture of independence means that when the watchdog and other functions are necessary, media will be more prepared. Free and independent media may organically arise in a mature democracy, but artificial steps are necessary in many transition contexts. Finally, one might argue, that there are strong ideological and instrumental implications that the emergence of democratic institutions in transition societies will come faster and with greater mass support and involvement if there are free and independent media to develop and inspire public opinion.

The instrumental and constitutive questions are rarely asked, however, about the intervening society. It is possible, as we will see in chapter 8's discussion of the history of Radio Free Asia, that foreign policy reflects domestic pressures. A policy that targets Cuban media space and tries to alter the nature of imagery and messages there might well be based on a desire to satisfy local internal constituencies in the US and win votes and support from them. A more distinctive instrumental consequence was discussed in this chapter: the introduction of an altered media sphere in a target society to achieve proximate or longer range stability, benefitting a global environment. It is a frequently asserted assumption that the fostering of a more democratic world is within US national security interests. On the other hand, enhancing trade may be the predominant instrumental function of efforts to alter media infrastructures in transition societies, and the argument for media law reform and its impact on democratic tendencies may by and large be a diversion.

Finally, one might ask whether media law reform efforts have a constitutive effect on the donor society. This turns out to be an interesting and important question. As a constitutive matter, the drive for media law reform is a kind of spiritual or quasi religious quest. In part, the notion of export of an idea may help reinforce faith in the idea at home. There is no question that the great press organizations, such as the World Press Freedom Committee, believe deeply in the goals of free and independent media (and with justification). The point here is only that their advocacy of these ideas abroad has implications for the spread of belief in a perspective of the First Amendment within the United States. There is the psychology of replication.

Do technical assistance processes work? Are they effective? Perhaps the answer turns on whether one is taking an immediately instrumental, rather than a longer-term constitutive approach. An abundance of new media entities in the short term may not necessarily turn into an enduring press sector as a society develops. Media assistance may implant the idea of speech and democratic growth in the bones of a society, even where there are no immediate tangible consequences. Now, more than a decade after the transitions began in post-Soviet countries, the inevitable process of review and evaluation, second-guessing, and hindsight begin. Yet, in comparison with economic reform where market indicators can be used to measure the impact of financial aid, foreign assistance to media institutions is far more complicated to evaluate.

The "stages of transition" approach is fundamentally diagnostic and based on a mechanical view that marries instruments of change to transformations in the political system. The market for loyalties argument, in contrast, explains technical assistance in a somewhat different way: most externally energized transitions seek to have represented in the cartel of loyalty suppliers not previously included (presumably a voice seen as useful by the assisting regime). The very essence of some transitions is the fragmentation or destruction of a previous monopoly or oligopoly of power. The questions then are which new or additional suppliers in the market for loyalties are supported by which sources of power or money and with what objectives?

The transition in Russia in the late 1990s, was an example of a transition in which media companies were, in large part, proxies for major formations of capital and political influence with each formation seeking its own group of media entities. If it is true that press regulation or intervention is designed to create, establish, or enlarge a particular cartel, then external support of particular media during transitions must have a similar function. In some transitions, press institutions are almost by design captured by disparate interest groups each of which has a commitment to a particular political outcome. Donor assistance (from outside governments or NGOs) is not a lottery. It is often designed to ensure that a specific voice, not previously heard, is reinforced or that a prevailing voice is stronger.

Creating democracy was the stated objective of the international effort in Bosnia, but the donor governments had an intermediate major goal, and one that implicates the market for loyalties: to undermine the harsh, conflict-prone nationalist parties and promote civic-minded opposition parties. Although support for democratization and journalistic inquiry were mentioned as policy goals as well, donor governments approved large expenditures with the hope of creating a new political reality in Bosnia.[54] "Free and independent media" may mean obtaining, in the marketplace of ideas, favored instruments for articulating values and summoning public support that might not otherwise have a chance to flourish. In some instances, and this was the case in Russia between 1990 and 1995, the private and privatized media can establish a pressure group reinforcing a government approach that favours their continued vitality and, therefore, a particular political program.

A different contrast can be made between the stages of transition approach and the Hirschman "stability" analysis. The philosophy behind the stages analysis is definite: to enrich civil society or render elections more legitimate so as to reinforce tendencies toward a more responsive, democratic state. The Hirschman stability philosophy is more value free. There may be an optimal mix of "voice" and "exit," but even if it is ascertainable and achievable, that optimum may not be tied to "democracy," especially as measured by the extent to which the government is elected. Rather, intervening states often have varying agendas about the relationship between voice and exit. Some states may prize stability over democracy and, indeed, conclude that too much voice will increase, and not reduce, instability and the likelihood of decline.

It is one thing to state the need to steer the old cartel of voices away from a monopoly or oligopoly. It is another to try to understand how external governments (for example, United States or the European Union) take steps or foster processes to encourage expansion (or contraction) of media voices and to facilitate entrants who will be favorable to a particular kind of change. Too often the term "independent media" is used indiscriminately as a substitute for thinking about the problem of monopoly and oligopoly in a society's set of available voices. For a foreign policy of media assistance to make sense, there must be an implicit or explicit conceptualization and classification of the circumstances in which particular models and particular forms of assistance are productive.

There is little articulation of such a conceptualization by the decision makers themselves, so what constitutes an environment that enables a suitable media must be deduced from a large number of examples. The very idea of an enabling environment for media reform assumes the importance of particular forms of law for free and independent media and presumes the necessity of a certain kind of media for the development of democratic institutions. Some may argue, however, that in a media environment that is becoming increasingly global, the development of indigenous media is not an essential prerequisite for the emergence of stable democratic institutions. Take, for example, the foundation requirement for free media that the government should not have a monopoly on information, as it often does with respect to the legitimate use of force. The very ability of civil society to have access, at critical times, to the Internet, fax, and phone might be sufficient for the checking function of media to be performed. At the least, this may mean that a society where there is an imperfectly developed private media sector but a porous capacity for citizens to gain Internet access is less in need of intervention or reform than a society that is bereft of both. Still, the existence of global voices is no substitute for local voices that can play constitutional roles in improving public debate.

Conclusion

I have sought to suggest various analytical frameworks that might account for efforts by one state, or a group of states, to alter the media and information flows in target societies, to change the structures in which speech takes place so as to change content and impact. I have focused on the search for stability, the desire to influence transitions and regime change, and to reorient the shares in a market for loyalties. These analytic approaches emerge from time to time in the next chapters and provide the basis for an overall framework for globalization and the media in chapter 9. Now, however, I turn to various aspects of the rhetoric of change, what I call tropes of restructuring.

II

Tropes of Restructuring

3

Metaphor and Model in Media Restructuring

In the last two chapters, I sought to describe a shift in thinking about laws and policy concerning media space, a shift away from considering rules and structures as the product of a single state, toward thinking about them as the dynamic result of multiple interactions, interactions among states and with transnational corporations among others. In this chapter, I ask how these shifts are reflected in language of policy formation.

The vocabulary developed in the past, in the context of relatively uncontested national sovereignty, itself exercises dominion over the conceptualizations of the future. It is as if people must sing the songs they know, even if the setting makes the music discordant and the lyrics less relevant. Basic verities—commitments to the right to receive and impart information—must be honored, but the structure and meaning of accepted principles is in flux. Inversions occur because of the complexities of the application of ancient concepts to new circumstances. Collective identities are threatened, democratic determinations of values are swamped by cumulative and individualized decisions, existing structures are found empty of significance and power. Traditions of control and censorship move from older language usages to the deployment of newer technologies. New media technologies arise or old ones must be redefined in radically different social and political circumstances. Given the pervasive remapping of media structures around the world, this task of conceptualization is a massive one. In this chapter, for example, I discuss how two techniques—the search for models and the invention of metaphors that provide direction to those involved in media assistance—have or can be used to think about and participate in the global restructuring of the media.

Drawing on the experience of others, proponents of one media regulation system or another invoke what they deem to be a "model" for imitation. Examples of "models" are the BBC model or what is described as a US model of market forces that control outcomes. Rarely is there discussion of how these models are defined, what sources of information govern beliefs about them, and how such models are used in legislative debate. The second technique for conceptualization discussed here involves the use of metaphor to articulate the path of change. Metaphor is used, especially, early in a process, often where there is no clear existing alternative model and a literary trope is an easy way to capture the unknown. Metaphor often loses its currency as greater familiarity with reality confounds the allusion. But metaphor continues, sometimes misleadingly, to be a mode of discourse that influences the shaping of law.[1]

In the particular case of new technologies, the search for models and metaphors is more desperate because things seem so lacking in coordinates. There is the lurking question, whether technology—especially transborder technology like satellite and the Internet—intrinsically confounds and resists law, makes law something different from what we know, perhaps a negotiation between state and supplier rather than an order from government to citizen. This series of doubts whets the appetite for an approach to certainty, a rhetorical ploy or a hint from the past that will tell us how to cope when apparent technological determinism makes ordinary legal steps seemingly irrelevant.

Throughout the enterprise, dealing both with the new technologies and the old, not only the translation of words, or even of concepts, but the translation of deeply-engaged settings and the machinery of administration must be taken into account. The terminology of all international norms relating to speech, all models, in this sense, is embedded in the particular context. In most modern societies, the elegant language of democracy and openness must be observed even while pursuing the restrictions and consequences of national interest described in the previous chapters. Each era has its style and vocabulary in statutes as well as in dress and modes of living. The style in the West is one of openness, pluralism, and freedom to receive and impart information. With very few national exceptions, that style is used to the extent possible in background documents, in speeches, in findings, or prologues to statutes. And the rhetoric or style of openness is, as indicated above, itself a tool of seeming inclusion.[2] This is the Orwellian point: the political use of language to cover behavior that is its opposite. The language of openness may be considered part of a strategy to convince governments and the public that a course of action, pursued for motives of self-interest, is wholly consistent with international norms. As put by Thomas Franck,

[G]overnment cannot govern by force alone. To be effective . . . law needs to secure the habitual, voluntary compliance of its subjects; it cannot rely entirely, or even primarily, upon the commanding power of a sovereign to compel obedience. Consequently, governments no longer blinded by the totalitarian miasma seek to validate themselves in such a way as to secure a high degree of voluntary public acquiescence in the governing process.[3]

There is a faith, too, in the portability of magical words, those with constitutional gravitas. It is sometimes difficult for those from Washington or Boston who market the First Amendment in Kiev, Kuala Lumpur, Bangkok, or Budapest to understand or translate the complexities of their adaptation. One cannot talk of "judges," of "neutral principles," or of "accountability of government officials to a rule of law" without sensitivity to the differences that may unravel the hidden meanings of these terms. And in the transformed global information space, concepts such as "freedom of speech" must be revisited in light of altered circumstances that belie their previous footing. Even sophisticated experts, schooled in the relativism of anthropology and sociology, find it hard to sort out the comparative aspects of all these questions and to help determine which element from the bundle of historically enacted statutes should be adapted to what context. It is easier to conclude that laws and institutions come in ready-made, almost modular packages, model statutes or constitutions. Yet, the analyst or observer is more than a naturalist working with cabinets stuffed with statutes, pinned like butterflies under glass. To examine change formally, the project of chronicling specific statutory drafts and laws, country by country, organizing them by category, and engaging in a textual analysis comparing proposed and achieved transformations in one state to those in another is necessary. But far more is required, far more understanding, far more context, and far more efforts to match the legal equivalents of modern technology to the situation at hand.

Models

By the use of models, I refer to something quite specific, namely the proposition that from one national practice, a scheme or approach can be abstracted and applied elsewhere. Models influence thought patterns; they expand or limit imagination. Because of their persuasive force and use in shaping debate, there are investments in furthering the appreciation of one model versus another. When applied to a new context, a model can be unitary, or presented in segments for study or adoption. The model can reflect practice accurately or it can be reshaped, abstracted, and represented in ways that camouflage imperfections or reflect political biases.

A model ordinarily suggests a construct that should be adopted because of its virtues, but it can also be defined for the purpose of rejection. Models function in one setting but are applied to another. As an example, in the United States, one could say about media that there is a "newspaper model" of regulation and a "broadcasting model" of regulation.[4] This is a shorthand mode for distinguishing between a medium where government regulation is deemed appropriate and one where government regulation is virtually forbidden. Media entities invest in furthering the idea of the "newspaper model" and for its extension to new and existing technologies.

A model, in this sense, is more than a set of words concerning the makeup of regulation or a version of what counts as law in a particular country. A model can convey a philosophical and economic perspective and it is often introduced into a debate for that purpose. At another level of abstraction, the model itself rests on higher models, like that of the "rule of law," a set of conventions about how the entire system in which the media-specific model should be seen. To further this superstructure of thinking, the United States and other Western democracies have had elaborate rule of law projects, sophisticated efforts to encourage the transplanting of the epiphenomena of law, but more than that, the shifting of fundamental patterns of thinking about the way law functions in the society. By the late 1990s the Department of State had a high-ranking official, Joseph Onek, in charge of encouraging the implementation of a rule of law policy in China, Central Asia, and in all societies where its influence could be usefully exercised.

Models can be shipped from one society to another at the request of the receiver. States, weighing different development strategies, act like consumers and shop in the supermarket of legislative alternatives. On the other hand as Julie Mertus observes, "the legal transplant process is generally marked by some form of coercion or at least heavy political and economic incentives. Those states that adapt their laws to conform with the laws of politically powerful states are rewarded with economic assistance, advantageous trade arrangements, and other political plums; while those that do not are penalized."[5] Between the voluntary and the coercive is what might be called the hortatory: a process of privileging one model over another by affecting the public debate, changing public opinion. The controversial New World Information and Communication Order debate of the late 1970s and 1980s was a collective effort to alter the perception of free market or Western models of media regulation and their relationship to other, often socialist, forms.[6] Similarly, what Samuel Huntington has called "the clash of civilizations" can be reread as identifying a debate in which some models, by some participants, are privileged over others.[7]

The process of transferring legal models—taking what is known and considered good by one group and transferring it to another—is far from novel.

There was the reception of Roman law in later Europe, the spread of English law through the colonies of the British Empire, even into parts of the United States which had never been under British rule, and the tremendous impact of the French Civil Code on other civil law systems in Europe and abroad, and latterly, the spread of American law to Europe.[8]

In modern times, war and victory have been the prime occasions for legal transplant. Occupation by victorious allies, at the end of World War II, was the occasion for the imposition of modified versions of democratic media laws in vanquished Japan and Germany. Of course, it was not only media laws but also entire systems that were transferred.[9]

The appetite for the transfer of legal models was repeated in the 1960s during a time labeled a "decade for development."[10] In a period of decolonialism, "departing colonial powers hastily imposed carbon copies of their own documents [and laws], which evolved from different cultural and historical backgrounds."[11] It was then that the legal academy nourished the taste for engaging in this particular export trade, funded by entities like the Ford Foundation, and later by government, to facilitate development through the transplant or adaptation of Western laws. The growth of a law component of the Peace Corps and the emergence of partnerships between American law schools and Latin American and African counterparts were part of an emerging machinery developed for problem solving and for promoting "a modern vision of law as an instrument of development policy along capitalist and democratic lines."[12] The project of transferring legal models was embedded in a set of beliefs about economic development, democracy, and the rule of law.[13]

The use of models in the transfer of media law to transition societies is similarly embedded in a grand view of the role of speech and society.[14] The task of the expert is often to emphasize the utility or ethical importance of openness in speech, find the bit of law that deals with the particular issue involved (e.g., cross-media ownership or control of obscenity) and then help to retool or modify that bit for adoption elsewhere. In the post–cold war world, this task of advocacy and transfer has been institutionalized and in Central and Eastern Europe, the former Soviet Union, and elsewhere financed by supplier governments. The export of broadcasting systems from the West is deemed important because of a deeply held belief that democratic media, under the rule of law, are central to the development of a democratic society. It may also be an aspiration, by the exporting country, that the adoption of a particular system of legal regulation results in continued relations and the export of television product.[15]

Gradations exist in the means by which the transfer takes place. James Gardner suggests the following as categories of a taxonomy of law-shifting methods: (1) direct transfer of legal institutions and instruments, (2) indirect transfer of legal concepts and models, (3) invited legal transfer, where the initiative and encouragement for the legal transfer process comes from the recipient legal culture, (4) imposed or uninvited legal transfer at the initiative of the "exporting" legal culture, (5) infused—"premeditated" or "planned"—processes of legal transfer, direct or indirect, wherein the initiative comes from the exporting legal culture, and (6) more occasional ad hoc borrowing.[16] While there is inevitably blurring among these categories—and they overlap as well as complement each other—some use of them to describe specific examples in the media area may be helpful.

India's debate over broadcast reform, straddling the millennium, is an example of a mix of these elements.[17] Models of mixed heritage loom in the Indian experience. Without question, aspects of Indian broadcasting policy are post-colonial and were influenced by two separate British models. The first model uses broadcasting as a quite specific instrument for the enactment of government policy. The second model is embodied by the BBC, its long-time monopoly over British broadcasting space, and its hard-to-replicate tradition of independence and nurturing of the public sphere. The Indian broadcasting system is also a reflection of the socialist models of media that the state fostered during the time when India had close ties with the Soviet Union. In this third model, broadcasting was instrumental in nation building, instruction, economic development, and shaping identity.

Now, the US model and elements of other systems are being brought to bear. In 1997, India was in the throes of a debate over what form new media legislation should take. Cable television had revolutionized the market for television programming, largely by bringing foreign satellite channels to a society that had been monopolized by state television. The prospect of direct-to-home broadcasting also threatened old ways and the Internet loomed after that. Those involved in the redrafting process explicitly invoked the notion of models as an aid to thinking about legislation. Proposals were framed in reference to US, British, or other models, but the multinational corporations ascendant in the market, comfortable with US precedents favored the model that embodied them. Those who had the greatest interest in change opposed how the government in its recommendations had presented the various foreign, models, on the ground that they had emphasized, and sometimes misrepresented, the restrictions that were included.[18] Models—the use of information from foreign practices—had been refashioned or re-imagined so that those in government could use them to justify solutions that extended the practices of the past.

In India, the use of foreign models for media reform was largely indirect (in the Gardner taxonomy).[19] In the period leading up to the introduction of legislation, the government, independently, undertook studies of the practices of other countries. A great deal of this was done in the Ministry of Information and Broadcasting, working from available literature. The government was acting under the prod of the Indian Supreme Court, which had found the existing system of regulation and state control constitutionally inadequate. The Court turned to American and British precedents because of their relevance to a model of speech in society as embraced in the International Covenant on Civil and Political Rights. In the decision in *Ministry of Information & Broadcasting v. Cricket Association of Bengal* in 1995, commonly known as the Hero Cup decision, Justice Reddy's opinion dealt with the exploration, in European and American jurisprudence, of the rights of viewers and listeners. He relied on human rights documents and interpretations of constitutional provisions from abroad not because they were binding, but because they provided insight from highly respected individuals who held positions similar to his own, dealing with fundamental documents much like Article 19 of the Constitution of India. Where there was a consensus among interpreters, and where that consensus has gained added sanction from being incorporated into international documents, they constituted an applicable model.[20]

Justice Jeevan Reddy's invocation, in the Hero Cup case, of European and American jurisprudence models to rethink Indian constitutional law, was a creative use of foreign concepts: not mechanical, not to further a particular private or cartel view, but rather, in a reasoned way, to determine an alternate idea of speech and the role of government. The opinion emphasized that Parliament and the government were mandated by the Constitution to restructure state broadcasting so that they would be under an autonomous public authority and, also, to have a form of media architecture that permitted independent competition with the government outlets. The court legitimated the invocation of foreign models reinforcing a tendency that may already have existed among those at the Ministry of Information and Broadcasting charged with designing the change.

Ultimately, in any context, whether or how models have persuasive power or whether foreign practices much influence media law is questionable. In India, at the very moment of debate in the 1990s, legal models from the West were widely accepted because of the predilections of the coalition then in power. Because no explicit compulsion (in the form of foreign aid conditioned on legislative conformance) existed, and only the rational or aesthetic appeal of any model weighed in its favor, domestic politics were determinative. Models served to enrich public discussion until a new and powerful Minister of Information and Broadcasting, Arun Jaitley, brought his own synthesis of ideas, informed by a political inclination to the market, to bear on the media statutory process. At that point the model moved up a level in abstraction, from external suggestion to a philosophy of the state.

The post-Soviet experience in Central and Eastern Europe, in contrast, in the Gardner taxonomy, veered more toward direct transfer or at least attempts in that direction. Just as "peacemakers" have replaced occupation forces in zones of conflict, a softer, more generalized, and expanded pattern of reshaping law has taken place in so-called transitions around the world. In Bosnia-Hercegovina, under the aegis of the Office of High Representative, the transfer of models for media regulation was essentially direct and coercive, even though the patina of consent was often employed.[21] Less coercive, but certainly direct, is the requirement that countries, like Hungary and Poland, conform to media regulation (as in other fields) in order to become members of the European Union. Their laws had to be audited, by authorities at the European Union, to determine whether they met the standard for entry.[22]

Throughout the transitions, the process of law transfer became more institutionalized, more administrative, more international, and more planned. The United States Agency for International Development (USAID) invested heavily in the process, as did the Soros Foundation's Open Society Institute and many others. The American Bar Association through its Central and East European Law Initiative (CEELI) organized lawyers around the United States to participate in what was deemed an important national opportunity to reshape law elsewhere. Funded by USAID, CEELI, and similar public and private organizations, established offices with full-time staff in a score of countries throughout the former Soviet Union, and dispatched volunteer lawyers to work with local parliamentarians, judges, law schools, and law offices there. Given the quantity of assignments and loci of contact, patterns of technical assistance emerged. CEELI organized workshops, trained and exchanged judges and lawyers, and, like a dry cleaning service, provided almost overnight legal assessments of draft legislation and of proposed structural changes in a legal system. Media law received a great deal of attention, although much of the focus was on matters similarly close to the American heart, namely commercial law, privatization, and the rule of law generally. Legal academics that have taken part in the process have often written about the process, sometimes self-critically.[23]

Whether the mode for transfer is direct or less coercive, there is another way of thinking about the transfer of media structures. An analysis might distinguish between the idea of law as the shadow understructure of a finished model, or, rather, as a set of spare parts, machine elements of a varying goal. There are occasions for transfer—as when an integrated system of financial transactions is contemplated—where the components that make up law on one end of the arrangement must be compatible with the components on the other end. Just as network compatibility is desirable among parts of a financial system, the distribution of imagery may have equivalent requirements. Law is not necessarily a set of modular components that can be taken from inventory after having been proved in practice in one setting and then moved to another. It is tempting to examine such components, and to some extent a checklist can exist.

Media law is an ensemble of practices and is composed, in its cabinet of wonders, of laws on defamation and libel, the licensing of broadcasters, accreditation of journalists, censorship or control of content, antitrust laws, tax laws, and others. These laws compose, enrich, and embody the model of media law, but transporting it as a model involves more than conveying machine elements of a deconstructible whole. The ideal model implies a philosophy that can carry across cultures, Particular statutes are difficult to transport if they had their source in certain local and idiosyncratic practices and traditions. Models are a combination of aspiration and approaches to achievement. Fully adopted in a society other than the one they were created for, they create problems in implementation. On the other hand, the best kinds of legal models are like an excellent architectural maquette. They incorporate an aesthetic, convey an idea, and provide a set of devices that allow the observer (client, architect, public) to determine how the material and intellectual ideas ought to be absorbed, altered, or rejected.

I have thought of the contrast between these various approaches: law as a set of models and law as a set of spare and interconnected parts in connection with efforts at telecommunications or media ownership reform in Russia in the late 1990s. In one example, USAID provided funds to the Moscow Center for Media Law and

Policy to help draft telecommunications-related legislation for the Duma. The US Congress had recently enacted the 1996 Telecommunications Act and Russia was engaged, at least at some level, in thinking through its telecommunications regulatory structure. As a result there were multiple requests to identify specific portions of the new US law that would be useful in Russia and then to obtain translations of those segments. The 1996 telecommunications law was thought to be useful because of its efforts to increase competition in the telecommunications sphere, both in long distance and local service, by facilitating entry into all segments, and to increase competition in video distribution. Whether it actually achieved—in the United States—what was claimed for the law, and whether it actually enacted the objectives that were attributed to it is unclear. It did, however, embody a model of what a telecommunication system should be, what role government and the market should play, and whether "convergence" between video and telephony could be advanced through changes in the market structure.

In reality, the specific provisions of the US telecommunications law itself were far less useful when transferred to Russia. The law was, in fact, a series of spare parts that fit the US context (and then, sometimes, badly) but would totally lack utility elsewhere. Telecommunications reform in the United States was designed specifically to take into account the consequences of the Bell monopoly breakup in the early 1970s and the fact that the industry was bifurcated into a dominant long-distance carrier and a series of regional monopolies. It was idiosyncratic. There were hundreds of provisions, but it is doubtful if any one of them could be adjusted for another context. In this way, the statute was the product far more of complex lobbying than of a philosophy or approach that could be shifted and absorbed as an ideal model would need to be.

One might wonder whether media law is so country specific, so tied to the mores, history, political structure, and regulatory style and state of the sector in a particular place that the application of laws from other contexts would be only marginally helpful. Or, on the contrary, one might conclude that media law and structures, especially in increasingly international or global societies, are so much a part of a transnational whole that any attempt at sharp local differences, unique in style and outcome, is virtually doomed. The need for uniformity can arise from cultural globalization or technology.

Without question, some aspects of media law are specifically local and tied, deeply, to their context. In India, concerns and experiences about religion and media are far different from those in the United States or Europe. Communal violence and its relationship to media has scarred memory. Language, too, has extraordinary variables that are so tied to social structure that media rules concerning them have to be dealt with carefully. An approach that consciously and affirmatively implements use of multiple languages on broadcasts so as to reinforce pluralism may be deemed useful in some national contexts, such as Canada. On the other hand, a policy that allows language pluralism to arise more or less from the market, as in the United States, may be far more suitable there. In the Internet, the affirmative effort to achieve language pluralism is both local and global.[24] Undoubtedly models can be fashioned that suggest language pluralism policies, but they would be vague, abstract, and complex.

Given the hazards associated with models, mistakes in transference are frequently made. Harold Bloom, the great literary critic, has argued that misreadings, rather than being a subject for scorn, are a vital element of the creative process. He was referring to the evolution of meaning in poetry or similar texts, but mistaken interpretations of foreign models and the fashioning of new domestic policies out of old and foreign texts are, almost certainly instrumental in legal growth.[25] Take one of the most frequent and most creative misreadings: vaunting the "British model," in contexts outside of the one that made the significance and uniqueness of the BBC possible, just at the very moment when British media structures are being substantially altered and subjected to critical review in the United Kingdom. The same is true of American practices. The unalloyed beauties of the "free market" model of the United States in relation to media can be and are vigorously questioned at home at the same time as they are elevated, enshrined, and uncritically propagated abroad.[26]

Misreadings may be positive or negative, intentional or subconscious. The agent of the transferor or the agent of the transferee may promulgate them. But, either way, such misreadings and mis-citations often become an integral aspect of legal evolution. How the model is interpreted is often as important as the model itself. Different readings of laws and legal practices can lead to different interpretations of the model with different consequences for ensuing legislative exercises. Representations of a model in a neutral and formal way often mask an argument for a result that is politically desirable or the result of the compromises necessary to accommodate various interest groups or parts of a coalition.

Misreadings are frequent because the complexities, technical details, and the very structure of media laws arise out of a specific tradition. In the United States, there is a complicated relationship between rules, licensing, and sanctions for the violation of rules. When the Fairness Doctrine that required broadcasters to provide the various sides of controversial issues of public importance was in full force, it was not enough to know the content of the doctrine to understand its implications.[27] Its true meaning could only be understood by knowing when and whether the Federal Communications Commission (FCC) enforced it, how much of a sanction would be imposed, and whether violation of the doctrine would be relevant at the time of a license renewal.

The fact that license renewals were virtually automatic in the United States, itself, affected the dynamic of the rule's meaning. At times, societies that enforce a rule readily and harshly claim that they are adopting a standard that exists in another place. But while these rules would have existed in the other country they might not have been enforced so stringently. Rules come fixed with an entire cohort of conditions, assumptions, and enforcement policies. A true adoption does not take place—and maybe never can take place—without adopting the surroundings along with the actual rule. Those who argue that the explicit limitations on the right to receive and impart information in Article 10 of the European Convention on Political and Human Rights ought to be eliminated make this point. A model for the protection of speech that can be sensitively interpreted in Western Europe might be used to justify state abuses in another part of the globe.[28]

Just as there are often dual judicial precedents leading in almost opposite directions as common law is interpreted, models can look two ways to different audiences as well.[29] Free speech models can be cited for their breadth or for their exceptions. This ambiguity may itself be a functional value for government officials who invoke foreign models. It is no surprise that in the contest over the extent of regulation, transnational media companies often cite those examples from abroad that serve their purposes or interpret models in ways most favorable to them. Models have a different point for them. They have a stake in common language in statutes, common philosophies in enforcement. Transnational companies desire predictability in investment and the consequences of programming decisions. Overlap, consistency, and the evolution of common forms of regulation, all lead to efficient and perhaps better products. Those companies that seek to do business globally, even if they program regionally, wish to have some common vocabulary, common approaches in the absence of a supranational authority. A desire for harmonization of media regulation may mean a specialized invocation of favored models.

However deferential or absorbing a society seems to be to models from abroad and however amenable the model is to local situations, the law will inevitably be shaped by the country's internal political and social structures. Even in the most difficult transitions—those from the authoritarian Soviet regimes to the democratic democracies—what went before was highly relevant to what went after. Language, thought patterns, and regulatory perspectives are ingrained and inherent. Even where models are specifically adopted—say the model of the BBC for autonomy of public service television—old relationships between governments and bureaucracies cannot easily be avoided. Creating, understanding, and communicating models is a delicate process, one in which the assumptions of superiority on the part of the purported transferor is not far from the surface.

Reflecting on this point, Julie Mertus has written that "Many US and Western European scholars have been compliant with [a] dominant one-directional process, studying the ways in which constitutions and laws in Eastern Europe can, should, and have been reformed to adapt to US and Western European standards. . . . Few critiques are made of the assumption that the US and Western European models should or can be transplanted."[30] In a period of globalization, when technology and the changes that technology mandates have so substantial an impact on practices around the world, comparative approaches become essential.

Metaphor: Trade Routes in the Sky

Statutes and fields of law have structures, often hidden. If they do not, they are a mere compilation of words, a stringing together of legal coping with anticipated events. Even when the task is almost impossible, the individual human scribe, or the society itself, trying to make sense out of these rude and artificial interventions, past or proposed, seeks to impose some pattern, some way of making sense of a regulation or set of regulations. In rejecting arbitrariness and striving for this idea of order, a statute or pattern of law is forced into the vocabulary of the familiar. Frequently that process involves the use of metaphor. Metaphors are necessary tools for taking what appears to be chaos and providing some comfort, some semblance of pattern. As metaphor affects reasoning, it facilitates the formation of restructuring and legislating that accompanies the new technologies.

The Internet is a prevailing example of this phenomenon. So difficult has it been to consider the appropriate regulatory architecture for the Internet, so forbidding is it to move from existing categories to a new form of analysis that the society is thrown back to previous ways of thinking. For its first public decade, Internet philosophers evoked the overwhelming "highway" metaphor. This metaphor drew on all of a highway's subcategories: entrances and exits, lanes, potholes, and speed limits. We do not know the ways that very strong metaphor controls thinking and, to some extent, policy. Certainly, in the Internet's first decade, the metaphor led to an idea of impersonality of information, streaming nameless data, like anonymous automobiles and trucks, subject to little in the way of interference and channeling. The content of highways is not directed from outside, nor is the destination of its users. On the other hand—and this has not always been considered—every car, every truck, is identified, tagged, and traceable.

In this chapter, I look at a specific metaphor for thinking about technologies of globalization. The metaphor of trade routes—used from time to time to describe the distribution of ideas and imagery—can nourish our conception of transnational paths of electronic communications delivery. Information became so valuable a commodity by the late twentieth century, and trade in information such an important part of world balances and deficits, that the metaphor of information trade routes can add to an understanding of current practices in law and regulation. Our minds are full of Rupert Murdoch and Disney, CNN and the BBC, as traders in information, great shippers of data, and distributors of huge slogs of sitcoms and news and advertisements. In the common reading of the world of electronic signals, media are considered "global," in the sense of a constant and ever-present net that can deposit information everywhere, disregarding boundaries.

Our most recent experiences with information flows seem to confirm and underscore a belief that data careen around the world from server to server, in patterns that seem virtually impervious to purposive planning or political and legal intervention.[31] Sender and receiver are linked in ways that appear indifferent to the route or mode by which they are connected. The obsolescence of boundaries, as I have already pointed out, is reinforced. So too has been the effect of the seamlessness of telephony, at least in the developed world, obliterating distance and time. In telephony, transmission pathways seemed invisible or at least irrelevant to the substantive decisions of most users. Although users are almost never conscious of it, establishment of the postal service, telegrams, and telephones required the construction of international systems of regulation. Assurance of adherence to worldwide standards was a condition for their formation and guaranteed their instantaneous nature and compatibility.

Central to this vision is the idea that the world's electronic penumbra makes information and data ubiquitous, capable of distribution everywhere, even if there are inequities in the manner and pattern of uploading and gaps in the earthbound infrastructure to receive them. One central component of the new global information field is satellite technology, but satellites are not ubiquitous. For satellites, at least generations of satellites now in use, location is everything. Satellite routes for the distribution of images—even though digitally communicated—are neither entirely random nor unaffected by the historic and arbitrary boundaries of nation-states. Rather, as with their nautical counterparts of ports of call, certain orbital slots for communications satellites have advantages over other information routes.

It is no longer fear of pirates or factors equally cinematographic that determines choice of passage. Still, issues of security in carrying goods (in the case of the satellites, information) over long distances exist now as they did in the historical trade. Satellite technology seems to generate zones of passage indifferent to content. But the emerging rules of orbital slots and satellite transponders show some similarities to rules of trade provided by ancient ports of call.[32] What the new factors are, and how governments and businesses interact to shape the value of one route as opposed to another, are still open questions. Because these routes leave no marks and little in the way of associated activity, how they develop and the impact of having one route rather than another have not been frequently examined.[33]

Satellite patterns are trade routes that have their own agonizing histories and their own differentiated impacts. In the past, a trade route formed along a set of points that permitted ships to travel, receive coal for refueling, and obtain water, food, and recreation for the sailors, in short, all stops necessary for goods to travel from point A to point B (and onward to C and D), usually in return of other goods such as raw materials or manufactures. A good part of the history of colonialism can be read as a set of efforts of manufacturing and trading states to gain power or sovereignty over the points that were key to the maintenance of trading routes.

The chain that linked these harbors was complicated. Often, first a monopoly trading company and then a colonial power gained full dominion and sovereignty over signal points along the route.[34] There were negotiations between the trader (or the government of the trader) and the local authority (king, tribe, city, or otherwise). The reliable existence of these points was essential to investment and to the success of trade. Sovereign entities often sought certain benefits for allowing others to use their ports, sometimes financial, sometimes otherwise.[35] Points on ancient trade routes were valuable because raw materials could be loaded there as vessels moved from place to place. Since ancient times, trade routes favored ports that opened up to large consuming markets as well as ports where raw materials could be acquired.

Today, satellites and their orbital slots constitute the points necessary for delivery of video (and other) signals over long distances. The trade routes for information are superficially very different from their nautical predecessors. Because the process is electronic, painless, free of manual labor, and invisible, no novels—science fiction aside—will be written about information trade routes; no Herman Melville of global transmissions will arise. Lives are not risked. Also, these trade routes do not have the same secondary benefits that the historic routes had. No coaling stations are required as intermediate stops between the original ports of debarkation and the ultimate ports of call, stations that once may have allowed some coastal towns to develop. The trade in information does not give the "colony" a chance to sell its goods the way it did in the historic model since after the new shippers deliver a manufactured product they do not need to return with raw materials.

Yet the similarities between ancient trade routes and modern ones have the potential to instruct. The first powerful generation of communications satellites was located in a precise and limited geostationary orbit above the equator, the only orbit that allows continuous contact between a satellite and a single ground station. Slots on this orbit are finite, and as a result contested, bargained for, and, to some extent, colonized.[36] Certain orbital slots are more important than others because they each have a particular terrestrial footprint. A footprint that reaches a vast, wealthy, or politically important population can be more valuable than one that does not. Governments seek to use such natural advantages as their terrestrial location to gain greater economic leverage and, for example, more favorable orbital slots.

Control of routes may also be used to control the nature of the cargo—what information, such as European programming, public service programming, anti-government programming, is carried. Control over the route may allow control over what legal constraints are imposed. For example, indecency regulation or prohibitions on subversion or the advocacy of terror may be enforced on some routes and not others. Improvements in satellites add further complexities, just as changing shipping technologies did in seventeenth- and eighteenth-century trade routes.[37]

There are moments, too, when existing patterns of trade routes are altered, sometimes permanently, by war, new technology, or changing patterns of consumption.

For the traditional trade routes, the opening of the Panama Canal or the Suez Canal reduced once important points on the trade route compass to impotency and brought new sites to prominence. Transitions from one direct broadcast satellite format to another or the introduction of communication satellite paths that do not rely on geostationary satellites change the relative value of orbital slots. Governments maintain the value of some orbits and preserve and enforce their preferred orbital slots and satellite systems (their favored ports) rather than others by out-lawing some receivers.[38] They pressure channel service providers (the new networks) to use favored carriers. Examples of this were the preference shown by Spain for Hispasat, Egypt for Nilesat, or Turkey for Turksat. These deliberate governmental interventions increase the value of some trade routes and reduce the value of others. Low earth orbital satellites, much greater in number, with very different characteristics may replace old technologies and, combined with the Internet, may render existing slots less valuable.

Trade routes have always defined markets. They enrich the immediate environments of the ports of call by creating subsidiary needs for commercial support, such as the building or maintenance of ships or the provision of housing for those who ensure the security of the routes themselves. The route itself implied a particular form and scope of trade and a set of needs that were a significant by-product of the route.[39] Satellite slots are quite different from trade routes in this regard. They are more modern in their technical coolness and have less impact on local economies. The opening of new routes in the sky for the distribution of images has radically altered the strategies of transnational corporations, just as the opening of new eighteenth-century routes altered the strategies of their equivalent business entities. These new routes also require new definitions of markets, as when states use the capacity of the new technology and the routes that are made available to reach out to their diaspora populations.

All of this suggests the need for a richer understanding of the geopolitical, economic, and technical factors that determine who controls which orbital slots, what satellites gain access to those slots and what program services are actually carried. Much of the literature of globalization deals only with the last point and its supposed cultural impact. An understanding of the infrastructure—the way satellite routes come into being and are regulated—is necessary for an assessment of the consequences of information and entertainment flows. One way to begin this process is to examine some examples—small case studies—of the differentiation of satellite patterns. These examples help show how the struggles of users, governments, and the international community mirror similar events in earlier efforts to control paths of commerce.

Tonga and Control of Orbital Slots

The Kingdom of Tonga is an odd pioneer in creating political control of orbital slots and turning that control to economic advantage.[40] In the late twentieth century, bureaucratic wiliness, not armed force, allowed Tonga to accomplish its objective of becoming a power, at least temporarily, in information routes. If a country wants to assert its right to control an orbital slot, their request must be considered and approved by the International Telecommunication Union (ITU) and its World Administrative Radio Conferences (now known as WARCs). Modern bureaucracies, not distant potentates, determine the existence of routes. It is neither papal decrees nor regal ordinances, but bland officials in Geneva that organize commercially consequential lines on maps.[41] Trade routes emerge because of complex compromises, not because of the exercise of cannons or the clever use of sophisticated maps.[42]

Tonga has been one of the most dramatic actors in the process of acquiring orbital slots. In the 1976 Bogotá Declaration, Tonga, along with other equatorial states, asserted that equatorial nations ought to have preferred access, almost by natural law, to the geostationary orbit in outer space above.[43] The industrialized West disagreed, arguing that outer space was a kind of public domain not belonging a priori to any state. International rules favored allocation of orbital slots to those highly developed nations that had the financial and technological resources to use the slots for satellites. In the 1980s, the ITU adopted a policy that, while rejecting the assertion of the equatorial states, established a process for claiming an orbital slot that sought to leave some leeway for developing countries.

The new global plan . . . represented a marked departure from the existing legal regime. Since the early days of the space race, the United States and other countries with the technical know-how and financial resources to place communication satellites into orbit generally . . . had their choice of orbital positions and frequency blocks. This system of 'first come, first served' has been bitterly resented by many developing countries whose satellite plans have only recently come to fruition. It is place, these countries . . . argued for the kind of *a priori* plan tentatively approved by the 1985 WARC.[44]

In ITU's new procedure, member states could file their intention to use a slot. Then, if they in fact used it within a reasonable period, they would be granted control of that slot.[45] Tonga used this paper-filing opportunity more than any other country. It obtained claims on seven valuable slots even without drawing on its status as an equatorial state. As with its counterparts in the terrestrial trade routes, Tonga transferred use of its space to others, private telecommunications corporations, for economic benefits. Because neither the ITU nor the "paper-satellite" countries had any means of policing the slot once a corporation launched its satellite there, the orbital slot was allowed to become a commodity controlled by the leasing corporate entity.

By 1997 the international community, at the ITU Radio Conference, modified the procedures for orbital slot allocation to lessen the likelihood of a Tonga-like occupation or warehousing of orbital slots in the future. The 1997 plan shortened the length of time a satellite application could remain on file from nine years (six plus an automatic three-year extension) to seven years (five years plus a two-year extension, conditional on an indication that a satellite was not launched despite good faith efforts to do so). Still, an effort to impose financial prerequisites for the posting of allocation claims was beaten back. Language endorsing "equitable access" was retained, recognizing some desire to ensure representation for developing countries. This compromise measure gained support from Tonga and other equatorial countries. It was also favored by satellite businesses that preferred using these countries as ports of entry, rather than other, more truculent and difficult holders of orbital rights.

In March 1998 the national satellite company of Tonga, Tongasat, together with Russian-owned and registered Inspace Corp., announced a plan to launch an ambitious fleet of satellites to serve the Asian Pacific region, and perhaps beyond, using Tonga's seven ITU-registered slots. This "paper-plan" to use "paper-satellites," if it were to occur, would have made Tonga a major telecommunications service provider. The country would have benefited from profits gained by using the orbital slots, far and above income collected from merely selling the airspace.[46] In the end, this plan was not realized.

Think of this Tongan experience, repeated elsewhere, in trade route terms. A geographical location (be it an ocean port or an orbital slot) might have the potential to be of great value to traders. For it to become an active site within a trading pattern, however, requires more: a degree of investment, security, and establishment of a physical port with attendant facilities. Tonga had gained the right to a slot, but only with further activity could that slot actually become part of a route that would bring financial and other benefits to Tonga.

Ironically, the United States, which had been one of the strongest critics of Tongasat on the international scene, indirectly acknowledged that speculation in orbital slots was acceptable. The United States did this in 1996 through the auctioning by the Federal Communications Commission of an orbital slot for direct broadcasting services (DBS), alleged at the time to be the last DBS slot capable of "seeing" all of the continental United States. MCI agreed in 1996 to pay $682 million for this slot—a staggering sum, reinforcing the idea that some points on trade routes are more valuable than others.

The story of Tonga is, of course, an anomaly. As with trade routes of the past, it was not only the actual, physical, terrestrial route or the points of transportation that ultimately counted but those factors together with the economic and political forces that controlled trade along those routes. Even if orbital slots are widely distributed among states, the arrangements to control satellites themselves, and the ultimate predominance of the West in the satellite trade, makes the analogy to the past more striking.[47]

Competition to Control the Satellites

Let us thus turn from the orbital slots themselves to the satellites that fill them. If the slots are the trade route equivalent of ports of call, then the satellites can be likened to the great trading vessels. They do not move from port to port but, in a metaphorical substitute, become the carriers of information goods through the system of uploading and downloading signals. At the outset, governments controlled both the orbits and the satellites that would occupy them. Private corporations ultimately sought to break government satellite monopolies, mirroring, perhaps, swashbuckling efforts to enter government-controlled trade in the seventeenth and eighteenth centuries.

The long struggle of Rene Anselmo, illustrates the point. He was the creator of the fiercely independent PanAmSat, a United States private satellite operator later associated with Hughes Electronics, which competed with Intelsat, the one-time monopoly intergovernmental body. Anselmo saw that Intelsat, concentrating on the satellite transmission of data and telephone messages, was ignoring a trade opportunity for the shipment and distribution of broadcast signals through satellites. He detected an unserved geographical market, as well, which could be served through satellites that linked the United States to Latin America and parts of Latin America to one another.[48]

Intelsat, like the trading companies of old, had deployed government power, treaties, discriminatory pricing, and other techniques in the late 1980s and early 1990s to maintain its monopoly and squelch PanAmSat and Anselmo.[49] In response, PanAmSat used a clever capability for navigating various government bureaucracies and banking firms to gain a foothold. The existence of PanAmSat's carriers meant new markets. The boom in global broadcasting channels, such as CNN, meant profitable cargo for PanAmSat.

The rise of the deregulatory mentality that endorsed the theme of competition and of multilateral trade agreements in which government restrictions would be reduced, magnified opportunities for PanAmSat to deliver its signals to earth stations in Europe and elsewhere. Mixing metaphors, Anselmo wailed about the monopoly in 1990 when he sought greater freedom to carry data over his system as well as video channels:

We were sent into battle with this monstrous worldwide telephone cartel with both hands tied behind our back . . . Intelsat's response to PanAmSat was to launch a global boycott of the company, lobby to prevent and stall the launch of our satellite, and start a war of predatory pricing to drive us out of the market. And that was only the tip of the iceberg of unfairness that they have thrown at us.[50]

Once the monopoly was avoided, Anselmo's company succeeded wildly, challenging the rules of access and use of trade routes in the sky.

There are many other stories about the use of control over satellites to gain the profits of the trade, other chapters in the drama of establishing empires of the sky. In the 1990s Luxembourg's Société Européene des Satellites (SES), newly established by a consortium of private banks with substantial public investment, began to offer the Astra satellite series, a series with access to a large European audience. This satellite company was responsible for more than 75 percent of Europe's direct-to-home audience. At the end of the twentieth century, SES was in high-stakes, fierce competition for a single point on the geostationary orbit, the valuable 29 degrees east satellite position that reaches Europe.[51] SES claimed the right to that airspace, based on varying interpretations of a 1997 World Administrative Radio Conference Agreement, but so did Deutsche Telekom. Both had already placed satellites in that airspace in dangerous proximity. Eutelsat planned to launch a third within that same 28–29 degree space by the year 2000, violating the norm that satellites are usually positioned at least three degrees apart.[52] With the ITU as decision maker, SES obtained the slot.

The Law of Satellite Trade Routes

One of the most intriguing questions is whether particular trade routes—historically or at present—are selected not just for their geographical span but because of the legal environment that surrounds them: whether there is a relationship of pathway to law, and law to cargo. Points within distribution patterns traditionally have barred certain cargo or put them in quarantine (animals, seeds, or people); such rules may have made some routes preferable to others. Now we can ask how governments that have control over an orbital slot regulate its use to affect the programming cargo.

This question implicates a third element of the infrastructure: the programming services that use the satellite, much like the shippers whose cargoes filled the vessels of seventeenth-century trade routes. Just as those ancient trade routes reorganized markets for goods, satellite footprints reorganize markets for information. The existence of new satellite routes made CNN, the Cartoon Network, and the many new diasporic channels possible, just as the existence of the new foci of Hudson Bay and Goa created new forms of commerce and among English, French, and Native American fur trappers and merchants in one instance or Portuguese, Asian, and African traders in the other. There are numerous examples of satellite trade routes that have created the possibility of trade and of physical distribution patterns that have inspired new approaches to content. One of many examples is Alfa TV.[53] Established by twenty-five countries in Central and Eastern Europe and the former Soviet Union, Alfa TV was proposed as a multilingual channel "to promote cooperation and reconciliation" in the region. With the support of the European Parliament and the European funding project called Eureka Audiovisuel, its task was to use films and other cultural programs to reach an audience estimated at 400 million viewers, from Finland to Azerbaijan. Like other trans-European channels, such as the German–French Arte and regional Euronews, Alfa-TV presented itself as an alternative to the oft-cited flood of US culture.

The application of law to route has yet to be fully articulated, but a few examples will help illustrate the increasingly important set of issues. In 1993 the Secretary of State for what was then National Heritage (now Culture, Media, and Sport) in the United Kingdom sought to block the marketing of subscriptions to allegedly pornographic broadcasts arriving in the country via direct broadcast satellite, that is, a signal that travels straight from a satellite to a small receiver at a person's home or place of business. The particular route selected for the delivery of the service, called Eurotica Rendez-Vous, involved "uplinking" (sending from the ground) the signal from France to a transponder within the Eutelsat satellite system for transmission into the United Kingdom.

The route selected meant that the legal structure of the European Union applied to this transmission, specifically the 1989 Television without Frontiers Directive. Under that regime the law precludes officials in the recipient country, in this case the United Kingdom, from unilaterally prohibiting the programming, though such a prohibition would not have been barred if the programming originated from outside the European Union. The European Directive gave member states the power to "suspend retransmission" of a service (originating from within the Union, in this case France) only if it "manifestly, gravely and seriously" harmed children by "impairing their moral development," as defined in Article 22 of the Directive. Though the United Kingdom and France may have sharply different views on what constitutes manifest and grave impairment of a child's moral development, the trade route selected by the programming source obliged the United Kingdom to mediate with France, to discuss its official finding that British standards were violated.[54]

It is still somewhat unclear what British officials had the power to do; even with a domestic law that allows the secretary of state to "proscribe" a foreign satellite service deemed to be "unacceptable." Many are the voices that say that regulation of programming as cargo is not only indefensible but also technologically impossible.[55] Still, the British government sought to preclude cable television operators from carrying a signal that arrived via satellite and violated UK norms; it ordered a ban on the sale of decoders, and it made it a crime to market a proscribed signal or to advertise in connection with such a signal. What it could not do was make the signal itself go away. As was true of different sea routes, the particular satellite passage selected bore within it a unique set of governing principles. Specific European laws governed the transmission of a satellite signal from France to the UK. Different laws would have governed a signal with different origins and destinations.

Shaping law for a satellite channel can be a matter of regional expectations. In 1999, in connection with the NATO bombing campaign, the board of directors of Eutelsat (composed of state representatives partly overlapping the membership of NATO) ordered the Serbian Radio-TV (RTS) signal to be taken off a transponder it controlled. Governments involved claimed that efforts to "end Serbian propaganda by bombing broadcast facilities would be diminished if Eutelsat transmitted similar programming within the Balkans and beyond."[56] The board action, singling out the removal of a signal because of its source or content, was unprecedented.

A different example lies with the broadcasts by Al Jazeera, the satellite channel made famous in 2001 but legally interesting before that. The channel was established in 1996 by Qatar's progressive emir, Sheik Hamad bin Khalifa al-Thani, as part of a move to introduce democratization there. The channel's practices caused controversy among the information ministers of the United Arab Emirates at a 1999 meeting of the Gulf Cooperation Council (GCC). A Bahraini government complaint to Qatar contended that Al Jazeera had hosted a fierce political attack by an opposition figure. Al Jazeera asserted that it was independent from all organizations and states and not controlled by Qatar as to content. Kuwait had earlier protested against the programs broadcast by Al Jazeera and accused the channel of supporting Iraq against the then-policy of the Emirates and, at one point, closed the channel's office there. Despite Qatar's refusal to interfere with the content of Al Jazeera, the GCC information ministers issued a decision, "regulating the external media," that called on members to discipline individuals and the media institutions that slander GCC states.[57]

MED-TV

A quite different story about the cultural and political implications of the choice of trade route involves the satellite service called MED-TV. MED-TV, as has already been mentioned, was established in London to distribute programming via satellite to the Kurdish population worldwide. MED-TV especially sought to reach Kurdish minorities in Turkey, Iran, and Iraq. Its programming, produced in large part, in Belgium, was a mix of news, entertainment, and education. The programming was aimed at a historically diasporic community of 35 million engaged, among other things, in trying to rediscover and redefine Kurdish nationhood and reaffirm its language and culture. Naomi Sakr has called MED-TV a "kind of Kurdistan in space," as it provided a culturally unifying function despite the lack of a Kurdish homeland or single territorial base.

In addition, satellite broadcasting, used by MED-TV, neither relied on high literacy rates (levels were low, especially among women) nor involved complications that can arise from print media, such as unstable mailing addresses, state censorship, and circulation prohibitions. The service was relatively inexpensive and obtainable even in remote villages.[58] It thus allowed a greater number of Kurdish people to participate in information exchange than would have otherwise been possible. But not all saw the implications of MED-TV in such a positive light. Turkish officials claimed that MED-TV was the media arm of the PKK, the separatist Kurdish force that has been engaged in armed conflict with Turkish government troops and has been deemed by Turkey to be a significant threat to the integrity and unity of the country.[59]

For an entity like MED-TV, selection of a trade route for the distribution of its images was a complex matter. It desired the least intervention, either directly by Turkey or by other governments at Turkey's behest. For example, its transmission was originally on a satellite nested in an orbit oriented away from the more commonly viewed Eutelsat satellites. MED-TV viewers had to turn their dishes in a direction different from those receiving traditional Turkish entertainment channel services. The authorities could see the difference in the attitude of the dish and could use that information to harass the MED-TV viewers. To protect them, MED-TV had to shift, therefore, to the more commonly viewed bird in the sky.

The location and ownership of the transponders on the Eutelsat system that would be used by MED-TV were also politically significant and affected MED-TV's choice of "trade-route." Eurovision, a cooperative effort of state entities, owns Eutelsat's transponders. Under Eutelsat's internal rules, these transponders are controlled by public agencies; the states that control those agencies have good bilateral relations with Turkey. Stories were told of MED-TV securing time on a Slovakian-controlled slot on a satellite only to have the Turkish Foreign Minister obtain a cancellation through bilateral discussions. MED-TV was unceremoniously bounced from various transponders on Eutelsat and their contracts for access canceled. Put in trade route terms, because of the contraband nature or status of the cargo, MED-TV's cargo arrangements were at risk.

One solace, an anchor, as it were, was MED-TV's British license. Whatever their political goals, the choice of a relatively secure legal and political system that would govern the delivery of their information seemed one of MED-TV's most important achievements and was a vital part of the strategy for obtaining transponder space to reach the relevant audience. The organization "established" itself in the United Kingdom, a technical term that meant that they were qualified to receive a license from the United Kingdom's Independent Television Commission. This resulted in MED-TV's being subject to the ITC's content standards. Receiving a British permit allowed MED-TV to claim that it met those standards. This was seen as a means for increasing the chances that its programming would be subject only to legal, as opposed to extra-legal, constraints. At the danger of pushing the metaphor too far, the MED-TV decision to obtain a license in the United Kingdom could be perceived as a rough equivalent of flying the British flag on the main mast.

Turkish officials mounted an extensive campaign to pressure the British government to withdraw MED-TV's license and close the producer down. They contended that MED-TV was a "political organization" and therefore, under United Kingdom legislation, precluded from obtaining a British license. In February 1998, the Independent Television Commission, charged with supervision of licensed entities in Britain, penalized MED-TV for three broadcasts, for a total fine of approximately $150,000. According to the Commission, despite formal warnings, MED-TV violated the impartiality requirements of ITC's programming code. In one breach, according to the ITC, a "40 minute long programme consisted entirely of a political rally organized by the PKK." The violation was that: "No context was supplied and there was no balancing material." In a second breach of impartiality requirements, MED-TV "seemingly endorsed" the on-camera condemnation of a US list of terrorist organizations. A third transgression of the ITC's rules (neutrality of journalists) involved " 'personal comments' from a MED-TV journalist in the field, namely a description of the more pro-government Kurdish Democratic Party as 'treacherous and murderous.' " Finally, in 1999 the ITC withdrew the license, finding that the station had too often violated standards of objectivity and impartiality. Soon thereafter, unable to attain a license elsewhere in the EU, MED-TV closed down.[60]

The point, here, is not the validity of the ITC decisions but the legal and political consequences for MED-TV in choosing (or being forced by circumstances to choose) a particular route for the origination and transportation of its satellite-borne information. MED-TV, in fact, could be the posterchild for the idea that the choice of transmission path has vital implications for the capacity to achieve a safe passage between sender and receiver. MED-TV's history has been one not only of British sanctions, but also, within Turkey, specific Army and police raids to destroy satellite-receiving antennas that would be capable of retrieving the MED-TV signal. Those in charge of the Kurdish broadcasting entity were constantly searching for alternative means of assuring a route in which access to production facilities, uplinking, satellite access, and downlinking into Turkey could be achieved as seamlessly as possible, free of government intervention.

Orbital Slots as Cultural Gateways

There are other examples, often trade related, in which countries have used slots, from time to time, to regulate access to information and entertainment by their populations, much as governments have often used ports of entry as a caliber of openness. Some countries, such as Malaysia, controlled trade routes by establishing a monopoly of information distribution in a favored orbital slot and restricting the use of the slot by limiting channel services to the control of those friendly to the government. Canada wished to encourage the creation of Canadian cultural content by prohibiting its citizens from gaining access to signals that travel through orbital slots not under Canadian control.[61] It has, in the past, sought to criminalize the sale of receivers that allow the receipt of signals from satellites in orbital slots of American origin.[62] Iraq has prohibited and confiscated satellite dishes capable of receiving signals from the West, particularly transmissions thought to be culturally subversive. There is some distant affinity to trade routes here, in the use of points of entry to control the kinds of products that would otherwise pass to affected populations, or in other words, the use of the power of the trade route for cultural screening. The BBC published excerpts of recorded prayer sermons at Teheran University on September 16, 1994, by an Imam for whom screening and banning was essential. The Imam states:

Satellite transmission, broadcasting the programmes of foreign television networks, is not designed to increase the scientific knowledge of nations. Rather it has been developed to mislead the youth. . . . They [the West] do not transfer their knowledge . . . [or] their experience of modernizing technology. What they transfer is something that drags families into corruption.[63]

Such cultural screening is by no means unique to the Islamic world. Almost two centuries ago, in its efforts to retain its tenuous hold on its American colonies, Spain prohibited the transport, sale, and distribution of subversive documentation inspired by Enlightenment philosophy.[64]

National and international regulation of trade routes is a complicated matter. The debates discussed in the ITU on actual control of orbital slots, the concept of "equitable access," and the debate between the developed and developing countries over a priori and a posteriori approaches to regulation are not unique. Twenty years ago, in the United Nations, countries were already debating whether an international regime could be established that controlled content in the trade of images. A sweeping draft convention would have imposed a set of substantive standards on satellite-delivered information, excluding from television programs transmitted by satellites "any material publicizing ideas of war, militarism, nazism, national and racial hatred and enmity between peoples as well as material which is immoral or instigative in nature or is otherwise aimed at interfering in the domestic affairs or foreign policy of other States."[65]

Conclusion

The complexity of corporate structures, the intricate relationships between business ventures and governments in the satellite field, and the difficulty of public accessibility of contracts for the transmission of program services, all turn the current intricate patterns of transportation of satellite images around the world into a black box of unknown content. Scholarship, partly as a consequence, has looked at what seemed most apparent about this traffic for a very long time, namely that programming has its source in values and in production in the West, often the United States, and its impact is felt around the world.[66] But as this picture changes, details will be far more important, including details about the ways trade routes in imagery and data are shaped and restricted. This will have to include closer examination of how governments use such powers as they attempt to control ways information is received within their borders, and how they use their control over orbital slots.[67] Not for nothing has the rhetoric of the global entrepreneurs, like Rupert Murdoch, changed from the claim of borderless skies to a claim of deference to states.

Trade routes, of whatever vintage, have always consisted of a series of physical points where ownership or control is vital. More than that, however, these points, taken together, have geopolitical implications as they transform into ports, concessions, warehouses, colonies, sources of raw material, and markets for products.[68] For the old trade routes, any government or power seeking to maintain the value of any particular point along the route was expected to struggle for that point's exclusivity, its competitive advantage, or its access to raw materials or markets. Trade routes in the sky, too, have their elements of exclusivity. Orbital slots have increased value if they or the satellites that occupy them do not increase in supply or if the demand for them keeps exploding in volume. For the satellite routes, as for their predecessors, technology increases supply while participants seek to retain control and quasi-monopolistic power.

In the broadcast era, when terrestrial transmitters were the exclusive technology, international concern had, historically, been to avoid the possible invasion of the domestic space of one country from its neighbor, especially for propaganda purposes. There were exceptions, such as the implicit acceptance of shortwave radio as a space for transnational services, symbolized by the use of spectrum by the BBC, the Voice of America, and many other external services. But bilateral agreements, for example, between Mexico and the United States, were designed to ensure minimal intrusion along the long borders. In the cold war, the Eastern bloc's choice of SECAM for its color television technology was a technological break with the West's PAL. With the recent inception of the post-Soviet era, the use of international pathways for external services, like Radio Free Europe/Radio Liberty, has been freshly debated. There are new disputes about Radio Marti, directed at Cuba, and Radio Free Asia, directed, among other places, at China and Vietnam, showing that traditional technologies continue to play an important role in the transportation of political imagery. For the first fifty years of broadcasting, the entire motivation of the international community was to establish trade routes that assumed a national gatekeeper. With some important exceptions, "harm" was largely defined as the intentional spillover of spectrum use from one national zone into another. Terrestrially, the use of directional antenna, the reduction of power, and the careful designation of spectrum were sufficient largely to achieve an international consensus.

Today, despite the fact that the technological capabilities of the satellite implicate issues of national identity, there is no international consensus on the rules that should guide the establishment of trade routes in the sky. The world remains divided into camps on how and whether to restrict routes by which that content gets delivered though technology. Some consider that transportation in images should (indeed, must) be subject to national controls. Malaysia required, as I have mentioned, that any information or imagery that is sent down from a satellite to people within its borders must first arise from within the territory, a so-called uplinking requirement. The tendency of some countries to require uplinking within their boundaries is an example of what Saskia Sassen has called reinstalling the local.[69] Despite the dizzying potential for free exchange of information available through satellites, some states are attempting to assert a sort of digital trade monopoly, exclusively controlling the exchange and distribution of information transmitted by satellite, or at the very least its points of entry and departure.

On the other hand, multilateral trade negotiations, which resulted in the World Trade Organization, have dramatically reduced barriers to free flow of services, including information and programs. The position has often been sounded that free trade in goods and economic growth are not possible without a free trade in information.[70] As part of the ideology surrounding these multilateral negotiations, government restrictions on transmission of imagery and programming whether tied to national assertions or not, are condemned as violations of the human right to receive or impart information. The US position, consistent with these views, is generally to assert that access to orbital slots, to licenses, and to markets should be as free as possible of public regulation. But, as we have seen, free trade does not necessarily mean random patterns of distributing information.

These new trade routes are not linear nor functionally evolved from prior methodologies. Invisible and "postmodern," the new routes are breaking some traditional categories, but reinforcing others. They crisscross regional lines, produce information spills such as pornography on the Internet, and allow diasporic groups to communicate among themselves. New trade routes, symbolized by the extraordinary disruption of traditional modes of distribution of music to consumers, cause turmoil in existing legal standards.[71] Seemingly indivisible by national boundaries, these routes prod existing sovereigns to search for ways in which borders can be rehabilitated. Enveloped in technology, masked by complexity, it is apparent that the configuration of these satellite routes has an important relationship to democracy and culture and to the spaces for public debate.

And this allows a return to "models," the subject of the first part of this chapter. Metaphors evolve into models, as the intuitive value of a figure of speech transfigures into a program for action. The world debate over media and communications policy is being shaped, in large measure, by a search for metaphors and, as well, a weighing of competing models. Companies and countries invest in the credibility of whole ways of thinking, ways of organizing media structures. Models are shorthand forms for persuasion, as, initially, are metaphors. This persuasion aims to translate preferred modes of the machinery of production, distribution, and reception so as to adapt them to new markets. Models now seem to be, like a range of automobiles, strikingly similar in function and design. But these similarities can be deceptive. In a stable world, competition for models is at the margin. But in a world where conflict reemerges, where differences gain ascendancy, models diverge and trade routes are scrutinized for the political, economic, and cultural impact of their cargo.

Metaphors are based on association, linking the unfamiliar to the familiar. Models are constructed of elements that purport to have explicit functions, elements that reflect ideologies. In the next three chapters, I examine some of the most famous or popular of these elements, packages of meaning drawn from these models. They include the move to privatization and self-regulation, the specific language of controlling illegal and harmful content, and the notion of "newness" as a vital element of regulating the introduction of technology.

4

Technologies and the Vocabulary of Change

There is a certain vocabulary of desire in the process of global media restructuring. Ideas, and the language that captures them, roll around the world, influencing action. At each moment, there is a repertory of such ideas and these I call tropes of restructuring. The tropes change as they are nourished, redefined, and deployed by governments, civil society, industry, and political parties. These terms reflect ideologies and specific sector-related goals. Included in the repertory are such terms as: "ensuring national security," "strengthening national identity," "guaranteeing the right to receive and impart information," "protecting the marketplace of ideas," "establishing free and independent media," "preserving public service broadcasting," "implementing communication for development," "removing trade barriers to data flow," or "reinforcing and reflecting pluralism." The origin, role in influencing government policies, and relationship to particular technologies of each of these ideas is worthy of exploration, though not all can be explored here.

Let us consider a relatively standard state response to media globalization in its information space. Assume that a government has established standards and enforcement mechanisms designed to regulate certain messages delivered via the old technologies. It may, for example, have special prohibitions on indecent programming on television and radio, regulate the representation of women, or require a degree of objectivity and impartiality in news presentations. Further, the state will have claimed that these standards and mechanisms were desirable or necessary for the health of the state and elements of its identity. In the instance of new technologies and the messages that flow from them, instinct may call for merely applying existing standards and enforcement mechanisms.

As we have seen, there is a dreamlike quality to this approach. Since much image-related law is media specific, with different standards for the printed press and radio, television, or film, decisions must be made about how to treat a new media entrant such as cable television or the Internet. And there are the daunting problems of jurisdiction and effectiveness. The unique nature of the Internet is at the heart of a broader argument against extending existing law to new technologies. Those promoting this argument contend that because the Internet provides a rare opportunity to develop a whole new practice of speech, even existing prohibitions should be reviewed and, if possible, eliminated. At a minimum, this position states that there should be resistance to the importation of restrictive speech standards.[1]

The extension of existing law into new media is at one pole in the range of tools for national response. The most complex techniques are what might be called *architectural*, a subject that is given further attention below. We have seen the architectural approach occuring where the state, with or without the support of law, tries to develop an elaborate infrastructure for the delivery of information that is most hospitable to state control. An example of the architecture of boundary construction is control of uplinking, the route by which programming gets to a satellite so that it can be downlinked to a target population. A multilateral approach provides for an international regime, often negotiated and achieved through informal mechanisms, in which the design of distribution systems facilitates the exercise of national jurisdiction.

There are variations on this architectural approach as a national or multilateral response to media globalization designed to protect internal space. Some governments employ strategies that are both technology driven and preemptive. In Singapore, for example, the government planned to build so modern, so comprehensive, and so total a cable television system that other options, such as direct-to-home satellites, could not easily compete. That plan arose as a result of the alternate physical embodiments that the new technology of multichannel video distribution can take. Through positive investment, structuring of licensing, and a prohibition on imports, a state might encourage the use of one technology over another specifically because that form of advanced communications technology protects its desired mix of images more than another does. A system, as Singapore would have it, in which all television homes are "wired," is more easily controlled than a system dependent on direct broadcast satellites. Monopoly- or oligopoly-structured concessions to manage cable and broadcasting systems are easier for the state to manage than a similarly technologically advanced system that is highly competitive.

An older architectural tool available to governments that seek to control the degree to which new technologies can permeate their societies is the imposition of limitations on foreign ownership of information distribution or programming channels. Because of the ease of adopting a rule that specifically targets foreign participation in media and its immediate public resonance, this form of national response was fairly common in the broadcasting era. It is the cheap and easy, but often least effective, strategy for facilitating control. And what does foreignness mean in the new global environment?

In the reform legislation of the late 1990s, the Indian government slightly loosened the state monopoly over terrestrial radio, but it limited new radio licenses to Indian nationals. Unusual among democracies, India also requires Indian citizenship for ownership of the printed press (though modifications of this rule are often under consideration). The United States maintains a ban on the control of broadcast licenses by foreign nationals. The extension of this practice to new technologies is complex. Nationality or citizenship requirements for the ownership of those Internet service providers marketing within a nation's boundaries are not yet common, though they do exist. Some states wish to restrict ownership of direct-to-home satellite platforms, or to provide advantages to nationals in access to domestic uplinking facilities. Many of the broadcasting systems in the so-called transition societies have requirements for one-third or more programming of national origin; often, as well, the extent of foreign ownership is restricted. Multilateral agreements, such as those leading to the development of the World Trade Organization, have, sometimes struggling, allowed such an exception to free trade principles.

The Meanings of Privatization

Because of its importance, it is desirable to spend time on the meanings, in the time of globalization, of the term "privatization." Perhaps clumsily, I place under an umbrella of "privatization" the collection of potent notions that include "enhancing the private sector," "encouraging self-regulation," or "decreasing the hand of government." A hallmark, both rhetorical and real, of the global restructuring process in broadcasting has been the effort to shift control over information spaces away from governments. This is true both for channels of distribution and for the programming that streams through those channels. What makes public broadcasting *public* is, in large part, a matter of ownership or control of the filter through which programming is selected for distribution. In addition, what renders public broadcasting categorically distinct is control of production of the programming itself. To be sure, there are still many societies where media, as a whole, are under the control of the government, but the tendency, fairly constant over regions of the world and even across forms of government, has been toward widely expanding the role of the private sector.

What is commonly thought of as globalism is, automatically, one of the great contributors to this process. By turning toward audiences abroad, the great multinationals, world straddling, many-homed, and of diffuse allegiances, have massively reoriented the relative distribution of content, in target societies, from the public to the private. Their dense array of privately produced programming allows the companies to profit only if the cornucopia of supply is tied to large-scale distribution mechanisms that yield massive audiences. Their very existence, hovering omnipresence, and accessibility inevitably alter information flow, inducing innovation in structures of delivery. More than that, in many of the post-Soviet societies of Eastern and Central Europe, and many other places besides, the partial or entire privatization of government channels or opening of public spectrum for private uses was part of the transforming landscape—almost a hallmark—of democratization.

Both advocates and opponents of privatization can agree that rendering entities as private encourages investment, often foreign, and with new levels of investment come new program strategies, including, in many areas, increased nonindigenous programming. While democracy-related goals may be espoused, government sale of frequencies or channels has deep fiscal motivations, stemming from powerful pressures to reduce government expenditures and debt. As with other aspects of the economy, privatization has to be considered if the state wishes to qualify for certain international money sources.[2] The World Bank and the International Monetary Fund often include conditions such as the design and implementation of a privatization plan in lending agreements. In this way they exert great pressure on transition societies and developing countries to privatize, though this is much more the case within the area of telecommunications than in the area of broadcasting.

The opponents of privatization argue that it leads to the intensification of the culture of the modern and a cosmopolitan globalization that detracts from sovereignty of the state and the strength of civil society. Proponents argue that the move can mean an expansion in the outlets of expression, more incentives to production, and an increase in creativity. As discussed in chapter 2, privatization can be a mask, disguising the fact that the elite often retains power through the new arrangements.

Implied in the drama of privatization is a uniformity of transformation. However, privatization has many meanings. Most simply it refers to the sale of a formerly government-operated enterprise to a buyer in the private sector, but even then, the process has many outcomes. Denationalizations have occurred, for example, in French broadcasting in the 1970s and 1980s.[3] In 1982, following the election of François Mitterand, the Law on Audiovisual Communication granted greater broadcasting autonomy and paved the way for further decentralization.[4] Existing public service broadcasters were restructured in more independent forms. Additionally, in the early 1980s private commercial radio broadcasters emerged.[5] At the outset, French law prohibited these entities from using advertising as a financing source, but this changed in 1984.[6] Private commercial television companies first appeared in 1984, with the founding of Canal Plus, a subscription television channel. Many television advertising restrictions were lifted in 1986.[7] Even with Canal Plus, however, the government retained broadcasting control through ownership of a significant stake in the enterprise.[8]

Privatization may take place when noncommercial channels are redefined as "commercial" or when traditional public service broadcasters, spin off entrepreneurial activities or, deploying subsidies, expand programming or other efforts that compete with the private sector.[9] These exercises are far from the wholesale recasting of a national system, but they share important similarities. The aspect that unites them is that privatization takes place when ownership or control patterns change to remove or substantially diminish state or public dominion of decisions concerning media space. A significant instance of such privatization was the decision in Russia to turn the principal television channel, and the channel which reached the whole Soviet Union (and was therefore the broadcasting symbol of Soviet identity), into a stock company with (at least for a while) substantial private ownership.[10] As with many things Russian, however, the transmutation to the private altered, but hardly eliminated, the fact of state intervention.

Conventional Privatization

Privatization, in a broad sense, also encompasses the kind of government decisions that took place in the transition periods of Poland, Hungary, and the Czech Republic.[11] There the spectrum that was unused, held by the military or reserved for state or public purposes was opened for licensing to commercial broadcasting. The former monopoly state broadcaster remained in existence (though itself, transformed), but private national or regional channels were licensed to compete with it and rapidly attracted audiences. In this way privatization was a matter of moving step by step from a government monopoly over the medium to a mixed system and then to one that is heavily biased in favor of those outside public ownership. Often a mixed system is the stated objective, but as is increasingly apparent, the introduction of private competition makes it difficult politically and financially to ensure the future stability of the public system.

In most transition societies, privatization is put forward as part of the shock treatment in the general move toward capitalism. Radically altering the ownership of the light bulb industry in Hungary or the automobile industry in East Germany had symbolic and democratic implications. In the area of information and entertainment, the significance of the act is tied to far more than efficiency. While there are substantial economic benefits to a freer flow of information, a major justification has usually been reducing the power of the state as part of the democratizing project.

The impetus to privatize broadcasting channels is thought to be particularly strong because it has resulted in a single step that literally removes the broadcasting or press entity from the direct control of government (or had the appearance of doing so). The 1990s were characterized by a substantial, but far from complete, shift in the production and distribution of images from public to private hands in transition state after transition state that altered the central engine of broadcasting. To a large extent, entry, for the transition society, into the global environment of news forms and data depended on this change in the structure of delivery of information and entertainment.

Thus media privatization was and is advanced for reasons that range from efficiency to speech and discourse principles. Privatization, it is argued, not only increases the operating efficiency of companies currently managed by government institutions but also affects content by making the operator more sensitive to demands of the audience. Arguments for the private often ignore the complexities inherent in measuring efficiency, especially if the media are supposed to serve such information-related functions as building the basis for responsible exercise of citizenship, enhancing pluralism, and strengthening national identity. While profit maximization is usually the central goal of a private sector firm, the government, when it operates the media, often commits to other goals, such as helping to create an informed electorate, protecting the sanctity of the local language, and ensuring access for minority groups.[12]

In some important instances, privatization was a fig leaf for a new relationship between the state and media. A significant example of this phenomenon, already cited, was the partial privatization of central state television in Russia where then-President Yeltsin decided to sell 49 percent of the First Channel to industrial groups he selected. This was a transaction, which, oddly, strengthened, not weakened, the president's role in program decisions. President Yeltsin placed private-sector figures, more beholden to him than the government figures previously controlling the channel, in charge of the broadcaster. The reorganization removed the broadcaster in part from the direction of a state bureaucracy, making it more subject to the will of the executive. Rendering a state or public service broadcaster more private may be a way those in power can weaken their opponents.

This type of power transferral happened again in Russia when a public frequency was turned over to a private corporation. Considered an exemplar of the private, NTV was critical of the Kremlin's policy in Chechnya and then supported President Yeltsin's re-election campaign in 1996. Laura Belin has described the interrelationships that ultimately came to haunt the broadcaster:

Given the hostility of various government officials to NTV during the Chechen war, it is easy to forget that state entities provided financial assistance to NTV, even during its first year on the air. A May 1994 government directive granted the National Sports Fund customs duty exemptions on broadcasting equipment imported on behalf of NTV. Other privately owned media outlets had to wait for the Law on State Support for the Mass Media and Book Publishing, which was adopted in late 1995 and took effect in January 1996, to receive customs duty exemptions on imported equipment. . . . A deal with the Communications Ministry allowed NTV to pay vastly reduced rates for transmissions services. Saving money on signal distribution gave NTV an advantage over other commercial broadcasters, because throughout the post-Soviet period, fees for transmission services comprised a huge proportion of expenditures for Russian radio and television stations.

. . . [D]uring the 1996 presidential campaign, NTV received a large cash infusion from Gazprom, which purchased a 30 percent stake in the network. The gas monopoly's investment provided the funds needed for an ambitious satellite television project—not an undertaking likely to pay for itself soon in a country where most people struggled to buy the bare essentials.[13]

Ultimately, the "independence" of NTV was destroyed by these and similar arrangements. Clearly, the state is unlikely to shed voluntarily its control over information space in a manner that would lead to significant weakening of the government itself. Thus the nature of the privatization arrangements is critical to its impact on the public sphere. It matters whether the "private" station is a mere surrogate or alter ego of the state—as was often the case in Russia, Malaysia, and Turkey—or whether it can claim a degree of independence. In Malaysia, MEASAT, the state-sanctioned monopoly over satellite broadcasting and the cable industry, was lodged in the hands of industrial or financial entities with extremely close ties to the government. This allowed flexibility for complex financial transactions and relatively autonomous decisions concerning what program channels would be carried. It also ensured that such decisions would be made in a manner consistent with the emphasis Mohammed Mahathir, Malaysia's prime minister placed on "Asian values." In Turkey, at the beginning of the era of satellite tech-nology, the president's son was the favored pioneer in terms of new alternatives to the state monopoly, starting with a satellite-delivered channel, but quickly turning that into a challenge to the existing terrestrial system. In Kazakhstan, the President's daughter became a principal figure in the private broadcasting sector.

It is useful to think of privatization as more than simply the conversion of a previously public or state entity into one that is privately owned. The circumstances and factors appropriate for analysis increase when an examination of privatization looks at issues of public control over production and distribution of content and, within those issues, direct state control as compared to autonomous public sway. For example, when state or public service broadcasting entities rely on advertising revenues, one could consider that in itself a move to the private. Increasingly there is criticism of public broadcasters who, while receiving public money, benefit from the market to the detriment of private competitors.

This kind of privatization has been an important factor in the transformation of Russian television, Doordarshan in India, and the former state television in Hungary and the Czech Republic. Dependence on advertising revenue inevitably affects programming decisions, and the nature of what the programming teaches is different in an advertising based medium. In some transition societies, in fact, public service broadcasters used discounted access for advertisers as a way of competing against independent competitors and were accused of unfairness. There were moments when legislation gave public service entities a monopoly, for example, on political advertising or on modes foreclosed to independent competitors, such as tobacco or liquor advertising.

Privatization sometimes occurs by intensification of an already private sector, rendering it, as it were, less public. Consider the historic existence of public interest obligations on American broadcasters, obligations, for example, to cover controversial events of public importance, or act as a voice for the local community.[14] The removal of these obligations through the process of deregulation could be said to be a form of rendering the private more private. Similarly legitimating home-shopping channels as in accordance with American public interest licensing standards or relieving stations of an obligation not to indulge in "overcommercialization" expanded the private nature of the system.

In the United Kingdom a change occurred in the balance when, in the early 1950s, Parliament authorized the creation of ITV, a private television broadcaster that would be a competitor to the BBC. Additional national or regional licenses for independent television also further altered the balance.[15] In many societies, systems became more private simply by becoming more open to foreign competition. This could occur through reducing limits on foreign ownership of terrestrial broadcasting or through tolerating satellite-delivered channels, usually foreign owned, on cable. In India, the arrival of satellite channels created a vast change in the mix of private and public as a whole affecting the state broadcasting system itself.[16] In Turkey, the reaction to the existence of foreign satellite channels coming into the country was to liberalize private broadcasting, thereby attempting to harness or regulate the processes of change.

Privatization can be an instrument to reflect changed constituencies or power groups in society. This might be especially true in periods of transition, where there has been a monopoly provider and a plural society. In some transition societies, privatization, or the emergence of private entities, is essential for breaking the stranglehold of the state broadcaster that, through its staleness and efforts to preserve the status quo, might itself be weakening state sovereignty. The existing state-controlled system may be outmoded precisely because it bespeaks an old, surpassed, and ineffective perception of the nation. Ingrained modes of thinking and the legacy of warehoused personnel and inherited and inflexible attitudes toward society may weigh down the broadcasting bureaucracy at the moment of transition, squeezing out the voices of difference. No matter how much the leadership of a massive broadcasting bureaucracy of the *ancien regime* changes, it can be an albatross against the efforts for change.

In addition, without the competition of the private, it may be difficult for the entirety of the enterprise to represent adequately new political forces or tendencies in the society. In India it required the competition from cable television and channels carrying satellite signals from abroad to force substantial changes in the programming strategies of Doordarshan.[17] In the Netherlands, competition from new quasi-pirate stations—some unofficially supported by the government—led to greater reflections of diversity in the information space. In Turkey, satellite-delivered private programming, pro-Islamic in nature, broke the monolithic and outdated state approach to information and culture. In each of these contexts, changes in the state monopoly and challenges from the private sector affected political identities and arguably also affected elections and their processes. For all these places, changes in media structure may have increased the viability of the state. An increase in private stations can weaken the power of the incumbent, but in the process redefine and reinvigorate sovereignty through pluralism. Many governments have viewed privatization as a potential attack on sovereignty when it is merely an attack on the status quo.

Privatization and National Identity

The instances discussed previously are cases where additional voices bring a critique or alternative perspective to that of the government. The move to the private can also be shorthand for the commercial, and in that sense, for avoiding controversy, pluralism, and involvement in the public sphere. It is possible that the benefits to the public sphere from the move to the private are exaggerated; privatizing broadcasting can be a means of reducing the possibility of dissent. In the case of the United States, during the Nixon administration there was an explicit effort to weaken the impact of public broadcasting on the ground that it had hidden partisan tendencies or, at the least, promulgated views of society that were thought inconsistent with the administration's goals.[18] In that instance, the administration did not attempt to render the public broadcaster more private but, rather, attempted to prevent it from becoming stronger and more centralized.

Privatization can affect sovereignty where, intentionally or not, programming on new entrants weakens cultural bonds. In some contexts, sovereignty depends on habits of culture and attitudes toward the centrality of religion, and on the preservation of language. State or publicly controlled broadcasters are caretakers of these values. At their best and most expansive, these institutions generate programming, make films, support orchestras, reinforce language, produce educational children's programming, and set a benchmark for news and public affairs. These practices can be undermined by long-term exposure to commercial programming and the erosion of audiences for public service broadcasting as a result of multichannel competition.

Privatization of the media can accelerate the incidence of cultural attrition that diminishes citizenship and loyalty. Of course, inadequate countercultural programming could and does take place on state or public entities as well. Left in a monopolistic, unchallenged environment, the public or state broadcaster would not reduce its output of state-reinforcing messages. And here, "state-reinforcing" is not a reference to the inevitable control of news and information that supports the regime. It is a reference, rather, to a mix of imagery that a democratic state might legitimately wish to deploy as an element of strengthening national identity. It is the benign side of the market for loyalties.

A variant on this fear of the private is censorial. The alleged subversiveness of modern culture is symbolized by the dangers uncontrolled media present to ancient customs and therefore to the very bases of the polity. Laws or practices limiting "representation of women," including rules that determine how women can dress as presenters, laws that render satellite-receive dishes illegal, and efforts to maintain an insular information space in other ways are hallmarks of this view. But the anti-modern is not restricted to the mullahs of Iraq and Iran. In the United States, it is reflected in the cries against "indecency" and violence on American television.[19] In South Africa, the dangers of the "modern," as depicted in the apartheid-free images of broadcasting, formed a major underlying argument delaying the introduction of television and later color television.

Privatization, Competition, and Public Service Broadcasting

Public service broadcasting in Europe provides an example of the influence of "privatization" on the structure of regulatory debate. The discussion that became a large-scale dispute in the late 1990s has roots in the question whether state aid to public service broadcasters constitutes a violation of EU competition rules. State funding of public broadcasters became an issue in Europe after a private broadcasting market was created, after the termination of a public service broadcasting monopoly. Prior to the existence of such a market, state funding did not distort competition, because there was no competition to be distorted. The emergence of the private sector caused the need for a more specific definition of the public service remit so that the law could be applied. It became the duty of member states to define public service if they wished to justify the continued subsidy.

How this has worked can be seen through court decision and Commission Directive. In May 2000 a lower court of the European Communities considered a charge that financial support from the Portuguese government constituted inadmissible state aid under European law. The Court of First Instance ruled in favor of the private broadcaster. The Court held that the decisive element in the concept of aid, and thus in determining its impact on the common market, is whether the state by granting support confers an economic advantage. State grants and other measures unfairly benefited a public operator who was present in the advertisement market and in direct competition with other television operators.[20] A further example of this line drawing can be found in a 1998 report called "The Digital Age: European Audiovisual Policy." The report states: "The funding of public service broadcasting must be in proportion to, and not more than, what is needed to discharge the public service remit," reinforcing the idea of a sharp boundary between what is public and what is private.[21]

Another way of examining the manner in which the existence of privatization redefined the nature of public service broadcasting is to study public broadcasters in Central and Eastern Europe a decade since the political turning point of 1989. In the light of competition from a growing number of commercial services, many found themselves facing serious financial difficulties. Lithuania's LRT was often in a crisis mode during the 1990s. In 2000, its bank accounts were frozen because of rising debts of nearly $4 million, and several leading managers resigned. There was a momentary danger that it would be taken off air.[22] In Latvia, the public broadcaster sought to restructure itself, but financial obstacles—including high tax obligations—destroyed its plans. Typically one solution was the proposed selling off of the public broadcaster's second channel. In Estonia, the public broadcaster, ETV, had to surmount harsh competition from three commercial rivals, each supported by wealthy foreign investors.

In the Balkans, public service broadcasters were an emblem of the region's political problems and the intervention of Western powers. In Bulgaria, the national public broadcaster BNT was particularly affected by privatization. In 1999 it lost the frequency reserved for its former second channel Efir 2 to the new News Corp-backed station bTV, and in 2000 the State Telecommunications Committee awarded the country's second national commercial license to New Television, a long-established regional station acquired by Greek interests. In Hungary, the public broadcaster MTV found itself in a decline since the launch of two national commercial stations in late 1997. By 2000 the two commercial competitors, both with substantial foreign investment and ownership, accounted for at least 80 percent of the country's TV advertising expenditure. Deprived of funds, MTV was forced into such measures as disposing of its historic headquarters in central Budapest and cutting its program budget by 15 percent. In Ukraine, for reasons of government control, the state broadcaster was more protected and more generously treated. In Poland, the publicly owned TVP was criticized for its mode of self-preservation, namely behaving like a commercial station while at the same time obtaining revenues from receiver licence fees.[23]

Privatization and Self-regulation

Because self-regulation has become so important and so tied to the trend toward the private (both in broadcasting and on the Internet), the term must be examined more closely. The position, history, pattern of growth, and mode of entry of the Internet means that the concept of "privatization" must play a different role there than in the case of terrestrial broadcasting. Because channels of distribution in the new information world are so decentralized, relatively inexpensive, and self-generating, there is not the same drama of shift from the public to the private. If the state is to have any purchase or consider what role is appropriate, the focus must be on control by regulation (or control through architecture of gatekeeping) rather than control through ownership of the channel of distribution. In the debate over the relationship between the state and Internet provider, "self-regulation" has become the central trope, allowing the idea of autonomy but implying some restraint.

Self-regulation is, at times, a privatizing of the institutions of law. The ideas involved in self-regulation allow a society that is comfortable about its commitment to a rule of law to find and develop space where private institutions or associations are charged with the formation, implementation, and enforcement of norms. In societies where the tradition has been one of arbitrariness, a gulf exists between the articulation of norms and their meaning and impact. Where corruption or nepotism have been a hallmark and where tools for testing and enforcing compliance are lacking, the very idea of self-regulation may be premature. Transitions are marked by a search for a legal framework in order to guarantee rights, including property rights, and that may mean specially sanctifying the use of law, and only the use of law, to legitimate the processes of change. The circumstances have to be appropriate for shifting certain elements of norm-creation and enforcement within association or community hands.

There has been a tendency to apply the term "self-regulation" indiscriminately across boundaries as though it means the same thing in different settings. This is, however, clearly not the case. The history of the relationship between business and government is very different even among the major Internet states such as the United States, Germany, and the United Kingdom. It is inevitable that the patterns of "self-regulation" will differ accordingly. An international practice of self-regulation will emerge, but it will be first an accumulation of national and regional experiences. Each state has different social demands, constitutional structures, and traditions of industry-government cooperation in the fields of media and speech. No account of the emergence of self-regulation can be complete if it is insensitive to these critical distinctions in practice. The expectation, function, structure, and culture of self-regulation in the Internet (and media generally) is different in each country.

One study of self-regulation and self-generation of standards in Canada and the United States demonstrates marked differences in the scope of cooperation with the government, shared standards, and the notion of self-regulation as a social and collaborative act.[24] In the United States, partly because of the First Amendment, self-regulation is distinctively a form of avoidance of confrontation with and studied separation from government. A comparative overview of media self-regulation systems in all EU member states identified clear differences in meaning and structure of the self-regulatory systems among them.[25]

Analytically, self-regulation means different things in different contexts because of the localized societal objectives for its use. Self-regulation can be solely policy making, namely enunciating principles that govern enterprises. It can be addressed by framing legislation or by self-generating rules for conduct. Self-regulation can focus on the enforcement stage, in which the institution of self-regulation prescribes and implements a mode of providing sanctions. This final step implicates adjudication, namely self-regulatory acts that help decide whether a violation has taken place and imposing an appropriate remedy.[26] It is necessary to determine, in each particular version of the exercise of regulation, how the roles are divided between the state and industry. For example, an industry may be responsible for the definition of standards for content (through developing a code of practice) but may leave enforcement up to the government. Industry may also put its mark on official state legislation with effective lobbying and use state power to obtain results unattainable through private agreement.

Self-regulation often means a division between the types of behavior that the state prohibits (incitements to violence, for example) and other kinds of speech behavior the industry defines, labels, and polices (indecent conduct). Similarly the state and self-regulating entity may divide the enforcement responsibilities, with the state prosecuting certain types of speech and the self-regulating entity self-policing and removing other types of speech.[27]

As a consequence of these differences in content and context, the reasons behind self-regulation initiatives also vary. Self-regulation can be a plea for more effective cooperation, or it can be a means for avoiding regulation (or a combination). Arguments for media self-regulation may appeal to national differences, or they may be part of an effort to harmonize practices across national boundaries. Self-regulation can mean, within Europe, different standards enforced differently in France, the United Kingdom, Germany, or Spain. Self-regulation could also mean giving more substantial power to existing subgroups in society, including religious groups, to set the standards for programming that is watched, heard, or read by its members.

Despite these differences, self-regulation has come to mean an approach to centralized standard setting within the corporations that produce and transmit program content. Self-regulation can be a move to transcend sectarian differences—clusters of traditional censors—and substitute secular, uniform transnational patterns. Self-regulation, particularly with respect to the Internet, means substituting for government the administration of standards by large transnational corporations that have a stake in harmonizing and unifying standards across national boundaries.[28]

Self-regulation of media becomes a kind of dance among media, government, and the public, sensitive to swings in opinion, perceived consequences of the conduct to be regulated (such as violence on television), and the responsiveness by the public to political grandstanding. Self-regulatory actions also reflect, though it is important to consider the limitations on this claim, a deeper, less opportunistic desire on the part of industry leaders that they function in a way that serves society and does not damage it.

Self-regulation becomes an important alternative when there is an effective public demand for regulation, but government, for constitutional or bureaucratic purposes, cannot adequately satisfy that demand.[29] In the sensitive content issues in media, and given aspects of the democratic process, this motivation for the use of self-regulation has been most evident. In the Internet context, as was true for other media before it, self-regulation was employed to control content where free speech norms make government regulation subject to question. Self-regulation of media practices, in fact, frequently exists for this reason, as do self-regulatory approaches to standards of programming for minors.

The US Congress put forth various efforts to pass a response to a perceived demand, in part through a child online protection law and Internet decency law. Early efforts proved unsuccessful.[30] If a framework for norm formulation and articulation were enforced by the state it might require standards and practices that would be unconstitutional. Without a law, industry may agree to such principles and come to a mutually negotiated understanding with the government, with the prospect of immunities or other benefits. Thus the self-regulatory approach allows the standards to be presented and enforced across the industry, even if the same standards would not be permissible in the hands of the state. Self-regulation as an alternative to a possibly inappropriate legislative outcome can be an attractive choice. The task of norm-development is converted into an informal negotiation between government and industry, with the legislature or the executive posturing for public acclaim and the industry engaging in sufficient self-regulation to avoid a harsher explicit legislative fate.[31]

Self-regulation similarly may be a compromise between media and government when the media organizations to be regulated have enough power to resist regulation and are able to produce a publicly acceptable substitute. Self-regulation may be deemed preferable for the Internet because it is still premature to choose a form of regulation that is hardened into law. Since there is social demand for some form of control or supervision of what seems, at times, to be beyond governance, self-regulation becomes an important alternative. This significant gulf between community aspiration and the perceived limits on government capacity forces each content provider and private intermediaries such as service providers to conduct a search for a remedy.

Another context for negotiated self-regulation occurs when a government is paralyzed, and cannot pass legislation, but has enough power to ensure the self-regulatory implementation of elements of a government legislative program. This has been true of India, for example, as the coalition governments in the late 1990s struggled to define broadcast reform legislation but were unable to gain a majority in the Lokh Saba. As part of an ongoing of discussion between the cable television industry and the government, certain parts of legislation, including programming and advertising standards, became, sometimes informally, a self-regulatory concern, at least for the foreign multinational channel providers.

Self-regulation and Transition

The main forum for self-regulation as classically conceived has been the developed societies. We have seen, however, that the doctrine is also increasingly invoked in transitional and developing societies. The broader the definition of self-regulation, the more universal the concept becomes. For example, there are many states in which the absence of law or the institutions of law lead to self-help and cooperative (or forced) efforts among competitors in the field. These yield self-regulatory bodies that operate not to prevent law but as a substitute for law. In the early days of any new media technology, before the government enters the picture, this form of self-regulation is ubiquitous. In many countries, early cable television growth was characterized by chaos, followed by consolidation, followed by control. Self-regulation, of a sort, was frequently the lubricant between chaos and consolidation. Later, when state power could assist or formalize self-defined relationships, legislation was invoked.

In this sense, self-regulation has a critical role to play in all societies, and even more so in states where the rule of law is absent. During the late 1990s, there was an effort to draft a law concerning the concentration of ownership of media in Russia. The draft was conceived at a time of extraordinary patterns of ownership. Russia, it was said, had a group of seven business oligarchs, each of whom controlled a banking and business empire with broadcasting and the press as part of their arsenal for exerting influence and protecting existing turf.[32] There was an informal balance of power among the oligarchs. Rules about such things as poaching on the other, market divisions, role in political campaigns, and the shape of the advertising profession (including who would control sales and reap revenues) undoubtedly grew among them. Unlike weak self-regulatory entities in developed societies, there was no limit to the means the giants used to enforce these rules, including violence.

Only in limited conditions can a law be implemented that contradicts or tries to undo the self-regulatory pattern of such an industry organization, and it is rare that a society can counteract custom of this kind unless the government has amassed considerable strength and authority or there is a perceived public crisis. In the absence of these extraordinary forces, it is doubtful a media law that is the product of external models, like the proposed Russian draft on media ownership, could be successful. In Russia a change in regime, the hounding and expulsion of two major media oligarchs, Vladimir Guzinsky and Boris Berezovsky, and the adoption of a relentless policy of change in control of broadcasting licensees were preconditions for destroying the existing patterns of "self-regulation."

Privatization and "Free Trade"

A logical consequence of privatization and the free market as tropes of restructuring has been the push toward elimination of barriers to global trade in films and television programs. An ultimate goal for many companies and governments on their behalf is to have cheap and easy international distribution (via satellites or through the Web) with the capacity for reaching local markets in an unencumbered way. Think of the great transnational ambitions of News Corporation, Disney, or Sony. The world, in this integrated sense, should be one in which there is a virtually universal scheme, based on private media entities that inter-relate, form alliances, merge, integrate with program providers, furnish efficient modes for distribution.[33] Accompanying the expansion of the private transnational corporation has been this impetus to create or facilitate a domestic infrastructure and a regulatory scheme that allows access to it. One method used is reducing restrictions on foreign investment ownership, and cross-ownership. But another is reducing quotas or other impediments to the flow of imagery and data across national boundaries. If the dominant rhetoric is to narrow a government's interference in the choice of imagery by a consumer, it is difficult to cabin that restriction to domestic product. The growth of transnationals has created fierce opposition to domestic cartels that not only control production but also conspire to protect each other's markets.

Largely to help foster these objectives of unrestricted trade, the United States, as the principal representative for the private sector in the production of imagery, has vigorously sought to extend free trade principles to cultural products. The asserted freedom of images from local restrictions was an issue that almost destroyed the capacity of the international community to reach accord as part of the 1994 Uruguay Round of the General Agreement on Tariffs and Trade (GATT) negotiations. In addition the United States had, at least temporarily, to back down, much as had been the case a few years earlier in the 1992 North American Free Trade Agreement (NAFTA) negotiations.

The dynamism of these events is reminiscent of the last big, global debate concerning transborder flows of information, in the 1970s and 1980s, that was centered on ideas and proposals framed by the so-called MacBride Commission Report.[34] The Report legitimated certain national restrictions and called for redress of a perceived imbalance in the flow of information from "North to South" and from the "First World to the Third." Recognizing the power of ideas to shape media structures, Western press institutions sought, fairly successfully, to drive a stake into the heart of MacBride, because of what was considered its dangerous potential to restrict freedom of speech as conceptualized by them.

Protecting the domestic private sector as a means of creating a stronger civil society can be justified under a "discourse" or "dialogic" conception of protecting national identity. As Professor Baker puts it:

The notion of discourse or dialogue makes participants, rather than content, central to culture. In this conception, the primary audience of a cultural product is other members of the same community . . . culture is a living practice . . . Protection of culture in this context means assuring that members of the cultural community have meaningful opportunities to be cultural "speakers."[35]

Canadian magazines (possibly tested by content rather than by ownership or management) may be important because "national periodicals allow people in the different parts of [the country] to understand one another's viewpoints, which is the first step towards cooperation and the removal of grievances."[36] Preservation of a Canadian private magazine sector was the justification for a law that prohibited Canadian advertisers from placing advertising directed toward Canadians in split-run (basically foreign) magazines.[37] These issues are discussed at greater length in chapter 7.

Privatization and Foreign Investment and Ownership

Concepts of the private are also tied to issues of regulation of ownership. Just as cultural exclusion efforts are read as protecting private interests (not imagery that advances identity), foreign ownership restrictions can be read with the same ambiguity. Arguably, a total commitment to the private would not discriminate between local owners and investors and those from abroad. Australian owners, French owners, German owners, Japanese owners, and Saudi owners would be all one and the same. Yet a dedication to ownership of terrestrial broadcasters by nationals remains particularly intense in many countries. The argument for privatization and the logical extension of its rhetorical flow has led to pressure to reduce national restrictions in many national settings. For example, the United States employs a rule of reciprocity to calibrate licensing determinations for certain kinds of licensed telecommunications systems.

The shaving of rules on foreign ownership of broadcasting entities is also the result of other pressures. For example, Poland, in late October 1999, approved a bill to liberalize ownership of the country's television companies as part of the process of meeting the requirements of European Union membership. The draft law would have allowed foreign investors to hold up to 49 percent of shares in television firms with terrestrial broadcast licences. Prior to the effort to comply with EU standards, investors were limited to owning stakes of no more than 33 percent. "Full liberalisation (majority foreign ownership) will take place at the time of our entry to the European Union," an adviser to the then prime minister, Krzysztof Marcinkiewicz, promised.

Those EU officials who monitored Poland's compliance criticized the existing law and claimed that it permitted the two channels of public television and the domestically controlled private station, *Polsat*, to dominate the market. Foreign firms were free to invest in cable and satellite television firms operating from abroad, but as was true in so many places, terrestrial broadcast stations, still watched by the majority of Polish households, remained subject to ownership restrictions.[38]

The creation of TV Nova in 1994 serves as a case study on the peculiar hazards of negotiating privatization and foreign ownership in transition societies. Nova was the star in the crown of Ronald Lauder's Central European Media Enterprises (CEME) empire. In the post-Soviet period, it was one of the first American-style private broadcasters to be introduced into a formerly closed environment. As in so many countries, Czech law had imposed a limitation on the extent of foreign ownership of a broadcast license, even though the very concept of the market-oriented station and the programming and engineering know-how that was needed, as packaged for Czech officials, all depended on outside investment. These dual and conflicting imperatives, the need for foreign capital and the desire to keep broadcasting in local hands, yielded a complex and eventually unworkable structure of corporate governance and guarantees.

The Czech license for TV Nova was granted to a company that was jointly owned by Vladimir Zelezny, a Czech citizen, and CEME. TV Nova soon became one of the most successful of the new television entities in Central Europe. In 1998, it earned $55 million, securing 75 percent of Czech advertising revenue. In 1999, CEME was about to be acquired by a larger Scandinavian company, SBS (in which the American company ABC was a shareholder), for over $515 million.[39] TV Nova was the treasure that made CEME attractive. But because of a variety of perceived slights, and in a sudden move, Zelezny exercised the right of the Czech citizen to have independent use of the television license, and decided to operate the license without his joint venturer, CEME.[40] By doing so, he pulled the rug out from under CEME and the entire SBS transaction. CEME stock slid from $30 per share to little more than $1.60. The transaction for the sale of the station collapsed and a period of litigation and intense bitterness followed.

TV Nova was a strong commercial station, perhaps the strongest private station in the region. Its success, as indicated above, weakened the state public broadcaster. Lauder sought to hold the Czech Republic accountable for losses to CEME. After CEME's falling out with Zelezny, Moody's Investors Service lowered the company's debt rating to a speculative grade, Caa-1, and warned investors that the rating might be reviewed again with the "direction uncertain." Then, in April 1999, CEME filed a lawsuit with the International Chamber of Commerce's Court of Arbitration in Paris to prove that it was the rightful license holder for TV Nova. It also sued in the Czech courts to get the license back.

In August Fred Klinkhammer, CEME's executive director in the Czech Republic, unsuccessfully asked members of the Czech standing parliamentary commission for the media to re-examine the granting of the broadcasting license to Zelezny's company. The arbitration action was based on the Czechoslovak–US agreement on bilateral protection of investment, signed by President Vaclav Havel in 1991. In the action, CEME demanded compensation for the suffered loses and a renewal of the previously agreed on contracts. Lauder also launched a major campaign to convince the Czech Republic that there would be long-term adverse financial implications if his investment in Prague was allowed to diminish in this way. The TV Nova saga, continuing in 2002, demonstrates the complexities of combining foreign investment and control with ambiguous regulations and licensing approaches.

Privatization, the Press, and Democratic Values

The use of the privatization trope is a strong example of the purposeful export of a concept to change the profile of global media regulation. It is also tied to notions of exporting the First Amendment of the US Constitution.[41] Accept the First Amendment and the theories of the state that it embraces, and much else follows. Those who seek a more favorable environment for market decisions, and those who have a passionate commitment to the enhancement of independent media can fight regulation and censorial policy by regulation step by step. Instead, or in addition, they can propagate and encourage the embrace of the general concept of "freedom of speech," and the idea itself does an impressive amount of the necessary work. Just as France sought to export a set of principles that embodied a perception of the Revolution (and also assisted in establishing French hegemony), there is an interest in establishing a universal commitment to free speech principles. It is under the umbrella of these ideas that global media structures take shape.

The interplay between models of democracy and theories of media reform come to light through the somewhat forgotten, but once much-praised report of the 1947 Hutchins Commission "A Free and Responsible Press."[42] The report of the Commission identified five functional descriptions of the press as a measure of performance:[43] (1) to provide "a truthful, comprehensive, and intelligent account of the day's events in a context which gives them meaning," a function that implicates objectivity and impartiality; (2) to serve as "a forum for the exchange of comment and criticism," a function that suggests "fairness" and a platform for disparate views; (3) to project "a representative picture of the constituent groups in the society;" (4) to present and clarify "the goals and values of the society," a function related to national identity; and (5) to furnish "full access to the day's intelligence," thereby serving the public's right to be informed.[44] These functions, representation of pluralism aside, can be telescoped into three summary tasks central to the polititical role of the media: to provide information, to enlighten the public so that it is capable of self-government, and to serve as a watchdog or check on government.

Each of these responsibilities and functions reflects varying aspects of democratic practice. Technical assistance for media development targets a particular function, which is in turn related to a conception of democracy. Visions of a democratic society that emphasize citizen participation, for example, would underscore the need for media that, as Professor Baker puts it, "aid groups in pursuing their agendas and mobilizing for struggle and bargaining."[45] On the other hand, an elitist version of democracy requires principally that media provide information, perform a watchdog function, and assist in inculcating and transmitting "proper values." A version of a democratic society that emphasizes pluralism would value more greatly the function of the press that sought to ensure that all groups felt represented or were in fact represented. The architecture of the press, the role of new technology, ownership patterns, and, of course, demand patterns and behavior of readers also are significant factors that respond to different versions of democracy.

Arguing for a press that *must* perform all these functions is unrealistic. US foreign policy cannot easily advocate a regulatory regime that requires newspapers and broadcasters to be comprehensive, intelligent, truthful, and objective since this involves a degree of regulation and monitoring that is inconsistent with its own domestic approach. Whether newspapers or broadcast media within a society carry sets of differing opinions or opinions that are different from their own also does not automatically define whether a society is democratic.

It is plausible to have a society of opinion, of diverse views, in which each particular instrument of the press is highly partisan. That is not within the model of a free press ordinarily exported, as it were, by the United States, but it is a model that exists. In the long term, having a press that is representative of various constituent groups in the society may contribute to a stable and plural democracy, but again, it has only seldom and grudgingly been a legal requirement of a "free and independent press." Indeed, in the United States any government requirements that a newspaper be "representative" in the sense that the content reflect specific concerns or specific groups have themselves been considered coercive and violative of free speech principles.

The Hutchins Commission wrote in the context of an already old and stable democratic society in which there were solid institutions, a rule of law, and a plenitude of means of communication. One could debate the conception of society that the Commission was furthering and the nature of the democracy that prevailed in the United States or Western Europe. It would be far more complex to transfer its logic to states in various degrees of transition. A legal environment protecting the exercise of speech freedoms, a journalistic tradition of professionalism, the economic underpinnings for the assertion of integrity, and the potential to finance the mechanisms of media—all of this is fragile at best in many societies. Perhaps a smaller claim is warranted: that a society that seeks to be and remain democratic can only be so if it has some engine that performs tasks of providing information, exchanging comment, and serving and sustaining diverse constituent groups. The press in such transitions may perform the traditional democracy-strengthening functions signified by the Hutchins Commission even if it does so in unorthodox ways.

Econonomic limitations make full implementation of press rights difficult. The absence of a broad-based availability of income limits the strategies for media survival and sustainability. Media can be dependent on subscriber fees, advertising, foundation, and similar support from sources outside the country, or from the government itself. Where poverty abounds, then the nature of survival suggests the restriction of alternatives. William Dunkerley, a consultant who was part of the technical assistance movement in Russia, argued at a time when Russia was mired or regressing in its democratization process that "there does not seem to be a close positive correlation between the amount of assistance that has been given and the degree of press freedom. Indeed, there is probably a negative correlation." His view was that USAID and others were "creating just another dependency" and were not likely to "encourage the emergence of an independent and self-sufficient media." Adequate media operations, he argued, cost more than consumers can afford to pay. While additional revenues must be found, the underlying economy and existing regulation often act as a damper on advertising revenue.

When a [foreign or domestic] government provides money, office space, etc., the media organizations acquire an indebtedness to something other than truthfulness and other than the interests of their readers, viewers, and listeners. The same thing happens if major sponsorship comes from commercial, industrial, or political organizations. Press freedom becomes a casualty to such forms of support. The media become subjugated by financial overlords. At best, any pretense of press freedom is merely at the largess of those who are paying the bills.[46]

Eric Johnson, a pioneer media assistance adviser who had worked with struggling entities across the former Soviet Union, has expressed sharp disagreement with this view. Of course, there was an inadequate economic basis for immediate sustainability: media assistance was designed to prepare the groundwork for independent media that could flower when economic developments allowed that to occur. "Private broadcasters in countries such as Georgia, Armenia, and Azerbaijan have become notably independent in their news when they achieve a certain level of economic sufficiency. The tiny amount of money spent on media assistance (compared to economic assistance) is in some way a form of insurance" that independent media would exist.[47]

In some parts of the world, illiteracy is also a partial enemy of a free press (at least for certain democratic conceptions of the term), though these might be sites for greater use of radio and other effective forms of communication. Moreover there are theories of democratic life, as we will see, where it is sufficient, even if barely so, for decision makers together with a broad set of opinion leaders to have access to comprehensive information. It became a significant fact that though newspapers in Russia were far freer from censorship in the post-Soviet era, the number of readers of the serious press fell precipitously, partly because of increases in the prices of newspapers (and a decrease in the effective average wage). Still, it could be argued that there was an expanding active civil society. But even holding the price of newspapers constant, after a period of euphoria, in some societies, the zest for news about public events declines.

Conclusion

Discourse alters the process of making law and policy, so we must pay attention to the ideas that shape structure. There is much else, of course, in the tabernacles of power that influences the way legislation and media structuring take place. Military force, capital, long-standing custom and tradition—all these are the hard-scrabble upon which ideas fall. It would be naïve to think that ideas alone, apart from political and economic forces control events (and much in this book is about such other forces). But the impact of language and the ideas that language reflects should not be underestimated. Ideas have their sway. And it is for this reason that, in addition to the movement in programs, films, and data, trade in these powerful ideas concerning media structure and media policy is a significant characteristic of globalization. All missionaries know the power of a concept, or a concept joined with an image. States, corporations, political forces, and religious groups bolster these competing concepts so as to alter modes of thinking and design.

The point is to see all advocacy, including advocacy of the First Amendment, in the context of multiple efforts coming from different directions at different times to affect media policies. One point worthy of analysis is the combined impact of the tropes of restructuring: the subtle but critical shift from the individual's "freedom to receive and impart information" to a different set of desiderata, the achievement of "free and independent media." There is a move from a preoccupation with the content of information (and its explicit consequences for national power) to a focus on the structure of ownership.

I want to link this discussion of privatization and the tendency to the private to the "market for loyalties" thesis I have already described.[48] I contended that media regulation frequently constitutes a government-enforced cartel among competitors for loyalties. Changes in media regulation often come about to reflect the necessity to fashion changes in the cartel itself. Most laws of this kind are designed to protect the cartel against competitors. They are modified to allow new members to enter or to eliminate (newly) disfavored segments of society. Globalization affects the processes of defining, redefining, and protecting the cartel. New technologies, fierce geopolitical realities, altered notions of human rights—all these external forces participate in determining the suppliers of loyalties and how they enter the media and imagery market. Governments, in reaction, will try to take steps to defend against destabilizing change, by gaining private entrants they control. States design systems to restrict entry and to proscribe suppliers of loyalties thought to be antithetical to their definition of national identity. Globalization tests whether or not strategies of regulation or prohibition can be effective at strengthening or retaining sovereignty.

Privatization of broadcasting has noticeable and global impacts in this market for loyalties. One mode of softening the danger of potential competitors to those who dominate the status quo is to encourage a depoliticized commercial set of messages, depoliticized in a way that deadens civil involvement. The existing cartel is composed of a range of manufacturers of identities, some public, some private, some domestic, some foreign. Altering the nature of the media sphere can make it far less volatile. In the United States, manufacturers of tobacco agreed (and obtained legislation) to eliminate battling for market share through the use of broadcasting. In an oddly similar fashion an oligopoly of producers of political loyalties may decide that a privatized, commercialized sphere leaves them less vulnerable. The increase in the private is, of course, an effective force in that highly celebrated market for loyalties, namely Samuel Huntington's clash of civilizations.[2]

The market of loyalties argument helps describe the posture of national law as it responds to global developments. If law is a tool for cartelization of identities within, it must seek to protect that cartel from competitors abroad. Thus postglobal reactions, not unlike their antecedents, are often tied to the nature of a political system and its organic responses of self-preservation. Everywhere there are such responses. The question is how to make a science out of them, how to determine the relationship of response to ideology, to language durability, and to geographical location, how to understand motivation, whether religious fervor or a desire to maintain a level of economic growth.

At present, in the transition societies of Central and Eastern Europe, the drama of globalization is being played out in fast-forward: institutional transformations, reduction in state control of the central broadcasting empire, introduction of transient independent programmers, formal opening up of the market to private competition, consolidation between domestic entrepreneurs and international investors and consortia, the arrival of multichannel transnational empires, and the flood of images of the global culture. For the audience, the consequence is the rapid remaking of the images on the screen almost from the beginning—what is vaunted, how people dress, and the narratives that are told. Television and radio become the handmaidens of the radical transformations on the street, the coming of McDonalds, and the reordering of what constitutes acceptable visions of the future.

I have tried to show how an idea—in this case the tendency to the private—moves through national debates concerning media restructuring and, as an element of persuasion and model of the good, affect legislative outcomes. The form of privatization selected, in combination, involves recognition of audience desire, an impulse toward pluralism or, perversely, a further effort by the government to maintain control. States invite private competition while simultaneously seeking to regulate the incursion of the global; while they honor consumer choice, they single out for regulation, self-regulation, or co-regulation specific zones for banning, for channeling (restricting to niches of space or time), or for rating and filtering systems). What is significant—at least for my general thesis—is that the invocation of this trope, the advancement of the private, is multifocal in its impacts and multilateral in its implementation. I have cited, in this chapter, the example of the European Union, under the Treaty of Rome, which compelled member states to define more closely the remit of public service broadcasters so that they did not unfairly compete with the private sector. As I have indicated, the World Bank and the International Monetary Fund encourage, often short of conditionality, the tendency toward the private. And governmental aid entities, like USAID, engaged in providing media assistance as part of the process of change, often favor the development of private media competitors. Ensuring that there is an expanding private media sector becomes an article of faith.

Privatization and the expansion of the private may strongly affect the market for loyalties. Encouragement of the private may be a means of including voices that demand to be heard but are not present in the existing media. Privatization may bring about an expansion of relatively weak and unthreatening views. It may provide for the means to inject new support for government where existing media are wanting. The relationship between the process of privatization and the strengthening of civil society is not clear or direct. Much more must be known about the context, motivation, and consequences. What is clear, however, is that the impetus to the private is one of the compelling engines for change—perhaps the most forceful—in the refashioning of global media space.

The force of the private is like a powerful virus, even if a benign one. Its existence and influence tend to position state controlled or public service competitors as outmoded and inefficient. Its capacities to innovate, to bring in personnel with new perspectives, to deliver more easily accessible programming, and to educate and meet public interest obligations free from state-imposed burdens usually mean that the existence of the private in a developed market imperils the existing nonprivate media. The spread of the private has led to a sense of drift among its public broadcasting counterparts.

I have attempted in this chapter to demonstrate how words developed in one context of media regulation, primarily concepts of privatization, are translated and employed in quite different circumstances, how these words shift as they cross borders and are required to perform a variety of camouflaging tasks. The tropes of restructuring, advocacy of national identity, assertion of the value of privatization, and even the advocacy of human rights and the freedom to receive and impart information, are decorations for efforts to affect stability; they move societies from one regime structure to another or assist competitors as they fight for shares in the market for loyalties. Privatization, self-regulation, and free trade in information, First Amendment and free speech: these are powerful ideas, powerfully expressed and together they compose a forceful argument for the adoption of an assembly or laws and policies. Each of these concepts is important in itself; each provides a platform upon which ideologies can ride. I continue the exploration of these tropes of restructuring in the next two chapters.

5
Illegal and Harmful Content

In the last chapter I concentrated on privatization as a motivating idea in media restructuring. Privatization is often taken as an emblem, a rhetorical sign, of efforts to lessen the role of the state. Now I turn to a category of assertions for regulation and control made by states as they strive to increase control. I have already alluded to those general claims that are connected to national identity. But, in these days of coming to grips with the Internet, the fear and loathing of content denominated "illegal and harmful" has marked efforts to establish norms. Here, I want to trace the way the words illegal and harmful have entered the public debate, received definition, and taken flight across the statutory landscape. The evolution of meaning for these words is a small part of a struggle, state by state, nation by nation, between those who see norms defined by law, those who wish the Internet to be as free of enforceable norms as possible, and those who seek to embed norms, through altered technology, in the actions of individuals.

This struggle is reflected in the structure of this chapter. In the first part, I focus on the articulation, within and across national boundaries, of standards to control illegal and harmful content. In the second part, I turn to the process of what is called empowerment in the US rhetoric, namely the use of technology instead of the definition of norms. I do this through examination of the V-chip. Here law gives way to a redefinition of the relationship between the individual and the image. The V-chip is a transitional and political bandage, the chief consequence of which has been to increase public understanding of the potential for labeling and filtering for gateways to information. In its singular format, it became limited in time and in international space. The debate over illegal and harmful content on the Internet, in contrast, is part of an ongoing, complex debate in national and international fora over the extent of power of the state, the norms that should influence speech, and the evolution of new forms of co-regulation between industry and government.

Illegal and Harmful

The words "illegal" and "harmful" have gained, in international debates, a secondary meaning, an association with pornography or similar material harmful to minors. But illegality and harm could include, and sometimes do by law, terrorist communications, hate speech, heightened violence, computer hacking, fraudulent advertising, speech that endangers national security or promotes war, defamatory slights on leaders or friendly neighbors, or even copyright violations. While all these areas, and more, lurk in the background of regulation debate, here the discussion is largely limited to the core meaning of the term, the way it is usually used when politicians seek headlines.

In the United Kingdom, a famous pop star is convicted for downloading thousands of images of child pornography. An American college professor is indicted for images stored in his computer. Dangers lurk behind the innocent-sounding exercise of a search engine's functions. Each time there is a prosecution and ensuing coverage there are renewed calls for more statutes, harsher penalties, and more perfect enforcement. The public demand for law increases. In the United States, as discussed at greater length in the next chapter, Congress and the courts have become locked in a theater of debate over what modes of defining popularly reprehensible content are constitutionally permissible. In India, Malaysia, and much of the Middle East, political attacks on media, linked to receipt of programs from abroad, emphasize the capacity of media to corrupt public morals. An entire international infrastructure of industry and other groups has developed to provide avenues for response and to furnish some sense that progress toward control is being made, consistent with maintaining openness on the Internet and in media.[1]

Norms are imprisoned in language, though language betrays the complexity of thought that lies behind most definitions. The phrase "illegal and harmful," or some variant, is increasingly the comfortable pairing used for describing content that should be controlled or regulated on the Internet. Forms of words that approximate this phrase in literature addressing the Internet and its future can be found in European Union documents, the laws of its member states, US statutes, developing law in Australia, and elsewhere.

These words roll off the regulatory tongue. But is there an iron distinction between illegal and harmful? Do the two words encompass the universe of what states seek, within their constitutional powers, to modify, regulate, or prevent in some way? More important, does the division of the world between illegal and harmful uncover some deeper problem in establishing norms for the flow of information, especially for the Internet? <u>The formula may be constructed because such laws cannot easily be enforced in cyberspace or because the norms applied elsewhere are not, pari passu, to be applied in a new environment.</u>

It is difficult precisely to trace the origins of this verbal pairing. The union of the two words seems to have entered the Internet world formally in EU documents in October 1996. That year, the European Commission adopted the Communication on Illegal and Harmful Content on the Internet.[2] The two words, illegal and harmful, fairly clearly stood for two pillars of content. The clearest distinction would limit "illegal content" to material whose utterance or publication would be subject to criminal penalties as defined by individual EU member states. "It is a matter for member states to define what is illegal by law and to enforce it by detecting illegal activity and punishing offenders." In contradistinction, the pillar, "harmful content," would cover a vaguer, but important, area of discourse: material not subject to criminal sanction but which "may offend the values and feelings of other persons." As the document put it:

What is considered to be harmful depends on cultural differences. Each country may reach its own conclusion in defining the borderline between what is permissible and not permissible. It is therefore indispensable that international initiatives take into account different ethical standards in different countries in order to explore appropriate rules to protect people against offensive material while ensuring freedom of expression.

There is an argument here that illegality resides in things that are almost universally prohibited (child pornography) while what is "harmful" is more relative culturally. As one might expect, this neat dichotomy is problematic. Even those things that are more or less banned in almost all societies (illegal) have differences in definition, penalty, or range of enforcement. There is hardly any standard that is absolute and universal.[3]

In the European context, the meaning of the term "illegal and harmful" was illuminated, obliquely, by the fact that, at the same time as its Internet Communication, the Commission issued a Green Paper on the Protection of Minors and Human Dignity in Audiovisual and Information Services.[4] This Paper—not specifically directed at the Internet—offered a variant on the illegal and harmful pairing used in the Internet-related Communication. The universe of concern is expressed as a distinction between material banned for all by particular member states and "certain material that might affect the physical and mental development of minors," that is, permissible for adults but harmful for children. One might assume that the "banned" material is congruent with the idea of the illegal, but the term was not central. The rationale for the variant was that different solutions are required for restricted access to the Internet and other media. The annex to the Green Paper adds one additional justification for the prevention of harm which broadens the meaning past minors, namely "the desire to protect sensitive people" from confronting offensive material. "Sensitive people" include "average" citizens who suddenly and unexpectedly see material from which they may wish to have been protected. It is worthwhile quoting the relevant section from the Green Paper:

> The arrangements made to protect minors and human dignity may vary from country to country and from time to time. But it is important to distinguish two types of problems relating to material: Firstly, access to certain types of material may be banned for everyone, regardless of the age of the potential audience or medium used. Here it is possible, irrespective of differences in national legislation, to identify a general category of material that violates human dignity, primarily consisting of child pornography, extreme gratuitous violence and incitement to racial or other hatred, discrimination, and violence. Secondly, access to certain material that might affect the physical and mental development of minors is allowed only for adults. These measures should not be confused with other objectives of general interest, such as consumer protection, which might help to protect minors (notably in terms of advertising, where exploitation of their credulity is to be prevented). The aim is therefore limited to preventing minors from encountering, by accident or otherwise, material that might affect their physical and/or mental development. The issues are sometimes confused for one reason or another, but it is essential to maintain the distinction between these different questions: they are different objectives that raise different problems and call for different solutions. Clearly, the measures required to enforce a total ban are different from those needed to restrict access by minors or to prevent chance access by adults.

Here again, the idea of bifurcation arises, bifurcation between minors and adults, bifurcation between material that is somehow *malum prohibitum* (universally disdained) and material that is only dangerous when minors (or other sensitive people) are exposed to it. It is a characteristic of television—as traditionally configured—that one could distinguish between material that was to be received by minors not only through scheduling but by dealing with a fixed group of distributors of signals. For example, material harmful for children would and could be subject to a watershed restriction (no broadcast prior to a certain time) on television or a technical device could be required that would aid parents in blocking and filtering.

However, the universe for regulation is wholly different for the Internet where time zones have no meaning and where content providers are legion. The technological imperatives of the Internet require a new mindset. When the European Parliament's Committee on Culture, Youth, Education, and Media reported on the Internet Communication, it reinterpreted the distinction with an intriguing approach.[5] A "fundamental distinction has to be made between illegal content, which appertains to the field of law, and harmful content, which concerns minors and appertains essentially to the domain of morals, whether it is conveyed by the Internet or by other modes of communication." The Committee reasserted that "it is crucial to differentiate between illegal and harmful content, which call for 'very different legal and technological responses.' "

The Committee pointed out that the main issues of concern with illegal content were traceability and detection, techniques of law enforcement, while with harmful content it was softer approaches that would be required, approaches like blacklisting (barring objectionable sites), whitelisting (putting a fence around approved sites), or the encouragement of neutral labeling. The assumption was that for the category called illegal, the consequence was forgone, while the principal difficulty was identification and finding the supplier of the material. For harmful material, the main issue was management. The report elaborated the distinction, demonstrating the scope of the illegal and the particular purpose of the category of the harmful:

It is one thing to talk of child pornography, which is illegal and punishable by the criminal law, and another to refer to the fact that children may have access to pornographic material intended for adults, which, while being harmful to their development, is not necessarily illegal for adult consumers. In the first case (deviant pornography), one is dealing with illegal content which is outlawed in all areas of society, whatever the age of the potential consumers and whatever the medium used, whereas in the second case what is involved is a form of harmful content, access to which is permitted to adults only and is, therefore, forbidden to minors. . . . Other types of content are considered to be illegal by the laws of most member states. These include paedophilia, trafficking in human beings, the dissemination of documents of a racist nature, terrorism and various forms of fraud (e.g., credit card fraud and offences against intellectual property).

All through the discussions lies this idea of distinction: enforcing a total ban and restricting access, the ying of illegality and the yang of coping with harmful material. Elaborate assumptions about the functioning of government and the industrial infrastructure that permits each side of the formula to be carefully implemented are inherent within the distinction. Also, the distinction harbors an important possible administrative counterpart. What constitutes the harmful is a matter that can be left for self-regulation and what constitutes the criminal—the subject of total ban or illegality—lies of necessity with the state (both for describing the conduct and enforcing the norm).

Not every society has the desire or the capacity to define specifically what constitutes the illegal and distinguish it from the harmful in the sense embedded in the EU approach. Not every society has the commitment to due process built into the idea of prosecuting the illegal, nor the full respect for the necessities of speech freedoms when determining whether a particular speech act is an illegal infringement. Similarly, to the extent the harmful is a matter for self-regulation, the validity of the concept depends on the techniques available in any society to engage in this softer form of law. If self-regulation is the alternative to the cruder force of law, there must be confidence in the machinery of self-regulation and the bona-fides and capacity of those who represent that certain protections will be delivered. The distinction between the illegal and the harmful may also be enlisted to describe another line between government and industry: broadcasters or the Internet industry (particularly Internet service providers) might have a duty to cooperate with law enforcement over illegal content (and there are statutes that so provide), more so than when the material is only arguably immoral.[6]

The world has not been uniformly satisfied (or uniformly conformed) with the distinction I have outlined, namely the two pillars of content, the illegal and the harmful, and its migration from Commission Communication or Green Paper to law is useful to examine. As the 1996 Communication permeated the member states, the distinction was reinterpreted. The European approach also interacted with efforts to determine standards in the United States, Australia, and elsewhere. Further, as standard went from document to implementation, the complexities of existing bureaucracies, constitutional limitations, and other domestic idiosyncrasies meant that a clear and overarching division would be difficult to sustain.

Within the member states, the Communication led to a variety of national studies (not all of which can be covered here). In Ireland, the Department of Justice commissioned a study called "The Internet: Tackling the Downside, The First Report of the Working Group on Illegal and Harmful Use of the Internet."[7] The ingenious authors found ten categories that they placed under the umbrella of potential illegality: (1) national security threats, (2) injury to children, (3) injury to human dignity, (4) threats to economic security, (5) information security breaches, (6) privacy betrayals, (7) damage to reputation, (8) gambling, (9) information on the sale of "controlled drugs," and (10) infringements of intellectual property. Several of these categories fit within the 1996 EU vision of material that could be categorized as harmful, though not illegal. These include injury to children and injury to human dignity. Having swept so much content into the definition of illegality, the subsection on harmful uses in the document from Ireland is relatively short. "Harmful uses are difficult to identify with any great precision since they involve an assessment of their effect on different individuals." The working group listed "material relating to sex, violence, discrimination, graphic crime reporting, drug addiction, and cult worship" as possibilities.

In the United Kingdom, there were many entities at work trying to formulate an internal standard that would be consistent with the EU Communication. As it happened, one of the interpretive documents relating to illegal and harmful content was written in the United Kingdom in an unusual way. An Internet Watch Foundation had been established as an "independent" entity to provide credibility for Internet service provider UK self-regulation and was subject to periodic government review. As part of that review, the government's Department of Trade and Industry (DTI) sought to explore the British embodiment of the 1996 EU envelope of illegal and harmful content. According to the DTI review, there should be *three* different categories of regulatory concern. These would be illegal, unlawful, and offensive.[8] Illegal material is that which is subject to criminal prosecution. Unlawful material infringes on a private right, recognized by law, although not subject to criminal law. Examples given include material that infringes on a copyright or breaches a contract. Offensive material is content that is generally not unlawful but "can be considered harmful or otherwise unsuitable, inappropriate to certain audiences, or offensive to their values and feelings." In the United States, the equivalent of "offensiveness," in this British reading, is the complicated regulatory cubbyhole, for radio and television, of "indecency."

In Germany, one of the industry associations, the Electronic Commerce Forum (ECO), worked on another form of interpretation and norm development. ECO established the Internet Content Task Force (ICTF) in May 1996 to promulgate and further self-regulating controls. Its analysis divided content into three different types: content criminal in most countries (for example, the banned or illegal content category of the EU), content criminal under German law, reflecting particular German needs (for example, laws banning Holocaust denial), and separately, content that is harmful.[9]

The problem of defining and establishing categories, is a worldwide phenomenon. In Singapore, the definition of illegal and harmful content was written to prevent the public from receiving a much broader panoply of materials. At least at an early stage in regulation, all Internet service providers were required to be registered by the Singapore Broadcasting Authority (SBA).[10] While Internet content was subject to general media laws such as the Defamation Act, Sedition Act, and Maintenance of Religious Harmony Act, an additional category of "undesirable content" was also established.[11] The Singapore Broadcasting Authority Act gave the SBA the power to pass Internet regulations, and in 1996 the SBA issued a notification that clarified what fit within the additional category. The restriction included contents that "threaten public order and national security, religious and social harmony, and morality." Examples of these categories underline the differences from the Western European models. Undesirable content, according to the notification, includes material that tends to bring the government into hatred or contempt, excites disaffection with the government, denigrates or satirizes any race or religious group, brings any race or religious group into hatred or resentment, promotes religious deviations or immorality (as defined by Singapore's value system), is pornographic or obscene, or depicts or propagates sexual perversions (for example, homosexuality and pedophilia).[12]

In Australia, neither the term harmful nor the term illegal was used in its landmark 1999 Online Services Act.[13] Instead, the vocabulary included terms such as "unsuitable" and "offensive" along with "prohibited." The question of definition was resolved in a way not used elsewhere. Content regulation was tied to standards adopted by the Office of Film and Literature Classification. Thus material would be prohibited if it would be classified RC or X by the Classification Office or if it was designated R and not protected by an approved restricted access system. The Online Services Act included provisions to restrict access to content "likely to cause offense to a reasonable adult," though there is little to explain the meaning of this open term, and it has provisions to protect children from content deemed unsuitable for them.[14]

The Australian Broadcasting Authority (ABA) actively negotiated an industry code of conduct, an age verification procedure for access to objectionable material and material unsuitable for minors, and a labeling scheme to alert users by threatening the adoption of one if there were no self-regulatory counterpart.[15] Australia is one of the few jurisdictions in which the statute distinguishes between content "hosted in" the country, and content that is "hosted outside." If the content is Australian, in this sense, the ABA may direct the content host to remove the content from their service. If the content originates abroad, Internet service providers have an obligation to follow procedures set out in an industry code of practice to block access to that material. If the material is illegal in nature (like child pornography), then law enforcement may have a role regardless of where the material had its beginnings.[16]

The Australian solution underscores the role of self-regulation and accompanying codes of conduct. These were instruments, as I have discussed in chapter 4, that frequently become part of the response of the Internet industry (especially the ISPs) to the demand for content control, and themselves reflect the complex and confusing initiatives taken by governments. Codes of conduct evolved into a means of mediating between the ambiguity of statutes (or government power generally) and the ambiguity of life. They can be explicit markers of agreed-upon norms, modes for defining misconduct, and methods for engineering enforcement. Codes constitute relatively transparent sites for negotiation between industry and government. Codes serve at least two functions: to establish and protect a space where ISPs would have no or limited responsibility and, in exchange, to describe the kinds of limited responsibility they might have in specific instances. They are often designed to counter the argument about the need for law by imposing standards themselves.

In the United States, the Communications Decency Act of 1996 embraced a duality similar to the illegal and harmful construct I have described thus far. It prohibited, on the Internet, obscene material, a category that had been held by the United States Supreme Court to be something other than "speech" and therefore unprotected by the First Amendment. What constitutes obscenity in American law does not thoroughly map to what constitutes illegality in the European scope of the term. It is undoubtedly narrower. As to the strange and difficult second category of harm to minors, Congress acted twice. In its first attempt, ultimately held unconstitutional, the category of harm was captured in the term "indecent," borrowed from its history of broadcasting regulation. As I recount in the next chapter, the Supreme Court struck down the statute penalizing entities that knowingly displayed indecent material.[17] In a seeming effort to plug the constitutional gap, the phrase "harmful to minors" was introduced in the second legislation ("son of CDA" or CDA II).[18] The lower courts have held this provision unconstitutional as well.[19] Obscene material, in this classic division, would be banned outright, and its distribution subject to criminal penalties. Material "harmful to minors" would be subject to restrictions more contingent on modes of verification and other matters.

The V-Chip

The interrelationship between government action, industry action, and the evolution of norms is illustrated, somewhat whimsically, by the experience in the late 1990s with the V-chip, a politically mesmerizing technical device designed to enhance parental consent over television, and enable content filtering and rating systems. The chip and its penumbra of self-regulation relates to television, not the Internet, but it was also part of the drama of the 1996 Communications Decency Act. As a tool for dealing with the amorphous category of the harmful or offensive, the V-chip seemed to be a magic wafer, a combination of wires and plastic that would help salve consciences, satisfy public responsibility, and resurrect parenthood. It would help persuade providers of programming to be more forthcoming about the content and impact of the material they purvey and thereby relieve pressure on government. The pattern of its evolution illuminates the many other areas where the existence of practical authority and the search for application of state power has been affected by transnational developments.

The V-chip debate (and the debate about content filters, labels, and ratings that preceded and accompanied it) is part of a painfully visible effort by states, against technological and constitutional odds, to alter the relationship between the consumer and producer of content. The debate and reception of these approaches is an especially interesting comparative study because of the way the process advanced from country to country, with a kind of conversation among states. One adaptation exerted influence on another, culminating in a regional or comprehensive study in the European Union.

The V-chip, or the concept of the chip, seemed to hit the marketplace of competing ideologies at a moment when elected legislators and decision makers in Canada, the United States, Australia, and elsewhere had a deep political need for this device, over and above the actual addition it could make in the architecture of program choice and screening. The technology permitted the inference that government was acting in a way that dealt with important cultural questions in the society while actually doing quite little to disturb the market. This presented an enormous political advantage. The genesis of the device was in Canada, but it was the kind of idea that mushroomed and spread, with a dramatic (and possibly forgettable) episode in the United States, Australia, Japan, and Europe.

In the mid-1990s a youngish Canadian scientist named Tim Collings wrote a short paper on a technology that, quite simply, permitted information about a program to stream down a little used aspect of the transmission system called the vertical blanking interval and trigger a mechanism in the television set—preset by its owner—to block unwanted programs. Originally the "V" stood for viewer: a chip to give the viewer a choice. The very first transformation in the ensuing international debate was over the meaning of the V: it has moved from viewer, in Canada, to violence in the United States (and, somewhat mysteriously, into sex or indecency). As they worked out a method for implementing the technology, the Canadian Radio-Television and Telecommunications Commission (CRTC) sought, systematically, to determine the best possible and most efficient means of classifying program content and conveying that classification to viewers. Industry and citizens together made decisions about what questions would be asked about a program, the subject matter of the information to be gathered, and the way in which that information should be conveyed.

In Canada, there was a period of experimentation, conducted under the supervision of the regulators that led, after hearings and industry recommendations, to the adoption of a comprehensive and relatively well-thought out public policy. At the beginning, in the United States, under the forced hand of Congress because of the design of the 1996 Telecommunications Act and the supposed implications of the First Amendment, it fell almost purely to the entertainment industry to fashion the implementation of the device. Only if the US industry failed to respond or develop an unacceptable labeling approach would there be a government-appointed commission to develop alternatives. This method, the result of political compromise and special US constitutional considerations, had a profound impact on the initial industry offering and the debate that ensued. In the end, the trails between the Canadian and American approaches seem to have converged, but that too is probably an indication of how narrow the possibility of fashioning an acceptable rating system might be.

In the United States, there was a melodramatic "second act," a consequence of interest group politics and the competition between industry-legislator alliances and legislator-community group alliances. In Canada, industry groups worked with public agencies and community entities during the planning process. In the United States, the initial industry-originated plan, mostly hatched behind closed doors, led to objections by public interest organizations and changes that—depending on the critic—did or did not have significance in the end.[20] The revised system took a leaf from the Canadian proposal and increased disclosure of content information at least as compared to the Motion Picture Association of America classification system, which was largely age based. Under the scheme, a three-year trial of a system would be implemented that would supplement age-based classifications with a V, S, L, or D rating, denoting violence, sexual content, coarse language, or suggestive dialogue. In a further departure, children's cartoon shows that contain cartoon violence would carry an FV for fantasy violence. As a central element of the negotiated settlement between major parts of the industry and the advocacy groups, key members of Congress were to agree to a three-year moratorium on legislation relating to television content.

The V-chip, in its basic form, is specific to television and is an episode in the very long series of discussions about whether the accessibility to children of violence or sexually suggestive programming on television (or broadcasting generally) deserves special attention. These discussions have an underappreciated prehistory in the labeling of comic books, rating of films, and proscription of books (each of which, in their turn, was supposed to have domineering and magical qualities of persuasion). In this V-chip embodiment, advocacy starts with the premise that radio and television have an even more particular power to affect conduct and, in the traditional free-to-air mode of distribution, a certain invasiveness.[21]

The V-chip approach has demonstrated a noteworthy and cultural capability for diffusion through other areas of distribution of imagery. These areas span the establishment of information that would allow filtering of violent and indecent television programming to far more expansive grounds for filtering advertisements concerning alcohol or tobacco or messages because of political content.[22] Labeling and rating schemes proliferate. They are no longer the province, primarily, of broadcasting and motion pictures. The video game industry and the music industry have responded to legislative pressure within the United States to develop labeling and rating methods of their own.

Labeling and rating methods have also spread to the Internet. The technologies of parental control schemes are far different and far more complicated than those embodied in the V-chip, but the principle is the same. A technical device should exist that enables parents to sort out (based on standards implanted in the electronic signature of content) which programs they wish to have enter the porous walls of their children's lives. School boards and libraries adopt policies that incorporate voluntary rating schemes into official regulation of access. In 2000, the US Congress enacted legislation requiring libraries to install filtering systems as a condition of obtaining favorable "e-rates" for connections to the Internet. Communities design criminal ordinances that use government sanctions to enforce these restless labels. The Internet Watch Foundation, founded in the United Kingdom, established an elaborate system of self-rating, partly to help Internet providers protect themselves from hostile government intervention. One of the most important discussions involved the development of PICS (the Platform for Internet Content Selection), a vigorous and still controversial approach to assuring a multiplicity of voluntary ratings, and an architecture freer of government involvement.

The V-chip philosophy has its gnarled roots in contested research and conflicting ideologies, where the interest groups are divided among those who oppose state intervention, those who consider it appropriate to preserve some version of values, and those who accept filtering and rating as the best that can be achieved, a compromise between government action and individual autonomy. The V-chip (and similar approaches) elide the heated debate between those, on the one hand, who think a connection between television programming and violence is adequately demonstrated and those, on the other hand, who think it is not proved sufficiently to justify government intervention.

The V-chip's introduction has been an odd occasion, as well, for a discussion, sometimes forced and artificial, about the role of parents in controlling the flow of images. There seems to be hardly any research on the relationship between parent (or caretaker) and child, and child and television set.[23] Yet speeches proliferate about the extent to which this device will enhance the parental or caretaking role. The technology's enthusiasts believed or claimed to believe that the V-chip "empowers" parents, to use the term of the 1996 US Telecommunications Act, though the evidence that parents either need empowerment (they probably do) or that this device empowers them, has been in slim supply. There is no question that the technology has its doubters, as to its inherent contribution, its neutrality and relationship to censorship, and to the plausibility of V-chip implementation. Among these are skeptics who believe that the V-chip merely allows legislators and policymakers to *appear* to be addressing a problem of imagery and society while in fact, nothing is done to address the virtually intractable issue.

While the initial concept of the V-chip was simple, its flow into the public realm has raised so many extraordinary questions that the introduction and production of the chip can serve as a case study in problems of law and public policy. Here are a few of the questions that have emerged: What research basis is necessary to require a framework for labeling and rating? What relationship between government and the image-producing industries can be characterized (for constitutional and other reasons) as voluntary as opposed to coercive? If images are to be evaluated, who should do the evaluation—the producers, the distributors, or objective third parties? In a society barraged by images, how feasible are rating or labeling systems? In television, should a rating system be scene by scene, program by program, series by series, or channel by channel? Indeed, how much information about content can be effectively redacted and communicated? There are semiotic questions about the nature of the logos, the on-screen signals used to alert viewers: What kind of label or logo informs, and what kind persuades? What kind of logo is neutral, and what kind bears its own shame-bearing or moral judgment? What kind of logo has a boomerang effect and attracts, as opposed to informs and repels, audiences for which it is to serve as a warning? What relationship is enshrined in the architecture of labeling between the industry that produces the images and the government that regulates them? How centralized or how distributed should the process of evaluation be? What guarantees of integrity are there in the evaluative or rating process? What assessment is there to determine whether filtering or labeling experiments, especially those reinforced by legislation, are successful?

It is also interesting to examine how a government introduces or furthers a technology of filtering. The different approaches in Canada and the United States toward the role of regulatory agency, industry, and government reflect political traditions and may demonstrate substantial distinctions in constitutional standards. Such a study of comparative processes—how different political and industrial systems evaluate these labels and mechanisms—has been of significance to the European Commission, the United Kingdom, and other entities studying rating arrangements after the US and Canadian adoptions.

Still, what is striking about these questions is that they assume a national ground for action. The data and experience can come from other societies, but it is almost always assumed that each society can absorb and render a decision for its own citizens. One can further read the interaction between the development of standards and approaches in the United States and in Canada quite differently. As a laboratory, Canada initially influenced the making of policy in the United States. The United States, later, affected the final Canadian decision by sheer dint of overwhelming neighborliness. US pressure groups obtained, through political activity, the absorption of various elements of the Canadian approach. The ultimate Canadian approach incorporated elements of the American system for reasons of pragmatic reality and the substantial presence of US programming on the Canadian screen.

It is hard to know how to read the aggregated results of industry proposal, group advocacy, and industry change in Canada and the United States. Did these plans rest on the notion that, whether self-enforced or not, the resulting techniques were ones that could be used effectively to alter the relationship between viewer and sender of messages? Or did the results indicate that in the modern world, any effort to intervene in the intimate, though industrialized speech practices of broadcasting, intervention was hopeless?

There were many, including in the creative community in Hollywood, who criticized the industry solution for compromising free speech values. In November 1996, for example, the Caucus for Producers, Writers, and Directors supported a ratings system similar to the one finally proposed by networks, with NBC adopting a slightly diffent system.[24] A year later, in November 1997, the Caucus, after inner turmoil, publicly voiced its opposition to the new television content ratings system and reversed its earlier position. "We actively oppose any interference with creative rights, whether it is the US government, studios, networks or special interest groups," the Caucus said in an advertisement. "We are appalled by the politically motivated tactics of legislators urging the FCC to reject the license renewals of television stations not using the new ratings system." Other critics claimed that the industry had too much control over the US rating system. Under its first proposal the implementation would be wholly within industry hands and would be designed to interfere least with the marketability of the industry's products. The summer 1997 revision adjusted membership on a monitoring board to assure representation from groups other than the networks and producers of programming.

No matter how much debate there was over the content of the labels, the size of their display onscreen, the number of seconds they would appear, and other details of hand-to-hand combat, the suspicion lingered that the whole exercise was merely a gambit. When Jack Valenti, the president of the MPAA and central negotiator, applauded the three-year moratorium on legislation that was decided in 1997, he charmingly grounded these suspicions. In vintage Valenti form, he candidly stated:

The purpose of doing a ratings system in the first place was to shut off this tidal wave of criticism. The gain, the singular gain, is that for three years we will keep the jaguars and bobcats off our backs, and have a period of legislative peace and perhaps a diminishing of carping and criticism in the marketplace.

This statement underscores the use of law as symbol, law used to demonstrate the effectiveness or seeming effectiveness of those in office when matters that cause public disquiet are on the table. The ratings system was the minimum concession by industry necessary to avoid a renewal of attempts at government content regulation. The V-chip expressed the appropriate level of official noise to demonstrate concern while avoiding intervention in the economic activity of major constituents. Insufferably mild an intervention for some, the American scheme, even in its indirect mode, constituted censorship and government control for others. The ratings system, and the legislation that brought it about, could, with some winks, be viewed as a good faith effort to meet a public need, or, on the other hand, as a brilliant preemption of legislation that might more effectively and dangerously intervene and impose binding moral standards.

No matter what the solution to the debate over the V-chip, at bottom, the public discussion generally glides over basic concerns about modern culture, modern mores, and the impact of the influx of images. The V-chip, though it exists largely because of unease about aspects of modernity, fixates on sex and violence, neglecting other effects of television on children, such as the loss of traditional kinds of literacy and the leveling of cultures. In this sense, the V-chip is an American-type formulation of false resistance to modernity and cultural change. It is a technical solution to a preoccupation with violence and indecency and a substitute for addressing concerns about fundamental trends in the way that children are acculturated.

The overarching, almost religious, questions that probably lie at the root of the most sincere expressions of social concern are reflected only indirectly in the many studies of violence and media. These studies cannot satisfactorily rehearse the question of whether images on television affect behavior, or which images on television, in motion pictures, or on the Internet affect behavior in what ways. As with much of the scholarship or research, the very point of the chip is to tweak culture at the margin, to provide a filter, not to dam modernity.

Transnational Implications

While the V-chip schemes, in the United States, Canada, and elsewhere look like domestic regulation of domestically distributed speech, there are several aspects of the V-chip that tie the national to the transnational. First, the shift, discussed in more detail below, toward "empowering" the listener may be a guerrilla response to the almost universal sense of diminishing state control over producers. Another way to put this is that at a time when the political power of the state seems, increasingly, to be declining, the state will relish a technique for monitoring that is synchronous with decentralization and deregulation. At a time when the institutions of law, in their traditional forms, seem to be weakened by transnational forces, the V-chip (and other filtering and labeling mechanisms) represents a mechanical deus ex machina. If the state cannot function through articulated norms enforced through traditional prosecutorial exercises of discretion, technology can provide a rescue. Just as highway cameras that trap speeding drivers and immediately impose a fine are part of the automation of traffic laws, the V-chip system can be part, even though an inelegant part, of a system of automating content norms.

Similarly the V-chip can be linked to self-regulation, as I have discussed it in the last chapter. The trend toward self-regulation is itself a product of the weakening of the state. There is an irony here. Only the most total of states could manage the logistics of reviewing, rating, and monitoring of all television programming, video games, and music. One could argue that the inability of authoritarian powers effectively to control all these forms of imagery is a basic reason for their decline. Without a mechanism of self-regulation highly dependent on industry cooperation and administration, so gargantuan a program of grading and review could not occur. In a world of lessening state power, industry participation and control is essential to the establishment of norms. This serves industry needs as well as state needs; it establishes the principle that government-industry cooperation should increase and contributes to the creation of transnational standards that expand opportunities for programming in the most restrictive of societies.

States or leagues of states act through an intensive kind of leverage, using the power of the corporations to achieve what cannot be achieved by the states themselves. Most important, the V-chip phenomenon (enlarged to incorporate the growing trend toward filtering and labeling techniques) reinforces important developments in the very conceptualization of speech in society. The ratings debate masks a theoretically changed relationship between listener and speaker. Speech rights have had an interesting use cycle. Mythologized as the domain of crusading pamphleteers and brave voices in Hyde Park corners, these rights have become, especially in decisions of the 1980s and 1990s, a shield for the major enterprises of entertainment: the rights of broadcasters, the rights of program suppliers, and the rights of cable operators.[25]

The V-chip debate seems, on the other hand, part of a slight tectonic shift to the infrequently articulated right of the listener or viewer. The European Convention on Human Rights and many of its counterparts in legal systems throughout the world include not only the right to impart, but the right to receive information. US law, in comparison, has been more inclined to emphasize the right to speak with slight attention to the right to receive. Rights of listeners or viewers might include rights to shape what is communicated, rights to a diversity of programming or information, access to public records and information, and, as in the V-chip, rights to information about information. In the new technologies the rights of listeners is shaped by interactivity as the function of listener and participant begin to merge. Essentially, these rights—in a modern world—are rights of consumers as compared to industrial suppliers of entertainment speech, advertising, and other products of the commercial broadcasting system.

One can say that labeling and rating systems either mandate or strongly encourage speech about speech. They do not seek to change speech but, it is said, like content descriptors on packages of food, only provide a sense of what the consumer is to receive. "This is a simple matter of truth-in-labeling," a US senator is quoted as having said. "We don't want Hollywood telling parents what is age-appropriate. We just want Hollywood telling parents what is in their shows." This is part of a reconceptualization of speech. Stated differently, almost all speech is contained in packages part of which is speech about speech. Television programs are often anticipated by information that tells the viewer, through promotion, what the program is about. Television guides contain capsules that are descriptive. The program itself has substantial text that attributes roles in its composition to directors, writers, and others. As listeners, we tend to put ourselves in positions where speech directed at us or speech we overhear is surrounded by clues on what to expect. Many individuals, by steadfast allegiance to certain messengers, shield themselves from messages that are deprived of clues. Most people, for example, are loyal to particular radio stations, inured, probably, to the nature of messages they will receive. The channel itself becomes a package of clues or descriptors. Readers buy *The New York Times* and not the *National Enquirer* because, by designating a particular framework in which messages will be transmitted, they ensure that a particular type of information will be delivered.[26]

The assumption here is that some speech breaks these rules or (and this is the stage in which we find ourselves) new batches of speech, new modes of distribution transgress previous understandings of listener or viewer discrimination. Advertisers and sellers of goods and ideas crave this advantage of surprise. But it is a temporary disequilibrium. In newspapers and television, one might argue, a history and tradition has developed in which the channel of transmission, itself, is usually sufficient to infer meta-data about the programming that is transmitted. Government intervenes, it may be hypothesized, when this equilibrium of understanding is destabilized. This occurs when structural aspects of transmission prevent or are perceived to prevent the traditional sort of branding or editorial familiarity in which meta-data about programs can easily be inferred. Skywriting could be taken as an odd example. Because there is virtually no defense against sky writing penetrating consciousness, the state may deem it necessary to impose standards that substitute for the existence of the capacity to edit.[27] People can turn off their television sets, but it may not be fair to require that they avert their eyes from the sunset. Indeed, it would be interesting to think how much of past government intervention into streams of speech can be explained by a desire to facilitate screening where what might be called the natural workings of the market do not advance that goal. Of course, almost every seller of ideas or products, in addition to wishing to service existing customers, wishes to reach out to new ones and expand the base. Often this requires breaking accepted patterns of distribution of information and exposing some to ideas, images, or modes of discussion that they would otherwise shun.[28]

As a machine of distribution, the very virtues of the Internet—its vaunted ideal of abundance, its ease of expansion and entry—conspire to render it primitive, primitive, that is, in its regression to an environment in which it is difficult for viewers to understand the channeling of speech or to create norms by which to discriminate. Much of the discussion and many of the actions of Internet service providers can be explained as providing informal methodologies to users to allow them to control how and when they wish to expose themselves to particular messages and images.

AOL, for example, has taken the position that it sponsors an array of mechanisms that provide the user with a large measure of control (and that there is no single mode that will accomplish the goal). It provides or encourages the provision of a variety of "whitelisting" search services that are delegates of this process of selection and monitoring. AOL has contributed to the growth of an entity called "NetWise" that provides instruction on how to be a sophisticated and discerning user of information present on the Internet. In its chat rooms, AOL has had "scouts" who patrol whether there are inappropriate uses of those facilities. There is something like an AOL-alert button that a user can employ if, of a sudden, some possibly harm-creating sender of words and images enters the information space unbidden and unwanted. These are all steps that have been taken toward developing a culture of discernment and attitudes on use, short of government banning and censorship. These steps, and the voluntary rating and filtering systems, become part of an evolving set of norms and an evolving mode for choosing among signals.

Is this activity of providing the surrounds for information enough or, to the contrary, is it too much? Just as information about nutrition on a package is designed to alter eating behavior, so the information on a rating or label is designed to influence what people see or hear. Furthermore there are problems with a system that is too much of a shift, and an artificial one, toward the listener. It is overwhelming to say that the listener's right cannot be fully implemented unless the listener knows, in advance, what is about to come into his or her ken. If the listener affirmatively chooses programming (as is the case in pay television), the information requirement is less pressing. But even there, the government's power to require information to assist the listener to be a better consumer may be what is at stake. In a world where listeners are atomized while speakers tend to be corporate, the corrective role for government may be growing. This slogan of listener empowerment, of providing the parent more authority to screen and select programming for the family, is politically persuasive. It seems to harmonize the desire to control with the bias against regulation. Yet, "user empowerment" recalls old attempts to move responsibility from the corporation to the citizen and to blame the citizen for collective acts, often the acts of businesses.

The place of the V-chip and Internet rating in this debate is significant; indeed, it may be argued that the V-chip's contribution to theories of speech and society are greater than its ultimate contribution to the relationship between children and imagery. Already the US Supreme Court has used the V-chip and related ratings approaches as reason to hold the Communications Decency Act unconstitutional because a less restrictive alternative might be available for achieving the desired result.[29] Bill Clinton, as president of the United States, pointed to the V-chip or other built-in rating technologies as a key to the design of a deregulated Internet. Already the European Parliament, as a result of considering whether the V-chip should be adopted, engaged in a broad-scale rethinking of the place that so-called technical devices, including digital electronic program guides, should have in the architecture of speech regulation.[30]

Another way to think about the V-chip and theories of free speech involves what I have elsewhere called the "open" versus "closed" terrain of speech.[31] Under this theory there is more government interest and more government activity in speech that is broadly open to public view and display. Speech on sites that are selective, chosen affirmatively by the user would not be considered so much as warranting regulation as content spread before the world in the traditional manner of broadcasting. The impulse toward content ratings would, under this mode of thinking, be more intense for broadcast television than for cable, more for basic tier or "free" cable channels than for pay channels. Ratings or labels are more important where the speech is not specifically the subject of contract or a careful degree of choice. Here the theory does not turn on whether or not children are listening and watching, but on the method by which information reaches a household.

Where does the Internet fit within this analysis? Part of the international debate is designed to influence the outcome to this question. If the Internet is fundamentally different from broadcasting, a matter predominantly of consumer choice, contractual, and personalized at the consumer's modeling, then, of course, it is closed terrain and should be treated as a private arrangement between customer and provider. If the Internet is deemed to be aggressively probing, "pushed" into the home, subversively entering the consciousness of children, and using that entrance for purposes of unanticipated dominance, then a different conclusion might be reached. It would fit the reigning theory of user empowerment and lack of regulation to adopt the view that the Internet, in this rhetoric, is predominantly a "closed" mode of speech. Material does not come uninvited to the home.

There is a third fashion of thinking about the increased emphasis on content ratings and labeling alternatives: we are witnessing a kind of "tobaccoization" of certain kinds of speech. Speech is treated as a public health question. Statutory findings and government statements concerning indecent and violent speech and images retrace the rhetoric concerning regulation for smoking and alcohol. Until recently not much had been written about a "public health" exception to free speech principles in the United States, but that is an area that deserves greater attention.[32] Article 22 of the Television without Frontiers Directive might be deemed a "public health" view of the power of the state to assure that particular forms of broadcasting do not jeopardize the development of minors.[33] The idea that there is a relationship between public health concerns and broadcasting is certainly more dominant in the European debate than in the American.

Labeling and rating schemes, as well as channeling proposals, are welcomed as alternatives to the more difficult and compromising interventions of blocking or censoring. This quality appeals to legislators who wish to appear proactive, to courts that seek interventions not so onerous, and to networks that seek to fend off criticism by adopting the mildest possible restrictions. But the beginning step of content labeling and filtering devices leads, inevitably, to other possible roles for the state. At some level content ratings may be so coercive that they amount to a ban or specific speech restriction. For example, a community could place sanctions on individuals, say with children, who refuse to use particular filtering systems, or whose rating choices are unsatisfactory. It is possible that disclosure of identities necessary for access to restricted channels unduly invades privacy. The state may be involved in monitoring the content rating decisions of producers or may determine that it should be, as in Australia, more deeply involved in the actual rating process.

In the case of the V-chip in the United States, the technology's significance and elaboration depend on the dominant role of the producer or network, as with the role of the Motion Picture Association of America (MPAA) in film. The American system may be a specific result of First Amendment elements that are not applicable in Europe or elsewhere in the world. The US V-chip system is built on the idea that there will not be effective competition in the market for classifications. The industry determines hegemonically what ratings are embedded in the program; licensees therefore are not common carriers obliged to carry all possible ratings or even a representative bouquet.

Implementation begs further questions. V-chip ideologies assume that over time almost all television sets (or computers) will be fitted with the technology. In the shorter term this will hardly be the case. In addition there are delicate questions about what program offerings should be covered by a rating system, news being the most important candidate for exclusion (news and sports are both excluded under the US plan). There is no question that news can be violent—there are those who believe that the primary modus operandi of the "late news" on American stations at 10:00 pm or 11:00 pm is to instill and build on the fears of the viewing public. If news is excluded, which programs, particularly those that are of the new "real life" genre or tabloid television can be characterized as news? It would be ironic but predictable to see violence and sexual innuendo come, even more, to shape news programming as a result of its exemption from a ratings scheme.

There is quite a lot of writing about the applicability of the US First Amendment to these systems.[34] A rather difficult aspect of that debate is the complicated, jurisprudentially brutal relationship between legislation or threatened legislation and private industry action, the coercive aspect of what is called jawboning in the United States. It was precisely the threat of legislation that called forth the "voluntary" action of the industry to develop a rating scheme, and as indicated above, the US industry extracted a moratorium on legislation and serious discussion of legislation as part of the deal for accepting the V-chip.[35] The US Telecommunications Act of 1996 was carefully drafted to respect an imaginary line between unconstitutional coercion and acceptably coerced voluntariness.

Thus are raised fundamental free speech questions about the way in which government interacts with industry. The manner of voluntary rating scheme adoption suggests a massive, moderately undisciplined, virtually unreviewable relationship between government officials and a particular set of industry speakers. How does society place bounds, rules, sense of appropriateness, to the range of this swing between voluntariness and coercion? In many countries, jawboning is not considered inappropriate government conduct and instead, shorn of a disparaging moniker, is constituted as a normalized ongoing interrelationship between the force of government and the self-regulation of industry. The ratings law is a useful moment for discussing changed modes of discourse between government and industry.[36]

All rating schemes and all public policy discussions about them contain some assumptions about the relationship of label to viewer or listener.[37] I have already referred above to what might be called the semiotics of ratings. How does the consumer perceive ratings? What differences are there among the various industries that have tried or are trying ratings in the nature of communication? A greater debate is needed on the exact impact of labels, comparisons among the icons from country to country, the drama or lack of drama of these icons, whether they are designed to communicate to the parent or to the child. There are practical questions about the shape and impact of the logo used as part of the rating system, how long it is on the screen, and the relationship between on-screen warnings and the reputed built-in screening capacity of the V-chip. In the future it will be useful to know what observed relationship there is between ratings—information—and behavioral consequences. Some symbols, in some industries, such as portions of the video game industry, seem almost designed to attract as well as inform the consumer. The proliferation of rating and labeling systems across content industries must be based on far more understanding of the psychological, institutional, and mechanical links involved.

The development of a labeling or rating system means that there will be a kind of common law of ratings or different common laws that depend on the industry. If ratings or labels are not arbitrary, rules will emerge. They may not be articulated in a published document or reduced to a code, but these rules will exist and be known to producers (this is somewhat the case today with films). Such a common law would indicate to producers exactly what conduct or display would receive what kind of label or rating. Over time such law will surely evolve, with finely drawn distractions concerning dress, vocabulary, and presentation of body.[38] One possibility is that the emerged common law will depend on the structure of the industry. An industry dominated by two or three providers may internalize a ratings scheme in a specific and documented form more rationally than an industry where there are many independents and constant testing of the limits and meaning of the ratings scheme.[39]

Clearing a Global Market

censorship etc.

Standards for what is "illegal or harmful" are everywhere evolving. National legislatures write their own dramas: as if they had discovered a problem of harm on the Internet or in broadcasting and feel they can fashion a national solution. Where images are clearly transnational or flow through the conduits of multinational corporations, there is informal pressure and aspiration for systems that have some uniformity in process and standard. At an international or regional level, representatives of industry and government deliberate, compare, examine, and borrow approaches. The interaction between government and industry that takes place within national borders enriches and mirrors interactions that take place among associations of industry and associations of governments at levels of higher abstraction. There are evolving norms of what constitute suitable levels of direct government intervention, what modes of policing will be expected of the Internet industry, and what processes of co-regulation or cooperation should be established. Through this process some other form of articulation, introduction, and enforcement of norms replaces law.

The global debate over the interpretation and application of free speech principles has to be seen as part of an historic development in which law tends to follow the market; or, better still, forms of law and a definition of constitutional principles are propounded that enable a market in Internet-powered speech (commercial and not) to grow. I have thought of this primarily with respect to the United States where the First Amendment initially bound only the US Congress and individual states could vary in the nature and extent of their own censorial standards well into the twentieth century.[40] A motivation for reinterpretation of the First Amendment as applied to individual states as well as the federal government was precisely the result of a need, in a national speech economy, for a national standard of noninterference. It was a necessary condition for the growth of a national communications industry and national market. The evolution was, some seventy years before the Television without Frontiers Directive, a successful attempt at regionalization and an architecture of regulation that recognized the need to "clear" a vast expanse for the creation of an information space.[41]

Now the question is how to "clear" or come closer to clearing a global market. Free speech principles are in the vanguard of this effort. The ascendancy of the right to receive and impart information is not new on the world scene. What is new is the emphasis on human rights principles as a means of furthering the expansion agendas of the multinational corporations. If one were to do a review of cases and arguments concerning Article 10 of the European Convention on Human Rights and the International Convention on Civil and Political Rights, one would find a transformation. The first stage focuses on the rights of the individual not to be suppressed; the second on the need to permit transborder flow of information within a region. Only as a third stage would there be the marshalling of free speech doctrine as a major argument against regulation of the large commercial entities. As a strategy this is an understandable evolution. Politically the end user in the communications chain is a more appealing subject for rights than the multinational corporations and the freedom of organized senders to communicate. The "right to receive and impart" information becomes more important as it becomes a higher and higher priority, with greater and greater geographical reach. Rights-affirmation becomes an important part of clearing a global information market. The right to impart information becomes more significant as funds for its definition and enforcement become more widely available and the staffs of nongovernmental organizations committed to its implementation become greater and more pervasive. The right to receive information by a villager in India becomes the right of a powerful consortium controlling international cricket matches to break through a government broadcasting monopoly.[42]

In a sense there are parallel lines of evolution that will determine how the debate over norms and technical devices develop internationally. First, the technology or architecture in which norms are embedded is evolving. The capacity of whitelists to be effective or for filtering systems to be comprehensive depends very much on the fineness of labeling and the sophistication of the software that underlies the material sent through the networks by content providers. Each year the software seems to allow greater discrimination and greater screening capability, though it is difficult to conceive that a perfect labeling and filtering system can ever be devised that will take into account the myriad of public concerns.

The second area for evolution is community norms. The relationship between norms and practices is a dynamic one. The history of taste is, often, but hardly always, of expanding tolerance, though there are, quite obviously, substantial national differences in what constitutes progress in taste and in the baseline itself. In general such norms change over time and a system of explicit regulation or self-regulation coupled with codes of conduct or of content rating, labeling, and filtering systems must take these changes into account. Those administering classification schemes have a variety of ways of plumbing changing public perceptions to determine how to exercise classificatory discretion.[43]

The shape of the industry of distribution is evolving as well. This can be seen in the division of roles among service providers, content providers, and competition in filtering and labeling systems. Major Internet service providers, such as AOL, play an affirmative and changing role in addressing content that might be deemed harmful. The extent to which there is further concentration among ISPs, and how those remaining or leading ISPs fashion their role will affect the standards and entire interrelationship of participants. Similarly how the market for content ratings evolves and the extent to which society sees itself as fashioning a more comprehensive system of trusted editors who rate or label programming so that filters can be effective will be important.

All of this will affect another area of evolution: the allocation of responsibilities between government and the various segments of industry. In the European Union, among member states, the relationship between administrative agencies and the self-regulatory bodies established by industry alters at a different pace, but there is an effort, at the European level, to harmonize the processes of evolution. One representative discussion of this change can be found in the Working Group study of Illegal and Harmful Use of the Internet of the Republic of Ireland. As the Executive Summary puts it with remarkable conciseness:

The downside of the Internet represents a common enemy that will only be defeated through partnership and cooperation. The new partnership approach will involve new structures and active participation by all parties, but with the service providers having a key role: . . . We believe it is not only impossible but also counter-productive to attempt to "regulate" the Internet in the sense of introducing new national statutory provisions to specifically control its illegal and harmful use.

All aspects of the debate over the meaning of illegal and harmful material on television and Internet reflect on this process. The existence of a plethora of inconsistent regulations across national boundaries jeopardizes the development of large-scale regional signals and therefore hampers global entrepreneurship. Just as it would have been difficult to have a US-wide network if enforceable standards for programming were different in Oklahoma and California, so it is a problem to develop programming for a transnational audience if there is the danger of prosecution in India for one kind of programming and in Malaysia or China for another. Inconsistency in the law of standards leads to lower investment in programming, more caution, and less diversity. Pervasive application of free speech principles provides the necessary market-clearing palliative.

The debate about ratings and labeling schemes demonstrates a shift from a law-based state to a "soft" or managerial state. Undoubtedly, this is part of a larger redefinition of the way in which governments function. In the case of the Internet, the move from law making to "influencing," "persuading," or "managing of the environment" is dramatic. While the most public aspect of the shift from a law-based to managerial state deals with Internet content, the move away from law is characteristic of other aspects of the introduction of the new technology as well. But what, in this sense, is "new"? Newness itself is another dramatic trope of restructuring and one to which I now turn.

6
Newness of New Technology

Every new technology reorders the world around it. A century ago, in a gentle preface to his novel *Under the Greenwood Tree*, Thomas Hardy wrote of the transformation of tiny church orchestras in village England. An "isolated organist" deploying a new invention, the harmonium or barrel organ, was displacing humble and amateur community instrumentalists. The new device presented certain advantages in control and accomplishment, but the "change has tended to stultify the professed aims of the clergy, its direct result being to curtail and extinguish the interest of parishioners in church doings." In these hamlets the technology of musical development had consequences for community participation, the life of the church, the nature of the music that was played and, Hardy seemed to be saying, for much of country life as well. Of these multiple and small transformations major changes in society takes place.[1]

Newness, a preoccupation with the unknown, a twinning of heralded benefits and fears of danger, is one trope of restructuring that is evident throughout the process of legal and policy transformation. Every candidate for new information technology has invited a superheated rhetoric of millennial social change, a ballooning of the claims Hardy made in his precise description of the effect of the harmonium. When wireless radio technology was introduced in the first decades of the twentieth century, world peace was said to be only a turn of the dial away.[2] *The New York Times* wrote: "Nothing so fosters and promotes a mutual understanding and a community of sentiment and interests as cheap, speedy, and convenient communication."[3] Then as now, investors, promised riches by hawkers of the new technology, poured lavish funds into fledgling, often nearly bankrupt, companies. Newness in information technologies seems almost always to embrace a simultaneous capability for fulfilling dreams, challenging existing institutions and mores, and disappointing expectations.

It is still possible that the satellite, the Internet, and other information technologies will lead to the "greatest revolution in information since the invention of the printing press."[4] The extent to which this will be the case is not the point of this chapter. Rather it is to ask how change in technology is conceptualized, evaluated, and manifested in the process of reshaping institutions and laws. Governments try to divine how the newness of information technology affects the porousness of boundaries, capacities of old institutions to regulate new realities, the cultural horizons that arise from altered patterns of data and image flows. Then, based on inadequate information, states probe ways to manage what they think are the consequences.

In the last chapter, I explored examples of the threat of the new: its articulation as a carrier of illegal and harmful content and the capacity of new information technologies to present or intensify potential mischief and dangers. Legislation to reshape modes of access and surveillance can be seen as an effort to deflect the use of new media for such purposes. In 1996, in the United States, President Clinton established the President's Commission on Critical Infrastructure Protection to investigate the potential for terrorism on the Internet and legislation ensued from that.[5] A President's Working Group on Unlawful Conduct on the Internet called for restrictions on anonymity in cyberspace, citing law enforcement's inability to trace online fraud, hacking, and dealing in child pornography, firearms, and drugs.[6] A society that fears revolutionary, destabilizing, and dangerous dissent was prepared to vest in its government extended powers to defend the status quo. Aside from the language I have already canvased, "terrorism" or radicalism of dissent becomes another trope that justifies greater state authority.[7]

Another quality of newness is how we describe the social structure by which information travels from those who originate content to those who consume it. New media technology famously disintermediates, or is said to, altering the power of traditional entities such as department stores, political parties, and television networks.[8] Policy makers who hope for a technology that destroys existing mediators—creating a freer path between consumer and producer of information—might be more tolerant of complexities of implementation than those who think that the new technology merely remediates (yielding slightly different institutional arrangements in place of the old). Legislative and judicial doctrines often build on a static concept of mediators or gatekeepers, dependent on actors who can be held responsible.[9]

Media technologies, as they are implemented, scotch the snakes of power but do not kill them. The language of technological determinism, as a descriptor of what constitutes the new, is overblown in this regard. Of course, it is true that states will lose some capacity for control as a result of the spread of communications technologies. There is no reason to privilege the existing arrangements of states and the distribution of power among them. Some states, however, will increase their capacity to monitor and control as a result of their means of marshalling the new technology. And there will be other shifts as well, yet unknown.[10] States where information is produced may gain power over states where information is consumed. It may be a hallmark of increased power to be a state where information is processed or uplinked to satellite. Power may come from control over vital elements of the hardware, such as the capacity to build microchips, or of software, as in encryption or filtering. States gain money and power when industries—gaming, pornography, or adventurous sale of pharmaceuticals—take advantage of technology that allows new zones of immunity, relocate, or establish themselves under the state's jurisdiction.

Throughout the global debate over new forms of producing and distributing information, the haunting question is whether technology overwhelms law and the capacity of a state to regulate. New technology changes the frame for negotiation, for decision making and for the formation and application of policy. It is much less the case that technological change eliminates either the need for law or reduces the capacity for establishing and enforcing norms to nothingness. What occurs, almost always, is a process of adjustment: norms and institutions that were created for one set of technologies adjust or erode. Where basic values and social needs are at stake, alternative modes of governance and standards emerge.

At the outset the transformation appears radical. An entire construct seems dependent on an old and decaying form of industrial organization and obsolescing assumptions about the structure of the media and its relationship to society. Or even if that is not the case, then the capacity of the governing authority to enforce is, itself, dependent on assumptions that are in the process of being undermined. Jack Goldsmith has challenged those who ridicule the possibility of law. He argues:

The skeptics make three basic errors. First, they overstate the differences between cyberspace transactions and other transnational transactions. Both involve people in real space in one territorial jurisdiction transacting with people in real space in another territorial jurisdiction in a way that sometimes causes real-world harms. In both contexts, the state in which the harms are suffered has a legitimate interest in regulating the activity that produces the harms. Second, the skeptics do not attend to the distinction between default laws and mandatory laws. Their ultimate normative claim that cyberspace should be self-regulated makes sense with respect to default laws that, by definition, private parties can modify to fit their needs.

It makes much less sense with respect to mandatory or regulatory laws that, for paternalistic reasons or in order to protect third parties, place limits on private legal ordering. Third, the skeptics underestimate the potential of traditional legal tools and technology to resolve the multijurisdictional regulatory problems implicated by cyberspace.[11]

Newness, then, has many faces. It can be newness within technology, as in the design of the interface or shifts in control over computational processes. Newness can be found in the impact on altering notions of distance or altering the speed of processes that in a slower environment could not be accomplished. Newness can mean altered institutional arrangements, as when states lose power or intermediating institutions lose force. Newness can have epistemological consequences, as when technology changes a person's idea of self or of collectivity and when it challenges existing ethical norms. We could speak of newness if technology brought to bear new narratives, new apocalyptic stories, and new ideas of perfection or immortality. The newness of new technology can be measured by whether its introduction alters, profoundly, human behavior. These broader senses of the new are important even as we turn to the narrow sense of introduction of technology that is the focus here. We need to be able to tell when a technological advance forces us to address a traditional problem in a highly altered fashion and whether the way of describing the problem itself has changed. And, often, the very newness drives us to search for ways to maintain (or seem to maintain) traditional customs notwithstanding the introduction of technological change.

Newness and Indecency

To look at this trope of newness in depth, I focus on a single judicial decision where a court was obliged to integrate what was presented as new media technologies into its existing patterns of thinking. The opinions in the 1997 decision of the United States Supreme Court in *Reno v. ACLU*, taken together with opinions in related cases, furnish a bouquet of opportunities for understanding.[12] The justices were addressing specific sections of the Communications Decency Act of 1996. The purpose of that legislation was to protect children from what its authors saw as "those who would electronically cruise the digital world" to engage them in inappropriate communications and introductions." Their goal too was "to protect citizens from electronic stalking and protect the sanctuary of the home from uninvited indecencies."[13] The CDA, as passed, extended various prohibitions on harassment, indecency, and obscenity from telephone calls to "telecommunications devices" and "interactive computer services." Under the law it became illegal knowingly to send to or display in "a manner available to a person under 18 years of age, any comment, request, suggestion, proposal, image, or other communication that, in context, depicts or describes, in terms patently offensive as measured by contemporary community standards, sexual or excretory activities or organs," regardless of whether the user of such service placed the call or initiated the communication. Among other offenses, violators were liable for "each intentional act of posting" as opposed to downloading or accessing since Congress sought to target content providers.[14]

When the constitutionality of portions of the law reached the Supreme Court, the justices felt obliged to determine whether the Internet, as a new technology, was such a departure from what had gone before that it demanded new forms of conceptualization. The justices would try to find a way to ride change—to make and define law while the technology to be regulated was still indeterminate and there was insufficient experience or knowledge to understand its actual impact and consequences.

In the US debate over media technologies and indecency, there is a specific rhetoric (not replicated in Europe) relating to the distinction between old media and new. As a consequence of constitutional tradition and judicial interpretation, every "new" media technology has to be dissected to see the way it functions measured against the template of the First Amendment.[15] One question often asked is, does the newness of the medium differentiate it or make it similar to newspapers, broadcasting, or cable? By so assessing the characteristics of the technology (and its surrounding social arrangements), its newness is tested to determine what features call forth doctrinal differences. This includes asking how a reader or viewer interacts with an image, whether the technology, coupled with the structure of distribution, renders the images on the screen more "invasive," or, rather, more subject to informed choice and selection.

The technology models for legislating for the Internet in the Communications Decency Act (CDA) were the telephone as well as radio and television. In coming to grips with its newness, one feature of the Internet was that it poses no obvious opportunity, as radio and television familiarly do, to establish parts of the program day that can be graded or zoned: no safe parts and "freer" parts, watersheds or time-based harbors for protecting children from inappropriate content. Such devices, familiar from European practice and earlier efforts in the United States, divide the schedule into spans when indecent programming could be broadcast for adults under the somewhat old-fashioned assumption that children would not watch television during certain late hours. Given global access, this approach would not work for the Internet. The architecture of the net currently precludes the comforting notion that society could protect itself by having family viewing times, or times of lower brutality and reduced sexual programming. The new qualities of the Internet (its global quality) require constraints that do not distinguish by time period. On this score much of the 1996 law is patterned after existing legislation prohibiting harassing calls on the telephone.[16]

A significant issue, in the US framing of the question, was whether anything new or different occurs in the interaction between child and image on the screen in the newer technology. Could it be the case, for example, that for all the complexity of distribution, for all the newness of new technology, there is little basis for distinguishing between what a minor viewer saw on a computer screen and what he or she saw on a television screen?[17] Qualities of technological newness in the hardware might not be sufficient to change the standard of what should be permitted or what banned in legislative treatment of other similarly received images. The psychological or cultural implications could be roughly the same.

It was in the context of this conflict between the old and continuous or new and differentiated that the 1996 statute came to the US Supreme Court. Assessing newness requires knowledge of context, but the Court made remarkably clear that too little is reliably known about the behavioral assumptions or legislative rationale concerning the Internet to determine how to conceptualize the new technology. In a footnote to his opinion for the Court, Justice John Paul Stevens sternly points out that no hearings were held in the United States Congress on the provisions at issue in the case until after their passage. He quotes at length one senator's dismay at Congress's "willy-nilly" intervention in the Internet.[18] Justice Stevens concludes his opinion by driving home the Court's dissatisfaction with "the absence of any detailed findings by the Congress, or even hearings addressing the special problems of the CDA."[19]

The Court thus found it difficult to rule decisively; its efforts were like a powerful automobile moving in a confusing dusk, forced to do something, but not necessarily in custody of all the relevant information. Justices had to assess the nature of newness at a time when the potential for change was great, but not yet realized, or even if realized did not exist in a manner that had an institutional filter. The Court was asked to furnish constitutional standards to guide Congress, but the governmental mechanisms for clarifying basic assumptions were still unclear. Fervent was the wish, among many in the technology world, for a recognition that the Internet was new in such a radical way as to call for a totally new jurisprudence that was wholly liberating. The forces for the new sought a ruling which would sweepingly defend the Internet from the hands of those inclined to regulate. Though the Court struck down the 1996 Act, an impulse to the categorically new was deflected by the ordinary notion of deference, or perhaps of deferral, to the legislative branch and to the pull of the constitutionally familiar.

Because these decisions came before a judicial tribunal, one with limited expertise in media effects (though often called upon to make assumptions about such effects), one way to read the Court's decision in *Reno* may be in terms of the rhythm of decision making. A proper rhythm or pace can be discovered by asking when, or under what circumstances, is it appropriate to evaluate the implications of a technology. The provocative writings of Lawrence Lessig, especially his views on postponement and readiness, have addressed this issue. Two articles, "The Path of Cyberlaw," and "Reading the Constitution in Cyberspace," both written before *Reno*, proved unusually influential in this then-young constitutional field.[20] Several ideas basic to Lessig's scholarship seem to haunt the justices' opinions. One is a plea for caution before policy makers impose a standard decision making grid on the use of new technologies. As Justice David Souter once wrote, taking Lessig's advice, "if we had to decide today . . . just what the First Amendment should mean in cyberspace, . . . we would get it fundamentally wrong."[21]

In a second suggestion, Lessig cautions that one must be careful not to be swept away by metaphors from the physical world when thinking about cyberspace.[22] Constitutional doctrines adapted from our preexisting environment may not be fully suitable in the brave, new context.[23] Circumstances, facts, and technology change. Existing conceptualizations (often based on metaphor) arise and may be necessary for day-to-day life. But transfer of category may be the mind's lazy approach to analysis. Taken together, these cautionary ideas suggest that the Court (or a court), muddling through, must wait and see before it prescribes solutions.[24]

Indeed these notions of time and the definition of newness have transcending and complex implications not only for jurisprudence in the Internet era but for all decision makers dealing with new media technologies. The idea that doctrine turns on a moment of assessment means that there are times in which insecurity about the wisdom of a rule ought to lead to nonexercise of power or to a fuzzy outcome. Yet that idea of caution and patience conflicts with strongly held views about the need for clarity and predictability. The tradition is strong that the Supreme Court (or equivalents in other societies) should render outcomes decisively so as to assist elements of society and institutions of the state in their accommodation of technology and constitution.

Doubt and caution may be reasons for the Supreme Court not to take a case, but once taken, it is hard to accept the Court saying "we don't know yet, but here's the best we can say." When the plurality in *Denver Area Educational Telecommunications Consortium, Inc. v. FCC*, a First Amendment case from the cable television medium, came close to saying just that, Justice Anthony Kennedy responded brusquely in dissent:

This is why comparisons and analogies to other areas of our First Amendment case law become a responsibility, rather than the luxury the plurality considers them to be. The comparisons provide discipline to the Court and guidance for others, and give clear content to our standards—all the things I find missing in the plurality's opinion. . . . We have before us an urgent claim for relief against content-based discrimination, not a dry run.[25]

Furthermore a position of doubt can conflict, as occurred in *Reno*, with an extraordinary pressure to categorize the new technology, *now* as a technology of freedom, unhinged from the ambivalent and government-justifying history of the regulation of broadcasting. The publishing industry, library associations, colleges, and universities—an enormously impressive list of plaintiffs—urged (unsuccessfully on this narrow ground) that the proclivity to regulate by Congress should be nipped in the bud by a clear decision applying the greatest possible protection to Internet communications. As the Court stated in a different context, "liberty finds no refuge in a jurisprudence of doubt."[26]

Lessig's scholarship suggests how complicated it is to adapt the metaphors and analogies that have influenced the constitutional doctrine of the physical world to the world of cyberspace, particularly when that world is itself still being constructed, both physically and conceptually.[27] Time may be necessary to transcend metaphor. This then is a further challenge, to acknowledge that many legal systems depend on metaphors that are fragile and limited and that misportray evolving circumstances. Implicit in this suggestion is a critique of the standard process of extending law, suggesting that shifting to cyberspace from more physical counterparts requires a rethinking of how categories are established, and who determines the character of the real world (in the US case, the respective role of Congress, administrative agencies, and the courts).

The opinion of Justice Sandra Day O'Connor, in *Reno*, illustrates the problem of adjusting to metaphors while assessing a new technology. She relates a wish to think of the Internet as a land, inhabited by a number of institutions, some of whom are purveyors of indecent material. For her, the relevant ways of thinking about the law are to consider the applicability of legal analogies. In her opinion she looks especially toward decisions concerning the more physical world of bookstores and their locations. There, the court has endorsed the establishment of "adult zones," specified physical sites that deal in pornographic materials and that can be segregated to particular parts of towns and cities, thus removed from children. By relying on the notion that this is a "zoning case," which is itself a vision of cyberspace, she makes her own leap, coping with the new but well within existing modes of fashioning principles.[28]

But Justice O'Connor demonstrates that she cannot be sure the analogy would work. Is zoning in cyberspace the same as zoning in the physical world? Justice O'Connor expresses doubts whether the received doctrine respecting speech-related zoning—rules that she finds acceptable in their traditional application to street corners in cities—should apply in cyberspace.[29] The image of the adult bookshop, with its masked windows, the forbidden entry, the lonely monitor working into the night, translates into cyberspace only with difficulty. "Before today," Justice O'Connor writes, there was no reason to question the approach of zoning, for before the Internet case "the Court has previously only considered law that operated in the physical world, a world with two characteristics that make it possible to create 'adult zones': geography and identity." This new layer of abstraction is what forces the rethinking of the constitution and basic principles in the world of cyberspace.[30] Thus Justice O'Connor retains her commitment to the architecture of her past constitutional doctrine but recognizes the complexity of extending it to the new technologies.

How does a decision maker act in such a moment of indecision—a moment when it is unclear whether the judicially accepted verities of a physical world exist in the cyberspace counterpart? Justice O'Connor concludes, "Although the prospects for the eventual zoning of the Internet appear promising, I agree with the Court that we must evaluate the constitutionality of the CDA as it applies to the Internet as it exists today. Given the present state of cyberspace . . . the statute's 'display' provision could not pass muster."[31] However, she justifies her belief that it will pass eventually by saying, "Cyberspace is malleable. Thus, it is possible to construct barriers in cyberspace and use them to screen for identity, making cyberspace more like the physical world and, consequently, more amenable to zoning laws. This transformation of cyberspace is already underway."[32]

Assessing New Technology

To determine the newness of a media technology one must have a description of it, fixing the points for a factual assessment. To achieve such a description involves notions of relevance. It may be important, for example, that new satellite dish technology is handkerchief sized, but the relevant question here is whether a reduction of diameter has legal and constitutional consequences. In societies where the state seeks to monitor or control the viewing habits of its citizens, the largeness or smallness of satellite dishes may be of great significance. What makes a new technology new for purposes of legal or constitutional analysis may often be a matter of the extent to which the new technology threatens, sustains, or even enhances a particular state's position in the marketplace for loyalties.[33] In this regard the concept of technological newness may function as cover for very traditional state concerns. What is new in a new technology may simply be those aspects of the technology that challenge state control or render current legal doctrine untenable.

Assembling facts to evaluate what attributes of significance have become realized, or are likely to exist within a period relevant to a societal decision, is central. Only with such facts can one rationally decide what is paradigm shifting about a technology. But these facts are ineffable. Almost by definition newness is often a series of claims, a series of promises, and a series of hopes. The questions of changing constitutionality or paradigm shift arise during times of aspiration, before industry structure and performance in the world are fully realized. The potential for stalemate is obvious. Financial investment in the industry may not be maximized until a reliable legal environment is established, but the decisions concerning norms cannot take place until there is sufficient information.

Let us turn to *Reno* again for an example of the relevance of a factual base. One background issue of significance was whether circumstances existed that allowed parents easily to control what their children saw on the Internet.[34] Danger to children, after all, was the big fear (justified or not) motivating Congress, the dark omen confounding the Internet's benefits. The 1996 legislative solution put the onus of keeping the Internet clean largely on the providers of information.[35] Providers or senders had to ensure, more or less, that only material "not indecent" flowed through the wires if young people would have access to it. Online providers were immune from responsibility only if they took specifically designated steps to assure that the recipient was not a minor. However, because of the shape of American First Amendment jurisprudence, this congressional approach would not be constitutional if less restrictive alternatives were available to meet the legitimate goals of Congress.

Thus, in the *Reno* litigation, one of the major questions was whether or not such solutions—less restrictive alternatives that would allow speakers to be unfettered (or less fettered)—were truly available. One of the revolutionary ways of thinking about "alternatives" was technology similar to the V-chip, the software-filtering systems discussed in the last chapter, which would allow screening by the user, rather than restrictions on the sender.[36] But a determination that a technology provides a "less restrictive alternative" is necessarily based on an assumption that the technology actually exists (or is very likely to exist) and is effective. The evaluation of which alternatives are viable or restrictive are questions concerning what the world is really like. Justices must determine what the world of technology and behavior is like at the moment in question and how to integrate a desired or imagined future into current constitutional doctrine.

In *Reno*, Justice Stevens, desirous of invalidating the burdens Congress imposed on the senders of information, had to stretch to make his point on the utility of alternatives. Outlining the anticipated types of devices available through the Internet, he writes, in carefully chosen words, "Systems have been developed to help parents control the material that may be available. . . . A system may either limit a computer's access to an approved list of sources that have been identified as containing no adult material, it may block designated inappropriate sites, or it may attempt to block messages containing identifiable objectionable features."[37] Justice Stevens noted that current technologies include parental control software that can screen for suggestive words or for known sexually explicit sites, though there is no software that can screen for sexually explicit images.[38]

The passive voice suggests the distance Justice Stevens places between his convictions and the description of reality that he presses into service. He also employs a device available to reviewing courts like the Supreme Court. On a "matter of fact" (like whether these devices are available), a justice of the Supreme Court can rely on the trial court, as a "finder of fact." Here, the District Court had, according to Justice Stevens, determined from the evidence that "a reasonably effective method by which parents can prevent their children from accessing sexually explicit and other material which parents may believe is inappropriate for their children will soon be widely available."[39] Note that the method is not yet available, and the "evidence" is probably a self-serving declaration by those who hope to introduce such software that it will be available.[40]

This technological meliorism has been criticized. One year after the Court handed down *Reno*, the prolific Professor Lessig published an influential law review article, "What Things Regulate Speech: CDA 2.0 vs. Filtering." In the article, he warned that even if the less restrictive means relied on by the Court became available in the form of effective filtering software, this technology would be more intrusive on speech than the provisions rejected in *Reno*. He stated:

My sense is that this first major victory—in *Reno v. ACLU*—has set us in a direction that we will later regret. . . . The "less restrictive means" touted by free speech activists in *Reno* are, in my view, far more restrictive of free speech interests than a properly crafted CDA would be. And unless we quickly shift ground, we will see Congress embracing these less protective (of speech) means, or worse, we will see the success of the President in bullying industry into accepting them.[41]

Professor Eugene Volokh was also dissatisfied with the reasoning.[42] In his view, the most troubling aspect of Justice Stevens's opinion was the statement that the CDA's burden on free speech "is unacceptable if less restrictive alternatives would be at least as effective in achieving the legitimate purpose that the statute was enacted to serve."[43] The important phrase, to Volokh, is "at least as effective." To him, no alternative could reach this standard. "None of the Court's proposed alternatives to the CDA—or any other alternatives I can imagine—would have been as effective as the CDA's more or less total ban. . . . The pregnant negative in the Court's reasoning is that, had there really been no equally effective alternatives (as in fact there are not), the CDA should have been upheld."[44]

The Social World of Newness

There are a few other areas, lurking in *Reno,* where decision makers have to decide what dignity to accord to those things that pass as "facts." What assumptions, for example, exist about the nature and functioning of the family that inform evaluations of the role of new technology? Since so much of the social concern over the Internet seems to be about the child, and so many of the remedies deal with interactions between that child and his or her family, one would think the empirical grounding for difficult decisions would be abundant, even if not wholly adequate.

There are normative questions such as whether a parent ought to be able to determine that his or her child should watch images that the state considers inappropriate. But there are factual questions that underlie proposals for change. Are filters useful? How do parents influence the viewing habits of children? In *Reno*, Justice Stevens visits, glancingly, the issue of whether Congress can protect children from indecent programming regardless of the desire of their parents. The United States, in its argument, had contended that the First Amendment does not preclude "a blanket prohibition on all 'indecent' and 'patently offensive' messages communicated" to a minor "regardless of parental approval."[45] The Court demurred, but in doing so, it seemed to raise a new kind of test. It is true, Justice Stevens writes, that protection of children was a "compelling interest" that, in some instances, justifies regulation. But a regulation that potentially overrules parental preferences, or even covers parental speech to children, "imposes an especially heavy burden" on Congress to demonstrate why less restrictive provisions would not be suitable.[46]

This "parent-protecting" test and the context in which this debate arises is intriguing. For just as moralistic as Congress (and perhaps the Court) seems to be in limiting the access of children to indecent material, it is similarly concerned about trenching on parent-child relationships. And this conflict drives Congress and the Court to make partially unfounded, ideology-charged and sweeping statements about parents and their relationship to children. The Court cites earlier decisions for the "consistent" principle that "the parents' claim to authority in their own household to direct the rearing of their children is basic in the structure of our society." This principle rests on an earlier pronouncement (having to do with foreign-language education) that, "It is cardinal with us that the custody, care, and nurture of the child reside *first* in the parents, whose primary function and freedom include preparation for obligations the state can neither supply nor hinder."[47]

Having decided that the CDA covers e-mail, Justice Stevens engaged in an elaborate conceit to indicate the constitutional infirmity of the legislation. "Many e-mail transmissions from an adult to a minor are conversations between family members," he says, setting a predicate for their special protection.[48] Under the CDA, Justice Stevens contends, "a parent who sent his 17-year-old college freshman information on birth control via e-mail could be incarcerated even though neither he, his child, nor anyone in their home community, found the material 'indecent' or 'patently offensive' if the college town's community thought otherwise."[49] To be fair, Justice Stevens's concern goes beyond e-mail. It seems wrong to him that under the CDA, a parent "could face a lengthy prison term" for "allowing her 17-year-old to use the family computer to obtain information on the Internet that she, in her parental judgment, deems appropriate."[50]

Here again, as with so much in *Reno,* it is a dependence on a specific and possible false understanding of the technological and social interaction that virtually controls how the new media technology is judged. The present state is such that the relationship between conclusions and available facts is dismal. Take just the vision of what we mean by "parents," what relationship there is (much less ought to be) between parents and children, and how in fact decisions are made to deploy sites that are considered "indecent" by Congress. To make a legal judgment, Justice Stevens must have a mental picture of how decisions to deploy indecent sites are made so he can tell whether there is a problem serious enough to warrant congressional intervention. His examples are somewhat class biased, to use an old-fashioned term that seems relevant here. The image that must be in the mind of the lawmaker is of the fractured, possibly "dysfunctional" family, what the government in its brief for *Denver Area* described as the condition of "absence, distraction, indifference, inertia, or insufficient information" that besets "innumerable parents" in America.[51] A view of the family that includes the imagined nonparent parent, incapable or unwilling to establish standards, "consenting" not in the active mode of reviewing and approving material, but acquiescing in an environment where the imposition of standards is impossible (for reasons of time, will, or culture) more clearly supports intervention.[52]

Newness and Jurisdiction

A recurring debate about Internet and newness concerns the utility of national law in an era of international and cross-border communications. Justice Stevens's opinion in *Reno v. ACLU* is not centrally about this subject, but there are fascinating asides. The issue is nestled in a footnote, ruminating within the Supreme Court decision. Justice Stevens cites an argument made by one of the plaintiffs, the American Library Association, that "Because so much sexually explicit content originates overseas, the CDA cannot be 'effective,'" as that term is precisely used in American jurisprudence. Justice Stevens fends off the argument, saying that it "raises difficult issues regarding the intended, as well as the permissible scope of, extraterritorial application of the CDA."[53] This is the Court's first careful encounter with an issue widely anticipated in legal literature on the Internet.[54] Because the Act could be condemned on other grounds, the Court suggests, it does not have to deal with it.

There is much within these few words worthy of comment. Let us first assume that "so much sexually explicit content originates overseas."[55] It is unclear, from

this terse discussion, what it is in foreign origin for some pornographic material that can limit the capacity of Congress to devise a set of satisfactory statutory prohibitions for indecent programming that originates in the United States. Justice Stevens indicates that perhaps the Communications Decency Act was not intended to apply extraterritorially.[56] Much more interesting is the question of "effectiveness." A law is not "effective" if it can only be enforced against domestic violators *and* much of the damage, unremediated, will be caused by those seemingly beyond the law's reach. And here the argument seems to be that these "overseas" violators are incapable of being prosecuted because of the special nature of Internet technology. Even if Congress had the power to enact legislation that is extraterritorial in its reach, technology and practicalities would render that law ineffective. In a world that cannot stop one source of illegal conduct, focusing on another might be discriminatory and therefore unconstitutional.

It is clear why the American Library Association would make this argument. Its members are among the possible available defendants, to be singled out though they are small instruments in a world in which the massive "real" wrongdoers are "overseas" entrepreneurs, clever commercial pornographers, largely beyond the nation's enforcement capacity. The Association has been at the forefront of efforts to fight local regulation of Internet speech, both as a matter of principle and because, in an irony of the "post-Gutenberg" age, public libraries are often sued.[57]

But the argument is extremely suggestive, perhaps disturbing, in its implications for the limits of law in a digital world and in a world of increasing cross-border capital mobility. Law will tend to be increasingly incapable of perfect enforcement where transactions and performances can so easily be moved "overseas." Here the laws that are putatively discriminatory because of difficulties of enforcement concern disagreeable images, and the argument could well be made that they should not be sanctioned at all. In the future, however, an argument based on inherent discrimination could be far more encompassing, including the disallowance of laws applying to electronic commercial transactions and possibly other areas, for example, aspects of family law, areas where enforcement might be thwarted if activities were moved offshore.

Could it be that US law becomes unsupportable because of this feature of newness: it is "impossible" to enforce, or difficult to enforce because of the structure of the Internet and the relationship between extraterritorial actors and US users? Certainly that argument is in the air, and it is one product of the facially attractive idea of preserving the Internet as a "regulation-free" zone.[58] At any rate it is not hard

to imagine, the contrary, that the result of incapacity or difficulty to enforce abroad would be discriminatory enforcement against those who, for reasons of lack of opportunity, economic capacity, willpower, or place-related reasons stayed within the power of the state.

How to think about these questions is not yet clear. Making law disappear is one answer, but not necessarily one that seems to have many institutional proponents or broad public support. In November 2000 a French court took issue with the question of practicality of enforcement. It gave Yahoo! Inc. three months to find a technological means to prevent Web surfers in France from gaining access to Web pages on its US-based auction site that featured over 1,200 Nazi-related items. Of course, unlike the invisible pornographic providers, Yahoo! had a French office and experts domorstrated the capacity of Yahoo! to filter content for the French users.

Taxation, copyright, gambling, and defamation law are all areas where, if care is not taken, discrimination may be the consequence of patterns of capacity of law enforcement. There will be suggestions that certain prohibitions that have been taken for granted within a society are no longer available. More likely it may mean that a different form of extraterritorial as well as domestic enforcement pattern must be devised.[59] What it certainly means is that, as Justice Stevens indicated, these are "difficult issues" indeed, and they may sometime come, in a ripe manner, before the Court.

Newness and the Rewriting of History

I have sought in this chapter to identify several areas where, using *Reno* as an example, new media technology is evaluated according to its relationship to existing constitutional standards. The *Reno* case is part of the Supreme Court's ongoing debate over the qualities in film, traditional television and radio broadcasting, cable, and the Internet that render their regulation subject to different degrees or kinds of constitutional scrutiny. In this last section, I want to examine another facet of the decision: the way the Court, as revisionist historian, uses its evaluation of new media technologies to replay and reorganize its justifications for the treatment of the technology's predecessors. All government agents are to some extent revisionists as they try to understand the power of the new in the context of the old. How the Court engages in revision helps us understand what it is about technology that is emerging as significant—from this constitutional perspective.

For example, Justice Stevens asserted a novel reading of past doctrine, namely that the "history of extensive government regulation of the broadcast medium" itself serves as a "special justification" for treating one technology (broadcasters) in restrictive ways not applicable to other speakers, in *Reno*. In his discussion he cites a case, *Red Lion Broadcasting Co. v. FCC*, that is so out of fashion that it had gone virtually unmentioned by the Court for years.[60] Another precedent, *Turner Broadcasting, Inc. v. FCC*, is cited for the novel observation that scarcity of available frequencies where such scarcity existed, for an information technology "*at its inception*" is a further justification for lower scrutiny of broadcasting regulation."[61] Justice Stevens also renews a somewhat controversial ground for justifying regulation and distinguishing broadcasting from other media, namely its "invasive" nature.[62]

What is interesting about Justice Stevens's citation of *Red Lion* is the subtle shift in the meaning that is implied. The previous standard understanding of *Red Lion* had been that broadcasting was more readily subject to regulation because scarcity of available frequencies made some form of rationing necessary and that necessity allowed the imposition of public interest standards. Because it is impossible for everyone who so wishes to get on the airwaves, government has to pick and choose. Almost from the beginning this reading of the Constitution, this prong of *Red Lion*, endured attack.[63] Economists argue that any scarcity shortage is government imposed, in that it was always possible to allocate more spectrum to broadcasting and technically possible to make spectrum accommodate more voices. This argument gained emotive power when cable television and other technologies made channels plentiful. In a world of abundance there seems no reason to pitch constitutional reasoning on a scarcity which, according to some versions, simply does not exist.

The Court, over the years, itself contested its *Red Lion* based justification in a variety of cases. Justices hinted (and more) that subsequent information and emerging technology might one day require abandonment of the doctrine. Its survival hung by a hair (or a vote or two). After *Reno*, the justification for regulation may have changed. Now *Red Lion* seems to stand for the proposition that the status of broadcasting as a more regulable medium is historically contingent, rather than solely technologically based. A medium that has had significant attention from the government from the outset will be treated differently from one that has not. Since most media technologies have close relationships to government in their development—and the Internet is certainly no exception—this reading of judicial history is important. Such a reinterpretation, if pursued, would bring American doctrine more in line with European counterparts.

The Court could be saying that traditional television and radio broadcasting meet three conditions, each of which is necessary for the peculiar susceptibility it has to regulation. These are: its history of extensive government regulation, the spectrum scarcity at its founding, and its special quality of invasiveness. A medium that does not have all of these qualities cannot be successfully compared with broadcasting so as to determine the category of constitutional analysis in which it fits. On the other hand, the Court could be arguing that these are relevant factors, not an ensemble of required conditions. Invasiveness, a history of extensive regulation, early shortages of frequencies, or their equivalents alone (or some combination of them), would be sufficient in this reading to justify a lower threshold for congressional regulation. The relevance of these factors to the Internet and to Justice Stevens's analysis in *Reno* therefore bears further analysis.

Justice Stevens recreates the jurisprudence of the broadcasting cases precisely so as to differentiate the historical electronic media from this new form of using wires and ether. His very explanation of cyberspace consists of facts designed to fit into a reinterpretation of the constitutional basis for regulation in broadcasting. The qualities of broadcasting that permit greater regulation, according to Justice Stevens, "are not present in cyberspace."[64] But is Justice Stevens correct, not in terms of his retrospective interpretation of the broadcasting cases, but in terms of the way he differentiates broadcasting from cyberspace? The first area for differentiation is "history." Justice Stevens makes the claim that broadcasting had a history of extensive regulation while the "vast democratic fora" of the Internet has not been subject to similar government supervision and regulation.[65] In one sense, of course, this is a false statement. The Internet, as the Court's decision traces, has a history rooted in federal supervision and largesse. It is an outgrowth of what began in 1969 as a military program to enable computers operated by the military defense contractors, and universities conducting defense-related research, to communicate with one another by redundant channels. The ARPANET is much more firmly rooted in a history of government involvement than was spectrum usage when radio broadcasting was relatively wild and open.[66]

Besides, the relationship between the Internet and Congress can be likened to the relationship between radio and the federal government at the time of the Radio Conference that led to the 1927 Act. Almost a century ago, as in the 1990s with the Internet, there was dynamism, ingenuity, and a period of unregulated innovation. With radio, explosive growth led to concern (though on different issues), federal study, and eventually legislation. Despite Justice Stevens's apparent desire, history cannot start when the historian wants it to begin. What has become the Internet originated with the Pentagon and involved an almost exclusively federally authorized network. Also it is hard to understand how one characterizes a medium by its history when it is the very nature of that history that is being fashioned.[67]

We also know, now that we have *Reno,* that the Internet is not invasive. Why? Because the District Court told us so and the Supreme Court accepts that finding. Justice Stevens concludes "the risk of encountering indecent material by accident is remote."[68] This is, as is said, a "constitutional fact."[69] Perhaps a constitutional fact is different from a garden-variety fact. To conclude, as Stevens does, that the Internet is distinguishable from broadcasting with respect to invasiveness, is a complicated matter. "Unlike communications received by radio or television," Justice Stevens writes, the Internet "requires a series of affirmative steps more deliberate and directed than merely turning a dial. A child requires some sophistication, some ability to read to retrieve material and thereby to use the Internet unattended."[70]

First meaningfully formulated in the dial-a-porn case *Sable Communications of Cal., Inc. v. FCC,* the notion of "affirmative steps" represents a patina on "invasiveness." Affirmative steps certainly enable a more accurate analysis of the emerging "interactive media model" in US telecommunications in which most content will be accessed rather than broadcast, pulled rather than pushed.[71] Yet even for current Internet technology there are problems with this innovative approach. It is true, for example, that, at least the first time, a child has to do more in a more directed and deliberate way, than turn the dial to get access to some particularly outrageous or erotic material. But once the place is saved, or "bookmarked," there is very little functional difference between turning a dial and gaining access to a Web site.

Odder still is the supposed distinction between those children with some "ability to read" and those without the ability. Invasiveness and uninvitedness may have to do with a child's sophistication, but in no previous case did this issue turn on actual literacy or its absence. Whom are we talking about: the 17-year-old deemed to be a computer wizard, or the 5-year-old who stumbles onto the satiric-erotic false-Disney program? How does the society make this decision? Can it? Are these questions about which we do not know the answer or is the District Court finding in this case sufficient, even against a congressional finding to the contrary? Where does Justice Stevens arrive at his factual understanding of a world that is interacting with the computer and how is such a world different from or similar to the world that interacts with radio and television? For constitutional analysis to be careful, we must know how doctrine is contingent on factual understandings and what constitutes adequate information supporting a notion of invasiveness or to the contrary.[72]

The third and most convincing difference between broadcasting and Internet questions whether spectrum scarcity exists. It is now almost an article of faith that whatever scarcity existed in the bad old days of analogue spectrum no longer exists. In *Reno* Justice Stevens puts a new and unexamined spin on the question, asking, for the first time in the Court's treatment of this subject, whether Internet is a "scarce expressive commodity."[73] He seemed to be inviting a refocus from an older, economic analysis of spectrum availability to a broader focus on the element of "expressiveness." Justice Stevens reveled in the Internet's plenty: "It provides relatively unlimited, low-cost capacity for communication of all kinds. . . . Through the use of chat rooms, any person with a phone line can become a town crier with a voice that resonates farther than it could from any soapbox."[74] All the magic elements are there: pamphleteer, town crier, and soapbox. No wonder this is Justice Stevens's clinching point before concluding that "our cases provide no basis for qualifying the level of First Amendment scrutiny that should be applied to this medium."[75]

Yet there are some factors to consider. We are at a stage in the development of the Internet—perhaps like early radio—where entry is certainly easy, inexpensive, and nondiscriminatory. But, as with radio, later developments in industrial organization and government action made entry more difficult and a broadly democratic means of becoming a town crier almost impossible. Radio spectrum was not really "scarce," though radio spectrum as an "expressive commodity" may have been. It would be wonderful if the Internet were to retain its capacity for expressiveness, as nonscarce as it seems currently to be, but we do not know yet whether that will be the case or whether the Court's limitations on congressional action will expand or restrict that zone. Certainly the history of radio would have been different if the Court had held the earliest forays into regulation and licensing unconstitutional because of the heady, egalitarian patterns of entry that characterized the time of basement radio transmission and ease of speaker entry.

The Court's decision also raises interesting questions about which numbers—what kinds of abundance—are relevant to the issue of scarcity, or scarcity of "an expressive commodity," to repeat again, Justice Stevens's novel and stunning phrase.[76] There are millions of radio receivers just as there are millions of computers. Penetration is obviously not the same, but moving in the same direction of universality. The important point for Justice Stevens, however, is that computers, unlike radios, are interactive. What is being compared is access or entry by *speakers*, not *receivers*. The end of scarcity with respect to "expressiveness" comes precisely because of the radical transformation of access to convey or impart as opposed to receive information.

Here the Court is committing to a particular conception of the Internet. Justice Stevens is assuming that the number of subscribers to the Internet is equivalent to the number of speakers, as is the case with the telephone, and that subscribing is a mark of entry as speaker. At the moment that may be a valid assumption. But the structure and custom of usage of the Internet could change. The behavior in the future might be that, other than for an e-mail function, 99 percent of subscribers act like passive receivers or dial turners: selectors at best but never, otherwise, as communicators. Information may come in packaged channels, with a market structure dominated by three or four giants. Then the question would be whether bottlenecks to entry exist, and whether analysis of the Internet (in terms of congressional power) should be assimilated to cases that justified regulation not on spectrum scarcity but on the difficulty of access by those who program channels and distribute them over cable.[77]

In one regard, this hypothetical future of packaged channels and a market dominated by oligopolistic producers has already come into existence, and the implications for "scarcity" have already begun to take shape. The abundance of the Internet has produced a new form of scarcity, one described by Jack Balkin:

All communications media produce too much information. So in that sense, all media have a problem of scarcity. But the scarcity is not a scarcity of bandwidth. It is a scarcity of audience. There is only so much time for individuals to assimilate information. And not only is there too much information, some of it is positively undesirable. As a result, all media give rise to filtering by their audience, or, more importantly, by people to whom the audience delegates the task of filtering.[78]

Information overproduction creates a problem not merely of unwanted offensiveness greeting an Internet user but also of unwanted irrelevance. Portals to the Internet, such as Yahoo! or Excite, exist to remedy this problem. Their front pages form some of the most expensive "real estate" in cyberspace. These portals provide free search engine technology to aid the user in finding desired Web sites. They also advertise Web sites. If a Web site is not listed by these search engines, it effectively does not exist, at least from the perspective of potential benefits to a general public. The search portals have become the dominant brokers in the "expressive commodity" of the Internet.[79]

Justice Stevens, in *Reno*, reopens questions of definition, exploring considerations that make one information technology more sensitive than another, more susceptible to regulation. He identifies history, scarcity, and invasiveness as criteria for decision. But his treatments of broadcasting and the Internet are not necessarily convincing, even as his own grid of analysis is applied. This is not surprising. "We are not the first generation," as Carolyn Marvin has written, "to wonder at the rapid and extraordinary shifts in the dimension of the world and the human relationships it contains as a result of new forms of communication, or be surprised by the changes those shifts occasion in the regular pattern of our lives."[80]

Conclusion

Examining this one case—in which the United States assessed the regulatory framework for the Internet so as to control indecency—has its analytic perils. Each society has its own distinct pattern of determining whether innovation in media technologies requires altered policies. Different societies have different mechanisms for rendering this judgment just as different societies have varied grids for determining which variables are significant. And in the United States, more than in many other country, judges are instrumental in the defining process. Just as the question of what constitutes "modernity," with its perils and opportunities, differs from context to context, so the question of what is "new" in terms of a grid of social decision making.

"Newness," as we have seen in *Reno*, is a sense of law filtered though concerns about the nature of the American family, the behavior of children, the availability of software, the history of regulation, ideas of the impact of broadcasting. Within the constitutional framework of American jurisprudence, these emblems of newness are salient. In other places, with other evolved law making mechanisms, the signifiers of newness would be different. They may not be about danger to children but about danger to the state or danger to religion. Fundamental questions about structure of society and the nature of human interaction determine what constitutes the new. In China, in the summer of 2001, over two thousand Internet cafes were closed "for examination." The purported reason had resonance with the Communications Decency Act: the main news agency reported that Internet bars were "flooded with pornographic or violent content" and that parents were very worried about the psychological and physical health of children and teenagers visiting them. "The examination has breathed a fresh breeze," said one user. "Bar owners are now trying to improve services and the environment according to our advice." The nationwide action of clearing up and rectifying the Internet bars was designed to regulate the Internet service market according to a set of rules jointly promulgated by the Ministry of Information Industry, the Ministry of Public Security, the Ministry of Culture, and the State Administration of Industry and Commerce.[81]

Technology has the potential to alter every institution, to provide even more access to education, to jobs, and to opportunities.[82] But things are new from a particular perspective. A new technology may be one that replaces or substantially augments a predecessor or establishes difference of a kind that must cross a hurdle of significance. We might reserve the notion of newness for innovations that have major significance for cultural developments, the distribution of power in society, the organization of the polity, or the recognition of new consumer markets.[83] Altered flows of information, resulting from new technologies, change the balances that previously existed in a legal framework in almost every case.[84] Defamation can be more immediate and more effective because of the Internet, but corrections and apologies can be as well. Copyrighted materials are more vulnerable because they are ubiquitous, easily downloadable, and their reproduction ridiculously easy, but new copyright protection software provides security against copying that might eliminate the breathing room that existed in fair use in an earlier era. Discourse via e-mail has the anonymity that can produce courage and vigorous dissent, but the capacity for tracing and identifiers can also furnish greater powers for the state to monitor and trace. Still, in the flood of novelty captured by the new technology, it is difficult to determine what attributes of change yield revolutionary consequences and what attributes merely expedite distribution.

I have discussed a set of judicial decisions that try to cope with these issues because of the insight they provide into the legal processes of assessing and assimilating new media technologies. Not every parliament will arrive at the same legislative decision, nor will every court follow the same analysis. Tribunals will attempt to decide what constitutes the newness of the Internet technology and what implications that newness should have for the existing ways of regulating imagery in society. Governments act as if it is a domestic decision to establish the rules of the new technology: not only that such rules can affect industrial behavior but that they can be decided internally. But, as it turns out, the entire subject of media space— the content of media and the structures that support them—is increasingly a subject of international debate. And it is to that quality I now turn.

III
Negotiating the Changed Media Terrain

Toward a Foreign Policy of Information Space

For several decades prior to the war on terrorism and prior to the events of September 11, 2001, there was no articulated US foreign policy of media space. Significant shards and important pieces of such a policy existed, as we will see, but little realization that these elements ought to cohere and be rendered more effective. The White House, through various administrations, showed no need for strong direction to make such a policy central to the achievement of US objectives. With the end of the cold war, long-standing US government efforts to help shape global public opinion on matters significant to national security had essentially been privatized. Respect for the United States Information Agency (USIA), the prime instrument for this function and descendant of the World War II Office of War Information, had declined, and it was robbed of its autonomy and merged into the State Department in 1999. On the other hand, Hollywood and Madison Avenue, CNN, and the Motion Picture Association of America, were celebrated as extremely effective carriers and projectors of US values.

All of this changed, at least temporarily, when fuel-laden airplanes crashed into the World Trade Center and the Pentagon. After September 11, it became the accepted wisdom that US national security turned on the effect that ideas and images, perceptions and beliefs, that could slowly coalesce into unanticipated danger would have on governments and a new global demography. Now a coherent and effective policy was seen as urgent. In November 2001, when Charlotte Beers was confirmed as the Under Secretary for Public Diplomacy in the US Department of State, she was immediately put in charge of a campaign to change "hearts and minds" globally and, in her articulation of the issues, to "rebrand" the United States and communicate its strengths more effectively around the world. She became part of a high-level team in the George W. Bush administration that would coordinate with British and other counterparts and shape a strategy for managing information affecting public opinion abroad.

Here, I try to place these intensified efforts in context. I have demonstrated, in previous chapters, the stake one state or group of states has in the media laws and policies in another state that foster political consequences. State strategies and techniques quite obviously differ depending on each country's history, position as receiver and sender of imagery, internal political and belief structure, and geopolitical ambitions and realities. In this chapter, I focus on the United States to ask a question less discussed, namely how a power or superpower brings together and renders coherent and effective its goals and objectives.[1] In doing this, I focus on several areas where different levels of information foreign policy have developed. I examine skirmishing in the Department of State to establish more directed and integrated policies and then turn to peacekeeping operations in Bosnia-Hercegovina as a zone where policies of forceful intervention into radio and television were tested.

Based on these experiences and others, including actions in the area of copyright, technical assistance, and trade, I ask whether there is a set of practices in the United States that could be characterized as its foreign policy with respect to global media space.[2] The United States, in this sense, serves as an example, but only as an example. For many states, an information and media-related foreign policy has evolved, though rarely explicitly. External attitudes toward media structures and the flow of images reflect many changes, only most immediately the concern about terrorism and national security. Among these are the shifts caused by the end of the cold war, the expansion of the free trade paradigm, the search for new alliances and new enemies, and changing approaches toward global involvement and humanitarian intervention. A study of emerging "foreign policies of media structures" (and US policies in particular) rests on the history of scholarship concerning international communications systems and the interplay between American power and the worldwide distribution of information and imagery.[3]

International Public Information Group

There is an imperfect but ambitious precedent for the making of a foreign policy of media space. It occurred within the US State Department during the Clinton administration. On April 30, 1999, the White House issued Presidential Decision Directive 68. The Directive sought to consolidate approaches concerning the use and shaping of information policies internationally. In the usual lulling terms of such directives, the document stated that the goals were "to improve [the] use of public information communicated to foreign audiences . . . [so as] to improve our ability to prevent and mitigate foreign crises, and to promote understanding and support for United States foreign policy initiatives around the world." The document went on to say, "Dramatic changes in the global information environment . . . require that we implement a more deliberate and well-developed international public information strategy in promoting our values and interests."

The drafters of the directive intended a far more aggressive use of information strategies where there is potential or actual conflict, including "effective use of our nation's highly-developed communications and information capabilities to address misinformation and incitement, mitigate inter-ethnic conflict, [and] promote independent media organizations." Achieving the capacity to utilize US information assets more efficiently would become "a critical foreign policy objective." Something in the way of "rapid-response" was envisaged. Under the policy, US international public information strategy would take on a heightened quasi-military rhetoric. It would include contingency plans, catalog the potential for information-based US responses, and predict the resources required for meeting US public information goals. The government would be affirmative in "preventing and mitigating foreign crises" while advancing US national interests. The directive imposed a duty to "use information assets—including those that reflect new and emerging technologies—in an innovative and proactive manner."

The directive found its bureaucratic embodiment in a new implementing structure. At the State Department, the Under Secretary for Public Diplomacy was made head of a newly formed International Public Information Group, the IPIG, whose mandate was directed at information abroad rather than at home. This Information Group was to have members from the State Department, USAID, the National Intelligence Council, the National Security Council, the Department of Defense, and the Joint Chiefs of Staff. The composition of this group, particularly the inclusion of members of the intelligence and military community, was designed to reflect the importance of media structure to foreign policy and national security.

Neither the words of the directive nor the composition of the group alone is sufficient to indicate the potential implications for a foreign policy of information space. The directive has, however, a more than usually explicit provenance and a franker articulation prior to its promulgation than is usually the case. While the fashioning of the directive was the work of more than one person, its essence sprang from the mind of an unusual young policy advocate, Jamie Frederic Metzl, a foreign policy specialist who had long campaigned for a redefinition of US capabilities in the information field and had written extensively about his objectives.

As part of the staff of the National Security Council, Metzl became involved in considering the reorganization of public diplomacy functions within and outside the State Department and the consolidation of the United States Information Agency under congressional direction. He wrote about the project for *Daedalus*.[4] He applauded the redefinition of public diplomatic functions and the forging of a closer relationship between substantive foreign policy decisions and the capacity to persuade key elements of a decentralized global public opinion of the desirability and efficacy of a US national interest initiative.[5]

Other critics had seen the controversial reorganization—in which the United States Information Agency was absorbed into the State Department—as flawed. They thought that the vestigial USIA would become less objective, less credible, more subject to direction by political leadership in the Department. Metzl, however, considered that, under the right conditions, the consolidation presented positive opportunities. The reorganization could begin a process of "reinvigorating the United States foreign policy establishment" by bringing public diplomacy and traditional diplomacy closer together. To engage internationally as effectively as possible in a decentralized world, a shift in foreign policy focus would be needed "towards a new vision, a new model, and a new culture."[6] Force, he appreciated, always required justification. "Without winning the struggle to define the interpretation of state actions, the physical acts themselves become less effective."

In his *Daedalus* article, which I cite because of its unusual openness about the issues at stake, Metzl also described the need to reach beyond governments and touch hearts and minds more directly. "With the rapid expansion and decentralization of information systems, including the growth of the Internet, satellite television and the sharp reduction in the costs of international communications, information assets have come to play an even greater role in defining the legitimacy of the use of force."[7] The particular impact of these new technologies, combined with other vectors of change, would redefine the relative importance of centralized and decentralized power as an object of persuasion. "How much effort should the United States put into relations with other governments compared to efforts to interact directly with foreign populations or with multilateral organizations or to facilitate nongovernmental contacts between sectors of the United States and foreign societies?"[8] Metzl called for a change in emphasis at the State Department for public persuasion rather than a system based on country contacts. His driving claim was that it must be a key element of US foreign policy to mesh public diplomacy with national interest decisions, and to have public diplomacy involved early in policy making as well as in a critical part of the execution of policy.

Fresh from his work helping to bring the International Public Information Group into existence, Metzl became its first director and had several opportunities to try to implement his philosophy. A useful example occurred in the period after the 1999 NATO military intervention in Kosovo. Under the prodding of IPIG, the United States took the lead in establishing a "ring around Serbia," a peripheral group of transmitters that pumped alternate voices into targeted parts of the former Yugoslavia. This aspect of "information intervention" provided a mode of distribution for reinforced Serbian language programming of the Voice of America, the BBC, the US surrogate, RFE/RL (a meshing of the former Radio Free Europe and Radio Liberty), and Deutsche Welle. The US government persuaded the leadership in Republika Srpska to allow transmitters there to be retooled for the Serbian information action. The "ring around Serbia" also included transmitters in Romania and Croatia that broadcast targeted messages into Serbia.

The concentration of energy, the ambition of the Information Group idea, and the implications for standard State Department practices attracted criticism. One basis was the fear that the Group would seek to manipulate American public opinion as well as opinion abroad. The argument was "that government cannot send one message to the international press corps and another to domestic media."[9] A different sense of concern arose from the very mode and comprehensiveness of the foreign policy objectives. *The Washington Times* sounded an alert based on what it claimed to be a leaked version of the charter of the new policy group.[10] The draft charter apparently indicated that the Group would control all "international military information" to influence "the emotions, motives, objective reasoning and ultimately the behavior of foreign governments, organizations, groups, and individuals."[11] Both the political left and right were concerned that the IPIG was intermixing military and civil foreign strategy considerations in a way that posed problems for the future.

In the 1990s, a sense of supportive urgency for the IPIG mandate was lacking. The cold war was over; propaganda seemed obsolete. But Metzl's philosophy, in its most extended form, anticipated the actions taken after 2001 by the Bush administration in its campaign to win "hearts and minds." Underlying the approach of the IPIG was the idea that the very means of distribution of information become a critical aspect of the way the United States represents itself in the world. And to accomplish such an integrated goal a foreign policy is necessary concerning media structures and the content and use of information space globally. Certain forms of global distribution of information will be more amenable to the exercise of "soft power" than others. In the wake of September 11, Charlotte Beers and her new apparatus scampered for new avenues to capture attention and to begin the process of reinforcing US policy through public diplomacy. The IPIG, to the extent it embraced Metzl's approach, recognized the special requirements of a decentralized information environment, where nongovernment organizations help shape public opinion across national lines. There, he thought, the critical element of any governmental effort would be flexibility and the capacity to adapt.

Such a foreign policy of media space began with the recognition that the institutions for delivering information had changed. During the time of monopoly state broadcasting authorities, with their substantial control over information space, the process of public diplomacy could be limited to influencing those broadcasters or trying to circumvent them. Now, the apparent shapelessness of transnational information networks, and especially the Internet, as it became a more significant means of immediate changes in information flow, compelled a different situational response. Any government engaged in these processes must be far more proactive as it deals with information distribution.

The point is not only that, as Metzl had put it, "foreign public opinion has become harder to influence as once jealously guarded state monopolies on information dissemination to home populations have been broken down by satellite dishes, telephones, fax and Internet links in all but the most repressive countries."[12] These dramatic changes could be turned to advantages. They did not mean that weak and powerful states no longer could use "public diplomacy" to achieve central national goals. Rather, as subsequent events demonstrated, effective public diplomacy required a wholesale rethinking of organization at home and modes of distribution abroad. States hoping to retain advantages in traditional areas of power, including military and economic, "must engage this decentralized environment in new and creative ways in order to retain these advantages ... To retain current levels of relevance into the next century, governments must recognize and internalize this [communications] transformation."[13]

The influence of the IPIG or of its underlying philosophy was never fully realized. The United States was not yet ready for so integrated a media-related foreign policy, at least not so explicitly, and not during peacetime. Still, it was, at least for the moment, administration policy that the greater the emphasis on public diplomacy, the greater the need for a far more comprehensive rethinking of the way in which information is distributed and received internationally. There was, again temporarily, recognition that developing a global media policy integrated into foreign policy required elaborate notions of how information is distributed.

Information Intervention

The approach to media after the World Trade Center and Pentagon attacks dramatized an obvious fact: that sensitivity to media abroad (as well as at home) becomes more visible and actions to affect such media more tangible and directed when war, or conflict that raises the threat of war, is involved. At such a time, the geopolitical stakes in the patterns of distribution of information are too high to be left solely to a market, often fictive, in which governments do not actively participate. In the 1990s, proposals began to be made, as they would be again a decade later in connection with the campaign against terrorism, for concerted action by the international community to forestall use of broadcast media that promoted or accentuated devastating, often genocidal, conflict.[14] These proposals commonally pointed to the explosive mobilizing role *Radio-Television Libre des Milles Collines* (RTLM) played in the Rwandan genocide with its repetitious and explicit incitement for Hutu to slaughter Tutsi. That became the textbook example where preventive intervention by the international community should have been deemed suitable and necessary.

Alison des Forges has written passionately about the maddeningly slow development of US foreign policy toward the Rwandan media space. Before the genocide, NGOs sought US assistance in jamming as a preventive measure. Though knowledgeable State Department officials agreed with the need, requests were denied on the ground that jamming went against the principles of freedom of expression and respect for national sovereignty. Des Forges points out that the United States had already engaged in jamming radios in arenas of combat, namely during the 1991 Persian Gulf War and in 1994 in Haiti.[15] "The State Department lawyers could have drawn on this precedent, given that the genocide was being executed during a war. They did not do so, almost certainly because the policy decision had already been made not to intervene and they knew that they were serving merely to endorse it."[16] With the crisis deepening, on May 4, 1994, the Pentagon concluded that jamming was an "ineffective and expensive mechanism."[17] The failure to stem the genocide in Rwanda would become a precedent for more rapid response in the future and a rallying cry for those who believed earlier intervention in the media space of Rwanda would have helped lessen the conflict.

What has emerged from Rwanda to the war in Afghanistan is a rich but insufficiently examined approach to critical elements of a foreign policy of media space which, together, can be called "information intervention." Information intervention includes a broader range of intermediary or information-related techniques available to the UN, NATO, or the United States as they engage in avoiding conflict, in conflict itself, and in peacekeeping operations. Both as a humanitarian and practical matter, proponents of information interventions consider it wise to avoid a stark choice between the extremes of massive, armed humanitarian intervention and mere symbolic action.

In war itself, as was exemplified in Serbia in 1999 and in Afghanistan in 2001, the elimination, through bombing, of domestic broadcast systems has become more customary, indeed frighteningly so. But what about interventions short of war? What media steps can be taken that lead to conflict avoidance or the encouragement of stability? The same Jamie Metzl who had been the young architect of the Information Policy Information Group has also written about the questions of blocking and interrupting transmissions, monitoring of local transmissions, or so-called peace broadcasting (the insertion of a channel of information that is "objective" and has as its goal defusing conflict).[18] He has argued that though sovereignty objections might be lodged to such aggressive nonforcible intervention, especially in internal strife, preventing such civil conflicts from becoming regional conflagrations is in the general interest. Permitting limited radio and television jamming in defense of human rights, while not a solution to all ills, still could be "a potentially effective and relatively low-risk tool for countering dangerous messages that incite people to violence." In 1958, President Eisenhower included in an address to the United Nations a proposal, for the monitoring of inflammatory communications. "I believe that this Assembly should . . . consider means for monitoring the radio broadcasts directed across national frontiers in the troubled Near East area. It should then examine complaints from these nations which consider their national security jeopardized by external propaganda."[19] Ultimately, as Metzl concluded, information intervention would be "one of a larger set of intermediate actions between neglect and armed intervention," that can increase the capacity of tools available for responding to potential conflict or genocidal calls to violence.

An Example: Information Intervention in Bosnia

Information intervention foreign policy can be divided into three segments: (1) attitudes toward the use of media pre-conflict (as in Rwanda), where war, instability, and massive human rights violations could be predicted; (2) attitudes toward manipulation of information in time of war (as in Aghanistan and the Gulf War); and (3) a foreign policy toward management of media in the wake of conflict when peacekeeping operations are initiated.[20] Here I focus on peacekeeping in Bosnia-Hercegovina because so many elements of information intervention played themselves out there. Bosnia-Hercegovina is significant for many reasons. One is that the ordinary foreign policy of supporting indigenous media was overtaken, in a time of crisis, by a desire to weaken embedded nationalist parties and strengthen the electoral prospects of candidates favored by the United States. Precedents established there became significant later in Kosovo and in Afghanistan. The creation of a machine of media-related peacekeeping would make a lasting impact on US policies toward the press and broadcasters in conflict zones.

Under the Dayton Accords, the NATO-led Stabilization Force (Sfor) and the Office of High Representative (OHR), together with the Organization for Security and Cooperation in Europe (OSCE) and a wide variety of nongovernmental organizations, took steps to reshape and reform the media space in Bosnia-Hercegovina, recognizing the critical relationship of altering media as part of reconstructing society. It became clear that a new approach was emerging, with vastly important constitutional, political, and structural implications. All of a sudden, the kind of machinery of administration over media was put in place that had not been seen as an imposition of the international community for almost half a century.[21]

NATO and the Office of High Representative (OHR) employed various modes, after the Dayton Accords, of creating a political environment with what might be deemed the desired democratic outcome. Control of the media continued to be important because hard-line Bosnian Serb "Srpska Radio Televizija Pale" (SRT Pale, after the city of transmission), controlled by Radovan Karadzic, was seen as fanning discord, creating the potential for renewed conflict and engendering opposition to the NATO mission. Responding to this challenge, NATO and OHR made a decision to address SRT aggressively. At its May 1997 semiannual meeting to review the progress of Dayton's implementation, the Steering Board of the Peace Implementation Council passed the Sintra Declaration, which stated that the High

Representative "has the right to curtail or suspend any media network or programme whose output is in persistent and blatant contravention of either the spirit or letter of the Peace Agreement."[22] This extraordinary provision of the Declaration established the right of the Stablization Force and the OHR to block media outlets throughout Bosnia-Hercegovina. It also provided the framework Sfor used to justify its later seizure of television towers in Republika Srpska.

On August 14, US Senator Carl Levin, the ranking Democrat on the Senate Armed Services Committee, suggested that American planes jam SRT signals while simultaneously transmitting "broadcasts that depict the true reasons for [the Serbian people's] isolation and poor standing in the international community" as a way of leavening their attitudes. Bosnian Serb leaders were furious. The Bosnian Serb information minister, Miroslav Toholj, stated that, "Any United States administration operation to jam SRT will be considered an act of war and will be treated as such." Only days later, in defiance of pressure by the OHR to broadcast the warning of the Sintra Declaration, SRT ran a report comparing Sfor with the Nazis and referred to them as "occupying forces." With the logo "SS-for" instead of Sfor, the broadcast alternated images of Sfor soldiers with World War II German storm troopers.

In a response on August 23, the new High Representative, Carlos Westendorp, sent a letter demanding that SRT broadcast, that day, an OHR statement explaining the internationally imposed obligations for the broadcaster included in the Sintra Declaration. In the letter, Westendorp wrote, "If this is not done, I am prepared to use my powers, including those stemming from the Sintra Declaration." This was essentially a threat to impose a protectorate over SRT. Westendorp called the broadcast comparing Sfor to Nazis "absolutely unacceptable." He suggested Sfor might take action by seizing television towers to stop the Pale media propaganda against the peace forces in Bosnia-Hercegovina. SRT promptly submitted to Westendorp's demand, and broadcast the statement before the deadline. However, immediately afterward, SRT announced that the High Representative's actions exceeded the bounds of the Dayton Accords and rebroadcast the clip comparing Sfor to the Nazis.

On August 22, in the next step of what became the transformation of SRT, US troops seized a television broadcast tower in Udrigovo, a northeastern town, under the pretense that they were trying to prevent possible clashes between supporters of Karadzic and supporters of Biljana Plavsic, a more moderate Bosnian Serb leader whom the international community and the United States backed in forthcoming elections. Political outcomes were surely a major element of the activities. But this desire had to be housed in a claim of neutrality. "Our aim is not to influence which programme will be broadcast via the transmitter. All we want is to prevent conflicts, but we will use any force deemed necessary at any attempt of violence," said Chris Riley, a Stabilization Force spokesman.

What followed was a negotiation resulting in a document known as the Udrigovo Agreement.[23] Sfor handed the tower back to the SRT authorities in Pale but on conditions designed to balance the information environment.[24] The Agreement required that the media of the Serb Republic stop producing inflammatory reports against Sfor and the other international organizations implementing the Dayton Accords, that SRT Pale would regularly provide an hour of prime time programming to air political views other than those of the ruling party, that SRT Pale provide Westendorp with a daily half hour of prime time programming to introduce himself and talk about recent developments, and that the Serb Republic agree to abide by all the rules being established by the international community's Media Support Advisory Group.[25]

Against a background of increased conflict on the airwaves of Republika Srpska, and the raised stakes for political control as the election drew nearer, the appeal for international jamming of SRT Pale gained currency. In fact the United States dispatched three Air Force EC-130 Commando Solo planes capable both of broadcasting information and jamming existing radio and television signals. These aircraft had been used for similar purposes in Haiti, Panama, and Grenada (and would be used again for jamming and transmission purposes in Afghanistan). US officials claimed that the primary role of the electronic warfare planes would be to broadcast "fair and balanced news and information" to the local population. Voice of America (VOA) broadcasts to Bosnia-Hercegovina also stated that the planes had the capability to jam pro-Karadzic transmissions. VOA reported the US belief that Karadzic supporters had violated the Udrigovo Agreement that mandated softened rhetoric against Plavsic and NATO peacekeeping troops.

The VOA broadcasts during this critical time also included an interview with Pentagon spokesman Dave Arlington who stated, "Commander Sfor controls the airwaves in Bosnia-Hercegovina, OK, so he is well within his mandate to be able to broadcast, and he will be the guy that's managing the frequencies and the broadcasts there within the theater." This contention made clear what had been only obliquely suggested before, namely that Sfor considered that it had ultimate authority over broadcasting in Bosnia-Hercegovina. This disturbed not only the Karadzic faction, but other political entities as well, all of whom became more vocal against what they called "media colonization." Western press freedom organizations also protested possible jamming. The planes were not put into immediate service but were held in readiness at bases in Italy.

More pressure to affect the flow of information in an election period resulted in the internationally brokered Belgrade Agreement designed to give more airtime for the station favoring Biljana Plavsic, the more moderate Serbian leader. The agreement stated: "President Biljana Plavsic and President Momcilo Krajisnik agree that the unified media environment of the Republika Srpska and free access to media by all participants in elections is vital for [elections to be] held in a democratic manner. They agree that news programmes be broadcast daily from studios in Pale and Banja Luka [the Plavsic station] alternately."

Hope for a harmonious implementation of the Belgrade Agreement was dashed almost immediately. A September 25 press release from the OHR said that SRT Pale was continuing to broadcast, as news, political announcements "devoid of any balance or alternative opinion." SRT Pale refused to soften its editorial content. On September 26, the chief prosecutor of the International Criminal Tribunal for the Former Yugoslavia, Louise Arbour, gave a press conference in Sarajevo, which was covered by SRT. The Bosnian Serb leadership had always maintained that the Tribunal was not a legitimate juridical body but rather designed to denigrate the reputation of the Serbs. Consistent with this view, an SRT Pale announcer introduced Arbour's press conference with a commentary claiming that the Tribunal was a political instrument and that it was prejudiced against the Serbs.

The United Nations, with substantial US involvement, considered this a breach of prior understandings, including the Udrigovo Agreement, and demanded that SRT Pale make a public apology on television. On September 30, SRT Pale did so, stating, "Serb-Radio-TV in this way wishes to apologize unreservedly for its misrepresentation of a news conference given by the prosecutor of The Hague Tribunal, Louise Arbour. We will read out a statement to this effect made by the prosecutor. The statement will be followed by the complete and unedited footage of the news conference given by Judge Arbour last Friday, during her visit to Bosnia-Hercegovina." Despite SRT Pale's apology, Sfor troops seized control of certain SRT transmitters the next day (October 1), thereby preventing SRT Pale from transmitting further broadcasts. Western governments also claimed that SRT Pale's repeated broadcast comparing Sfor troops to Nazis constituted a threat to the safety of the Sfor soldiers and therefore needed to be silenced.

Sensitive to the potential for condemnation of the seizure, Sfor and OHR announced that SRT Pale could regain access to the transmission network and resume operations, but only if strict conditions were met. SRT Pale would be obliged to agree to "criteria for its reconstruction and reorganization, as well as for editorial control of broadcasting, as suggested by the Office of the High Representative in Bosnia-Hercegovina and the international community." In protest of the silencing of their station, employees at SRT Pale went on strike. They then held a meeting with twenty local radio stations in the Serb Republic and sent an appeal to the international community to "lift the blockade of the SRT transmitters."

The High Representative dictated the criteria SRT Pale needed to meet in order to go back on the air. He demanded that all politicians withdraw from SRT's board of directors and give up their right to control the station. In a letter, the High Representative went on to say that a "transitory international director-general" and two deputies would be appointed by the OHR to head SRT Pale.[26] He also stated that the OHR would draft a statute and editorial charter for the station, that SRT Pale would be obliged to broadcast programs requested by officials from the international community without editing or commentary, and that a team of journalists and editors would be brought in to train personnel and supervise the programming of SRT Pale. He added further that the international representatives would evaluate the SRT journalists and editors and that "only those who are positively evaluated will be able to get a job again."

On October 10, the editor of SRT Pale announced, "the international community is planning to introduce a protectorate over Serb Radio-Television and to destroy it."[27] Both Krajisnik and the Bosnian Serb prime minister at the time, Gojko Klickovic, rejected Westendorp's demands and challenged the OHR's legal basis for seizing the TV transmitters and reorganizing the board of directors of SRT Pale. Meanwhile, the staff of SRT, deprived of their normal distribution methods and allegedly on strike, kept trying to devise ways to get around the NATO blockade, and much to the chagrin of Sfor (the NATO troops), they did so. The staff of SRT Pale also disabled signals transmitting programming supporting Plavsic. SRT Pale then used special military vehicles fitted with broadcasting and jamming equipment to transmit its programs on the pirated frequency in contravention of the NATO blockade. NATO responded immediately by deploying one of its Commando Solo electronic warfare planes to jam the mobile SRT Pale broadcasts. The plane also transmitted a message to Serbs in eastern Bosnia-Hercegovina that the Pale authorities were responsible for the interruption of regular SRT Banja Luka programming.

On the same day, a mysterious explosion destroyed a transmitter in Bijeljina that was key to SRT Pale's ability to circumvent the NATO blockade. SRT Pale's broadcasting ability effectively was destroyed. Several days later, Western diplomats in Sarajevo suggested broadcasting SRT Banja Luka to eastern Bosnia-Hercegovina via a US satellite. By October 31, this was done and Serbs in eastern Bosnia-Hercegovina could watch only SRT Banja Luka.[28]

This brief history demonstrates the use of information intervention instrumentally to affect the outcome of a key election. This could be justified on the grounds that the distribution of media power was severely biased toward the encouragement of conflict and, as well, was in the hands of the state. Sfor and the Office of High Representative could determine that it was proper to weaken the undergirding of the nationalist politicians and supporting the media power of those who, to a greater extent, supported a more democratic society. Bosnia-Hercegovina saw the use of almost all the instruments of information intervention. The international community provided assistance to rebuild the infrastructure of existing media, established an alternate media network, set requirements for the electoral regulation, forced "corrective" and official broadcasts, jammed broadcasts and transformed the staff and leadership of broadcasting entities. Internationally designed and staffed media regulation bureaucracies, some tied to elections and some not, were all introduced in Bosnia-Hercegovina. Finally, the Office of High Representative, attempted to rationalize the process and created a comprehensive new regulatory scheme for a post-NATO pluralistic unified multi-ethnic state.

The Law of Information Intervention

What was the basis for the intervention by the United States and the international community in Bosnia-Hercegovina's media and information space? A part of foreign policy is articulating justifications, and as the international community increasingly uses media-related intervention as part of its peacekeeping arsenal, greater attention must be paid to its legal framework.[29] The idea of supporting one side in an election over another, or one set of parties over another, or of creating a whole new political class may be a superb one, but it fits with difficulty into acceptable forms of media subvention. Various groups within Bosnia-Hercegovina questioned whether the international community had the legal power to reshape the information space in Bosnia-Hercegovina. Outside press organizations, some from Europe and the United States, expressed grave reservations as to whether the international community's actions in Bosnia-Hercegovina were consistent with international norms.

The legal justification for media intervention in Bosnia-Hercegovina is nowhere clearly stated and the United States and other parties neither sought nor articulated such a legal justification as they responded to practical realities. But it matters what legal principles are invoked. If the United States and its Western allies acted as "occupiers," then a particular body of international norms would govern their powers and the limits on them.[30] If they acted, on the other hand, under a consent regime, then the shape of their authority would be governed, in large part, by the conditions of their particular entry into Bosnia-Hercegovina.[31]

The United States and its allies belligerently occupied Germany and Japan after World War II.[32] The Allies refashioned the radio broadcasting systems in Germany and Japan, as part of the larger mission in constructing a democratic society in the former Axis nations.[33] In Germany, the Allies split up and decentralized the dominant media outlets in order to prevent a dominant national voice from arising.[34] In Japan, the US government sought to eradicate all elements of militarism and nationalism from the national voice.[35] The first Memorandum of the Allies asserting that Allied actions reestablished freedom of speech and press required that news be true to facts, be faithful to the policies of the Allied Powers, and refrain from skeptical criticisms of the Allied Forces.[36]

In Bosnia, the international community set in place a legal system governing all media, established licensing requirements, and invested in a public service broadcasting network with a governing board that meticulously attempted to reflect the various segments of the society. Institutions and legal systems were introduced to emphasize and encourage harmony and unification not separation. But Bosnia is not Japan or Germany and under current norms the term "occupiers" does not describe the status of the international presence in Bosnia. The historic examples provided by occupation strategies in Japan and Germany may inform, but they do not justify the actions of the Office of High Representative or Sfor.[37] Occupiers have the power to act in lieu of a sovereign, though those actions are constrained by the duty to serve as a surrogate for the local sovereign and to do so in accord with internationally established standards.[38]

In the Bosnian context, exploring the legal basis of intervention, other than occupation, must start with the General Framework Agreement for Peace, the Dayton Accords themselves. The significance of the Dayton Accords was that essentially the Republic of Bosnia-Hercegovina, the Republic of Croatia, and the Federal

Republic of Yugoslavia all consented to let the international community enter Bosnia-Hercegovina. In other words, the powers of NATO, the OSCE, and the Office of High Representative, to the extent they arose from the Dayton Accords, came from the parties to the Accord, not from the use of force or from other international doctrines. The powers thus described were, however, extensive. For example, Annex 6 of the Dayton Accords provides that the parties "shall secure to all persons within their jurisdiction the highest level of internationally recognized human rights and fundamental freedoms," including freedom of expression. Restructuring the media, including displacing some media outlets and building new ones, was deemed, in a radical sense, as securing freedom of expression.[39]

In the Accords, Annex 10 recognizes that fulfillment of each party's obligation under the terms of the treaty requires "a wide range of activities" including "the establishment of political and constitutional institutions in Bosnia-Hercegovina, "and the creation of a High Representative whose duties are "to facilitate the Parties' own efforts and . . . coordinate the activities of the organizations and agencies involved in the civilian aspects of the peace settlement." This general architectural commitment could be read to include the kinds of powers that Sfor and NATO exercised in reshaping the media of Bosnia-Hercegovina.

In Annex 1-A, the Agreement on the Military Aspects of the Peace Settlements, each party recognizes that NATO would establish a multinational military implementation force (first known as IFOR and then as Sfor) "composed of ground, air, and maritime units from NATO and non-NATO nations, deployed in Bosnia-Hercegovina . . . to help ensure compliance" with the Accords. The Annex authorizes IFOR to "take such actions as required, including the use of necessary force . . . to ensure its own protection." In Annex 3, the parties agree to ensure "free and fair elections in . . . a politically neutral environment" and, in that connection, they ensure "freedom of expression and of the press." The Parties invite the OSCE to "supervise, in a manner to be determined by the OSCE and in cooperation with other international organizations the OSCE deems necessary, the preparation and conduct" for specific elections, including the elections involved in the post-Dayton media disputes.

The Accords are, thus, a charter of authority, a specific and bounded invitation to particular actors in the international community to participate in the peace process in explicitly limited ways. They grant the international community three important fonts of power. The first font of power is election-specific and flows from Annex 3 of the Dayton Accords.[40] Many of the aspirations embodied in the

Dayton Accords and much of the international community's involvement in Bosnia-Hercegovina concern the political process and the indispensable involvement of media in this process. The authority of the international community in this area lies with the OSCE.

The second font of power involves the authority of the military to accomplish its mission and, to protect and preserve itself. If troops were endangered as a result of inflammatory media statements, authority to act could be inferred. This power stems from Annex 1-A and other portions of the Dayton Accords and is in some sense self-evident, but its apparent simplicity masks difficult questions surrounding the authority of individuals and groups to take specific actions in Bosnia-Hercegovina. In some instances NATO troops acted as a result of military command decisions. NATO troops were not subject to the direct authority of the High Representative, though the OHR had coordinating responsibilities.

The third font of power is the broadest. It stems from the executive power of the OHR itself and, as we have seen, overlaps with the other two fonts of power. The Accords were parsimonious in assigning specific powers to the OHR and, as a consequence, the OHR's powers sometimes grew organically, due to broad interpretations of the Accords mandated by the circumstances on the ground. With respect to media, however, the OHR emerged as an idealized "information intervention unit" backed by the support of the international community. OHR encapsulated the contradictions, the constitutional dramas, and the struggle over standards that determined what actions to take towards media. It was the OHR that became the receptacle for international hopes.

In its Bonn Statement, the Peace Implementation Council "reiterate[s] its firm commitment to establish free and pluralistic media throughout Bosnia and Hercegovina." More important, it "support[s] the High Representative's overall media and telecommunications strategy." This broad focus on the OHR as manager of the Bosnian media strategy emerged from the Sintra Declaration. The Contact Committee, the six-country coordinating committee of NATO powers, expressed confidence in the OHR and its role in regulating media in Bosnia-Hercegovina in the Sintra Declaration. The Declaration is an example of the formulation of law as a post hoc clarification of power and extension of authority necessitated by circumstances on the ground.

In Bosnia-Hercegovina, finally, the international community intervened by establishing a new media regime and relicensing all existing broadcasters. Ultimately, law reform plays a key part in legitimating and facilitating change. Law becomes the vehicle for articulating goals and establishing the machinery for meeting those goals. In Bosnia-Hercegovina, whatever the original authority for intervention, the OHR, in an effort to create a moral plural medium, found it necessary to develop a system of media regulation that was clear, transparent, and available to all the actors in the region.[41]

This case study of the role of the international coalition in shaping the Bosnian domestic media space helps us understand the context, limitations, and techniques of information intervention. It illustrates how the international community struggles to define and implement a policy, including developing justifications for initiating an intervention or increasing the scope and bite of existing interventions.

In spring 1998, Sfor handed the seized towers to the newly elected Bosnian government with one explicit condition, namely that Sfor had a right to retake the transmitters at any time.[42] On April 14, 1998, the Serb Republic Prime Minister, Milorad Dodik, and Sfor Commander, Eric Shinseki, signed a memorandum of understanding in which Sfor agreed to stop "provid[ing] security protection for TV transmitters belonging to Serb Radio and TV."[43] The episode of transmitter seizure was over. A graphic incident, the enactment of a specific set of integrated foreign policies to affect the media and information space of Republika Srpska and Bosnia-Hercegovina, had concluded at least as to one episode of it.

Elements of an Information Foreign Policy

I have suggested, in my discussion of the US State Department's International Public Information Group, that a foreign policy of media space had to be flexible, involve many tools, and respond to local needs. If this approach is plausible, we should be able to identify and describe an ensemble of methods used to implement such a policy. In the next chapter, I look at a major historic piece of such an articulated policy, namely the deployment of state-sponsored broadcasters like the Voice of America. But a foreign policy of media space incorporates many elements that have percolated in earlier parts of this book. It includes the use or management of media to prevent conflict, to conduct war, or to engage in peacekeeping. An information-related foreign policy incorporates issues of trade in cultural policy, media-related assistance to change regime structures abroad, and, generally, the persuasion of a global audience of the value of national policies. New information technologies have created novel media-related foreign policy questions, such as structuring new governance needs on the Internet,[44] regulating "terrorism,"[45] gaming,[46] or issues of copyright.[47]

I have also already mentioned many techniques employed in implementing such a foreign policy: providing subsidies for favored forms of media; sponsoring the export of legal and policy models regarding media structures (and rewarding those states that adopt the favored model); expanding or altering state-sponsored international broadcasting; using the World Trade Organization and related mechanisms as means to force changes in media-related trade practices; reinvigorating the international copyright regime to affect domestic intellectual property regimes; developing regional agreements, treaties, and customary international law as measures to shape or limit state media law enactments; increasing "information intervention" by the international community especially in postconflict situations; encouraging an international environment that fosters new technology (including addressing the digital divide). The United States has such a signature role that fragments or elements of such a foreign policy in all these areas are more explicit than elsewhere.

Trade and Media Policies

Of course, one increasingly important component of a multilateral policy concerning media structures are trade agreements. Debates concerning the World Trade Organization have been a major forum for describing the relationship between trade, flow of programs, and concepts of identity. It was a post–cold war slogan for Western democracies to advance a "dual transition to democracy and market economy," and the foreign policy of many Western democracies was designed to assist in this conjunction.[48] The compatibility of the two objectives was supported by the logic that in time, countries with strong civil societies and institutions can manage and reduce domestic conflict and will be more stable." Also "nations that deregulate and privatize their economies are much more likely to achieve economic growth and be competitive in the global economy. A participatory political system supported by a rule of law culture and democratic institutions will enable sustained economic growth over time."[49] Trade, and especially trade in information, produces democracy, stability, and peace.

In the 1980s and 1990s, during the Uruguay Round, the United States forcefully advanced measures extending the idea of an all-encompassing international economy, grounded in free trade. For much of the 1990s the question was whether broadcasting and cultural production should be subject to its sweeping religion. The international debate focused on whether information is a "commodity," whether there should be cultural exemptions, and how broad those exemptions should be.

Regional agreements dealt with whether there could be changes in foreign ownership restrictions for the media and whether national quotas, protecting national program producers, should be retained.[50] As new rounds of negotiations were planned for the first decade of the twenty-first century, both Canada and Europe (especially France) sought alliances that would help them resist free trade rules for cultural products.[51] They did this, they claimed, to protect cultural industries vital to their social and democratic development, and possibly even to their survival as a nation.[52] Large monetary stakes are involved—cultural products are the second largest export item of the United States.[53] Although some rounds of the dispute have been settled, the struggle continues.[54]

The US position has been that free trade generally benefits consumers worldwide and provides incentives for workers and firms who are more productive and efficient. For media products, as for tires, steel, or chewing gum, the system as a whole (and presumably most countries) is better off when resources now used in comparatively inefficient sectors are moved to economic activities where they hold a comparative advantage. C. Edwin Baker has written an extensive and sweeping critique of the free trade position that notwithstanding the fact that media products (including newspapers and magazines as well as television and film) are integral to the formation of public opinion and political discourse, they should be treated no different from other consumer goods.[55]

Marc Raboy has also set forth the case for the competing, so-called protectionist approach. His concern rests on the determination that:

The mass media, cultural industries and communication and information technologies have become the major catalysts for cultural activity, mass consumption and participation in public life. . . . Access to the resources that facilitate communication can be seen as part of the basic building blocks of citizenship and raises policy issues that are central to the development of civil society.[56]

Much of the world, often including the United States itself, sees Western (usually US) programming, as being message laden and at least as persuasive politically as the programming of the state-sponsored international broadcasters. MTV, CNN, and the treasured library of US film are persistent carriers of a specific culture, effective ambassadors of a point of view about the individual in society and ultimately, therefore, of ideas of allegiance and political values. Advocacy of free trade means easier access, it might be argued, for these perspectives to compete in a global "collision of cultures."

There is a related idea. One must look at the First World as developing two distinct but related products. Major developed societies, including, of course, United

States and Japan, have shaped an entertainment industry with global aspirations, manufacturing software, news, films, television series, and other elements of content. Developed societies generally have not only facilitated the achievement of this industrial goal but shaped two other, equally important export products: a style of trade-regulated regulation and a set of doctrines or ideologies of democratization that facilitate an attitude toward trade. The export of models of regulation serves as a policy housing to facilitate the export of goods. The export of ideology functions to legitimate the infrastructure for trade. Indeed, much of this book has been about the export of regulatory doctrine from the United States and the West.[57]

Copyright

National policies toward international intellectual property agreements are also a measure of attitudes concerning media and information space. TRIPs (Agreement on Trade-Related Aspects of Intellectual Property Rights) relies on national treatment and nondiscrimination principles to set minimum standards for international protection of intellectual property.[58] The agreement, which took effect as an element of the WTO process, established something closer to a global approach to global rules.

Copyright—itself a mode of affecting the flow of information and imagery—is an area where multilateral negotiations over rules that limit or shape national policies have intensified. In the last century, the scope of intellectual property rights was largely a matter for national definition though within an international framework. Now, reliance on an adequate degree of protection in distant markets, without support of international policy, seems increasingly less possible, and there have been several efforts to augment the working of the Berne Convention, the great older international effort that established standards for its members. The Convention itself never adequately adjusted to new technologies or the extraordinary changes that arise from a global spread of information and media.

Neil Weinstock Netanel has eloquently written of the impact of the TRIPs Agreement on this state of affairs. "In a seeming blink of an eye, international bodies applying international law have effectively become the arbiters of domestic copyright law."[59] Globalization of copyright might, in Netanel's view, be a superior outcome, because of his view that intellectual property serves fundamentally to underwrite a democratic culture. By according creators of original expression a set of exclusive rights to market their literary and artistic works, "copyright fosters the dissemination of knowledge, supports a pluralist, nonstate communications media, and highlights the value of individual contributions to public discourse." If authoritarian states and developing countries are compelled to institute a full-fledged Western system of quasi-proprietary copyright, "TRIPs effectively unleashes copyright's democratising force, even if the Agreement's primary goal is the furtherance of trade."[60]

The point here is not whether Netanel is right or not (expanded copyright protection restricts the public domain, for example) but rather the intricate relationship between one country's foreign policy toward another's copyright laws and the potential effect on political systems. Bruce Lehman, then US Commissioner of the Patent Office, articulated a part of the reasoning behind intellectual property protection's connection with foreign policy. In one congressional hearing, he put administration attitudes pithily, "people from my office are [daily] in several countries in the world, often times along with representatives from the United States Trade Representatives Office, or from the State Department . . . making it very clear to foreign governments that there will be a price to pay if they do not respect our intellectual property rights."[61] For him, and the information industry in the United States, what constituted adequate enforcement by China, Mexico, or other countries was a foreign policy issue.

An overly rigorous copyright enforcement policy, paradoxically, can hamper efforts in developing countries to nourish "free and independent media" and halt the spread of parasitic start-ups. These start-ups often depend on the bounty of Western programming and have little immediate capacity to pay. Even so, they challenge existing, often state-financed, broadcasters. In the Internet era the expansion of intellectual property protection is viewed, by some, as problematic, and possibly inconsistent with the democratic potential of the new medium.[62] Thus, while meticulous arrangements further certain aspects of US foreign policy (those related to trade), they may not always work to support the immediate and instrumental development of plural and abundant media in transitional societies. Places where a viable economy to sustain media in a Western marketplace fashion does not exist are places where copyright niceties are likely to be ignored. If there is a foreign policy need for plural media—during a period in which multiple voices are desirable—then raising the cost of entry is counterproductive.[63]

Technical Assistance

In chapter 2, I touched upon financial assistance and other forms of technical aid to media as a means of addressing stability issues and achieving desirable outcomes in terms of regime structure. The United States and Europe in the 1990s mounted many efforts to foster transitions to democracy and these continue into the new century.[64] The goal was to establish a media sector supportive of democracy, one that would have a substantial degree of editorial independence, was financially viable, reflected diverse and plural voices, and provided information necessary for citizenship to be meaningful.[65] Technical assistance is a basic tool of foreign policy.

I start with a time-fixed categorization of transition or transition-related states in Central and Eastern Europe prepared at the turn of the millennium for USAID.[66] It provides insights into problems in delivering media assistance. The five categories in box 1 are in the form of descriptions, almost report cards, but the manner in which the categories are articulated have implications for the policy directions of the external "assisting" state.[67]

A number of elements are interesting in this description of the world, or at least in this description of Central and Eastern Europe. Categories are formulated in order to explain different media assistance priorities and then to use those priorities to shape future action. Thus, for example, USAID may conclude that aid to media has a lower priority or is unneccessary in states characterized as "consolidating democracies." It might limit forms of assistance to those considered worthwhile in consolidating authoritarian states. The description suggests areas in which previous assistance patterns were probably helpful (the consolidated democracies) and areas where instability implies the need for immediate attention. The presentation is one in which there is no built-in sense of automatic progressivity. Failed states and weak or unstable states demonstrate the tentative nature of transformation and the complex factors that are involved in shifting toward a more democratic culture. Failed states may also require wholesale international intervention, of the kind that occurred in Bosnia-Hercegovina. The description of the qualities of a consolidated democracy provides at least a partial list of media-related goals. Assistance should include ways of encouraging "strong political and social consensus," a decentralized government that has passed acceptable media laws, presumably fairly administered, a diversity of information sources, and the capability of journalists to lobby for change.[68]

The document lists barriers. These include the existence of weak economies where, as a consequence of the lack of economic support and independence, media would be too dependent on local politicians and others with "narrow interests." In such a weak economy, "publishers and editors are forced to accept the demands of

Box 1
Media Assistance and Transition States

1. **Consolidating democracies (Estonia, Czech Republic, Hungary, Poland, Latvia, Lithuania, and Slovenia)** A strong political and social consensus exists. There is a relatively high level of government decentralization. Government has passed acceptable media laws, private media flourishes, and citizens gain access to a variety of different sources of information from both broadcast and print media. Associations lobby on behalf of journalists.

2. **Unstable states/divided states (Albania, Armenia, Bulgaria, Croatia, Georgia, Macedonia, Montenegro, and Romania)** Powerful ethnic/clan divisions and loyalties sharply impede nation building and divide citizens at the local level. "Liberal" media laws may exist, but politics still control media regulation. State media are not independent from the governing political party, although reform efforts could have started. Print media generally plentiful.

3. **Weak states/weak societies (Moldova, Russia, and Ukraine)** A stagnant or contracting economy, a lack of proactive support from a generally passive and/or disinterested government, and an increasingly cynical public hamper democratic transition. In the case of Russia, the government, under President Vladimir Putin, is actually taking a more active role in trying to manage independent media. This includes challenging private media more often in court, arresting so-called media barons, and writing policy that may result in more restrictive media laws.

4. **Consolidating authoritarian states (Azerbaijan, Belarus, Kazakhstan, increasingly Kyrgyzstan, Serbia, Turkmenistan, and Uzbekistan)** Elections used, but increasingly represent little more than plebiscetary endorsements of state power; society remains almost completely state dependent, monoculture economic development (oil, cotton, etc.) with prime businesses in the hands of a political/business elite. National broadcast media completely controlled by the state; local broadcast media in the pockets of local politicians. Media laws—even if on books—are not followed, as government takes extreme measures to control, censure, and even shut down any independent voices.

5. **Failed states (Serbia, Tajikistan, and international protectorates of Bosnia and Kosovo)** Economic stagnation and weak governance, civil war, and ethnic conflict have interrupted transitions. Basic questions of identity, community, and control of boundaries remain unresolved. Government's capacity to control policy and provide services is limited. Media are either in an embryonic state, receiving complete support from international community (e.g., Kosovo broadcast media), or professional journalists are working but are hampered by authoritarian regime, as in Serbia under Milosevic. Networking among media outlets is essential in media defending themselves against a powerful state apparatus.

local governors and less-than-honest business interests that run underground economies." A second barrier to the development of independent media is "outdated, socialist or communist-style media regulations." A third factor of concern, listed by USAID as a barrier to the nurturing of a transformative media is the "political vulnerability" and instability of governments. Because of deep insecurity, such governments invoke "fear, [and] harass, imprison, and sometimes kill dissenting journalists and media managers." And weak governments might also lack the political will "to break up state media monopolies." Less basic, but still a factor, is "substandard equipment in both broadcast and print media, which creates a substandard product." Without better programming, independent media would be "unable to compete with the usually better financed State media." The USAID document notes that "disquietingly," in a number of countries independent media has "made great strides and then slipped back, as a result of changing economic and political circumstances."

This set of USAID categorizations is studiously agnostic about the inevitability of change, inherently pessimistic, perhaps, about the potential for change. It recognizes the complexity of world events as chastening and limiting. But the diagnostic aspect of this approach to technical assistance implies a direction for foreign policy: the relationship between a "stage" or status of society and the mode of technical or media assistance that might contribute to the democratization process. Dr. Beata Rozumilowicz, in a study of media assistance across widely varying regime types,[69] linked stages to forms of fulfillment of foreign policy. As to what might be called a pre-transition stage, for example, Dr. Rozumilowicz suggested that foreign policy might include a series of steps, as outlined in box 2.

These elements of a media-related foreign policy, taken together as "technical assistance," sound neutral and virtually mechanical. But the bases for determining what assistance should be provided can be electric in controversy in the target community and far from neutral in its administration. Its theoretical grounding is often connected to difficult issues of political theory and communications policy. A foreign policy of technical assistance for media reform is a mix of idealism and realpolitik, of advocacy of principle and extension of national interest. Each element of assistance (financial aid, organizational assistance, and legal reform) touches on choices concerning the meaning of democracy and the role of media in the enhancement of a political process. Each element assumes a structure of laws and administration in which assistance is embedded.

Box 2
Pretransition Media Support Measures

1. Identifying the soft-liners or reformers within the ruling regime and providing them with material, informational, and moral support in disseminating their opinions and views.
2. Persuading the regime to recognize an opposition (either structured or unstructured) through diplomacy or economic measures (tying such actions to financial loans, packages, or debt remission).
3. Providing a targeted opposition group (directly, indirectly, or through regime support) with resources that will allow them to disseminate their opinions and views.
4. Persuading the regime to allow greater levels of open criticism without fear of reprisal (tying such actions to financial loans, packages, or debt remission).
5. Attempting to minimize reprisals when they occur (again, as above).
6. Upgrading the use of international broadcasting.
7. Providing constructive media infringement critiques (or more general human rights critiques).
8. Developing multilateral efforts to assist move toward the next stage.
9. Identifying a future civil society or potentially active civil sector and, in like manner to the other groups above, providing it with support.

Mostly, this discussion of the dynamics of transitions has been about the policies of states, especially the United States, and the public international community. But it would be wrong to ignore the importance, in policy setting and implementation of nonstate actors. A great deal has been written about globalization from above, "the restructuring of the world economy on a regional and global scale through the agency of the transnational corporation and financial markets."[70] But increasingly important, both the formulation of policy and its implementation, is the rise of transnational social forces concerned with environmental protection, human rights, peace, and human security from below.[71]

Benedict Kingsbury has made a broader point about the relationship of state activity and the "dense matrix of transnational interactions involving other states, intergovernmental institutions, corporations, and a whole range of cross-border groups and networks that are slowly evolving into a transnational civil society." Participants in the human rights decision-making process include individual states but also individual participants, NGOs, intergovernmental organizations (IGOs), and other voluntary associations. This means that the formulation and implementation of human rights standards now involves more than the state; it involves many non-state interests as well.[72]

Ten years after they have begun, these processes of media assistance are being subjected to resistance and criticism even as they continue to expand.[73] Concerns extend to administration and execution, such as lack of coordination among donor governments and lack of an implementing strategy. Differences between European and US assistance patterns may turn, for example, on the extent public service broadcasting should be favored as compared to private commercial media. Sustainability of newly encouraged media initiatives is also a serious problem. In addition there are doubts about the theoretical basis for the activity of shaping civil society itself.[74] Critics argue about the capacity of external governments to implant the elements of democratic society.

The receptivity of target societies to aspects of media reform has also become more complex, with reactions ranging from active rejection to an integrating acceptance. After a decade of efforts to plant democracies in relatively hostile terrains, and in an environment affected more and more by new technologies, the grounding, organization, and implementation of media assistance is in need of more systematic examination, study, and possibly revision. Still, "media reform" remains an important technique by which the media structures of a target society are influenced by external efforts.

Conclusion

Government responses following September 11 reinforce an emerging realization: that there are information foreign policies everywhere. In Armenia, there is an information foreign policy concerning Azerbaijan. In India, there is an information foreign policy concerning Pakistan. In Turkey, there is an information foreign policy concerning the use of media by Kurds abroad.

Governments, democratic and authoritarian, have long concerned themselves with the impact of competing narratives on their capacity to function in a complex world order. Prior to the Gorbachev era in the Soviet Union and to the fall of the Berlin Wall, the United States and the West had a foreign policy toward the use of information and media that (especially in retrospect) was clearly articulated and implemented. This was a policy specific to the cold war, its institutions and technologies. But now the scale has changed and the stakes have altered. There have been repeated instances where the United States and other countries cite the need to influence media, ranging from presidential statements concerning hearts and minds in the Middle East to ambassadorial urgings in the Balkans. This is an approach to information space that seeks, in a wholly new context, to maintain stability, further democratic values, and, to some extent, limit the use of media for infringing human rights.

The extraordinary power of modern information techniques, yielding an enhanced role of imagery, news, and culture in world politics, has turned what may have once been deemed an arguably domestic set of preoccupations into an international concern. Governments are no longer passive, if they ever were, in the light of changing media realities. Altered structures and roles for the media result in modified responses by governments. What appears in the media establishes political priorities. Governments, as a matter of course, will as always seek to influence what media report. More than that, they increasingly understand that they have a stake in the process by which information and cultural signals are developed and communicated and the machinery through which that occurs.

These reactions, as events move from the ad hoc to platforms of consistency, from the anecdotal to the deliberate, become elements of policy, and should be discussed as such, whether or not the governments involved explicitly recognize what is occurring. Indeed, this process of turning the occasional to the frequent is one possible outgrowth of the often-empty notion that "media are global." What once constituted primarily the domestic concern of local regulatory activities, such as the use of Internet by groups labeled terrorists by other states, the propounding of hate speech, general determination of free expression levels, and attitudes towards investment and ownership, now have external consequences and are increasingly subject to international norms and bilateral and multilateral pressure. Ironically, while countries are increasingly frustrated at the task of controlling the flow of information into their own boundaries, they try, unilaterally or multilaterally, to affect the mix of information that streams around the world through satellite and the Internet.

8

Public Diplomacy and the Transformation of International Broadcasting

In the last chapter, I described a variety of elements that, together, compose a foreign policy of media space. In this chapter, I focus on one of the instruments of such a policy, namely international broadcasting. Until the events of September 11, 2001, and the war in Afghanistan, there was precious little public attention to the place of international broadcasting in the armament of external influence. Scholarly treatment of international broadcasting has recently lagged.[1] But international broadcasting encapsulates many of the conflicts and difficulties that are central to understanding the need that one society may feel to shape the information space of another. We will see the struggle to harmonize goals of "objectivity" with the need to act as an effective instrument of propaganda, the potential split between advancing national policy and acting as a credible journalistic enterprise and the tension between promotion of favorable regimes and the nourishment of dissent. International broadcasters have a range of styles, and additional styles are now emerging. International broadcasting embodies capabilities described in earlier chapters. Among these are the power purposefully to alter the mix of voices in target societies, to affect the composition of their markets for loyalties, to destabilize, to help mold opinions among their publics, and otherwise to assert "soft power" for the purposes of achieving the national ends of the transmitting state.

After September 11, there is something else. All of a sudden, "hearts and minds," the mental and emotional kilns in which hatreds are stoked and positive attitudes formed, burst forth as a meaningful and urgent battleground for large-scale state concern. After the attack on the World Trade Center and the Pentagon, the debate on the significance of a "clash of civilizations" was no longer confined primarily to academic institutions. It became clear that military responses were insufficient to counter reservoirs of intensely inculcated belief that nourish future terrorists or aggressors against the West. As part of any broader strategy, the United States and other states would be required to be actively involved in the way opinions across the world toward the West and its policies were shaped.

Increasingly, political figures paid close attention to the mix and content of voices in other states, concentrating on the power of media, to be sure, but also examining such previously off-limits areas as the nature of religious education and the policies of leadership in tolerating or quietly reinforcing harshly anti-Western speech. The discovery that minds were being honed over years in ways unseen and unanticipated, in ways that could convert individuals into instruments of violent destruction forced a response. The United States and others reexamined the role of public diplomacy, including international broadcasting as tools in a long process of countereducation and counterprogramming.[2]

In this chapter, I review transformations of international broadcasting as an element of the foreign policy of media space, focusing particularly, though not exclusively, on the United States. I conclude with a discussion of the impact of September 11. But, to understand the limits and discourse in which immediate pressures to change take place, other transformations must be reviewed. These include the changes brought about by the end of the cold war, the domestic pressures to transform international broadcasting as a fiercer tool of surrogacy, the responses to the ethnic conflicts before the turn of the century, and the implications of changed technology.

Histories and Definitions

"International broadcasting" is the elegant term for a complex combination of state-sponsored news, information, and entertainment directed at a population outside the sponsoring state's boundaries. It is the use of electronic media by one society to shape the opinion of the people and leaders of another. It involves what was once with pride called propaganda.[3] The Voice of America, Deutsche Welle, and the BBC World Service are the best-known exemplars, but the practitioners are legion. Lines, of course, are blurred. Newer satellite services are often linked to government or regional policy but are not "state sponsored" in the literal sense. There are those who argue that CNN is an instrument of US hegemony, consciously or unconsciously, but it is not an international broadcaster in the club-like definition of the term. Similarly Al Jazeera has been described as bearing the heavy bias of its regional political setting, but it is not, at least officially, state sponsored nor does it appear to be state financed.[4]

The category is not defined by the technology of distribution. International "broadcasters" have traditionally used shortwave radio as a dominant mode of distributing their signals, but now many technologies, including FM, Internet, and satellite to home, are involved. A line is usually drawn between "international broadcasters" who are transparently such and so-called clandestine or "black" radios, instruments of information transfer that are secretly sponsored by governments, intelligence agencies, or state-linked political movements. There are varying styles in international broadcasting, a British style, a French style, and one or more American styles (reflecting the division between US sponsored broadcasters).[5] These differences in style track broadcasting histories, varying foreign policy objectives, responses to the nature of societies targeted, political involvement at home, and deep-seated domestic cultural proclivities.

Histories of international broadcasting often seek to answer—usually inconclusively—whether international broadcasting accomplished or assisted in the accomplishment of the goals assigned to it.[6] Accounts of the effectiveness of international broadcasting are often told through justificatory memoirs and rarely by the disaffected.[7] The claims of achievement among the most avid believers are expansive. A book by Michael Nelson, former chairman of the Reuters Foundation, eloquently summarizes the position of many who support international broadcasting and are confounded by the underappreciation of radio as a tool in altering the global political landscape. Nelson asks rhetorically, "Why did the West win the cold war? Not by use of arms. Weapons did not breach the Iron Curtain. The Western invasion was by radio, which was mightier than the sword. 'Those skilled in war subdue the enemy's army without battle,' wrote Sun Tzu."[8] Among the contrarians, a former Voice of America correspondent criticizes those in Congress who think, "simplistically that United States broadcasts of otherwise unavailable news and information poison authoritarian regimes and fertilize the intellectual, if not revolutionary soil so that Western democratic ideals and free markets will blossom."[9] In 1927 Harold Lasswell wrote: "The truth is that all governments are engaged to some extent in propaganda as part of their ordinary peacetime functions. They make propaganda on behalf of diplomatic friends or against diplomatic antagonists and this is unavoidable."[10]

The Voice of America, through World War II, was the symbol of US international broadcasting. In the postwar era, as a response to the cold war, with CIA backing and ultimately virtually full CIA funding, the surrogate radios then called Radio Free Europe (targeting Central and Eastern Europe) and Radio Liberation (targeting the Soviet Union) came into existence. For a very long time, the Radios maintained that they were wholly independent of the government, privately funded, and, until the issue was forced, the government denied its clandestine relationship to them. Later the Radios merged (Radio Liberation had become Radio Liberty) and the federal government acknowledged its financing role. The advantages of the two (increasingly similar) styles—VOA "full service" broadcasting (largely telling America's story to the world) and the Radios' highly targeted surrogate style (narrating for the targeted society an account of events transpiring there)—have been debated in Congress for several decades, and this intensified when resources became scarcer in the post-Soviet period.

The depth of public interest in international broadcasting is cyclical. In the early 1960s, President Kennedy sought to build up Voice of America broadcasting for the "peaceful evolution" of socialist countries. The President aimed to make the broadcasts "leap national borders and the oceans, the 'Iron Curtain' and stone walls, in a life-and-death competition with communism."[11] A US Congress report then noted, "Radio broadcasting is a most valuable means of promoting foreign policy." "We need to re-acknowledge the strategic role of broadcast stations, considering our strategic superiority, to conscientiously reappraise radio broadcasting. . . . Radio broadcasting is the only way to overthrow socialism."[12] During one of the many congressional subcommittee discussions concerning support for Radio Free Europe, Representative Edward J. Derwinski stated, "the American people must be educated to think of the Radios as weapons—albeit nonlethal key elements in our national security."[13]

The cold war was a time when international broadcasting raised specific issues of negotiation, unilateralism, and multilateral agreement in affecting media space. When the use of ideologically inspired radio broadcasting was at its height in the cold war, the United States maintained a strong condemnation of radio-jamming technology in many contexts, a legal position that still exists and is invoked. Jamming is the blocking of programming through co-channeling on the same frequencies or the "deliberate use of interfering radio signals sent from one or more transmitters to garble emissions from other transmitters in order to make them unintelligible at reception."[14] The United States and the West generally claimed that their right to broadcast putatively objective radio programs abroad meant that an interference with these transmissions was a breach of international law in terms of both specific radio conventions and broader rights of free expression.[15] With regard to the older technologies, the Soviets and the Cubans had quite a different understanding. To them, and to many developing countries, state sovereignty precluded such undesirable foreign transmissions, and jamming was, and for Cuba remains, an often-used countermeasure.[16]

The legal status of jamming has been much discussed, especially in connection with Radio Marti and disputes between Cuba and the United States over the legality of US broadcasts and subsequent retaliations.[17] In the case of Cuba and the United States, legal relations were established by the North America Radio Broadcasting Agreement (NARBA), which became effective in 1960. It is a "treaty among certain North American countries providing a system of priorities and engineering standards designed to minimize interference and to promote the orderly use of the AM channels in the North American region."[18] NARBA established power levels at which broadcasting stations were required to operate to avoid objectionable interference. In addition the ITU Radio Regulations have provided that the shortwave band is "the internationally accepted method in which information can be transmitted across national borders," while the AM band is for domestic use. Radio Marti operates on the shortwave and AM band.

The US basis for Radio Marti's operation is declared in section 2 of the Radio Broadcasting to Cuba Act of 1983, which provides (1) that it is the policy of the United States to support the right of the people of Cuba to seek, receive, and impart information and ideas through any media and regardless of frontiers, in accordance with article 19 of the Universal Declaration of Human Rights; (2) that consonant with this policy, radio broadcasting to Cuba may be effective in furthering the open communication of accurate information and ideas to the people of Cuba, in particular, information about Cuba; and (3) that such broadcasting to Cuba, operated in a manner not inconsistent with the broad policy of the United States and in accordance with high professional standards, would be in the national interest.[19] It is interesting that built into the justification is the reference to article 19 of the Universal Declaration of Human Rights that grants all people the freedom "to seek, receive, and impart information and ideas through any media and regardless of frontiers." Despite the assertion it is not clear that article 19 provides any government the affirmative right to make information and ideas available to whomever it chooses on the basis that the host government is engaged in a deprivation of the right.

Transformations in the Wake of the Cold War

As the cold war ended and with it the established basis for this ethereal penetration of sovereign borders, fundamental geopolitical change has required the reconfiguration of international broadcasting as new targets, new justifications, and new purposes were explored. Until resuscitated by the war on terrorism, international broadcasting underwent a deep crisis of purpose and credibility in the mid-1990s. Budget considerations, new technologies, and new industrial modes of distributing information were influential in the reassessment process.

During this time, Canada and Australia came close to eliminating external broadcasting. The Australians had a lesser involvement in classic European cold war politics and, instead, had specialized as a major source of information in Southeast Asia and Oceania. Still, as would be true in the United States, Australian external broadcasting was the victim of a general budget cutting process. Australian commercial broadcasters also objected to the continuation of the service. Companies, like those of the media mogul Kerry Packer, sought to extend their sphere of influence into places such as Vietnam and Cambodia where international services operated. Ultimately, after Australian troops took a dominant position in peacekeeping in East Timor, and after an effective public outcry at home, Radio Australia's budget was restored and, to some extent, expanded. A unique effort to couple an Australian international television broadcasting presence in cooperation with a subsidized commercial channel failed, with international radio becoming the favored survivor.[20] In Canada the budget cuts were more lasting.[21]

In 1999, Deutsche Welle, the German external broadcaster, was required, also for budget reasons, to dismiss staff for the first time since 1949. In October 1999 its director announced a new strategy for DW in light of these budget cuts. The declared principles were similar to changes marked for many other external broadcasters. Radio broadcasts would continue for regions with significant information deficiencies (broadcasting to the Balkans would continue and programs for Indonesia and crisis areas in Africa and Asia would be expanded). DW Radio would be discontinued in liberalized regions that were well served by privatized information markets (Japanese language programming for Japan and Spanish radio programs for Latin America were therefore cut). DW television would be maintained and Internet offerings expanded. As a kind of plaintive cry, the Director justified DW's existence because "growing Anglo-American media domination requires consistent offering of foreign language services and increased international cooperation."[22]

In the United Kingdom, after outliving the spasms of fascism, cold war, and decolonization, it became necessary for the BBC World Service to find a more inclusive definition for its long-term purposes. In 1993 John Tusa, the outspoken former head of the enterprise, argued that international broadcasting from the United Kingdom should not "turn on the hinge of a particular political dispute or ideological difference, nor one particular period of history or the immediate needs of a particular part of the globe." Defining the criteria for a sustained World Service, he added: "It must be relevant to all audiences worldwide. . . . It must appeal to a global rather than an elite audience. It must be 'international' rather than foreign." The Service's broadcasts, Tusa wrote, can do a multiplicity of different things for different people. "In part, the broadcasts operate like aid, transferring knowledge and skills; they have an element of cultural advertisement; they are an instrument of informal diplomacy; they bring individuals in touch with a nation."[23]

Threatened cuts in the early 1980s nearly forced the closure of BBC services like the Burmese, though it typified the function most readily justified, providing transmissions to people whose oppressive governments deprived them of access to other reliable sources of news. Later in the decade capital budgets actually increased, enabling a dramatic improvement in transmission facilities, and a consequent jump in the listening figures. With the collapse of communism in Eastern Europe and the Soviet Union, as with the American Radios, the Service redefined opportunity and found itself with another new role, namely assisting in transitions in the old Soviet bloc. Attentive to warnings not to allow itself to become too defined by particular disputes or historical events, the BBC World Service survived the passing of the global crisis of confidence with almost all its European services intact.[24]

In the United States, the invention and growth of CNN caused some to raise monetary objections to the continued existence of such entities as the Voice of America and the so-called surrogate radios.[25] After the collapse of the former Soviet Union, the once-vigorous Russian international broadcasting efforts deteriorated markedly. Shortly after coming to office, President Bill Clinton called for the consolidation of all US international broadcasting. This was a low point in the prospects for international radio. Consolidation was to be an opportunity to reduce budgets, rethink missions, and question assumptions. Under his initial proposal, the budget of Radio Free Europe/Radio Liberty (RFE/RL) would be slashed, as a prelude to later elimination of the Radios. On April 30, 1994, the President signed into law the US International Broadcasting Act. The Voice of America and the Radios, including Radio Marti, would report to the International Broadcasting Bureau within what was the soon to be abolished United States Information Agency (USIA).[26] In obeisance to history, the surrogates, RFE/RL and Radio Free Asia, reported directly to the Bureau's Board of Governors as privately incorporated, federally funded grantees. Their employees were not part of the US civil service as were those of other components, the VOA and Radio-TV Marti, for example. The legislation also authorized the Broadcasting Board of Governors (BBG) to oversee the Broadcasting Bureau, establish and maintain broadcasting standards, set broadcast priorities of the different language services, and assess the quality, effectiveness, and professional integrity of all activities. Typical of the mood of the time, the act, ominously, expressed the sense of Congress that the private sector should assume all funding for the radios not later than the end of fiscal year 1999.

The tenor of government and society was far less supportive than it would be less than a decade later. In the mid-1990s the institutions of international broadcasting were under pressure from the great private media moguls and their political counterparts. They argued that international broadcasting was unnecessary in the "age of CNN." The Radios and the VOA were, together, considered gold-plated cold war relics, with high salaries and an obsolete mission. That year, too, the President certified that significant national interest required relocating the operations of RFE/RL from Munich, Germany, to Prague in the Czech Republic.

In the face of this effective opposition, the Radios began to rethink their missions. No longer facing an authoritarian regime where they served as surrogates expressing the views of dissenters, they created a new role for themselves: facilitating transitions. The Radios' missions, they claimed, had evolved from the purely surrogate task of providing news and analysis on internal events where no such media were available, to compensating for the limitations of domestic media and setting a standard by which emerging free media could judge themselves.

RFE/RL asserted three primary missions for itself in the transition period: (1) to act as a traditional broadcaster by providing information and news on important issues such as democracy and political organization, the environment, and economic growth; (2) to provide assistance to indigenous radio stations; and (3) to train indigenous radio personnel and broadcasters. RFE/RL offered itself as a "model of Western journalism, an alternative news source, and insurance against resurgent government censorship abroad." It developed bureaus in all former Eastern European target countries and the former Soviet republics and rebroadcast on stations licensed within those states.

Geoffrey Cowan, then director of the Voice of America, articulated the VOA's comparable purposes in 1996 as follows: to help transform authoritarian societies, to encourage freedom of media as practiced in the United States, to foster appreciation for US values, to increase educational opportunities, to explain US policies to the world and to serve US culture, trade, and tourism. Increasingly, the mission of the Radios overlapped with that of the Voice of America, causing growing friction and competition between the constituents of the International Broadcasting Bureau.

The mood of the times would affect bureaucratic predilections. Lobbying groups and public officials favored "surrogacy" or a more hard-hitting approach by tax-supported international broadcasting institutions. This bias tipped ardor and revenue, ardor's manifestation, to the Radios over the Voice of America. On October 30, 1997, two new US-funded radio services to Iran and Iraq began transmitting.[27] Produced by RFE/RL, these services originated in Prague. The service to Iran was originally to be called Radio Free Iran and had its political sources in Congress rather than in the State Department. In May 1997, after the election of President Khatami, the State Department sought to postpone or cancel the Iranian service as part of a general diplomatic overture. By April 1998, the State Department, under intense congressional pressure fostered by RFE/RL and those who favored the surrogate approach, justified the new service as designed to enrich domestic political debate inside the country and not to undermine the government.

As a semantic manifestation of this delicately articulated purpose, the authorities agreed to change the name of the new entity from Radio Free Iran to the Persian-language service of RFE/RL. This importance of nomenclature would repeat itself, as we will see with Radio Free Asia. In the case of Radio Democracy in Africa, original congressional pressure had been for a surrogate named Radio Free Africa. This was avoided in favor of a VOA division; rather than have an ethic of "opposition" or dissent, the African service would engage in conflict prevention or conflict resolution and "civic reporting and civic building" where there were "moves toward democracy." The service would adhere to the VOA charter commitment to general objectivity and impartiality, and the newscasts were to be determined by VOA.[28]

The implications of global change and increased private competition on the Radios can be seen in the emphases for the continuation of national services as articulated by Congress:

It is the sense of Congress that Radio Free Europe and Radio Liberty should continue to broadcast to the peoples of Central Europe, Eurasia, and the Persian Gulf until such time as (1) a particular nation has clearly demonstrated the successful establishment and consolidation of democratic rule, and (2) its domestic media which provide balanced, accurate, and comprehensive news and information, is firmly established and widely accessible to the national audience, thus making redundant broadcasts by Radio Free Europe or Radio Liberty. At such time as a particular nation meets both of these conditions, RFE/RL should phase out broadcasting to that nation. [29]

Transformations and Radio Free Asia

Radio Free Asia is a case study in the focused effort to transform international broadcasting to affect information space in target countries.[30] This surrogate service, established in the US International Broadcasting Act of 1994, was designed to target China, Vietnam, Burma, Laos, Cambodia, and North Korea.[31] RFA is a modern iteration of cold war use of the airwaves, emphasizing a turn from the traditional cold war targets to new ones. The debates about Radio Free Asia echo those about other surrogate radios. These debates are important within the United States, as well, because of a general shift to purposeful, designated, and sharper-edged surrogate approaches.

Radio Free Asia is also an example of another hypothesis: instruments of international broadcasting are a reflection of the priorities and internal politics of the sending nation. Most foreign policy, it is said, including international broadcasting, can be described as shaped by domestic politics.[32] There are a number of themes in the RFA story that illustrate the relationship between domestic politics in the United States and the design of international broadcasting. For example, what emerges from the debate is the introduction of Radio Free Asia as a domestic trade-off to build support for "most-favored nation" treatment for China. In the 1990s, when there were numerous objections to China's human rights policies and a liberalized trade policy was held hostage to a more aggressive attitude toward China, RFA was a convenient technique for gaining votes: those who favored free trade could demonstrate their loyalty through the fist of radio at the same time as facilitating the glove of opening economic markets.

Aside from the debate over trade, much of the congressional debate that focused on Radio Free Asia was about the nature and purpose of international broadcasting. Often congressional statements focused on such questions as the similarities and differences between China in the 1990s and Eastern Europe of the late 1940s to 1960s. Advocates of RFA recited the account of the end of the cold war that assigned a major role to the impact of Radio Free Europe and Radio Liberty in bringing about the fall of Soviet dominion. Opponents responded that whereas the European societies under Soviet dominion were ostensibly "tightly closed," today a "flood of information reaches China."[33] European listeners risked their lives to listen to RFE, while in China leadership policing, it was contended, was not so strict.[34]

Opponents of RFA argued that the best strategy to combat human rights abuses and to institute political freedom and democracy in Asia was by focusing on economic engagement. US credibility in Beijing, they claimed, would be undermined by the establishment of RFA because "the PRC leadership would see creation of a Home Service radio as confirming that the United States follows a policy of attempting to displace them by promoting 'peaceful evolution.' "[35] Such a response would "undercut US influence and our ability to moderate People of Republic of China policies to which we object."[36] Finally, opponents denied the claim that the Chinese people did not have any available source of news about domestic affairs. They asserted that informal alternative sources of domestic news were abundant in China.[37]

Proponents hoped that RFA might provide the "hope and knowledge needed to change conditions in China" by fostering an increased "understanding of the meaning of political and economic freedom and democracy" and thus forcing "the Chinese government to allow greater measures of each."[38] In arguments claiming a special obligation on the part of Americans to support democracy and freedom abroad, the proponents stressed that RFA was necessary to "show our commitment to these countries' citizens."[39] Some went so far as to say "the fate of America is intertwined with [propagating or advancing] the faith of American ideals."[40] Others made the more strategic argument on behalf of RFA claiming, "that the spread of democratic ideas serves the interests of the United States because democracies are far less prone to launch wars of aggression."[41] For this reason RFA would serve "[a]s a prime vehicle for the dissemination of democratic ideas" creating "a cost-efficient, nonviolent means of communication."[42] Some argued that RFA was not only the most efficient means for democratization and prevention of physical destruction but also for saving money, feeling that due to budget restraints, "it is cheaper to fight some of these conflicts and wars with words rather than weapons."[43]

The debate exposed fault lines between supporters and opponents of the Voice of America as compared to the approach of the surrogates. Partly this was a philosophical debate over goals and methods, over what US international broadcasting should be like. But it was also a struggle over declining resources. Advocates of the Voice believed that the creation of RFA would lead to a proportional cut in VOA services. In the midst of this battle, VOA submitted a compromise plan in which it would satisfy the need for "surrogate service"-type broadcasting. This plan was based on the assumptions: (1) that unlike VOA, RFA would require a "new structure and staff;" (2) that VOA already had a audience, and it would take years for RFA to "find an audience and establish credibility with a loyal listenership"; and

(3) that augmenting VOA would be "a much more efficient and less expensive way" of accomplishing the objectives—that VOA, even though many assert it focuses only on "news from the United States and international developments" and cannot do targeted broadcasting, is capable and has demonstrated that it can provide specialized programming.[44]

Despite the numerous objections, the International Broadcasting Act of 1994 brought RFA into being and provided for its support.[45] RFA's obligation was to furnish a service for Asian countries "which lack adequate sources of free information," in a way that would "enhance the promotion of information and ideas, while advancing the goals of US foreign policy."[46] The legislation listed target countries: the People's Republic of China, Burma (Myanmar), Cambodia, Laos, North Korea, Tibet, and Vietnam.[47] Under the Act, the "surrogate" function of RFA was specified, that is, to construct a service that would give "accurate and timely information, news, and commentary about events in the respective countries of Asia and elsewhere and be a forum for a variety of opinions and voices from within Asian nations whose people do not fully enjoy freedom of expression."[48]

In May 1994 the President announced that renewal of most-favored nation status (MFN) was contingent upon increased "international broadcasting."[49] Soon thereafter, he suggested that talks on reducing the Chinese jamming of Voice of America were progressing.[50] In March 1995, the BBG attempted to rename the RFA as the Asia Pacific Network. The attempt angered some in Congress who thought the radio was meant to be confrontational and so should keep the name "Radio Free Asia." The original name was restored.[51] In September 1996, broadcasts began in Mandarin into China, and soon thereafter a Tibetan language service was added.[52] In 1997, broadcasts were begun to Myanmar, Vietnam, and North Korea. In 1996 and 1997, the debate over MFN status to China was renewed, and RFA again became an important bargaining chip. Representative Porter introduced legislation to make RFA a twenty-four hour a day service, as a kind of relief valve for opposition to continued extensive trade relationships with China. The President and Speaker supported the legislation.

The international debate over the broadcast of RFA took on the character of many past battles over US international broadcasting to older target sites including the Soviet Union and Cuba. On the one hand, the United States argued that its privilege to broadcast was contained within article 19 of the Universal Declaration of Human Rights giving everyone the right "to seek, receive, and impart information and ideas through any media and regardless of frontiers."[53] These arguments assumed, as has already been mentioned, that the "right" of individuals in target countries gave the United States the correlative power or duty, under the international legal regime, to satisfy legal and informational disabilities that such individuals might have. China, Korea, and Vietnam argued that such broadcasting violates international tenets and agreements on domestic sovereignty.

I want to turn, briefly, to a rhetoric of response, accounts from the societies RFA was designed to reach. These responses include (1) a critique of the free flow of information argument as being instead a form of cultural imperialism or (2) claims that the broadcasting efforts violate domestic sovereignty. For example, a report from Vietnam, commenting on the US congressional debates, argued:

It is obvious that the Free Asia Radio is a tool of psychological war, a typical tool of the cold war period, and at the same time a direct interference in the internal affairs of Asian Nations. In other words, the Radio Free Asia is a form of cultural colonialism. . . . Supporters of Radio Free Asia consider it an effective tool to . . . entice the Asian people to overthrow their regimes. . . .[54]

The *China Youth Daily* reported:

Although the cold war has been over for years, the United States and other Western nations rely on the superiority of their communication and information technology to increasingly launch cold war propaganda. . . . The real goal of setting up Radio "Free Asia" is to use news media to interfere in the internal affairs of China and other Asian nations, to create chaos, and to destroy the stability of these countries.[55]

In 1999, a report from China attacked VOA's increased broadcasting in Tibetan as a new escalation in the US radio infiltration of China.

A look at a series of most recent actions in US broadcasts against China shows the new United States "smokeless war" strategy. The United States has gradually installed around China a series of relay stations and transmitters . . . United States officials asserted that, "these . . . relay stations enable all of mainland China to hear the VOA," "making Beijing's jamming ineffective." After President Nixon's 1972 visit to China, particularly after the establishment of Sino United States diplomatic relations, United States officials in charge of foreign propaganda held that: this was the arrival of "an absolutely unprecedented opportunity since 1949 to really subject China to Western ideological influences and values." So we need to seize the "unprecedented good" opportunity, launching propaganda against China, to make up "its gap in Western ideology and values." The VOA has adjusted its programming in line with changing circumstances on one hand, while going all out to expand its real broadcasting might against China on the other.[56]

Similar statements emanated from North Korea. Shortly after the initiation of Radio Free Asia in 1994, a spokesman for the DPRK Foreign Ministry objected to the legislation and stated:

Passage of the bill . . . is a criminal act of interfering in the internal affairs of and hostility against our country and other Asian countries. . . . The true intention of the United States in initiating Radio Free Asia is to infuse the so-called United States style democratic values and the toxin of bourgeois ideology into our country and other Asian countries in order to crush socialism in this region and demolish the independent governments there from within. The United States was able to use this machination and propaganda effectively to demolish from within the former socialist countries in another region in the past and to have them turn to capitalism, but it is far from workable in our country.[57]

Another typical passage objecting to Radio Free Asia is as follows:

The US plan to establish an Asian Pacific broadcast to control our people with Korean-language broadcasts is as foolish an act as attempting to crush a rock with an egg. The US maneuvers to establish an Asian Pacific broadcast cannot be anything but a childish farce [*yuchihan norum*] that will only bring disgrace in the United States. It is better for the United States to maintain relations with Asian countries through a sound way of thinking, instead of adhering to shabby slanderous broadcast propaganda. This is also the demand of the United States people. The United States should not kick up a useless racket.[58]

Arguments from Vietnam had much the same tone. *Nhan Dan*, a leading Vietnamese newspaper, strongly criticized radio efforts of the United States, saying they were detrimental to the recent efforts to improve Vietnamese–US relations. In a commentary, the paper called the US efforts to open Radio Free Asia "a move to renew the psychological warfare in the cold war period, using the pretext of democracy and human rights to launch a war of ideological and cultural invasions and interfere into Asian countries' internal affairs." The papers said that from the idea of its establishment to preparations for the start of is broadcasts, "Radio Free Asia has exposed itself as a wicked political instrument and a product of the cold war period," which is designed "to oppose socialist countries, including Vietnam."[59]

The second, related, set of arguments against RFA from Asian countries focuses on the international legal framework for national sovereignty, as well as political rhetoric emerging from this framework. A Vietnam radio commentary against Radio Free Asia is one such example:

One of the fundamental principles of international law is the principle of respect for national sovereignty. In existing international law, this principle has become a rule and a condition already engraved in almost all-important international legal documents, especially in the UN Charter and in various documents of the UN General Assembly, by which all nations have full and ultimate authority to make decisions on foreign and domestic policies. Therefore, the use of Radio Free Asia by the United States to spread its propaganda and impose its political will, and to pressure other countries into changing their national policies and lines constitutes a violation of the sacred sovereignty of these countries.[60]

In the official *Quan Doi Nhan Dan* (People's Army) newspaper, the United States was accused "of seeking to undermine stability in Asia, but also expos[ing] deeper sores from a war that ended nearly 22 years ago." The paper went on to say:

You [the United States] should know that for the Vietnamese people, for a long time, whenever the adjective *free* is used by you it implies no beautiful meaning. . . . The Vietnamese people don't want to repeat that whenever the adjective *free* has been applied to us by you, it's linked with "free aggression," "freely bombing," "freely spraying toxic chemicals," "freely killing and jailing patriotic people," "freely distorting the truth" . . . and "freely interfering in the internal affairs of sovereign countries."[61]

Transformations and Information Intervention

Transformations in international broadcasting were also occasioned by the ethnic conflicts that closed the twentieth century. I have discussed the complicated balance the international community seeks to find as it alters media space to prevent future conflict and the potential for genocide. Training journalists, fostering new voices, and sparking local, indigenous media are all steps toward increasing stability and enhancing the plurality and diversity of political participation. But there are contexts where the ground for these more advanced measures was barren. In countries such as Cambodia and Rwanda, at particular times, the deployment of international radios may be a major mechanism for introducing a mood hospitable to peace or to help initiate useful

political shifts. Combinations of monitoring, so-called peace broadcasting (neutral, outside efforts to provide information), and jamming are now emerging as elements of formulae for preventing conflict and promoting healing after war and genocide.[62]

In Cambodia, in the mid-1990s, when the international community entered, there was little in the way of indigenous media and UN radio was created to ensure that there was a "fair" information source during the first elections. But afterward, the UN radio ceased. In order to fill what was perceived as a void, Radio Free Asia sought to establish an FM relay station in Phnom Penh.[63] The Hun Sen controlled Information Ministry agreed to allow the station, but before the agreement was concluded and the station actually took concrete shape, the station's authorization was put in doubt. Newspapers charged Hun Sen with fear of RFA and VOA broadcasts "because the RFA broadcast constitutes a powerful missile that can destroy all tactics conducted by the dictatorial clique in the twinkling of an eye." With RFA's FM broadcast in Phnom Penh, "people can be informed immediately of what the

Hun Sen government has done whether for national development or national destruction." The argument, hyperbole aside, was that RFA would provide pluralism of views:

Everyone is now aware that Hun Sen and his entourage have spent millions of dollars on FM radio stations to disseminate misleading information aimed at deceiving the people. Most of the radio stations controlled by Hun Sen—except Beehive Radio—represent the voice of injustice, immorality and dictatorship. Nevertheless, the overwhelming majority of people do not believe the news broadcasts by those stations because RFA or VOA rectifies them promptly. This is the reason why Hun Sen and his cronies have revoked their decision to let the RFA set up a relay station in Phnom Penh.[64]

In Rwanda, the international broadcasting community was initially paralyzed as to how it should affect media space where media agents were in some part contributors to genocide.[65] There was a residue of shame and resulting inertia partly because or earlier inaction, partly because of the horrendous complexity of the postgenocide society, and partly because some Rwandan journalists, trained by the West in the skills of radio production and audience building, had used those skills during the genocide to drum up fervor for the Hutu to slaughter the Tutsi. Later, as a relatively minor contribution, in the wake of genocide, the BBC World Service launched an FM relay in Kigali in March 1998. External donors including the UN High Commission for Refugees, the British government's Department for International Development, Christian Aid, the British Red Cross, and Save the Children Fund funded this special service for the Great Lakes region (Rwanda, Burundi, and the Democratic Republic of the Congo). Included in the program would be news and current affairs for the region, development and rehabilitation features and messages from refugees and displaced people. Because of "growing competition from local, national, and international broadcasters and satellite television and the Internet," said the BBC World Service managing director, "it is no longer enough for the BBC to broadcast on shortwave alone; we have to be more accessible to our audience, more relevant and more aware of our listeners' needs."[66]

International broadcasters, in these newly altered conflict resolution and peace-keeping roles, often must work with concurrent efforts to block disfavored communications, altering the position of the international community. Especially in the contexts of threatened genocide or potentially large-scale deprivation of human rights, different forms of intervention have been found warranted. These modern interventions are even more drastic than jamming and not within the standard definition. The airwaves have to be—or so it seems—affected negatively and positively. In the bombing of transmitters in Afghanistan, before the international broadcaster took over the air space, local transmitters were destroyed on the ground that they were used for the spewing of speech that incited or intensified conflict.[67] In another example, in May 1999, at the height of the conflict in Yugoslavia, the Eutelsat Board of Directors, as I have discussed in chapter 3, discontinued transmitting the Radio-TV Serbia (RTS) satellite program and thus made RTS inaccessible in European countries.[68]

In November 1999, the United States reiterated its displeasure that Israel continued to permit the Yugoslav authorities to broadcast RTS on an Israeli satellite. After the Secretary of State raised the question, the private Israeli company Spacecom, which owns the Amos-1 satellite, announced that it stopped broadcasting the Yugoslav program, following orders from the Israeli government.[69] According to the Serbian authorities, "the decision [to discontinue RTS broadcasts] is a culmination of the hypocrisy of the policy pursued by Western powers, which in words urge the freedom of the media while most grossly preventing the flow of information in the world and, thereby, consciously violating the Eutelsat founding principles."[70]

For the first time since the founding of Eutelsat, one of its members has been denied the right of transmission of its programs, which poses a most serious threat to others, too. Today it is Serbia and it is only a question of who will be the next. The Eutelsat Board of Directors have explained their decision by saying they wanted to prevent the spreading of religious and national hatred, which they are in fact precisely doing with their own decision.

There are many who suggest that the international community should have jammed "hate" programming or programming inciting conflict in Rwanda and the former Yugoslavia, this being the other side of the power to inject a new set of images into a designated context. International broadcasting exists within this overall strategy of shaping, denying, and inserting words and images into a target society. Implied as well is an international order in which these processes can take place.

Transformations and New Technologies

One important question for the themes of this book is how international broadcasting is affected by new technologies. There are innovations, but one could also conclude that external broadcasting remains a primarily low-tech enterprise and that radio, and shortwave radio at that, is its most effective tool. In the postwar review of how to build up Afghan media, one approach was to sponsor a series of low-power transmitters that would reach local areas rather than seek a national audience. Changes, such as the expansion of VOA into television, satellite feeds to a large number of independent or state-owned FM radio stations around the world, the introduction of monitoring, jamming, and broadcast aircraft as part of a means of introducing messages, often during war, and, of course, the turn to the Internet have suggested that modernization is necessary and useful. But do these new efforts make a difference? Do new technologies make states particularly permeable to the extensions of other states, and have the sending states used new technologies in ways that have affected the strategies of international broadcasters?

The geopolitical and technological changes affecting international broadcasting in the 1990s have been substantial. Partly, there was a shift from reliance on traditional shortwave and mediumwave transmissions. An increasing number of intended recipients were turning to TV, the Internet, and the national and local FMs carrying relays of the international broadcasts tolerable to the host country. The international broadcasters, like their domestic counterparts, have had to learn new skills and new modes of attracting attention.[71] There is a greater stress on "multimedia" in this new environment, and competition for listeners' attention has increased in the emerging multichannel world. A shift in the nature of conflict itself to internal war and hostilities rather than conflict between nations has affected the role of media.

As to technology, one observer has noted, "The Internet and digital transmission by satellite will make obsolete the old shortwave broadcast system, with its expensive and cumbersome relay transmitter stations."[72] Without question, the VOA, Radio Free Asia, and all other international broadcasters are seeking to adjust to an Internet-literate world. The then-chairman of the IBB's board of governors, Marc Nathanson, was quoted as saying, "technology of shortwave is outmoded. We need to get into modern technology. Congress needs to fund it as we go to satellites, the Internet, and FM broadcasting."

Listeners with access to the Internet in China, Serbia, or Russia can download radio broadcasts in real time. Because of the demography of Internet use, American and other foreign global broadcasters, such as the BBC and Germany's Deutsche Welle, will find an audience slightly different from what they had before, with an increasing proportion of academics, students, and government officials. Television is also an important altered venue. Though international broadcasting remains substantially a radio service, radio listening shrinks everywhere where television is available. Consider the adjacent states of Indian Bihar and Uttar Pradesh. According to VOA research studies in 2000, in Bihar, the BBC obtained a 20 percent listening rate for their shortwave broadcasts. In Uttar Pradesh, which has five cities of national consequence with available television, the BBC only had a 4 percent rate. It is possible that other factors related to urban life affected this result, but generally, shortwave radio listening recedes under pressure from television. For the VOA, this means that its competition may not be primarily the BBC World Service but, instead and ever increasingly, television and local radio, especially FM. Consider it as a market for attention. International radio listening is traditionally an evening activity. Families listen during what is commercially considered to be prime time. As television becomes more generally available, it draws these families away from the international radio hearth.

Direct-to-home (or to village) satellite television has potential in some circumstances to transform institutions of international broadcasting. It certainly requires that the audience both has satellite dishes and is information poor or information denied. This combination may not frequently exist. Where it does, or where information poverty relates to information about local events, a third condition is that individuals feel that they can watch without real fear of interdiction. Iran became a case that satisfied these conditions. Satellite radio has promise, but to date it predominantly means distribution of a radio signal by satellite to a terrestrial rebroadcaster. A great deal of planning and experimentation—along the lines of WorldSpace's ambitious plans in Africa, Asia, and the Caribbean—must be undertaken before there are satellites regularly and effectively distributing programs directly to radios. Problems with shadowing in target regions proved difficult to resolve, as was the cost of radios that can receive direct from satellite. Digitalization is not yet a functional low-cost option for receivers, though there are experiments, conducted by WorldSpace, to provide for a dedicated service for digital radio receivers in Africa.

In late 1996 and early 1997, the then president of Serbia, Slobodan Milosevic, cracked down on independent media during opposition rallies protesting his regime's annulment of opposition victories in fourteen municipal election contests across Serbia. The BBC, VOA, and RFE all sought to fill the information vacuum. VOA not only expanded its Serbian language broadcasts on shortwave and medium wave to reach more listeners in Yugoslavia, it leased time on a Eutelsat TV transponder to simulcast its Serbian language radio broadcasts within ten days after Milosevic attempted to close down independent Serbian radio station B-92.[73] The Serbian language VOA radio-TV simulcasts were pioneering efforts for planned expansion in VOA-TV programming of the late 1990s and beyond.

The 1999 NATO campaign against Yugoslavia provides additional insights into adaptation to new or different technologies. During the campaign, the Yugoslav government closed down all foreign broadcasting and banned the retransmission of international broadcasters on domestic radio stations to the extent they could. In October 1998, during the period of threat of NATO attacks, the then Serbian information minister, Aleksandar Vucic, issued a decree that banned the "rebroadcasting of foreign media reports that aim to spread fear, panic, or defeatism." He singled out Deutsche Welle for its "numerous fabrications" about events in Kosovo and claimed that the Voice of America was conducting a propaganda campaign against Serbia.

This is a way to prevent the psychological-propaganda war which some foreign countries have waged against us either by broadcasting their programs or parts of their programs on domestic radio and TV stations or by directly or indirectly influencing the editorial concepts of certain media companies, especially if this originated from countries which are directly threatening to use military force against us.[74]

With the Voice of America and Radio Free Europe's broadcasting taken off the air on stations inside Serbia, in April 1999 the chair of the International Broadcasting Board announced that the US government had decided to join in building the "ring around Serbia," described in the last chapter. The decision was to deploy FM transmitters so that the US agencies could get signals into Serbia and communicate to the Serbian people. The FM transmitters would beam into Serbia from surrounding countries though, at the time, international broadcasting officials were not specific about which countries were involved. The FM transmitters were constructed with funds provided by USAID. Though FM has a limited range, is problematic in hilly terrain, and more vulnerable to jamming than shortwave, the policy makers resorted to FM because it is the radio medium of choice in Serbia.[75] The construction of any strategy to transmit FM signals required a complicated effort to obtain rights to use of transmitters. In the case of Serbia, use was made of facilities in Kosovo and Republika Srpska, the Bosnian Serb entity.

The Internet yields other transformations, in the summer of 2001, the United Kingdom announced the curtailment of shortwave transmissions of their international broadcasting arm to the United States, Canada, Australia, New Zealand, and the Pacific Islands. Listeners instead would have to access the World Service on the Internet or listen to a limited service rebroadcast on FM by local stations. The move ended the tradition, established in 1932 when the Empire Service, as it was then called, first went on air, of punctuating each hour with the familiar signature "This is London" and providing many listeners with their first live voice from a distant land.[76] The Voice of America cutback on its shortwave services as well and expanded its Internet content, though not so systematically and successfully as the BBC. The context in which the BBC World Service and the Voice of America functioned had changed, and changed dramatically. New technologies, including the Internet, now in specified locales, had greater audiences than traditional modes for distributing their messages. Virtually for the first time, because of the boundless nature of the Internet, a congressional rule that the VOA could not be directed at a US domestic audience was technologically threatened in a meaningful way. There was muttering at that and other decisions to alter priorities. But times and technologies had made some rules unenforceable.

Transformations and September 11

There is little question that the events of September 11, 2001, had a profound impact on all of public diplomacy, including the institutions of international broadcasting. The war in Afghanistan was a moment in which military strategies were rethought and new ideas tested. Similarly it would be a critical episode in assessing the significance of doctrines of long standing in the arena of propaganda and use of information. There had long been talk of a Revolution in Military Affairs (RMA), but rarely discussion of a Revolution in Public Diplomacy.[77] Now there were the elements and the demand for performance that might lead to further transformations in international broadcasting. Previous scrutiny—arising out of the end of the cold war, the opportunity presented by new technologies, the demands of the ethnic conflicts, the challenges put by young critics like Jamie Metzl (discussed in the last chapter)—had shaken the institutions of international broadcasting but not fundamentally altered their behavior.

In short order, various underpinnings of the classic commitment to international broadcasting were questioned, not out of indifference but rather out of a new sense of necessity that propaganda goals were vital to national security.

One such underpinning had been the celebrated (though repeatedly questioned) commitment to objectivity by the Voice of America as that term came to be interpreted in US journalism. A VOA charter, drafted in 1960 and signed into law in 1976 by President Gerald Ford, addressed the need to protect VOA's integrity (an ambiguous need to maintain a profile that would relay the national message while still upholding national values like impartiality).[78] The Charter provided as its first principle that "VOA will serve as a consistently reliable and authoritative source of news. VOA news will be accurate, objective, and comprehensive."[79] The harsh reality of September 11 caused an immediate conflict with this principle. A little more than a week after the suicide attacks, William Safire, the influential columnist for *The New York Times*, questioned the utility of adherence to the principle of objectivity as practiced by the VOA. He skewered "evenhanded journalists", and mockingly condemned "fine impartiality" as " the wrong voice" for a state-sponsored international broadcaster in wartime. Prompting Safire's ire the VOA had included a discussion of various views, including those of Taliban leaders, in a program concerning the potential war. Safire quoted the VOA's news director as stating that "for the agency to remain 'a credible news organization' such interviews with terrorists 'will be part of our balanced, accurate, objective and comprehensive reporting, providing our listeners with both sides of the story.' "[80]

For Safire—and then for many who identified with what he wrote—the irrelevance of adherence to the Charter's first principle was clear: "Which US government broadcaster should be charged," he wrote, "with stirring anger among Afghans at rulers eager to bring further devastation to their country? That mission of countering Radio Shariah's propaganda should go to RFE/RL, the 'radio free' outfit experienced in acting as a surrogate free press in repressive nations like Iran, Iraq and China."

"In the climate of today's undeclared war," Safire had concluded, "private media in democracies are free to take either or neither side, but US taxpayer-supported broadcasting is supposed to be on our side." The Safire column created its own volcano of additional objections and soon combined with a second incident in which the State Department placed pressure on the VOA not to feature an exclusive interview with a leading Taliban figure, Mullah Mohamed Omar, even though it was, by all accounts, an important news story.[81] A much-vaunted characteristic of VOA–State Department relationships had apparently been violated, a corollary to the principle of objectivity: the existence of a "firewall" which was supposed to protect Voice programmers from intervention from Executive Branch officials. The VOA had striven to present itself to the world as largely insulated from political control. Yet at this moment of national security fears, the qualities that VOA considered vital to its international reputation seemed to be ephemeral, incapable of resisting the significant anxieties of the moment.

And then there was a third kind of faltering. During the Afghan War, the VOA was broadcast from military aircraft, the Commander Solo planes that were substituting the VOA signal for the destroyed Taliban radio. The VOA had stead-fastly refused during the Gulf War and Kosovo crisis to permit its programming to be relayed via US Defense Department aircraft or terrestrial "psywar" stations. This policy, too, had been put in abeyance. For some, these events were part of the process of conflict; for others it was a further deterioration in the idea of independence.

Finally, a sign of all these pressures was that Congress, rarely subtle when it is passionately in pursuit of newfound truths, tried, instantaneously, to recast the inter-national broadcasting structures. Senator Joseph Biden, the chair of the Senate Foreign Relations Committee, proposed a half-billion dollar initiative for a satellite television channel that would compete with Al Jazeera to reach "younger Muslims who are seen as anti-American." Congress raced, as well, to establish a new surrogate Radio Free Afghanistan at the beginning of the US bombing campaign. According to Congressman Ed Royce, this station was necessary "to do what was done with Radio Free Europe in Poland and Czechoslavkia. When we talk with leaders [there], they say that the hearts and minds of those people in those countries were turned by the opportunity to listen daily to a radio broadcast which explained what was actually happening in their society."[82]

In addition there was enthusiasm for a new Middle East Radio Network (MERN) targeted at young Arabs with a "musical mix [that] will run from Madonna and the Backstreet Boys to popular Middle Eastern Singers like Egypt's Amr Diab and Cheb Mami of Algeria."[83] The origins of such an approach can be found in the months prior to September 11, but it was rushed into prominence as a result. As implemented, MERN was the embodiment of a Revolution in Public Diplomacy, especially when joined with other emerging stratagems to "rebrand" the United States. MERN would have radical implications for the VOA and international broadcasting.

MERN was the brainchild of Norman Pattiz, a highly successful radio entrepre-neur (he was the major shareholder in Westwood One—a large-scale information and entertainment radio content supplier) and a member of the International Broad-casting Bureau's Board of Governors. Because of his background in the commercial radio industry, Pattiz had been asked to co-chair the committee charged with under-taking an extensive review of the effectiveness of the VOA. What he learned, he said in post–September 11 testimony before the US Congress, "shocked" him.[84] "I was astounded to see how poorly we did in areas of vital concern to US foreign policy." He was disturbed, especially, by listening rates in the Middle East. He faulted the VOA for having "no targeted programming for the region, just a generic, one-size-fits-all Arabic stream." He considered the distribution mechanisms outdated and fatally flawed: "We had no local FM or regional AM distribution, the radio channels of choice, just outdated shortwave. We scarcely had a presence in the region, only a few very small news bureaus. In short, we really had no chance of being successful."

The remedies he outlined could be seen as a significant critique of international broadcasting as it had previously developed. First, as have the commercial broadcasters who now dominate US radio space, the MERN would have more specific demographic analysis and objectives. "We're going to know the audience and program to that audience." For the Middle East Radio Network, the determination was that the target would not be the elite of the target society, not an older politically involved audience, but "the new young mainstream of educated Arabs under 30 and the emerging Arab leadership."

Not surprisingly, the programming and marketing to be used would approximate those of the urban stations, which Pattiz had helped develop. His solution to VOA's problems—in its broadest terms—was for US international broadcasting to use "the same techniques and technologies that drive US commercial media today." These would include an approach to radio as "a medium of formats not shows." The US listener tunes "to a particular station because we like what that station offers overall." Modern radio is constructed so that there are stations known for the kind of music they play, thematically, all day long. These are highly engineered formats designed to attract and keep audiences.

Such a model would be radically different from the programming schedule of the traditional VOA. US international broadcasting, Pattiz contended "still uses radio largely the way it was used fifty years ago. The sixty language services present collections of programs, packaged into programming blocks of varying duration. Not only is this sound dated but it robs our broadcasting of one key advantage of formatted radio—a clear identity the audience can relate to and easily recognize." To accomplish his results, there would need to be a different organizing mentality, different staffing, and a different set of incentives. The content and approach to content would be transformed, just as American radio was transformed by the rise of highly managed, highly targeted, sensitive to ratings radio that emerged after the 1970s. Genres would change, with implications, probably, for competition among international broadcasters, with new satellite services and local commercial competitors.

In his testimony, Pattiz argued that a specially designed MERN would "present a consistent, uniform format that achieves a clear identity the audience can relate to and easily recognize." His words recalled urban radio in Detroit or "easy listening" formats in Los Angeles. "We're going to be a force in the market—on the air 24/7 on multiple channels that the audience uses and that we own. Being on around the clock establishes a fixed, prominent profile as opposed to sporadic broadcasts at different times during the day. We want to maintain a constant on-air presence and be available whenever the audience wants us." The nature of the target audience would affect format and content. "We're going to attract an audience by creatively using entertainment and music. We have to be realistic." His indication of ownership suggests a different technology of distribution, with more local transmitters and local FM or AM outlets obtained by the US international broadcaster.

A significant question would be the status of news and information, areas that have been central to the VOA's existence. Noting that the target audiences for the Middle East Radio Network would be young adults 15 to 30 years old, Pattiz argued "They are not news-seekers first and foremost. We have to attract them with the programming they want to hear and drop in the news and information we want them to get. This means strategic use of music and entertainment. A major competitive advantage of the Middle East Radio Network is access to specialized music researchers who use state-of-the-art techniques to stay up to the minute on changing audience preferences. Since music will be a vital to our programming appeal, it must be absolutely current."

Pattiz might have had in mind, as a model, Radio Maximum, a decade-old radio station in Moscow. The station had been developed, in part, by Bert Kleinman, who was selected by Pattiz and the International Broadcasting Board of Governors in 2001 to develop a "master plan" for MERN. Chosen, apparently, because he possessed "unique capabilities" in providing ethnic and Middle East–specific broadcast consultative services, Kleinman would provide "branding and marketing strategies." A joint venture between the US-owned Storyfirst Communications and the Moscow News publishing house until it was sold in 2001, Radio Maximum was number six in the Moscow market and number two in St. Petersburg with a format described by its managing director Mikhail Eidelman as "cool rock and smart pop." The strategy is to have an image as "a young energetic station for forward-looking people." Mostly in the 18 to 30 age bracket, students and young businessmen, who have a higher than average income, Eidelman sought an audience better educated, "generally more open-minded to the world," very much the equivalent of the desired demography in the Middle East. Significantly, according to the managing director, a characteristic of the Russian programming strategy was: "No politics, no hard news, no sport, only short reports with a good sense of humour. Our audience has enough brains not to be told what to think—they are well-informed people who can get other kinds of news elsewhere. We are an entertainment station."[85]

All of this suggests why Pattiz's vision for the Middle East Radio Network contains seeds of transforming change. Pattiz foresaw MERN as breaking through the traditional distinctions between the Voice of America and the so-called surrogate radios. Debates about international broadcasting in the United States, as we have seen, have been filled with vicious divisions between those (essentially the Voice of America) who contend that the task is to provide an objective and impartial view of the United States in the world and those, the surrogates, who deploy international broadcasting to provide a view of local news in the target society as framed by those employed by the surrogates.

Pattiz's vision transcends this divide by relying on a new model, one that would draw on commercial counterparts to overcome any ideological obstacle. There would be a "a global, research-driven US government broadcasting network" that fulfills the missions of both the surrogate radios and the Voice of America by broadening the distribution mechanisms and bringing them under one mode of control. He predicted a time when the component parts of current US international broadcasting efforts—surrogates and VOA—would be content providers supplying programming. This network would be maintained by the International Broadcasting Bureau, which also operates under the Broadcasting Board of Governors and has had since 1994 the function of consolidating broadcasting operations. Presumably the network would also be able to gain content from other suppliers if the task of reaching the target audience would be enhanced.

The Afghan War, the sharper focus on hearts and minds, rendered the model of the Middle Eastern Radio Network more likely of achievement. It would provide, if all the aspirations of Norman Pattiz were to be realized, an astonishing, sweeping change in US international broadcasting. It would bring the techniques of the marketplace much more to the fore, and with it, radical changes in genre and technique. The VOA office warrens of displaced diasporic dissidents, the Pashtos, the Serbs, the Azerbaijans, would find that their preserves were severely jolted and their places taken by the inevitable MBAs and managers with experience in commercial radio. As Pattiz concluded his testimony. "We know how to make US international broadcasting robust in every quarter of the world. We simply have to use the same broadcasting techniques and technologies that drive the best commercial broadcasting today. These have worked everywhere they have been tried."

Conclusion

The events of September 11 brought to the foreground debates over the future of public diplomacy and international broadcasting. These debates sharpened an understanding of the interest one society has in the media space of others. There are few other contexts in which there is so direct a discussion of a national purpose to alter the mix of voices, to affect the market for loyalties, to achieve greater civic participation in target societies, and, finally, to win over hearts and minds. If there is a "revolution in public diplomacy," international broadcasting will be one critical site for its implementation. The move may be toward "rebranding," to use a current hot-button phrase, from an emphasis on a general process of representing the United States to one far more instrumental in its emphasis on specific content. International broadcasting may move from being an active proponent of the relationship of media to democracy to a function more closely tied to issues of media and global security. The very institutions of international broadcasting could begin to mimic their commercial counterparts. There may be a move from news to entertainment, from "objective and impartial" reportage to promotion of a particular culture or style. New technologies, new genres, new kinds of partnerships—all these will certainly characterize the future of international broadcasting as we have seen in the example of the Middle Eastern Radio Network. The revered Canadian activist and writer Graham Spry had a relevant warning (though he was speaking of domestic public service broadcasting): "To trust this weapon [the shaping of public opinion through electronic media] to advertising agents and interested corporations seems the uttermost folly."[86]

9

Media Globalization: A Framework for Analysis

My effort, in these pages, has been to explore the range and play of forces that exist in the vast project of global media restructuring. I have resisted the relatively easy conclusion, more prevalent prior to September 11, that the day of the state is past, or that regulation is impossible in a time of new technologies. Something too important is lost in the denial of national power and the deprecation of state capacity to make and enforce law: the organic, complex, yeasty, contradictory, often oppressive forms of adjustment that are everywhere occurring. But it is one thing to record skepticism concerning the imminent disappearance of the state and the triumph of decentralized information flows. Some substitute approach is needed.

In part I, I sought to prepare the groundwork for a framework that might help explain the combination of forces that result in the remapping of media space. I tried to show how media structures, media spaces, and information policies are increasingly negotiated, the product of subtle arrangements among states, between states and multinational corporations, between international entities and states, and encompassing other vectors. Not only technologies, but a vast number of political, economic, and social influences converge. Part II addressed the rhetoric of change, the immense difficulty of matching novel challenges with the vocabulary of the past. I looked at the use of models and metaphors as a path to policy formation, and to the articulation of concepts of "newness," privatization, and self-regulation, among others, to explore the uses of the language of the law. In part III, I turned to the realpolitik of information space, the exercise of power, the efforts by one state to influence the structure and content of media in another.

In this last chapter, I bring a number of these perspectives together, emphasizing an interlacing process by which states, religions, corporations, and individuals help shape media structures and the content that flows through them. A portrait of a dynamic world emerges, a world in which states experiment with various techniques as they try to maintain some degree of control over the changing imagery that enters their political spaces. The stories I have told about Canada, South Korea, India, Bosnia-Hercegovina, Turkey, the United States, and elsewhere, demonstrate the international implications of domestic media law and policy decisions. They show how, in a time of global media interconnections, it is almost impossible to reach decisions or adopt practices about broadcasting or the Internet in one state that are not the consequence of or do not affect the political life of other states. This catalog of incidents leaves the question of how and why states act as they do open for inquiry. This inquiry should in turn yield a framework for analyzing national responses to media globalization.

Before I turn to this framework, it is worth reflecting on the inquiry into why and how states respond and interact with one another (and with other entities) in the information sphere. At some level of international abstraction, whether housed in human rights discourse or ethical standards, knowledge of the entire context of national responses to transnational information flows may help distinguish between states that pursue appropriate, or internationally acceptable goals and those that do not. A society that wishes to maximize the availability of data and imagery while addressing specific problems of cultural impact should be considered and treated differently by the international community from one that is purposefully, willfully, and harshly closing off flows of information. A multilayered set of categories might help in discovering or validating certain assumptions, such as the possible correlation between national response to global media and stages of economic development, religious and communal division, or per capita income.

Understanding patterns of response may also be helpful in stabilizing areas of conflict, preventing deprivations of human rights and protecting national security concerns. Just as the alchemy of technology and industry creates whole new ways of conceptualizing the media and the spread of information, the alchemy of geopolitics and national identity will lead to a range of regional regroupings, national responses, and a redefinition, at times, of how norms are formulated and enforced. The world is a kind of force field where blazing technologies interact with gargantuan media entities and transformed geopolitical realities. Together, these lead to new forms of social and governmental response. Well-chronicled modes of establishing censorship regimens will remain in some societies, but variants, such as enforced self-regulation through codes of conduct, negotiated standards linking performance of state behavior to trade benefits, and the use of force and international intervention to alter information space will develop and are much more intriguing.

Our models of the past have been nationally oriented in character, based, as I have said, on the memory (perhaps invented) of a national "bubble of identity," inside which each state more or less sets the rules and controls or tolerates a set of narratives within its borders. I have proposed a shift to a different model, in which the set of narratives within any state is the result, and increasingly so, of multilateral transactions, transactions among states and between states and multinational corporations and other entities. In this sense the relationship between state and media must be recharacterized to emphasize this biological organic process. No framework that tries to capture these modes of action and interaction by and among states can be adequately comprehensive at this stage. It can only point the way. Such a framework facilitates the formulation of policies by those committed to improving civil society through the alterations of speech-related practices in target societies.

I start with a distinction I developed in chapter 1, dividing national responses to the complexity of information inflows into two categories or types, one where the state protects its own information space and the other, where the state attempts to influence or alter media structures and their impact outside its own borders.[1] I use this distinction—between state efforts directed inwards and state efforts directed to other states—to underscore a move away from a static conception and toward a more dynamic model of regulation of government efforts aimed at shaping the stream of messages and content that affects political and social life.

In my discussion in chapter 1, I suggested that each of these two categories of state activity can be divided further. Domestically the state can act unilaterally (using law or force or adopting technological approaches) to alter the media in its own country. I distinguish that case from the increasingly likely set of circumstances where the state, to address the flow of messages within its boundaries, must deal with other states (or with major major media conglomerates) that have goals and influence there. The textbook unilateral approach is for one state to establish and maintain a monopoly over imagery. An ideal way for the state unilaterally to act is to ensure the existence and enforcement of standards for a robust and public sphere. In the second category, where states attempt to alter external information space, international broadcasting began as unilateral efforts to penetrate information space, and has evolved into efforts that are negotiated among countries. The bombing of transmitters in Serbia and Afghanistan (or the destruction of the offices, in early 2002, of the Palestinian Broadcasting Corporation by Israel) is an extreme and modern example of the use of force by one state or a coalition to change the information space in a target society.

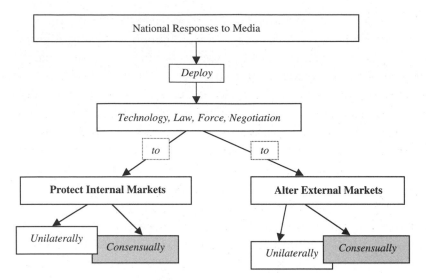

Figure 9.1
Taxonomy of analytic approaches showing categories of state activity

There are also interesting examples of bilateral efforts to limit the use of radio space for national purposes. In the 1948 Agreement between India and Pakistan, the parties promised that their respective publicity agents (including for radio and film) would "refrain from and control: (a) propaganda against the other Dominion, and (b) publication of exaggerated versions of news of a character likely to inflame, or cause fear or alarm to, the population, or any section of the population in either Dominion."[2] Similarly a dispute between Santo Domingo and Haiti was settled, in the early 1950s, with a document that included a commitment by both parties not to "[t]olerate in their respective territories the activities of any individuals, groups, or parties, national or foreign, that have as their object the disturbance of the domestic peace of either of the two neighboring Republics or any other friendly Nation."[3]

My hypothesis in this book has been that there is a general tendency to move from the unilateral to the consensual, the negotiated, and the multilateral. The argument is illustrated in figure 9.1. Of course, to describe a state's response in terms of its external or internal effects is only a first step, a bit mechanical, if taken alone, as a way of classifying national interactions with media globalization. How this basic building block plays itself out—the type and mode of national response—

Table 9.1
Taxonomy of analytic approaches

	Paradigm of state-based structuring	Multilateral shift
Market for loyalties	Netherlands and pillarization	Turkey and Kurdish voices
Processes of transition	Singapore and information modernization	Post–Soviet Czech Republic and broadcasting competition
Achieving stability	Soviet Union and control of dissent	Kosovo and information intervention

requires elaboration of the framework I propose. The framework then provides assistance in understanding state trends, possibly yielding some predictive qualities and also helps clarify distinctions that relate to human rights norms and developing international law. Table 9.1 presents a taxonomy of the analytic approaches I have used in earlier chapters.

Market for Loyalties

In chapter 1, and elsewhere in the book, I used a "market for loyalties" analysis to indicate that a period of re-regulation or remapping occurs when existing modes of control have led to an uneasy cartel of political allegiances, one that can no longer maintain its position of civil authority. The permeability of borders creates a regulatory crisis if barriers to media entry are lowered for those excluded from the old political cartel, especially if they could be threats to the dominance of the *ancien regime*. In addition media globalization may foster the crisis if, for other reasons, previously excluded or marginalized competitors now have a more feasible claim for entry. Under this model, a national response can take the form of redefining the cartel and accommodating new entrants or taking effective steps, through law or force, to try to raise the barriers to entry again. A state's mode of altering regulation may reflect pressures to alter its internal cartel or may reflect pressures from outside to increase competition and alter those who compete for loyalties on a regional or global basis. The market for loyalties approach also explains actions of external entities (corporations, states, and diasporic groups) to use technology or international norms to force a state to modify the membership of a local cartel.

The Netherlands supplies an example of an internal approach to achieving a desired market structure for a regulated oligopoly of competing suppliers of loyalty and national identity. There, the long-standing approach of pillarization, dividing the market among differentiated loyalties (religious, political, and lifestyle) was reflected in a self-contained set of broadcast regulations. The permeability of borders made this practice difficult, and the capacity of the state to enforce an arrangement of existing participants in such a market virtually disappeared. More typical of the new environment is the MED-TV example, as discussed in chapters 1 and 3, where Turkey was required to negotiate with other states to help slow or control the transmission of signals by satellite to minorities within its borders.

Stages of Transition

A second analytic approach for understanding media remapping is founded on an analysis of state activity as it relates to the state's place in the transition from authoritarian, for example, to more democratic structures. State actions, especially interactions among states, are often implemented with the purpose of facilitating or resisting movement from one stage to another in mind. As an analytic approach, the "staging" strategies are useful to explain specific interventions aimed at altering the political life of the target society, usually seeking to render it more "open" or "democratic." The idea of transition and the ideal that one can move societies along a continuum by enhancing the functioning and structure of the press are at the heart of this "stages" explanation for restructuring efforts.

Singapore, with its emphasis on regulated high-capacity information systems is an example of a state that uses unilateral control of the architecture of information distribution to hasten the pace and direction of transition. In contrast, the Czech Republic is an example of the shift to multilateral approaches to affecting transition. There, the shaping of private broadcasting, the role of foreign investors, and the commercialization of the broadcasting sphere are a result of internal decisions, negotiations with the Council of Europe and the European Union, as well as media assistance from the West in the early post-Soviet period.

Affecting Stability

In this book, I have suggested a third and related approach to understanding global patterns in media restructuring based on a general motivation for strengthening stability (and occasional efforts to destabilize governments). Albert O. Hirschman's little gem of a study, *Exit, Voice, and Loyalty*, indicates how each organization, tribe, and state has the ability to respond to perceptions of decline and to readjust its message to meet the needs of its consumers or citizens. Some societies get the balance "right" (by meeting citizen needs or successfully avoiding them) and are therefore stable; some regimes may not achieve the optimal combination of "exit" and "voice" and decline. As discussed in chapter 7, the stability of individual states, whether or not they decline or transform, has external consequences. As a result there may be a general interest in the manner in which states cope with problems of internal dissent and miscommunication. The extent to which state and society structures meet the needs of a plural population and sufficiently buffer or accept dissent has security implications for other states. The patterns of media restructuring, particularly the efforts of one state to change the media space of another state, may be analyzed through this approach.

Frequently, as is exemplified by US efforts in Bosnia-Hercegovina and in Kosovo, these interventions are designed to facilitate stability, though in some instances, as in the case of US policy toward Iraq, the interest of the external state may be to destabilize a target regime and enhance its decline. Destabilization can be accomplished through subsidizing dissent, through instituting clandestine radio stations, and through more sophisticated psychological operations. The Soviet Union (or almost any authoritarian state) was an example of attempting to achieve stability, in part, through maintaining a monopoly over media.

Taxonomy of Influences

How a state responds (whether it can best be explained through the market for loyalties approach or other aspects of the analytic framework) is a function of historic and pervasive influences on the particular decision maker. Thus the analytic framework must be augmented by an account of the relationship between influences and outcomes.

Societies that have a lower degree of privatized media, longer history of religious tension, lower exposure to advanced and innovative technology, greater concern about terrorism, or more authoritarian past may tend to be less open and more fixed on control than those that have a different history. Rather than grade correlations, it is more intelligent to say that the complexity of reaction and response has some degree of relationship to a specific combination of these factors. I discuss seven

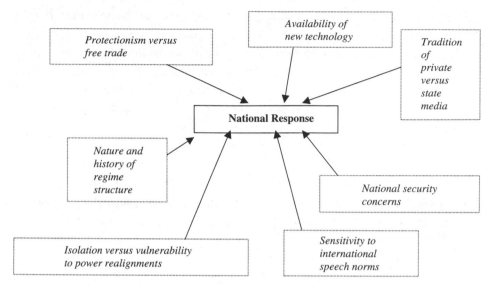

Figure 9.2
Taxonomy of influences

such influences: approaches to free trade, the influence of the shift to the private, the influence of new technologies, the influence of prior and existing regime structure, the influence of national security concerns, the influence of power realignments, and the influence of international norms (see figure 9.2). Others, or subcategories of these elements, of course, exist.

Protectionism versus Free Trade

Much of the formal, apparent process of national response to media globalization is a consequence of the nature of the debate over free trade. Should free trade be limited where there are direct adverse consequences for national identity? Just as there is a global debate over the consequences of trade globalization for employment, including issues of child labor, trade discussions incorporate questions of national control of "cultural products." In chapter 7, I have discussed aspects of the debate over free trade in goods and in intellectual property as they affect national responses.

To advocate free markets in information abroad, a country would be expected to adhere to free market principles within. Symmetry and consistency are not, however, essential characteristics of state policy, and it would not be the first time that principles were put forward in foreign climes and ignored at home. But the advocacy of free markets may sit uneasily with the need to regulate domestically. Even the most market oriented of states can suffer recriminations if the state tries to change the ownership rules of others while its own rules are deemed too restrictive. A country can find itself suddenly encumbered by its own internal curbs on content when trying to affect the content regulations in another country. Numerous examples of these troubles exist in areas such as content standards in broadcasting, foreign ownership for terrestrial broadcasting stations, and restrictions on particular uses of the Internet.

Influence of the Shift to the Private

I have suggested throughout the book, and particularly in chapter 3, that media globalization involves the establishment of a localized receiving infrastructure for the distribution of imagery increasingly produced and controlled by multinational corporations. Multinationals require growing markets, and these usually necessitate patterns of terrestrial distribution to complement other patterns of satellite networking. Law or the rule of law is an integral part of the effectiveness of such a localized system. The national responses determine whether the global system for the distribution of information will be embraced.

To some extent, we may be moving to a pattern of international production comprised of regional or national wholesaling and local retailing. Another characteristic of this system, driven globally by large private corporations is that so long as multichannel video distribution opportunities are available locally, the multinational sector seems relatively indifferent to the technology for such distribution (cable, direct broadcasting, Internet, etc.). As this system matures, the impact of concentration at the multinational scale becomes clearer: the fewer the competitors at the production and distribution level, the fewer are the alternatives for states negotiating the nature of a national response.

Influence of New Technologies

While there is much in this book that is resistant to technological determinism, especially in its most enthusiastic forms, it is obvious that the pace and pattern of introduction of new technologies has a major impact on national responses. Societies must shift their strategies of control to take into account shifts in the way ideas enter or circulate within their boundaries. Because so much has been written about this influence on the nature of national law, I do not need to expand upon it here.[4]

Influence of Regime Structure

As I explored in chapter 7, the nature and history of the regime have an enormous influence and predictive quality on the response of the state to media globalization. Not only the current status—whether a state is a Western-style democratic society or a religiously based quasi-authoritarian regime—but also the form and mode of transition substantially affect attitudes toward the structure of media.

Regime structure can be described by asking questions about the nature of the domestic civil society, attitudes toward the rule of law, issues of authority and democratic structure, and whether or not there are effective nongovernment organizations. National response is determined by the extent to which those in control dominate levers of social change, whether they have substantial power over existing forms of information flow, and the number of traditions that favor including opposition voices.

Influence of National Security Concerns

Traditional national security concerns color many aspects of state response to media globalization. After the more strident 1950s and in the controlled cold peace in the West, internal security concerns at least momentarily diminished in Western Europe and the United States. The idea of a dangerous domestic world in which speech could ignite terror directed at its population—with noticeable exceptions—declined, only to reappear with a vengeance after September 11, 2001. Concepts of tolerance and the expansion of speech rights flourished in an environment of international stability. Now, however, ideas of global terrorism, unsettled notions of a new set of enemies have restored national security concerns in all national settings. States' responses may be categorized by the way in which a predominant and contentious religious history, a relationship to conflict and anxiety, or terror and national security affects media policy.

It is sometimes difficult to differentiate those states that exploit the invented myth of danger to suppress political dissent from those states where the potential for centripetal dissolution is actual and great. Fear of images and messages deemed to be subversive and information capable of endangering national security spreads. It was the basis for British prohibitions against showing the faces of members of the IRA. This fear emerged in the United States as the White House sought to control exhibition of videos of Osama bin Laden, and it surfaced as government responded to sensed dangers of cyberwar and Internet terrorism.[5] Terrorism has become a new trope for the restructuring of regulation, especially of the Internet, as it becomes a forum for the potential cohesion of groups inimical to the political order. It is an irony that Western democracies so long condemnatory of speech restrictions in states like China are beginning to look at its architectures of control for potential ways to regulate what is deemed terrorist expression on the Internet.

Influence of International Norms

The clash of national security with free speech standards brings us to the continued and changing use of human rights doctrine as an influence in the remapping process. Elements of an international community, including NGOs, invoke article 19 of the Universal Declaration of Human Rights and other similar doctrines to measure compliance as a restriction on national responses to media globalization. The US State Department, the Organization of Security and Cooperation in Europe, the Organization of American States, other regional organizations, and the United Nations increasingly all have special officers who monitor compliance with international norms in the speech and press areas.

There is a transformation of rights language in the zone of media. Since the 1990s the assertion of speech rights has been tightly linked to the rising influence of private media corporations. Companies seeking to minimize government regulation of media enterprises, marshalled speech rights most effectively. In the United States, speech rights, though most popularly associated with political dissenters, were deployed, often successfully, to restrain the capacity of Congress to shape the structure of cable television (for example, when deciding whether cable systems should be required to carry public service television channels), to limit the power of the legislature to force an access right in newspapers, to limit cross-ownership between cable companies and telephone companies, or to set public access requirements for direct broadcast satellites or other media. Human rights principles are used to clear a global space for commercial media.

In Europe, human rights principles were successfully advanced to force states to alter the way in which they licensed radio frequencies to the private sector. Free speech norms have become effective rallying points for urging change in societies that assert the most control over their speech environments. In the international sector, as within each state, media institutions are, in some part, surrogates for individuals. As a result, to some extent, freedom from constraint for the media means enhancement of the right of people to receive and impart information. But that is not always the case. Regulation may also increase the zone of speech, enlarge the flow of information to citizens, and enhance their right to communicate.

Table 9.2
Aspects of restrictive national responses

Justifications for restrictions
Mode of communications technology restricted
Object of restriction
Intensity of restriction

Influence of Power Realignments

Part III of this book underscores how changes in spheres of influence and political alliances affect media restructuring. Orthodoxies of regulation reflect geopolitical shifts. Regulations concerning language usage mirror political needs and specific transitional realities. During the cold war, the West used human rights doctrine to justify international broadcasting that violated state borders by saying that these transmissions were fulfilling the right of individuals to receive information. In a changed world, where stability is increasingly important, attitudes toward the privileging of shortwave or clandestine radios, and condemning jamming may change. The Stability Pact for Southeast Europe is an example of shifts in thinking about the mode and role of media structures. States, or parts of states such as Kosovo, Chechnya, Bosnia, Rwanda, and Cambodia are subjects of direct information intervention. In these cases wholesale reorganizations of media space occur as part of great changes in political power.

Aspects of Restrictive National Responses

Every country, even one committed to free speech principles, is engaged in some form of regulation or restriction relating to media. And many of these restrictions or actions are a consequence of or affected by transnational concerns. Freedom House and others often classify states along a hypothetical grid that reflects how they deploy (or do not deploy) restrictions on the flow of information. In considering this kind of classification (table 9.2), one might look at the justifications a state provides as its grounds for restrictions (its characterization of its own needs and the way it checks the conformity of that justification to principles of law); the mode or modes of communications technology that the state restricts (reflecting probably its evaluation of which technologies are the most important tools of persuasion); the object of restriction (content provider, distributor, gatekeeper, consumer, or other states); its techniques of restriction (the extent to which it uses law or other forms of coercion); the intensity of restriction (the extent to which it either intends to or has the capacity to fulfill a mandate); and the influence of time (the pattern by which restrictions and their enforcement evolve). Let me describe, briefly, each of these in turn.

Articulated Basis for Restriction

National responses can be classified on the basis of reasons given by governments to protect their own media space. While the consequence (though sometimes unintended) of any form of regulation is to restrict speech, one might gain insight into the nature of a state's response through the category of justification: whether, for example, there was a claimed national security threat that justified a particular form of regulation.[6] Among the tropes for restriction (somewhat overlapping) are protection of children, preservation of morals, protection of domestic industry, strengthening of national identity, protection of religious beliefs or a favored church, and avoidance of sectarian violence.

The permissible areas for restriction are sometimes defined by international treaty or convention, and these modes of definition and limitation are becoming more influential. Certain of these motivations for restriction (national security, territorial integrity, and prevention of disorder, for example) are memorialised in section 2 of article 10 of the European Convention of Human Rights and that document gains greater force as the Council of Europe expands, and as application of the ECHR norms and European Court jurisprudence spreads to settings outside Council of Europe states.[7]

Analyzing national responses on the basis of the justifications given for restrictions also opens a path for determining the validity of such justification. This process generally occurs through internal challenge in domestic courts or through regional tribunals (such as the European Court of Human Rights). The justifications permitted and the standards used by tribunals to determine whether the restrictions are justified are both relevant to the analysis. In addition there are evaluations by nongovernment organizations or other governments, as in the annual survey of compliance with human rights by the US Department of State that must be considered.

Medium of Restriction

Another axis for sorting restrictions would be classifying national responses by the technology that is controlled. Some states, for example, claim to have an unrestricted press but regulated broadcasting.[8] Some states have newly focused regulation on the Internet. There are states where radio has the most significant impact and so is the most significant target of control. It is important therefore to understand which medium, for which state, is deemed most effective or most threatening at altering the state's information space.

Choice of medium for restriction may be the result of a variety of factors. Some modes, forms of image making, may be thought to be invasive or too powerful, almost mystically mesmerizing. This idea exists even in American jurisprudence.[9] The intrinsic power of broadcasting has been a basis for distinguishing radio or television from press, just as it has been a favorite instrument for international propaganda. Some modes are favourably treated because they reach only elites and are therefore considered less dangerous. Modes of distribution, such as satellite to home, may be especially feared because of the lack of a regulable gatekeeper or intermediary and the potential for shifts in strengths among ethnic groups and communication between ethnic groups and outside diasporas.

The capacity of nongovernment organizations, such as multinational corporations (or broadcasting sponsored by another state) to reach into a society through satellite or powerful transmitters or through other means (song or sermon incorporated in audiocasette) would potentially be reflected in the nature of governmental response. A medium may be singled out for regulation if it appears to be an instrument of groups labeled as terrorists. Finally a medium may be singled out for regulation for historical reasons, for competitive reasons, or for regulatory reasons of a global tradition in that medium.

Objects of Restriction

An evaluation of where in the chain of production, distribution, and consumption of information a restriction is aimed is critical to understanding national responses. Censorship laws can be aimed efficiently at gatekeepers (newspapers, broadcasters), but strategies of control alter as the capacity to identify and regulate such nodes diminishes. States may respond by negotiating with content providers or by increasing control of consumers through tracking what they read or watch. States may enter into agreements that restrict what third-party states can do to alter the mix of voices in a target society.

Just as families sometimes consider they have the right to think, in a wholesale way, about the education of their children and their exposure to images, states do not always stop at blocking only some programs or regulating a particular entity. For some, their perspective on images and messages is more systematic and overwhelming, just as their attitude toward governance is more total. There are states that believe that the rhythm, pattern, and comprehensive impact of media generally provide a worldview and culture antagonistic and inconsistent with their own. The very style of Western television, the very presentation of women, the beliefs implicit in its programs—all these are as significant as the words uttered and the cultural boundaries crossed. The specific emphasis on a secular living, different from one that may be religiously mandated, could violate community norms. Eyes should be shielded from those who make such life choices, and certainly children should not be exposed to them. In a future of seamless communications and permeable borders, national restrictive responses shift from control of gatekeepers to control of users.

Intensity of Restriction

Another axis for analysis is the intensity with which a state enforces techniques of restriction or promotes a diversity of speech sources. Regulatory mechanisms and their institutions of implementation can be designed to provide great or narrow openings to the information of the world, and formally stated restrictions do not always reveal actual experience. Articulated norms always have an influence, but the extent of the value depends on notions of enforcement or related coercion. Courts use norms to measure whether national responses to media globalization should be upheld or subjected to criticism.[10] There often is a gulf between explicit legal norms and actual practice, with restrictions being more or less intense than the statutory language would imply. States may establish harsh formal restrictions but do so as a means to buttress customary practices or religious attitudes. States may not have the capacity to enforce standards that they erect. Formal commitments against censorship are often belied by practice. Conversely, a reputation for speech restrictive legislation may be belied by the existence of an active marketplace of ideas and widespread and accepted disregard for formal rules. One might want to ask which states—despite the structure of impediments—embrace an actual public sphere in which there is a broad pluralism of views and perspectives from without as well as from within the state's boundaries.

Methods of Implementation: Law, Negotiation, Technology, and Force

All comes down to means of implementation. I have canvased many techniques and modes of implementing national responses in this book, and they are legion: enactment of domestic laws of censorship, the negotiation of and invocation of international human rights laws, manipulation of laws governing the allocation of spectrum, use of laws providing for licensing broadcasting stations, design of the architecture of signal reception, intervention through technical assistance, and even bombing. I have devoted attention to international broadcasting and adjustment of trade practices. One could focus only on emerging state responses to the Internet, from adjustment of copyright to regulation of the sale of pharmaceutical products, coping with issues concerning gaming, and, as has been an important subject for this book, programming not considered suitable, in some cultures, for children.

A final way of parsing these techniques—in terms of evaluating, predicting, or understanding national responses—is to asssign them to one of four categories: adopting law, entering into negotiations, implementing technology, or engaging in the use of force. There are, of course, deep conceptual difficulties with this form of categorization: law, for example, can itself be said to be a form of force, negotiation is often the consequence of the exercise of power. The line between technology and law, as Lawrence Lessig has famously reminded us, is increasingly fine.

Aspects of this grid are important, however. Calling a means of implementation the exercise of "law" has different implications than if the action were characterized as an exercise of (naked) force. When the United Nations establishes a Temporary Media Commissioner to regulate certain aspects of the content of broadcasting in Kosovo, the actions of the office can be evaluated according to traditional standards derived from the rule of law.[11] We have seen that those who enter a zone of conflict under the doctrine of "belligerent occupation" have different privileges from those whose entry occurs as in the Dayton Accords. The introduction of technology presents special problems. General international principles that are based on the enactment of law need to be adjusted to address the use of software design or novel regulation by governments to circumvent those norms. It is more difficult to assess government policies that function through system architecture than through explicit policy tools like broadcast licensing. Negotiation, too, as when a government and a multinational corporation agree upon areas of restriction, falls beneath the traditional evaluative radar screen.

In addition to the use of law, force—sometimes subtle, sometimes brutal and coercive—is used both internally and without. I have discussed the growing practice of what has been labeled "information intervention," a new term for a collection of measures available to the international community to alter media content within a country where uncontrolled information flow is thought to be inconsistent with multilateral objectives. Jamming, monitoring, bombing of offending broadcasting outlets, and seizing control of transmitters to prevent conflict-producing media are the stuff of this emerging practice.

But there is an even more pervasive turn. We have seen that one modern response of states is to replicate the old system and ensure that, to the extent possible, information is funneled through regulable intermediaries. But, if information leaks around intermediaries, then the next step will be to try to regulate the content providers. They, too, are elusive in the Internet era. The result may be increased emphasis on regulating the ultimate user, a crude return to punishment of the consumer, the citizen, the subject. In highly organized and religious societies where there are intense community pressures, peer observation and reporting becomes a prelude to a social enforcement tool. In the United States, cases involving downloading computer files of child pornography demonstrate some slight shift in prosecutorial attention from the distributor or intermediary to the ultimate user.

Governments can, with only partial success, construct an information version of a star wars defense to block out unwanted images. They seek to control information by alliances, secret or otherwise, with the purported owners of means of distribution. An approach that can serve as a basis for understanding certain national responses involves the use of rating and filtering techniques and the ability to resort, as a response to the newer flows of content, to meta-information in order to regulate certain kinds of unwanted content. Technological approaches that identify information, allow it to be classified, and that determine to whom it goes and from where it comes are an area for expansive involvement by states acting alone, in concert, or with private corporations. It will be important to analyze the shift from traditional regulatory modes—such as censorship and criminal prosecution—to regulation that is rooted in identification and control of flows of information. Modes of surveillance and encryption are related to this general issue.

States exult in burying value choices in the neutral pitch of unfathomable code and the complexities of system architecture. In the new technologies, it is the design of code that often is the prelude for the potential and the desire of the state to regulate. The turn to software provides the infrastructure for ideology, not ideology itself, and has become a significant factor in regulation. Terrorism and its prevention will be one area where the use of filtering technology will become a greater tool.

The architecture of rating and filtering will be an approach of choice not only in authoritarian societies but also in those states that are committed to private broadcasting and seeming deregulation. Ideas in the future may be required to have identity cards or passports, in the form of technical meta-information, that determine where such ideas can travel, to whom they can be addressed, by whom they can be received, how much they cost to access, and whether they should be banned entirely. The rhythm of change moves in unusual directions as states seize the opportunities that technologies provide to answer dangers that technologies pose.

It may seem eccentric to suppose that ideas will have "passports," but consider the notion against the background of history. One of the purposes of national control over personal movement across borders was to limit disturbances to the status quo and control against the hazards of dissent and subversion. In a simpler world, limiting movement of people performed or supplemented (imperfectly) the task of limiting movement of ideas. On the side of technology, the impetus of states (and of corporations, it should be added) has been to move to the kind of tagging of content with meta-information that allows ideas to be filtered and restricted in ways similar to the methods used to restrict free travel across boundaries of individuals. It does not take much imagination to put these two trends together. Indeed, scholars and critics of technical advancement have pointed out the ethical and speech-restriction potential of many code-related innovations.[12]

Technology is also allied to force. Technology can be an instrument of force, in one sense, when it allows the state to control without the mediation of a legal regime. The capacity of government to have more complete dossiers on its citizen is a form of national response to the seeming chaos and individuality—increasing attractiveness of new technologies. More, rather than less, governmental surveillance and power appears to be an almost certain outcome of the newest technologies of freedom.

Technology and force unite in cyberwar. Here one can mention the transformation of military strategies, the rise of altered theories of combat, and the impact of so-called psyops (psychological operations). Cyberwar involves actual disruption of the enemies' information space.[13] The US military defines psyops as:

> Planned operations to convey selected information and indicators to foreign audiences to influence their emotions, motives, objective reasoning, and ultimately the behavior of foreign governments, organizations, groups, and individuals. The purpose of psychological operations is to induce or reinforce foreign attitudes and behavior favorable to the originator's objectives.[14]

More and more, training encompasses the idea that in an information society, military operations, like those of governments and corporations, should be constantly working to affect perceptions and loyalties. General Wesley Clark, responsible for much of the Kosovo campaign, in a postconflict speech, suggested that an information war, earlier commenced and effectively conducted, might have been preferable to the bombing campaign that was actually implemented.[15] "[A]chieving information dominance over an adversary will decide conflicts long before resort to more violent forms of warfare is necessary." Much of psyops is contingent on new technology, though the monitoring aspect of military strategy has developed more than the transmission side. Often the last mile or last hundred miles, such as the distribution of information in Bosnia and Afghanistan, is dependent on old models—not Internet, but radio—while the organization and distribution of information to reach that point depend on a revolutionized and more pointed technological capability. The development of psyops, including antiterrorism efforts and cyberwarfare is a part of an information policy that is rarely transparent. Yet, it will become an increasingly significant aspect of the way in which one society seeks to shape the information and media space of another.

Each element of the framework—influences, restrictions, analytic approaches, methods of implementation—demonstrates a movement from the state specific to the multilateral and negotiated. A set of influences is reflected in a package of restrictions. The behavior of governments can be characterized in terms of the appropriate relationship to one of the analytic frameworks. Governments act defensively and actively to influence the media world around them. Analyses along these multiple vectors, and over time, could demonstrate a number of interesting trends or possibilities for evolution. But there are limits on any grid or conceptual approach to analysis.

The response of any given state, at any given time, involves a unique combination of the factors I have just described. As a result governments differ markedly as they face the elements of media globalization. These government styles (often inconsistent and incoherent within any single state) can be seen as arrayed in a spectrum of national response. For example, there are those countries, like the United States, that focus primarily on the export potential of the transformed media landscape; with few if any formal restrictions on the receipt of foreign messages and, until the concern over terrorism and its consequences, seeming but hardly total indifference to the political and cultural impact of such signals at home.

For some countries, there is merely a rhetorical aversion, officially stated, to the deemed fallout of media globalization, but little in the way of state action to affect the distribution of information. In contradistinction, there are those states, often condemned for human rights violations, that fear the impact of unmediated information on their political authority, or those that have a strongly articulated objection to many images of mediated modernity and take action to limit their cultural impact. The Taliban in Afghanistan exhibited their mode of response, at one time, by building bonfires of television sets. Lawrence Rosen, the law and anthropology scholar, has suggested, at least in conversation, that even the most speech restrictive of states—Libya, Iran, and Iraq—increasingly realize that their populations are (relatively speaking) awash in information. These states, Rosen contends, seek to establish or reinforce a set of norms that distinguish between freedom to receive information (where there is more acquiescence by the state) and freedom to express a wide range of views (where controls are retained).

We have seen examples of states that search for ways of allowing the greatest access to global information that would still be consistent with existing content standards. Singapore is emblematic of states that limit—at the direction of the authorities—specific kinds of information, such as pornography or speech, that would be politically destabilizing from coming within their boundaries but, at the same time, actively and aggressively, allow societal access to global databases. They justify their policy choices by reference to a chaotic, rancorous, and now virtually suppressed past. The techniques of restriction that violate specific international norms are important because they are architectural. Singapore comes close to universal access and dense supply of information, but has designed a system in which gatekeepers have a significant tie to the power structure. These states are laboratories to determine whether seemingly conflicting goals can be harmonized. Some countries use the garb of cultural identity to mask economic protectionism. One can invent a category of responses for those countries, and there are many of them that seem to be in no position in terms of power or purpose to block information from coming in and are not positioned to expand, in any significant way, their external programming.

Conclusion

Having described a framework, I conclude with some brief indications of its implications for policy and public understanding. Each element of the framework should reflect global processes of remapping, reconfiguration, and rethinking of media institutions. Most significantly, each element can be evaluated or suffused with a commitment to the freedom to receive and impart information. But inherent in the framework is the idea that as the context for these freedoms alters dramatically, the rhetoric of rights-assertion and the machinery and institutions of defending and defining those rights will have to change as well.

An internationalized set of free speech principles will become more sensitive to what I have called, in this chapter, objects, instruments, justifications, and techniques of restriction. Sensitivity does not mean tolerance to restriction but rather an adjusted means of comprehension and criticism. I have sought to indicate how such a transformation in the structure of distributing imagery, actually occurring in practice, affects the comfortable absolutes that have historically guided analysis. I have emphasized the need for more attention to bilateral and multilateral approaches to speech and speech restrictions, restrictions arrived at, for example, by tacit agreement, convention, or military alliance. It is in recognition of the move to the global and multilateral that international nongovernmental organizations have seized a much more vital role in evaluating media structures and assessing the conduct of governments. At the same time these groups have been actively intervening to modify the environment for the creation and distribution of information. "Media assistance," the process by which funds are channeled, usually from one government to the media sector of a target society, is becoming a larger and more elaborated enterprise. NGOs recognize that in a world where "regulation" is less effective than before as a mode of affecting imagery, positive intervention is often necessary.

Another energizing need, resulting from the restructuring process, is to make the hidden prescriptions of the new information order more transparent. These efforts include spreading the doctrine of freedom of information acts, encouraging scrutiny of emerging rules in transition societies, and, more widely, focusing on areas of less visible rule making, such as customer service agreements with Internet service providers, self-regulation codes of conduct, and technical value-laden code that exists in software. Still too opaque are contracts or their kin reached between states and multinational corporations or informal agreements among states concerning permissible restrictions and enhancements of media institutions There is too little analysis and capacity to react regionally and internationally to the rapidly changing structure of concentration and convergence in media industries. The European Union may informally communicate with the US Department of Justice, but that hardly yields a sufficient global discussion about concentration policies. Nor is it clear that a policy emerges even from that limited process. In the area of "national identity" and free trade, a lively, multilateral debate, with consequences for the shape of the WTO definitely exists.

One possible approach would be a plan of integration leading to a single over-arching international agency with regulatory powers, a glorified and empowered International Telecommunications Union. The articulated commitment to further-ing, yet regulating freedom to receive and impart information is found in a wide array of world capitals. But that does not mean that there will be an effective inter-national regime for enforcing these commitments. Governments are pragmatic; they seek to retain control over information in their countries. Nor are there always the conditions for obtaining an international regulatory regime. As one economist has put it, "Where there have been disagreements about basic principles and norms and where the distribution of power has been highly asymmetrical, international regimes have not developed. Stronger states have simply done what they pleased. Radio broadcasting and remote sensing offer the clearest examples."[16] On the other hand, where the states have a need to coordinate, and where there is agreement on elim-inating mutually undesirable consequences, the chances of international agreement increase.

Much is and should be made of "convergence," in which technological change erodes old categories of thinking. Principles of freedom of speech and of the press (especially of the press) deconstruct as technological change and commercial reali-ties wreak havoc with existing categories of "news," "journalists," and the very institutions of media that have claimed the mantle of the fourth estate. As media, constituting a vital element of the public sphere, transform, it is essential to reex-amine the very authenticity of the surrounding democratic institutions themselves. Media are often key to the way in which political practices are legitimated. If the nature of media changes, then those ultimate practices become subject to challenge as well.

Recent events have revived public discussion on the role of state-sponsored inter-national broadcasting, and this book deals in depth with the patterns of diffusion of its messages across state boundaries (including the use of new technologies and the reinvigorated use of FM). But this study of genres, technologies, and messages of international broadcasting is just the beginning of what is urgently needed: namely a far-reaching discussion about the relationship between state and imagery as opposed to denying that such a relationship exists. In this respect the analytic framework I have outlined suggests that the "marketplace of ideas" or free trade in imagery may now less characterize the relationship between state and imagery than do increased concerns over national identity, national security, and terrorism.

Indrajit Banerjee, reimagining Benedict Anderson and others, has written that "the formation of a nation-state not only requires political and economic solidarity and a sense of shared destiny but also the creation of a collective identity, a symbolic web of shared beliefs, values and norms. . . ."[17] It is that recognition that has justified much of state intervention in the realm of speech and regulation, especially in new and transitional societies. What I have tried to demonstrate in this book is that the identities shaped in this process often have such elaborate consequences for many outside the nation-state that regional and global superpowers, among others, seek to affect their formulation. The existence of external consequences for internal identities, the importance of these symbolic webs, means that such institutions as public service broadcasting have to be reinterpreted. They increasingly have global and diasporic functions as well as their functions within the boundaries of a state. While these directions suggest animated possibilities for their revitalization, the competition from the global, the private, the commercial, points in a less positive direction.

In the spring of 2002, *The New York Times* published a story about Al Jazeera, the transformation of Arab television, and the radicalization of its regional and global audience. The story featured Essam al-Sayed, a neighborhood lawyer in Cairo, as a harbinger of a new transnational audience. After the Israelis began their offensive, al-Sayed and his wife abandoned their normal social life, and each night after he returned from work, "s[a]t and sample[d] the endless Arab programming devoted to Israel's military offensive in the Palestinian territories." They turned off the set only when they heard the first call to prayer, at dawn.[18] *The Times* claimed, somewhat hyperbolically, "The Arab world ha[d] never seen a television moment quite like it," but instances of the power of imagery to cross boundaries and motivate passions are hardly new.

Such permeating images, with their galvanizing effects, have been widely applauded as wholly outside the control of even the most authoritarian leaders. Yet that impulse is incomplete. It is an implication of this chapter's framework that to understand the flow of imagery, one must identify the history of state acquiescence in the new distribution patterns, how governments exploit the transcendence of boundary and hone their methods of control. The system of states reacts and readjusts to a world in which imagery and narrative profoundly affect the regional and global whole. Hearts and minds are shaped in regions, in global sectors, in diasporas, in living rooms, and village viewing spaces everywhere. It does not take much to remind governments that the shape, content, and delivery of speech—especially through television—orchestrates passions and inflames loyalties. Leaders can act free of the pressures caused by public opinion. But more often they seek, separately and together, to affect that power.

Words seem ethereal and ideas ephemeral next to bullets and bombs, but the two modes of interaction seem increasingly linked. Histories of the twentieth century, and now the twenty-first, will rehearse the disparate struggles for the political and religious soul of the world and the violent competition over values and ideas that accompany them. In these struggles, issues of transition, stability, and control are as permeating as principles of freedom, individuality, and creativity. New media giants, new regional alliances, new geopolitics, all conspire in the remapping of information space. The defining interactions of image and society may be in technological flux, but the issues that underlie them never disappear.

Notes

Chapter 1

1. See, for example, David J. Elkins, *Beyond Sovereignty: Territorial and Political Economy in the Twenty-first Century* (Toronto: University of Toronto Press, 1995); Brian Kahin and Charles Nesson, *Borders in Cyberspace* (Cambridge: MIT Press, 1997); David R. Johnson and David Post, "Law and Borders—The Rise of Law in Cyberspace," *Stanford Law Review* 48 (1996): 1367.

2. Of course, all this has a long history. For one survey of twentieth century aspects of the phenomenon, see Fred Fejes, *Imperialism, Media and the Good Neighbor: New Deal Foreign Policy and United States Shortwave Broadcasting to Latin America* (Westport, CT: Ablex Publishing, 1986). The book was published in a series, "Communication and Information Science," edited by Melvin Voigt and included various titles relating to the "cultural imperialism" analysis of Professor Herbert Schiller. See, for example, Kaarle Nordenstreng and Herbert Schiller, *Beyond National Sovereignty: International Communications in the 1990s* (Westport, CT: Ablex Publishing, 1993); Glen Fisher, *American Communication in a Global Society* (Westport, CT: Ablex Publishing, 1987); Howard Frederic, *Cuban–American Radio Wars: Ideology in International Telecommunications* (Westport, CT: Ablex Publishing, 1986).

3. Howard Witt, "US channels voice to wider Arab audience; media war room occupants battle for hearts, minds," *Chicago Tribune*, 23 Dec. 2001, p. 4C.

4. Fouad Ajami, "What the Muslim world is watching," *New York Times Magazine*, 18 Nov. 2001, p. 48.

5. "Australia says no to RFA relays," BBC Summary of World Broadcasts (Nov. 14, 1997, Friday). Section: World Broadcast Information; Australia/US/Vietnam; WBI/0046/WB. Source: Voice of America, Washington, in English 1730 gmt, Nov. 8, 1997.

6. "Angola between war and peace; Arms trade and human rights abuse since the Lusaka Protocol," *Human Rights Watch Publication (HRWP)* 8:1a (Feb. 1996), and "Angola-Peace: Negotiators suspend dicey debate," *Inter Press Service* (Mar. 28, 1994).

7. "Greek radio's new programme for foreign workers," BBC Summary of World Broadcasts (Apr. 17, 1998), Greece/US; WBI/0016/WB. Source: Athens News Agency Web site, in English (Apr. 6, 1998).

8. Announcing that in order to keep reactionary broadcasts off the air, a contract will be signed with broadcasting establishments that have won the tenders [for broadcasting licenses], the Turkish official added: "In that contract I will tell them to sign the following undertaking: 'You will be closed down for good if your broadcasts take aim against the indivisible unity of the state, country, and nation, and if you exploit our sublime religion to promote various interests in violation of the constitution and the laws.' Once they sign that, they cannot say anything if I close them down. But for now we do not have such a signature." World Broadcast Information; Ukraine; WBI/0016/WB Milliyet Web site, Istanbul, in Turkish (Apr. 8, 1998).

9. "Minority issues; Hungarians complain about 'alternative educational system,'" BBC Summary of World Broadcasts (Feb. 8, 1995), Wednesday, World Broadcast Information; Slovakia; EE/222/A. Source: Czechoslovak Press Agency, Prague, in English (Feb. 6, 1995).

10. "RTHK accused of being a 'mouthpiece of the BBC,'" BBC Summary of World Broadcasts (Apr. 10, 1998), Friday, World Broadcast Information; Cyprus; WBI/0015/WB. Source: Wen Wei Po, Hong Kong, in Chinese (Apr. 8, 1998).

11. "Moves against Russian media in CIS reviewed," BBC Summary of World Broadcasts (Apr. 11, 1997), Friday, World Broadcast Information; WBI/0015/WB. Source: *Nezavisimaya Gazeta*, Moscow, in Russian (Mar. 27, 1997).

12. "'Repressive measures' against Russian media," BBC Summary of World Broadcasts (Apr. 18, 1997), Friday, World Broadcast Information; WBI/0016/WB. Source: Voice of Russia, Moscow, in English 1810 gmt (Apr. 10, 1997).

13. "Georgia pulls plug on last remaining Russian channel," BBC Summary of World Broadcasts, (Apr. 2, 1999), Friday, World Broadcast Information; Germany/Yugoslavia; WBI/0014/WB. Source: 'Krasnaya Zvezda', Moscow, in Russian (Mar. 24, 1999).

14. "Information minister defends relay ban," BBC Summary of World Broadcasts, Friday, Oct. 16, 1998, World Broadcast Information; Serbian Ban on Relaying Foreign Broadcasts; WBI/0042/WB. Source: Tanjug News Agency, Belgrade (Oct. 10, 1998).

15. For the text of the communique, see "Communique on North Korean TV viewing decision," BBC Summary of World Broadcasts, Friday, Oct. 29, 1999. World Broadcast Information; Latvia; WBI/0044/WB, Source: South Korean Ministry of Unification communique, Seoul, in Korean (Oct. 22, 1999).

16. Graham Spry, "The decline and fall of Canadian broadcasting," *Queen's Quarterly* 68 (Summer 1961): 213–25.

17. Quoted in Marc Raboy, *Missed Opportunities: The Story of Canada's Broadcasting Policy* (Montreal: McGill–Queen's University Press, 1990), pp. 152–53.

18. Canadian Radio-Television and Telecommunications Commission (CRTC), "Canadian broadcasting—A single system" (1971), pp. 22, 38, 41; Raboy, pp. 215–16.

19. Note, "The country music television dispute: An illustration of the tensions between Canadian Cultural Protectionism and United States entertainment exports," *Minnesota Journal of Global Trade* 6 (1997): 585.

20. Ronald G. Atkey, "Proceedings of the Canada–United States Law Institute Conference: NAFTA Revisited: Canadian Cultural Industries Exemption from NAFTA—Its Parameters," *Canada United States Law Journal* 23 (1997): 177, 185–86.

21. Michael Richardson, "Freeing up Malaysia's airways: Satellite TV grows, but state will retain some control," *International Herald Tribune*, in Neuilly-sur-Seine, France (Jul. 28, 1995).

22. "There is a limit to what the government can do to safeguard the interests of the public. Ultimately, the onus is on each individual to exercise caution and discretion in selecting what is best for himself and his family." Eileen Ng, "Malaysia inches open its airwaves, aims to be top broadcast hub," Agence Presse, Kuala Lumpur, Oct. 6, 1996 (Lexis file).

23. Sabry Sharif and Adrian David, "A giant step in broadcasting for Malaysia," *New Straits Times* (Malaysia), (Jan. 10, 1996): national, 5; "Over RM1.5bn for facilities," *Business Times* (Malaysia) (Jan. 10, 1996): 1.

24. See, for example, Robert Waterman McChesney, *Rich Media, Poor Democracy: Communication Politics in Dubious Times* (Champaign: University of Illinois Press, 2000).

25. See David Atkinson and Marc Raboy, *Public Service Broadcasting: The Challenges of the Twenty-first Century* (Paris: UNESCO, 1997); Michael Tracey, *The Decline and Fall of Public Service Broadcasting* (Oxford: Oxford University Press, 1998).

26. See, for example, Monroe E. Price, A. Richter, and P. Yu, eds., *Russian Media in the Yeltsin Era* (The Hague: Kluwer Law International, 2002); Sevanti Ninan, *Through the Magic Window: Television and Change in India* (New Delhi: Penguin, 1995); and David Page and William Crawley, *Satellites over South Asia—Broadcasting Culture and the Public Interest* (New Delhi: Sage, 2001).

27. See, for example, David Lerner, *The Passing of Traditional Society: Modernizing the Middle East* (New York: Free Press, 1958).

28. See, for example, Anthony Smith, *The Geopolitics of Information: How Western Culture Dominates the World* (London: Faber and Faber, 1980).

29. Pakistani satellite television PTV2 aired freely in India in 1989, but during the Kargil war, the Indian government banned transmission of the channel by the Indian cable broadcasters. See "Telecast of Pak TV banned," *Times of India*, Jun. 11, 1999.

30. See, for example, Colin Sparks and Anna Reading, *Communism, Capitalism and the Mass Media* (London: Sage, 1997).

31. See, for example, Ellen Mickiewicz, *Changing Channels: Television and the Struggle for Power in Russia* (Durham: Duke University Press, 1999).

32. See Emmanuelle Machet, *A Decade of EU Broadcasting Regulation: The Directive "Television without Frontiers"* (Düsseldorf: European Institute for the Media, 1999); Stefaan Verhulst, "European Responses to Media Ownership and Pluralism," *Cardozo Arts and Entertainment Law Journal* 16 (1998): 421, 422.

33. An example of support: Treaty of Amsterdam, section II, chapter 8, (Protocol to the Treaty establishing European Community). Online [Jul. 2001], available: *http://www.itcilo.it/english/actrav/telearn/global/ilo/blokit/eutre4.htm*.

34. See, for example, Rachael Craufurd Smith, *Broadcasting Law and Fundamental Rights* (Oxford: Clarendon Press, 1997); Jay G. Blumler and Wolfgang Hoffmann-Riem, "New roles for public television in Western Europe: Challenges and prospects," *Journal of Communication* 42:1 (1992): 20–35.

35. See, for example, Robert W. McChesney, "Media Convergence and Globalization," in Daya Kishan Thussu, ed., *Electronic Empires: Global Media and Local Resistance* (London: Arnold, 1998), pp. 27–46; and Chris Barker, *Global Television: An Introduction* (Oxford: Blackwell, 1997).

36. See Sevanti Ninan, "History of Indian Broadcasting Reform" in Monroe E. Price and Stefaan Verhulst, eds., *Broadcasting Reform in India—Media Law from a Global Perspective* (New Delhi: Oxford University Press, 1998), pp. 1–21.

37. David Page and William Crawley, *Satellites over South Asia: Broadcasting Culture and the Public Interest* (London: Sage, 2001).

38. See Joseph Man Chan, "Television in greater China: Structure, exports, and market formation," in John Sinclair, Elizabeth Jacka, and Stuart Cunningham, eds., *New Patterns in Global Television: Peripheral Vision* (Oxford: Oxford University Press, 1996), pp. 126–61; Daniel C. Lynch, *After the Propaganda State: Media, Politics, and "Thought Work" in Reformed China* (Stanford: Stanford University Press, 1999).

39. See Shanthi Kalathil and Taylor C. Boas, *The Internet and State Control in Authoritarian Regimes: China, Cuba and the Counterrevolution*, Working paper, Information Revolution and World Politics Project, Carnegie Endowment for International Peace, 2001.

40. For a baseline study of the issues that may arise, see Stephanie Farrior, "Molding The Matrix: The Historical and Theoretical Foundations of International Law Concerning Hate Speech," *Berkeley Journal of International Law* 14 (1996): 3.

41. See, for example, Christopher T. Marsden, ed., *Regulating the Global Information Society* (London: Routledge, 2000).

42. See, for example, Herbert Schiller, *Communications and Cultural Domination* (New York: M.E. Sharpe, 1976).

43. Federal Communications Commission, *A New FCC for the 21st Century* (Washington: 1999).

44. See, for example, Richard W. Leeman, *The Rhetoric of Terrorism and Counterterrorism* (New York: Greenwood Press, 1991); Alex P. Schmid and Janny de Graaf, *Violence as Communication: Insurgent Terrorism and the Western News Media* (London: Sage, 1982); David L. Paletz and Alex P. Schmid, *Terrorism and the Media* (London: Sage, 1992).

45. Monroe E. Price and Mark Thompson, eds., *Forging Peace: Intervention, Human Rights, and the Management of Media Space* (Edinburgh: University of Edinburgh, 2002).

46. RFE/RL was previously Radio Free Europe and Radio Liberty.

47. In the United States, the Telecommunications Act of 1996 purported, in part, to deal with the consequences of new technologies for existing structures and modes of regulation, though it was, in many ways, as much a barrier to transformation as window to change. Monroe E. Price and John F. Duffy, "Technological change and doctrinal persistence: Telecommunications reform in Congress and the Court," *Columbia Law Review* 97 (1997): 976, 992.

48. David Post, "Anarchy and state on the Internet: An essay on law-making in cyberspace," *Journal of Online Law* (1995): art. 3. Online [Jul. 2001], available: *http://www.wm.edu/law/*

publications/jol. Robert L. Dunne, "Deterring unauthorized access to computers: Controlling behaviour in cyberspace through a contract law paradigm," *Jurimetrics: The Journal of Law, Science, and Technology* 35 (1994): 1; I. Trotter Hardy, "The proper legal regime for cyberspace," *University of Pittsburgh Law Review* 55 (1994): 993. For a different argument on the issue, see Keith Aoki, "(Intellectual) property and sovereignty: Notes toward a cultural geography of authorship," *Stanford Law Review* 48 (1996): 1293; Julie Cohen, "A right to read anonymously: A closer look at 'copyright management' in cyberspace," *Connecticut Law Review* 28 (1996): 981; Dan L. Burk, "Federalism in cyberspace," *Connecticut Law Review* 28 (1996): 1095; Lawrence Lessig, "The zones of cyberspace," *Stanford Law Review* 48 (1996): 1403; Margaret Jane Radin, "Property evolving in cyberspace," *Journal of Law and Commerce* 15 (1996): 509.

49. See, for example, A. Michael Froomkin, "The constitution and encryption regulation: Do we need a 'new privacy?'" *New York University School of Law Journal of Legislation and Public Policy* 25 (1999–2000): 3.

50. "Uniting and strengthening America by providing appropriate tools required to intercept and obstruct terrorism" (HR 3162, the "USA Patriot Act") is one major element of post–September 11 antiterrorism legislation. It limits judicial oversight of electronic surveillance by (1) subjecting private Internet communications to a minimal standard of review, (2) permitting law enforcement to obtain what would be the equivalent of a "blank warrant" in the physical world, (3) authorizing intelligence wiretap orders that need not specify the place to be searched or require that only the target's conversations be eavesdropped upon, and (4) allowing the FBI to use its intelligence authority to circumvent the judicial review as might otherwise be required by the probable cause requirement of the Fourth Amendment; see Nat Henthoff, John "Ashcroft v. the Constitution," *Village Voice* Dec. 4, 2001, p. 30. The foreign ministers of the forty-three states of the Council of Europe, in a related legislative act, formally approved a Convention on Cyber Crime in November 2001. The treaty is intended to facilitate the collection of information by requiring companies that provide Internet services to collect and maintain information in case it is needed by law enforcement agencies. It would permit international access to such information by governmental authorities in participating jurisdictions.

51. See Glen O. Robinson, "Symposium: Telecommunications law: Unscrambling the signals, unbundling the law; Article: The new video competition: Dances with regulators," *Columbia Law Review* 97 (May 1997): 1016.

52. See, for example, Stuart Cunningham and John Sinclair, eds., *Floating Lives: The Media and Asian Diasporas* (St. Lucia: University of Queensland Press, 2000); Dona Kolar-Panov, *Video, War and the Diasporic Imaginations* (London: Routledge, 1997); Robin Cohen, *Global Diasporas: An Introduction* (London: University College London Press, 1997); Nicholas Van Hear, *New Diasporas: The Mass Exodus, Dispersal and Regrouping of Migrant Communities* (London: University College London Press, 1998).

53. See Benedict Anderson, *Imagined Communities: Reflections on the Origin and Spread of Nationalism* (London: Verso, 1998 [1983]), instrumental in fashioning discussion of these questions.

54. See, for example, Jamie Frederic Metzl, "Rwandan genocide and the international law of radio jamming," *American Journal of International Law* 91:4 (Oct. 1997): 628–51.

55. See Michael Nelson, *War of the Black Heavens: The Battles of Western Broadcasting in the Cold War* (Syracuse, NY: Syracuse University Press, 1997); John B. Whitton and Arthur Larson, *Propaganda: Towards Disarmament in the War of Words* (Dobbs Ferry: Oceana Publications, 1964).

56. For example, in 1997 the Indian government banned the use of DTH (direct broadcast satellite) technology within India, claiming that it would lead to a cultural invasion. See Ninan, "History of Indian broadcasting reform," in Price and Verhulst, eds. *Broadcasting Reform in India*.

57. John T. Delacourt, "Recent Development: The International Impact of Internet Regulation" *Harvard International Law Journal* 38 (Winter, 1997): 207, 215–18. Delacourt discusses China's attempts at regulating Internet content including their use of firewalls.

58. Act of Apr. 29, 1942, ch. 263, 56 Stat. 248. The US Supreme Court has upheld the Act and its requirement that certain documentaries be labeled as propaganda. See *Meese v. Keene*, 481 US 465 (1987); Note, *Duke Law Journal* (1989): 654.

59. International Convention Concerning the Use of Broadcasting in the Cause of Peace (Sept. 23, 1936): 186 LNTS 301. Article 2.

60. "Principles governing the use by states of artificial earth satellites for international direct television broadcasting," UN General Assembly Resolution, A/RES/37/92. Adopted at 100th plenary meeting, Dec. 10, 1982.

61. See Craufurd Smith, *Broadcasting Law and Fundamental Rights*.

62. Page and Crawley, *Satellites over South Asia*, p. 86, David Mellor "Silence is Golden for Murdoch," *The Guardian*, Apr. 1, 1994.

63. "GCC information ministers voice concern at activities of Al Jazeera TV," BBC Summary of World Broadcasts, Oct. 15, 1999 Friday. World Broadcast Information; Romania; WBI/0042/WB. Source: *Al-Ra'y*, Amman, in Arabic (Oct. 10, 1999). Al Jazeera generated complaints, at the time, from Algerian, Moroccan, Saudi Arabian, Kuwaiti, and Egyptian governments.

64. See Philo C. Wasburn, *Broadcasting Propaganda: International Radio Broadcasting and the Construction of Political Reality* (Westport, CT: Praeger, 1992).

65. See Nelson, *War of the Black Heavens*, and Lawrence C. Soley, *Clandestine Radio Broadcasting: A Study of Revolutionary and Counterrevolutionary Electronic Communication.* (New York: Praeger, 1987).

66. See, for example, Henry P. Pilgert, "Press, radio and film in West Germany 1945–1953," Historical Division of the Office of the United States High Commissioner for Germany, 1953, pp. 74–75; Gerard Braunthal, "Federalism in Germany: The Broadcasting Controversy," *Journal of Politics*, 24, no. 3 (1962): 545–61.

67. Page and Crawley, *Satellites over South Asia*, p. 263.

68. Jack L. Goldsmith, "Against Cyberanarchy," *University of Chicago Law Review* 65 (1998): 1199.

69. International Convention Concerning the Use of Broadcasting in the Cause of Peace (Sept. 23, 1936): 186 LNTS 301. Article 2.

70. Barred programming was that which included material "publicizing ideas of war, militarism, Nazism, national and racial hatred and enmity between peoples as well as material which is immoral or instigative in nature or is otherwise aimed at interfering in the domestic affairs or foreign policy of other States." *Draft Convention on Principles Governing the Use by States of Artificial Earth Satellites for Direct Television Broadcasting*, UN Doc. A/8771 (1972). Article IV.

71. See, for example, David J. Elkins, *Beyond Sovereignty: Territory and Political Economy in the Twenty-first Century* (Toronto: University of Toronto Press, 1995).

72. David Morley and Kevin Robins, *Space of Identity: Global Media, Electronic Landscapes and Cultural Boundaries* (London: Routledge, 1995): 121. A useful discussion is in Marjorie Ferguson, "The mythology about globalisation," *European Journal of Communication* 7 (1992): 69-93.

73. William J. Drake, "Territoriality and Intangibility: Transborder Data Flows and National Sovereignty," in Kaarle Noerdenstreng and Herbert I. Schiller, eds., *Beyond National Sovereignty* (Westport, CT: Ablex Publishing, 1993), pp. 259, 270.

74. Ithiel de Sola Pool, *Technologies of Freedom: On Free Speech in an Electronic Age* (Cambridge, MA: Belknap Press, 1983).

Chapter 2

1. See, for example, Jerry Everard, *Virtual States: The Internet and the Boundaries of the Nation-State* (Oxford: Routledge, 1999).

2. See Julian Borger "Cyberwar could spare bombs; NATO Commander Wesley Clark boosts the case for telecom assaults with a vision of how they might have been used in Kosovo," *Guardian*, Nov. 5, 1999, p. 17.

3. One of Ronald H. Coase's early economic analyses of law showed how regulation in Britain was used to limit competition from radio signals originating in France and Luxembourg. See Ronald H. Coase, *British Broadcasting: A Study in Monopoly* (Cambridge: Harvard University Press, 1950). What became the British Broadcasting Corporation emerged, in part, as a legal expression of fear that unregulated transborder data flow might injure British nationhood.

4. See "President pushes TV Marti; ITU pushes back," *Broadcasting*, Apr. 9, 1990, pp. 37–38, reprinting message from International Frequency Registration Board (IFRB), an arm of the ITU to the State Department concerning the legality of TV Marti, the American initiative to bring its television to Cuba. See also S. Ruth, Comment, "The regulation of spillover transmission from direct broadcast satellites in Europe," *Federal Communications Law Journal* 42 (1989): 107.

5. For a general illustration of different approaches to the problem, see Daya Kishan Thussu, *International Communication: Continuity and Change* (London: Arnold Press, 2000); Denis McQuail, *McQuail's Mass Communication Theory*, 4th ed. (London: Sage, 2000); Mike Feintuck, *Media Regulation, Public Interest and the Law* (Edinburgh: Edinburgh University Press, 1999); Arjun Appadurai, *Modernity at Large: Cultural Dimensions of Globalization*

(Minneapolis: University of Minnesota Press, 1996); Tony Spybey, *Globalization and World Society* (Cambridge: Polity Press, 1996); Philip M. Taylor, *Global Communications, International Affairs and the Media since 1945* (London: Routledge, 1997); Paddy Scannell, Philip Schlesinger, and Colin Sparks, eds., *Culture and Power: A Media, Culture and Society Reader* (London: Sage, 1992); Annabelle Sreberny-Mohammadi, Dwayne Winseck, Jim McKenna, and Oliver Boyd-Barrett, *Media in Global Context: A Reader* (London: Arnold, 1997); Ian Clark, *Globalization and Fragmentation: International Relations in the Twentieth Century* (Oxford: Oxford University Press, 1997); Peter J. S. Dunnett, *The World Television Industry: An Economic Analysis* (London: Routledge, 1999); Francis Fukuyama, *The End of History and the Last Man* (London: Hamish Hamilton, 1992); Nicholas Garnham, *Capitalism and Communication: Global Structure and the Economics of Information* (London: Sage, 1990); Peter Holding and Phil Harris, *Beyond Cultural Imperialism: Globalisation, Communication, and the New International Order* (London: Sage, 1997); Edward S. Herman and Robert Waterman McChesney, *The Global Media: The New Missionaries of Corporate Capitalism* (London: Cassell, 1997); Samuel P. Huntington, *The Clash of Civilizations and the Remaking of World Order* (New York: Simon and Schuster, 1996); Thomas L. Friedman, *The Lexus and the Olive Tree* (London: HarperCollins, 1999); Stephen Krasner, *Sovereignty: Organized Hypocrisy* (Princeton: Princeton University Press, 1999); Robert O. Keohane and Joseph S. Nye, *Power and Interdependence*, 3rd ed. (London: Longman, 2001); Ronald Robertson, *Globalization: Social Theory and Global Culture* (London: Sage, 1992).

6. See Monroe E. Price, *Television: The Public Sphere and National Identity* (Oxford: Clarendon Press, 1995).

7. In developing a framework for comparative analysis of European media, Karen Siune et al. defined policy making as "a reaction to a challenge, a reaction that is intended to find a reasonable balance between 'forces of change' and 'forces of preservation.'" The authors also stated that "[i]n the current process of adaptation to technological progress public action strategies in most European countries may seem to be a reaction to the risk of disintegration, especially in cultural matters, in the broadest sense." See chapter 2 of Denis McQuail and Karen Siune, eds., *New Media Politics: Comparative Perspectives in Western Europe* (London: Sage, 1986).

8. Monroe E. Price, "The market for loyalties: Electronic media and the global competition for allegiances," *Yale Law Journal* 104 (1994): 667, 669–70.

9. See, for example, Huntington, *The Clash of Civilizations*. The rush for various states to have a satellite channel presence is evidence of this competition.

10. See Margaret A. Blanchard, *Exporting the First Amendment: The Press–Government Crusade, 1945–1952* (New York: Longman 1986).

11. Michael Keating, *Nations against the State: The New Politics of Nationalism in Quebec, Catalonia and Scotland* (London: Macmillan, 1996).

12. See, generally, Kenneth Dyson and Peter Humphreys, eds., *The Political Economy of Communications: International and European Dimensions* (London: Routledge, 1990).

13. Especially the quota measure (e.g., 50 percent of European works) was controversial. Immediately after the Broadcasting Directive was formally adopted, the United States

objected that some parts of the measure were contrary to the General Agreement on Tariffs and Trade (GATT). Shortly thereafter, US officials filed a trade complaint with GATT to protest the Directive's quota clause as an "unfair trade practice." Responding to the US complaint, the EC argued that the Directive did not come within the scope of GATT, since, first, GATT rules did not apply to services and, second, the quota principle was intended to protect cultural sovereignty, and thus could well be exempt from the usual GATT restrictions. See, Kelley L. Wilkins, "Television without frontiers: An EEC broadcasting premiere," *Boston College International and Comparative Law Review* 14 (1991): 195.

Other issues discussed at the 1994 Uruguay Round (GATT), at which the United States regarded the EU as behaving in a discriminatory fashion, were (1) subsidies for the sector and (2) the blank-tapes levy. At the last moment, the audiovisual sector was removed from the GATT at the request of France.

14. Sevanti Ninan, *Through the Magic Window: Television and Change in India* (New Delhi: Penguin, 1995); David Page and William Crawley, *Satellites over South Asia—Broadcasting Culture and the Public Interest* (New Delhi: Sage, 2001); Monroe E. Price and Stefaan Verhulst, eds., *Broadcasting Reform in India: Media Law from a Global Perspective* (New Delhi: Oxford University Press, 1998).

15. Price and Verhulst, *Broadcasting Reform in India*, p. 275.

16. Quoted in Page and Crawley, *Satellites over South Asia*, p. 266.

17. In particular, the Indian government was critical of BBC's decision to broadcast a news feature about Muslim–Hindu communal violence in 1992, claiming that their reporting and programming contributed to resulting riots. See Bob Drogin, "Profile: The BBC's battered Sahib; Mark Tully has been expelled by India, chased by mobs and picketed. He loves his job." *Los Angeles Times*, Dec. 22, 1992, p. 4; "Religion and Communications; Feeding Fundamentalism," *Economist*, Aug. 21, 1993, p. 45.

18. See Sevanti Ninan "Part I: Background; Chapter 1: History of Indian broadcasting reform," *Cardozo Journal of International and Comparative Law* 5 (fall 1997): 341; Mark N. Templeton "Part II: The Bill and comparative media law; Chapter 4: A human rights perspective in the broadcasting bill debate," *Cardozo Journal of International and Comparative Law* 5 (fall 1997): 401; Committee of Secretaries, India, Appendix I: Minutes of the Meeting of Committee of Secretaries, *Cardozo Journal of International and Comparative Law* 5 (fall 1997): 669.

19. Asu Aksoy and Kevin Robins, "Gecekondu-style broadcasting in Turkey: A confrontation of cultural values," *InterMedia* (Jun.–Jul. 1993), 15. See also Haluk Sahin and Asu Aksoy, "Global media and cultural identity in Turkey," *Journal of Communications* 43 (1992): 31.

20. Eli Noam, *Television in Europe* (Oxford: Oxford University Press, 1991), p. 258.

21. Noam, *Television in Europe*.

22. For an understanding of these issues, see Steven H. Shiffrin, *The First Amendment, Democracy and Romance* (Cambridge, MA: Harvard University Press, 1990).

23. The notion of elasticity of demand comes into play here. Sellers of ordinary goods often want to know whether and how much an increase in price will decrease demand for their

product. Manufacturers of national identities, including the state itself must (in the economic model) ask the same question.

24. See Cecelia Tichi, *Electronic Hearth: Creating an American Television Culture* (Oxford: Oxford University Press, 1991).

25. See, for example, Report of the President's Task Force on United States Government International Broadcasting: Hearings before the Subcomm. on International Operations of the House Committee on Foreign Affairs, 102d Congress, 2d Session 9 (1992). See Charles F. Gormly, "The United States Information Agency domestic dissemination ban: Arguments for repeal," *Administrative Law Journal of American University* 9 (1995): 191.

26. See Marika N. Taishoff, *State Responsibility and the Direct Broadcast Satellite* (London: Pinter, 1987), p. 13, for a discussion of states that see advertisements as a threat. "Foreign-made" images are usually labeled "American" for convenience, though they may originate from many sources and from companies that are not controlled by US citizens. The influence of Western television and foreign made images are certainly considered subversive in many parts of the Islamic world.

27. Theodor W. Adorno, *The Cultural Industry: Selected Essays on Mass Culture* (London: Routledge, 1991); Theodor W. Adorno and Max Horkheimer, *Dialectic of Enlightenment* (London: Verso, 1979); Thussu, *International Communication*, pp. 68–70.

28. Albert O. Hirschman, *Exit, Voice, and Loyalty* (Cambridge, MA: Harvard, 1970).

29. Hirschman, *Exit, Voice, and Loyalty*, p. 30.

30. In some contexts "voice" may be effectively exercised through song or sermon or smuggled audiotapes.

31. Hirschman, *Exit, Voice, and Loyalty*, p. 82.

32. Hirschman, *Exit, Voice, and Loyalty*, p. 79.

33. "Only as countries start to resemble each other because of the advances in communication and all-round modernization will the danger of premature and excessive exits arise, the 'brain drain' being a current example." At that point, "a measure of loyalty will stand us in good stead." Hirschman, *Exit, Voice, and Loyalty*, p. 81.

34. Duncan Campbell, "Bush goes looking for love—Among illegal immigrants," *The Guardian*, Tuesday, Aug. 7, 2001, p. 16.

35. Daan Everts, "Speech on the occasion of the opening of the new studios of the Radio Television Kosovo," Feb. 16, 2000.

36. This more aggressive approach was without regard to distinctions between different forms of media (electronic or print).

37. See Larry Diamond, *Developing Democracy: Toward Consolidation* (Baltimore: Johns Hopkins Press, 1999). Related is the "modernization" theory, the notion that "international mass communication could be used to spread the message of modernity and transfer the economic and political models of the West to the newly independent countries of the South." See Thussu, *International Communication*, p. 56. For modernization literature, see Daniel Lerner, *The Passing of Traditional Society* (New York: Free Press, 1958); Wilbur Schramm, *Mass Media and National Development: The Role of Information in the Developing Countries* (Palo Alto: Stanford University Press, 1964).

38. See Monroe Price, Beata Rozumilowicz, and Stefaan Verhulst, *Media Reform: Democratizing the Media, Democratizing the State* (London: Routledge, 2001).

39. See Juan J. Linz and Alfred Stepan, *Problems of Democratic Transition and Consolidation: Southern Europe, South American, and Post-Communist Europe* (Baltimore: Johns Hopkins Press, 1996).

40. See Zbigniew Brzezinski, "Polska scena obrotowa," *Polityka*, no 44 (Oct. 29, 1994). Brzezinski's analysis is set forth by Karol Jakubowicz, "Media in transition: The case of Poland," in Price, Rozumilowicz, and Verhulst, eds., *Media Reform*.

41. See, Mark Drumbl, "Post-genocide: From guilt to shame to civis in Rwanda," *New York University Law Review* 75 (2000): 1221 at p. 1306; Richard Joseph, ed., *State, Conflict, and Democracy in Africa* (Boulder, CO: Reiner, 1999), pp. 339, 339.

42. Diamond describes the role of the press in Nigeria, a country with an intermittent history of authoritarianism as opposed to a linear unidirectional transition. He writes, "the press has kept alive the commitment to democracy and has sought to establish some kind of accountability during periods of authoritarian rule" (pp. 388–89). Larry Diamond, "Nigeria: Pluralism, statism, and the struggle for democracy," in Larry Diamond, Juan J. Linz, and Seymour Martin Lipset, eds., *Politics in Developing Countries: Comparing Experiences with Democracy* (Boulder, CO: Riener, 1990).

43. See Monroe E. Price and Peter Krug, *The Enabling Environment for Free and Independent Media* (Washington: US Agency for International Development, Office of Democracy and Governance, 2002). Online [January 2002] available: *http://www.usaid.gov/democracy/pdfs/pnacm006.pdf*.

44. Katarina Tomaševski describes the focus on elections as follows: "Compared with the investment necessary to develop human rights infrastructure and protection, elections offered a fast and easy option. Donors' accomplishments are easily quantified by the number of countries, which have been transformed into democracies, and their number increased accordingly. *Parkinson's Law* would classify such numbers as fiction, or perhaps as ideology, because they disguise rather than describe reality." Katarina Tomaševski, *Between Sanctions and Elections: AID Donors and Their Human Rights Performance* (Washington: Pinter, 1997). Similarly Slavko Spichal writes: "The process of democratization in Central and Eastern Europe is still primarily related to the issue of the formal right to participate in decision-making (that is, general elections). The representative parliamentary system (re)established after political revolutions is seen as the sufficient condition required for democracy to flourish. For genuine democratization, however, the extension of *contexts* in which citizens can exercise their right to participate in decision making is of paramount importance." Slavko Spichal, *The "Civil Society Paradox" and the Media in Central and Eastern Europe* (Greenwich, CT: JAI Press, 1993), pp. 85–109.

45. Speaking of foreign aid in general, Rubén Berríos writes that the "political self-interest argument is based on the notion that aid will strengthen the political commitment of the recipient to the donor. Since foreign aid is often utilized as a tool of foreign policy by a donor country, the allocation patterns often reflect national self-interests. In the case of the United States, strategic political considerations have been a major motivation for aid." Rubén Berríos, *Contracting for Development: The Role of For-profit Contractors in US Foreign Development Assistance.* (Westport, CT: Praeger, 2000), p. 19.

46. Blanchard, *Exporting the First Amendment*, p. 1.

47. See, for example, Lawrence E. Harrison and Samuel P. Huntington, *Culture Matters: How Values Shape Human Progress* (New York: Basic Books, 2000).

48. Diamond, Linz, and Lipset, eds., *Politics in Developing Countries*.

49. Thussu, *International Communication*, ch. 2.

50. There is a different kind of instrumental utility. It may be instrumentally useful for an authoritarian society to adopt a progressive media law if that is the price of entry into world trading markets or the obtaining of foreign loans or benefits; it may be instrumentally useful for Western democracies to insist on competition so as to weaken the hold of a former monopoly state broadcaster.

51. For a discussion of the relationship among domestic structures of a target state, the nature of its political institutions, state–society relations and values or norms embedded in its political structure, see Thomas Risse-Kappen, "Ideas do not float freely: Transnational coalitions, domestic structures and the end of the cold war," in *International Organization* (spring 1994): 185–214. This is developed by Jessica Stalnaker in "International media assistance and Bosnian civil society: Localization as the missing link" (unpublished paper, American University, 2000).

52. Bryant Garth and Austin Sarat, eds., *How Does Law Matter?* (Evanston, IL: Northwestern University Press, 1998), p. 2.

53. See Rudolph W. Giuliani, "The next phase of quality of life: Creating a more civil city" (speech, Feb. 24, 1998) Online [Jul. 2001] Available: *http://www.nyc.gov/html/om/html/98a/quality.html*.

54. See Mark Thompson and Dan De Luce, "Escalating to success? The media intervention in Bosnia and Herzegovina," in Monroe E. Price and Mark Thompson, eds., *Forging Peace: Intervention, Human Rights, and the Management of Media Space* (Edinburgh: Edinburgh University Press, 2002).

Chapter 3

1. Bernard J. Hibbitts, "Making Sense of Metaphors: Visuality, Aurality, and the Reconfiguration of American Legal Discourse," *Cardozo Law Review* 16 (1994): 229; Paul Ricoeur, *The Rule of Metaphor,* trans. by Robert Czerny (Toronto: University of Toronto Press, 1981), pp. 207–15; Milner S. Ball, *Lying Down Together: Law, Metaphor and Theology (Rhetoric of the Human Sciences)* (Madison: University of Wisconsin Press, 1985).

2. See the arguments of those who contend that freedom of expression and openness is employed as an ideology to be used or abused by different groups in society. F. Schauer, "The First Amendment as ideology," in David Allen and Robert Jensen, eds., *Freeing the First Amendment* (New York: New York University Press, 1995).

3. Thomas Franck, "The Emerging Right to Democratic Governance," *American Journal of International Law* 86 (1992): 46, 48.

4. See, generally, Jonathan Weinberg, "Broadcasting and Speech," *California Law Review* 81 (1993): 1103; Eric M. Barendt, *Broadcasting Law: A Comparative Study* (Oxford: Clarendon Press, 1993).

5. Julie Mertus, "Review of *Human Rights: Group Defamation, Freedom of Expression and the Law of Nations: What International and Domestic Laws Can Teach the United States,* by Thomas David Jones," *Houston Journal of International Law* 21 (Spring 1999): 581. See also Alan Watson, *Legal Transplants: An Approach to Comparative Law,* 2nd ed. (Athens: University of Georgia Press, 1993). Legal transplants involve "the moving of a rule or a system of law from one country to another, or from one people to another."

6. Michael J. Farley, "Conflicts over government control of information—The United States and UNESCO," *Tulane Law Review* 59 (1985): 1071; Kusum Singh and Bertram Gross, " 'MacBride': The report and the response," *Journal of Communication* 31 (1981): 104, 113; Mustapha Masmoudi, "The new world information order," *Journal of Communications* 29 (1979): 172, 178; Fred H. Cate, "The First Amendment and the international 'free flow' of information," *Virginia Journal of International Law* 30 (1990): 401.

9. Samuel P. Huntington, *The Clash of Civilizations and the Remaking of World Order* (New York: Touchstone, 1998).

8. See Peter De Cruz, *Comparative Law in a Changing World* (London: Cavendish, 1995), pp. 486–87.

5. See, for example, John M. Maki, "The Japanese constitutional style," *Washington Law Review* 43 (1968): 893, 898.

10. There was a "development" model for broadcasting, less about freedom and the public sphere and more about the distribution of information about farming, skill development and education. See, for example, G. C. Awasthy, *Broadcasting in India* (London: Allied, 1965), pp. 98–110.

11. Lis Wiehl, "Constitution, anyone? A new cottage industry," *The New York Times,* Feb. 2, 1990, p. B6. James A. Gardner, *Legal Imperialism: American Lawyers and Foreign Aid in Latin America* 14 (1980) [quoting from Karl N. Llewellyn, "The crafts of law revisited," *Rocky Mountain Mineral Law Institute* 15 (1942), pp. 1, 3]: "The essence of our crafts-manship lies in skills, and wisdoms; in practical, effective, persuasive, inventive skills for getting things done, any kind of thing in any field; in wisdom and judgment in selecting the things to get done; in skills for moving men into desired action, any kind of man, in any field. . . . We are the trouble shooters."

12. Mertus, Review of *Human Rights,* p. 585.

13. A thorough and critical account appears in Amy L. Chua, "Markets, democracy and ethnicity: Toward a new paradigm for law and development," *Yale Law Journal* 108 (1998): 1.

14. For a relatively early discussion of these models, see Charles A. Siepman, *Radio, Television and Society* (New York: Oxford University Press, 1950), p. 114.

15. See Monroe E. Price, B. Rozumilowicz, and Stefaan Verhulst, *Media Reform: Democratizing the Media, Democratizing the State* (London: Routledge, 2001).

16. James A. Gardner, *Legal Imperialism: American Lawyers and Foreign Aid in Latin America* (Madison: University of Wisconsin, 1980), pp. 21–22.

17. Monroe E. Price and Stefaan Verhulst, eds., *Broadcast Reform in India: A Case Study in Comparative Media Regulation* (Oxford: Oxford University Press, 1998).

18. "Survey of national broadcasting, cable and DTH satellite laws," *Cardozo Journal of International and Comparative Law* 7 (1997): 715.

19. As indicated in chapter 1, the US ambassador helped support a coalition of US television interests who sought to shape the Indian legislation. In that sense a more direct effort at bringing the US model was in play.

20. *Secretary, Ministry of Info. and Broad. v. Cricket Ass'n of Bengal* (1995) 2 S.C.C. 161 (Hero Cup case).

21. Mark Thompson and Dan De Luce, "Escalating to success? The media intervention in Bosnia and Herzegovina," in Monroe E. Price and Mark Thompson, eds., *Forging Peace: Intervention, Human Rights, and the Management of Media Space* (Edinburgh: Edinburgh University Press, 2002).

22. Enlargement of the European Union, Enlargement Task Force: "The European Parliament in the Enlargement Process," Briefing no. 47, Audiovisual Policy and the Community *Acquis*. Online [May 2001], available:
http://www.europarl.eu.int/enlargement/briefings/47a2_en.htm.

23. I have written about this subject in chapter 5 of my book, *Television, Public Sphere and National Identity* (Oxford: Oxford University Press, 1996). See also Marina Ottaway and Thomas Carothers, eds., *Funding Virtue: Civil Society Aid and Democracy Promotion* (Washington: Carnegie Endowment for International Peace, 2000); Molly Stephenson, "F.Y.I.: Real property lawyers promote reform in Central Europe," *ABA Section of Real Property, Probate, and Trust Law, Probate and Property* (May–Jun. 1997): 12; Joan Davison, "America's impact on constitutional change in Eastern Europe," *Albany Law Review* 55 (1992): 793, 793–94; Charles-Edward Anderson, "Exporting democracy: US lawyers help Eastern Europe draft new constitutions," *ABA Journal* (Jun. 1990): 18; Gianmaria Ajani, "By chance and prestige: Legal transplants in Russia and Eastern Europe," *American Journal of Comparative Law* 43 (1995): 93.

24. For a few representative examples, see Arthur Goldstuck, "Non-English net user numbers increasing," *Africa News*, Aug. 13, 1999; "Multilanguage Web addresses in final test phase," *Agence France Presse*, Jan. 23, 2001; and "End English monopoly on Internet: Prof. Menon," *The Hindu*, Mar. 4, 2001.

25. Harold Bloom, *A Map of Misreading* (Oxford: Oxford University Press, 1980): 69.

26. See, for example, C. Edwin Baker, "Giving the audience what it wants," *Ohio State Law Journal* 58 (1997): 311.

27. For a general essay on the decline of the Fairness Doctrine, see Thomas G. Krattenmaker and L. A. Powe Jr., "Comment: The Fairness Doctrine today: A constitutional curiosity and impossible dream," *Duke Law Journal* 151 (1985).

28. Dana Bullen and Rosalind Stark, *Perverse Result: How the European Convention on Human Rights Supports Global Restrictions on Press Freedom* (Reston, VA: World Press Freedom Committee, 1997).

29. William Powers Jr., "Commentary: Judging Judging," *Valparaiso University Law Review* 28 (1994), p. 857.

30. Mertus, Review of *Human Rights*, p. 586.

31. See, for example, Eugene Volokh, "Cheap speech and what it will do," *Yale Law Journal* 104 (1995): 1805.

32. The ancient definition of the port (i.e., *portus*) is "a place through which merchandise was carried." In this sense the routes and ports of the system of satellite communication can be compared to their terrestrial predecessors. Karl Polanyi, "Ports of trade in early societies," *Journal of Economic History*, 23 (1963): 30; Phillip D. Curtin, *Cross-cultural Trade in World History* (Cambridge: Cambridge University Press, 1984): pp. 13–14.

33. For an interesting early article, see The Georgetown Space Law Group, "DBS under FCC and international regulation," *Vanderbilt Law Review* 37 (1984): 67.

34. Eugene Van Cleef, *Trade Centers and Trade Routes* (New York: Appleton-Century, 1937).

35. A. H. Quiggin, *Trade Routes, Trade and Currency in East Africa: The Occasional Papers of the Rhodes-Livingstone Museum*, Rhodes-Livingstone Museum (1949); A. Kumar, *Java and Modern Europe: Ambiguous Encounters* (London: Curzon, 1997); T. Raychaudhuri, *Jan Company in Coromandel, 1605–1690: A Study in the Interrelations of European Commerce and Traditional Economies* (Dordrecht: Martinus Nijhoff, 1962).

36. Michael J. Finch, "Limited Space: Allocating the Geostationary Orbit," *Northwest Journal of International Law and Business*, 7 (1986): 788.

37. The focus of this section is on geostationary satellites, which, for a long time, had been virtually the only kind of satellites operating commercially. Commercial operations by low earth orbit (LEO) satellites have now been added. For these satellites the concept of orbital slots is entirely irrelevant, but the concept of orbital planes may nonetheless make the trade route metaphor relevant. The orbital paths taken by LEO constellations are not randomly selected but rather are intended to traverse the major population zones of the world. In addition the satellites themselves typically are designed with steerable antennas, which enable them to focus on populated areas even as the satellites move in and out of direct viewable range.

38. Monroe E. Price, "The market for loyalties: Electronic media and the global competition for allegiances," *Yale Law Journal* 104 (1994): 667.

39. The classic example is the "spice trade," the route from China and Southeast Asia through to Europe developed by Asian, Middle Eastern, and Mediterranean traders. Only comparatively small quantities of pepper and spices, in comparison to other cargoes, were transported along this route. Their high ratio of value to weight not only made the trips worthwhile (even circumnavigation around Africa or across the Pacific) but determined the routes and stops at ports of call as well. Phillip D. Curtin, *Cross Cultural Trade in World History* (Cambridge: Cambridge University Press, 1984), pp. 131, 143–44.

40. Jonathan I. Ezor, "Costs overhead: Tonga's claiming of sixteen geostationary orbital sites and the implications for US space policy," *Law and Policy in International Business* 24 (1993): 915–16.

41. Jannat C. Thompson, "Space for rent: The International Telecommunications Union, space law, and orbit/spectrum leasing," *Journal of Air Law and Communications*, 62 (1996): 279, 288; M. L. Stern, "Communications satellites and the geostationary orbit: Reconciling equitable access with efficient use," *Law and Policy of International Business* 14 (1982): 859, 864.

42. The ITU (originally the International Telegraphic Union) was established in 1865. It has sought to encourage cooperation among its member countries to improve global

telecommunications and offer technical assistance to developing countries. Its Radio Conferences, held every second year, allocates orbital space to member countries. The classic history is G. Codding Jr. and A. Rutkowski, *The International Telecommunication Union in a Changing World* (Norwood, MA: Artech 1982).

43. Stephen Gorove, *Developments in Space Law: Issues and Policies* (Dordrecht: Martinus Nijhoff, 1991).

44. Gregory C. Staple, "The new world satellite order: A report from Geneva," *American Journal of International Law* 80 (1986): 699.

45. The ITU structure that exists for registration of orbital slots developed in a telecommunications environment in which each country, including the United States at the outset, was the single monopoly carrier for virtually all telecommunications traffic. This "club" of carriers created Intelsat as a cooperative intended to establish satellite links among the monopolies, much as the same club members had created undersea cable links among themselves. The theory was that each country, through (typically) its government-owned monopoly, would control the domestic orbital slots over its own region, while Intelsat would control the international slots. The ITU orbital slot registration process made more sense when a telecommunications monopoly model existed than when a more open, competitive approach evolved.

46. Robert Keith-Reid, "Tonga pushes for Pacific-owned communications network," *Associated Press Newsfeed*, Mar. 11, 1998.

47. Phillip D. Curtin, *Cross-cultural Trade*, pp. 251–52.

48. In the late 1970s and early 1980s, as the owner of the largest US Spanish-language television network, Anselmo sought to import Spanish-language programming from Latin America. Because the transmission of this programming would be international, the FCC required Anselmo's network to use Intelsat for the transmissions, even though US domestic satellites were technically capable of carrying the traffic and would have done it at rates that were 50 percent or less of Intelsat's. Although the US government eventually allowed some transborder communications via US domestic satellites, Anselmo became so enraged that he decided to compete directly with Intelsat in the provision of international satellite services.

49. "PanAmSat lobbies FCC for greater freedom." *FinTech Telecom Markets*, Jul. 26, 1990.

50. There is an important relationship—illustrative of the legal creation of sites—between Anselmo's PanAmSat and the legal adventurousness of Tongasat. When Anselmo and others filed at the FCC in the early to mid-1980s for what were then called "separate system" licenses (because they were "separate" from the Intelsat system), the issue of orbital slots serving international routes first arose. If, indeed, it would be possible to compete directly with Intelsat, then orbital slots over the oceans—which theretofore had been of interest solely to Intelsat—were suddenly of great potential value. Tongasat, led at that time by an American entrepreneur, was one of the first to recognize this potential, and to recognize that the ITU's procedures essentially allowed any nation, no matter how small, to file for large numbers of these valuable slots.

51. This slot was valuable even though Astra already had six satellites at 19 degrees East for two reasons. First, they needed to have three degrees of separation or they have to share

frequencies, reducing their value; second, because most DBS dishes are in a fixed position, the introduction of competition in delivery to those dishes undermines monopoly rent.

52. "Eutelsat promotes 290 East slot," *Cable and Satellite Express* (Mar. 26, 1998): p. 9, available in LEXIS World Library, ALLWLD File; "Hostilities resumed in SES-Eutelsat Star Wars," *Cable and Satellite Europe*, Apr. 1998.

53. "Alfa TV—a multilingual satellite TV for Europe and FSU," BBC Summary of World Broadcasts, Jan. 16, 1998.

54. *Regina v. Secretary of State for the National Heritage ex parte Continental Television BV* (Apr. 30, 1993): [1993] CMLR 387 (dismissing an appeal from a denial of injunction to prevent the United Kingdom from banning reception, viewing, and advertising of pornographic channel Red Hot Television emanating from Denmark).

55. The point is significant from a constitutional perspective. See Eric B. Easton, "Closing the barn door after the genie's out of the Bag: Recognizing a futility principle in First Amendment jurisprudence," *DePaul Law Review* 45 (1995): 1.

56. "Satellite Circuit," *Satellite News* 22, no. 22, May 31, 1999.

57. "GCC information ministers voice concern at activities of Al-Jazeera TV," Al-Ra'y, Amman, in Arabic Oct. 10, 1999 (BBC World Media Monitoring Service). Al Jazeera was long championed by *New York Times* columnist, Thomas L. Friedman. "[I]n a region where the evening news for decades has been endless footage of Arab leaders greeting each other at the airport, and singing each other's praises, it is no wonder that Al-Jazeera, with its real news and real opinions, has every Arab with a satellite dish trying to bring in its signal and every Arab leader gnashing his teeth. Libya, Tunisia and Morocco have all broken diplomatic relations with Qatar at times after being criticized by Al-Jazeera." Thomas L. Friedman, "Glasnost in the Gulf," *New York Times*, Feb. 27, 2001, p. 23.

58. Naomi Sakr, "Frontiers of freedom: Diverse responses to satellite television in the Middle East and North Africa," *Public/Javnost: Journal of the European Institute for Communication and Culture* 6: 1 (1999): 102–103.

59. "Turkey calls on USA to end MED-TV broadcasts," BBC Summary of World Broadcasts, Friday, Aug. 30, 1996; "MED-TV off the air after UK, Belgian police raids," *BBC Summary of World Broadcasts*, Friday, Sept. 27, 1996; "Turkish premier discusses MED-TV with Tony Blair," *BBC Summary of World Broadcasts*, Dec. 19, 1997; A. Hassanpour, "Med-TV, Britain, and the Turkish state: A stateless nation's quest for sovereignty in the sky" (unpublished paper presented at the Freie Universitat Berlin, Nov. 7, 1995).

60. A successor, Medya-TV, opened in the summer of 1999, but under different legal circumstances. Source: BBC: Monitoring research (Jul. 30–Aug. 3, 1999). "A new Paris-based Kurdish satellite television station identifying itself as Medya TV has been observed since 30th Jul. It broadcasts via the Eutelsat Hot Bird 4 satellite at 13 degrees east (10853 MHz vertical polarization, audio subcarrier 6.65 MHz). This transponder also carries Kurdish and Christian programming from the UK-based CTV (Cultural TV). News bulletins formerly carried on CTV appear to have transferred to Medya TV along with some of the presenters. . . . Medya TV carried a live relay of its official launch ceremony in Paris. The ceremony was held in a hall with the Medya logo depicted in laser lights as the stage backdrop. Two large screens on either side of the stage showed the musicians and the announcers, who spoke in

Kurdish. What appeared to be a message marking the launching of the station by Kurdish National Congress President Serif Canli was carried at 1710 GMT. It was followed by a similar message in Kurdish from Yasar Kaya, president of the Kurdish parliament-in-exile." WBI, Oct. 21, 1999.

61. Ronald G. Atkey, "Canadian cultural industries exemption from Nafta—its parameters," *Canadian-United States Law Journal* 23 (1997): 177, 193. "In the recently concluded WTO negotiations on basic telecommunication services, Canada retained a 46.7 percent limit on foreign ownership, a requirement for Canadian control of basic telecom facilities, and a routing restriction to promote the use of Canadian facilities for domestic traffic. The routing restrictions are with regard to both domestic Canadian and international traffic, but the international traffic restrictions will be phased out over time. These restrictions have implications for cultural industries given the likelihood in this age of convergence of the telcos being permitted to be carriers of entertainment product in competition with the cable companies." Atkey, "Canadian cultural industries exemption from Nafta," p. 192.

62. For a news account, see David Orenstein, "Border feud foils broadcast venture," *Albany Times Union*, Nov. 16, 1996, p. B11. For a more formal discussion of the ownership issues, see Robert L. Hoegle, "Foreign ownership caps and the WTO agreement: The movement toward 'one size fits all'," *CommLaw Conspectus* 6 (1998): 65.

63. Ayatollah Mohammed Emani Kashani, "West interested in transfer not of technology but of corruption," BBC summary of world broadcasts, Monday, Sept. 19, 1994; The Middle East; Iran; ME/2104/MED.

64. John Lynch, "The origins of Spanish American independence," in Leslie Bethell, ed., *Cambridge History of Latin America: Bibliographical Essays*, 3rd ed. (Cambridge: Cambridge University Press, 1988), pp. 41–46.

65. Draft Convention on Principles Governing the Use by States of Artificial Earth Satellites for Direct Television Broadcasting. UN Doc. A/8771 (1972), art IV.

66. Herbert I. Schiller, *Communication and Cultural Domination* (White Plains, NY: International Arts and Sciences Press, 1976); Jeremy Tunstall, *The Media are American* (New York: Columbia University Press, 1977).

67. For a discussion of human rights and the Indian Broadcasting Bill, see Mark A Templeton, "Human rights perspective in the broadcasting bill debate," in Monroe E. Price and Stefaan Verhulst, eds., *Broadcasting Reform in India: Media Law from a Global Perspective* (New Delhi: Oxford University Press, 1998).

68. Satellite channels are both "deterrestrialized," meaning that they address audiences from space in multiple geopolitical territories, and "deterritorialized," in that they may be based abroad, target primarily foreign audiences, and hire foreign nationals. Stefaan Verhulst, "Diasporic and transnational communication: Technologies, policies and regulation," *Public/Javnost: Journal of the European Institute for Communication and Culture* 6:1 (1999): 31–32; Sakr, *Frontiers of Freedom*, pp. 91, 94–95.

69. Saskia Sassen and Kwame Anthony Appiah, *Globalization and its Discontents: Essays on the New Mobility of People and Money* (New York: New Press, 1998); Saskia Sassen, *Losing Control? Sovereignty in an Age of Globalization* (New York: Columbia University Press, 1996).

70. C. Edwin Baker, *Media, Markets, and Democracy* (Cambridge: Cambridge University Press, 2001).

71. For a judicial discussion of the Napster case, see *A. M. Records v. Napster*, Inc., 239 F.3rd 1004 (9th Cir. 2001). For the refiguring of trade routes of music as consumers searched for alternatives, see Matt Richtel, "With Napster down, its audience fans out," *The New York Times*, Jul. 20, 2001. Online [Jul. 2001], available: *http://www.nytimes.com/2001/07/20/technology/20MUSI.html*.

Chapter 4

1. See Brian Kahin and Charles Nesson, eds., *Borders in Cyberspace*, (Cambridge: MIT Press, 1997).

2. *See* Mark Baker, "Privatization in the developing world: Panacea for the economic ills of the Third World or prescription overused?" *New York Law School Journal of International and Comparative Law* 18 (1999): 233, 234. "[P]rivatization has increasingly become a component of conditionality requirements attached to institutional lending . . . seventy percent of structural adjustment loans and forty percent of sectoral adjustment loans made by the World Bank during the 1980s contained a privatization component."

3. Wolfgang Hoffman-Riem, *Regulating Media: The Licensing and Supervision of Broadcasting in Six Countries* (New York: Guilford Press, 1966), p. 160.

4. Hoffman-Riem, *Regulating Media*, p. 161.

5. Virtual Institute of Information, *French Regulation of Media Ownership*. Online [Jul. 2001], available: http://www.vii.org/pcmlp/france.html.

6. See Hoffman-Riem, *Regulating Media*, p. 161.

7. See Hoffman-Riem, *Regulating Media*.

8. See Hoffman-Riem, *Regulating Media*.

9. Document on transparency: Commission Directive 80/723/EEC of 25.6.1980 on the transparency of financial relations between member states and public undertakings, OJ L 195 of 29.7.1980; amended by Commission Directive 85/413/EEC, OJ No L 229, 28.8.1985 and Commission Directive 93/84/EEC, OJ No L 254, 12.10.1993.

10. For discussion of Russian television broadcasting and licensing regulations, see Peter Krug and Monroe E. Price, "Russia," in Global Report Series, *Media Ownership and Control in the Age of Convergence* (London: International Institute of Communications, 1996), p. 186. For more detailed discussions of legislation affecting the Russian media and the application of the relevant laws and decrees, see Monroe E. Price, Andrei Richter, and Peter K. Yu, eds., *Russian Media Law and Policy in the Yeltsin Decade* (The Hague: Kluwer, 2002).

11. For an overview of privatization in the telecommunications markets of Poland, Hungary, and the Czech Republic, see Daniel J. Ryan, *Privatization and Competition in Telecommunications: International Developments* (Westport, CT: Praeger, 1997).

12. C. Edwin Baker, "Giving the audience what it wants," *Ohio State Law Journal* 58 (1997): 311.

13. Laura Belin, "The rise and fall of Russia's NTV," *Stanford Journal of International Law* 38 (2002): 19.

14. See, for example, Donald W. Hawthorne and Monroe E. Price, "Rewiring the First Amendment: Meaning, content and public broadcasting," *Cardozo Arts and Entertainment Law Journal* 12 (1994): 499; Erick Howard, "Debating PBS: Public broadcasting and the power to exclude political candidates from televised debates," *University of Chicago Legal Forum* (1995): 435; Howard A. White, "Fine tuning the federal government's role in public broadcasting," *Federal Communications Law Journal* 46 (1994): 491.

15. Thomas Gibbons, "Aspiring to pluralism: The constraints of public broadcasting values on the de-regulation of British media ownership," *Cardozo Arts and Entertainment Law Journal* 16 (1998): 475.

16. See Nikhil Sinha, "Doordarshan, public service broadcasting and the impact of globalization: A short history," *Cardozo Journal of International and Comparative Law* 5 (1997): 365.

17. Ibid.

18. David M. Stone, *Nixon and the Politics of Public Broadcasting* (New York: Garland, 1985). Ralph Engleman, *Public Radio and Television in America: A Political History* (Newbury Park, CA: Sage, 1996).

19. Monroe E. Price, ed., *The V-Chip Debate: Content Filtering from Television to the Internet* (Hillsdale, NJ: Lawrence Erlbaum, 1998).

20. Court of First Instance, First Chamber, Judgment of 10 May 2000, case 46/97, *SIC Sociedade Independente de Comunicação, SA v. Commission of the European Communities.*

21. See also Document on transparency: Commission Directive 80/723/EEC of 25.6.1980 on the transparency of financial relations between member states and public undertakings, OJ No L 195 of 29.7.1980; amended by Commission Directive 85/413/EEC, OJ No L 229, 28.8.1985 and Commission Directive 93/84/EEC, OJ No L 254, 12.10.1993.

22. "Lithuania: State radio, TV threatened with closure," BBC World Monitoring Media Service, Nov. 24, 2000. Source: ETA news agency, Tallinn, in English (Nov. 23, 2000).

23. This information comes from a summary editorial prepared by BBC Monitoring, Dec. 6, 2000, available from BBC Monitoring. Also see Monroe Price and Marc Raboy, *Public Service Broadcasting in Transition: A Documentary Reader* (Düsseldorf: European Institute for the Media, 2001).

24. Stephen McDowell and Carleen Maitland, "Developing Television Ratings in Canada and the United States: "The Perils and Promises of Self-regulation," in Price, *The V-Chip Debate.*

25. Jörg Ukrow, *Self-regulation in the Media Sector and European Community Law* (Saarbrücken: EMR, 1999).

26. Angela Campbell, "Self-regulation and the media," *Federal Communications Law Journal* 51 (1999): 711.

27. Several major service and content providers, such as AOL and MSN, have developed explicit guidelines and user protection guarantees, particularly for minors, often labeled

"Netiquette," in order to establish and maintain confidence among their users. Industry corporations also worked with public interest groups such as the Internet Education Foundation, *http://www.neted.org*, and America Links Up, *http://www.americalinksup.org*, to further consumer choice in content selection alternatives.

28. AOL, for example, has established a hotline and "notice and takedown procedure" and works in cooperation with the UK's Internet Watch Foundation.

29. US courts granted a preliminary injunction against the enforcement of the Child Online Protection Act. *Reno v. ACLU*, 31 F. Supp. 2d 473 (E.D. Pa 199), Affrmed, 217 F. 3d (3d Cir. 2001).

30. Ibid. See also *Reno v. ACLU*, 520 US 1113 (1997). See chapters 5 and 6.

31. In Australia, the Internet Code of Practice was created in 1999 by the Internet Industry Association, a trade body covering different sectors of the Internet industry, as a product of the enactment of the Broadcasting Services Amendment (Online Services) Act 1999. The industry became much more proactive in self-regulation when the Online Services Bill was going through the legislature in an attempt to cushion the potential impact of the legislation, which many in the industry considered "heavy-handed." Mr Patrick Fair, chair, Internet Industry Association, Senate Select Committee on Information Technology (SSCIT), Evidence (Apr. 27, 1999): 13.

32. Geoff Kitney, "Moscow: Russia's 10 most powerful people are seven oligarchs and three regional governors," *Sydney Morning Herald*, Australia, Apr. 1, 2000; David Remnick, "The real new Russia: A democracy it isn't. It is a nascent state with some features of democracy and many more of oligarchy and authoritarianism," *The Vancouver Sun*, Dec. 19, 1997, editorial, p. A21; "After the meeting: What new realities?" *Current Digest of the Post-Soviet Press* 49: 37 (Oct. 15, 1997): 8. Source: Nikita Kirichenko, "The big seven: The president and the six oligarchs," *Moskovskiye novosti*, no. 37, Sept. 14–21, 1997, p. 5.

33. D. Rothkopf, "In Praise of Cultural Imperialism, *Foreign Policy* (Summer 1997): 38–53: 43, 52; Daya Kishan Thussu, *International Communication: Continuity and Change* (London: Arnold, 2000).

34. See William Harley, *Creative Compromise: The MacBride Commission: A Firsthand Report and Reflection on the Workings of UNESCO's International Commission for the Study* (Lanham, MD: University Press of America, 1993). See also Michael Farley, "Conflicts over government control of information—The United States and UNESCO," *Tulane Law Review*, 59 (Mar. 1985): 1971.

35. C. Edwin Baker, "An economic critique of free trade in media products," *North Carolina Law Review* 78 (Jun. 2000): 1360, 1366; C. Edwin Baker, *Human Liberty and Freedom of Speech* (Oxford: Oxford University Press, 1989); C. Edwin Baker, "Of course, more than words," *University of Chicago Review* 61 (1994): 1181 [reviewing Catharine A. MacKinnon, *Only Words* (Cambridge: Harvard University Press, 1993)].

36. Ted Magder, "Franchising the Candy Store: Split-Run Magazines and a New International Regime for Trade in Culture," *Canadian–American Public Policy* (Apr. 1998): 7; Mary Vipond, *The Mass Media in Canada* (Toronto: James Lorimer, 1989, p. 27), quoting Frederick Paul, Editorial, *National Periodicals or Annexation*, Saturday Night (Toronto), Mar. 20, 1926, p. 2.

37. Magder, "Franchising the candy store," p. 50. In Magder's view magazines, "are an important forum for the expression of the ideas, attitudes and values of the reading communities they represent."

38. Under the draft law, pay television services, such as France's Canal Plus and Dutch-owned Wizja TV, could not buy exclusive rights for important social, cultural, and sporting events.

39. "SBS Broadcasting System acquires Central European Media Enterprises Ltd." Newsletter, Communications Media Center at New York Law School, Mar. 31, 1999.

40. Jan Culik, "Nova TV: Commercial success or embarrassing failure?" *Central Europe Review* 1: 6 (Aug. 2, 1999).

41. See Margaret A. Blanchard, *Exporting the First Amendment: The Press-Government Crusade of 1945–1972* (New York: Longman, 1986).

42. The Commission on Freedom of the Press, a Free and Responsible Press: A General Report on Mass Communication: Newspapers, Radio, Motion Pictures, Magazines, and Books (1947) [hereafter Hutchins Commission Report]; see also Everette E. Dennis, "Internal examination: Self-regulation and the American media," *Cardozo Arts and Entertainment Law Journal* 13 (1995): 697, 698–99; Lee C. Bollinger, "Why there should be an independent decennial commission of the press," *University of Chicago Legal Forum* (1993), pp. 1–25.

43. One attempt to clarify the link between mass media and nature of the political society was presented in F. S. Siebert, T. B. Peterson, and W. Schramm, *Four Theories of the Press.* (Urbana: University of Illinois Press, 1956). These were the authoritarian, the libertarian, the Soviet, and the social responsibility models.

44. Hutchins Commission Report, pp. 21, 23, 26–28; see also Theodore Peterson, "The social responsibility theory of the press," in *Four Theories of the Press*, pp. 87–91.

45. C. Edwin Baker, "The media that citizens need." *University of Pennsyivania Law Review* 147 (1998): 317, 351.

46. This statement was part of a colloquy that originally took place on the listserve of fsu-media. See William Dunkerley, "The efficacy of American assistance to the media in Eastern Europe and the former Soviet Union: Have strategic objectives been achieved—And what should be the next step?" *Post-Soviet Media Law and Policy Newsletter* 54 (Apr. 1, 1999): 45; Eric Johnson, "A response from Eric Johnson," *Post-Soviet Media Law and Policy Newsletter* 54 (Apr. 1, 1999): 46; Catherine Fitzpatrick, "Why such sad cruelty," *Post-Soviet Media Law and Policy Newsletter* 54 (Apr. 1, 1999): 46. All subsequent quotations are from this document.

47. Johnson, "A response from Eric Johnson."

48. See Monroe E. Price, "The market for loyalties: Electronic media and the global competition for allegiances," *Yale Law Journal* 104 (1994): 667.

49. Samuel P. Huntington, *The Clash of Civilizations and the Remaking of World Order* (New York: Simon and Schuster, 1996).

Chapter 5

1. See Jens Waltermann and Marcell Machill, eds., *Protecting Our Children on the Internet: Towards a New Culture of Responsibility* (Gütersloh: Bertelsmann Foundation, 2000).

2. See European Commission, *Illegal and Harmful Content on the Internet: Communication to the European Parliament, the Council, the Economic and Social Committee and the Committee of the Regions*, COM(96) 487, Brussels, Oct. 16, 1996. Online [Jul. 2001], available: *http://www2.echo.lu/legal/en/internet/content/content.html*.

3. The EU document specifically suggests that "harmful content" could include the expression of certain extreme political opinions, religious beliefs, or views on racial matters. If these are carved out for noncriminal treatment by member states, they must do so in a manner consistent with the right to freedom of expression provisions of the European Convention on Human Rights.

4. European Commission, *Green Paper on the Protection of Minors and Human Dignity in Audiovisual and Information Services*, COM(96) 483. Online [Jul. 2001], available: *http://www2.echo.lu/legal/en/internet/content/gpen-toc.html*.

5. European Parliament Committee on Culture, Youth, Education, and the Media, *Report on the Commission Communication on Illegal and Harmful Content on the Internet*, A4-0098/97, PE 219.568/DEF.

6. This cooperation could take the form of monitoring to assist in detection, ensuring an architecture of the system that aids in tracing and that minimizes anonymity so that transgressors can be more easily apprehended, and other forms as well. It is in this question of relationship to law enforcement that the device of the hotline has gained respectability as an instrument of self-regulation and coordination with law enforcement. "An effective way to restrict circulation of illegal material is to set up a European network of centers (known as hot-lines) which allow users to report content which they come across in the course of their use of the Internet and which they consider to be illegal. Responsibility for prosecuting and punishing those responsible for illegal content remains with the national law-enforcement authorities, while the hot-line aims at revealing the existence of illegal material with a view to restricting its circulation." *Action Plan on Promoting Safer Use of the Internet*, Decision no. 275/1999/EC of the European Parliament and of the Council, Jan. 25, 1999, p. 7.

7. The Working Group on Illegal and Harmful Use of the Internet, *The Internet: Tackling the Downside, The First Report of the Working Group on Illegal and Harmful Use of the Internet*. Online [Jul. 2001], available: *http://www.irlgov.ie/justice/Publications/internet%20submissions/intrep.pdf*.

8. Department of Trade and Industry and Home Office, Review of the Internet Watch Foundation 1999. Online [Jul. 2001], available: *http://www.dti.gov.uk/cii/iwfreview/*.

9. The German Federal Act Establishing the General Conditions for Information and Communication Services (Information and Communication Services Act) was passed Aug. 1, 1997. It extended the Law on the Dissemination of Publications Morally Harmful to Youth to the Internet. A fairly interesting initiative was a section that required the appointment of "youth protection ministers."

10. Sarah B. Hogan, "To net or not to net: Singapore's regulation of the Internet," *Federal Communications Law Journal* 51 (1999): 429.

11. Ibid., p. 436.

12. Ibid., pp. 437–39. See also the Singapore Broadcasting Authority Act, Internet Code of Practice, at Prohibited Material. Online [Jul. 2001], available: *http://www.sba.gov.sg/work/sba/internet.nsf/pages/code.*

13. Broadcasting Services Amendment (Online Services) Bill 1999 ("Online Services Act"), no. 99077.

14. These provisions to restrict access to content "likely to cause offense to a reasonable adult" are set out in section III of the Act. The bill was widely criticized as interfering too extensively with the Internet and has been called the "Net Oppression Bill" by groups in Australia. See Electronic Frontier Australia's Web site on the legislation. Online [Jul. 2001] available: *http://rene.efa.org.au/liberty/nchistory.html.*

15. For age verification procedures, see Internet Law and Policy Forum, Content Blocking Working Group, *Content Blocking Report, Self-regulatory Initiatives.* Online [Jul. 2001], available: *http://www.ilpf.org/work/content/selfreg.htm.* The industry's code of practice must be written after "appropriate community consultation" and must "contain appropriate community safeguards." See *http://www.aba.gov.au/what/online/overview.htm.*

16. In New Zealand, as in Australia, the focus of Internet content has been on "objectionable" material as defined by the New Zealand Films, Videos, and Publications Classification Act, 1993. The Act defines a publication as objectionable "if it describes, depicts, expresses, or otherwise deals with matters such as sex, horror, crime, cruelty, or violence in such a manner that the availability of the publication is likely to be injurious to the public good." A publication is deemed objectionable for the purposes of the Act if it "promotes or supports, or tends to promote support of" a list of six different categories, including the exploitation of children, torture, and certain sexual conduct. Self-regulation has been the standard mode so far in New Zealand with regard to the Internet. A New Zealand Internet Code of Practice (ICoP) was adopted Jun. 26, 1999. Its aims include ensuring "information and procedures are in place for the protection of minors from accessing objectionable material over the Internet" and "so Internet users know how to limit access to protect a user from accessing inappropriate or objectionable material."

17. *Reno v. ACLU*, 117 S. Ct. 2329 (1997).

18. See Child Online Protection Act ("COPA"), Pub. L. no. 105–277, 1401, 112 Stat. 2681 (1998). The only place the words "harmful to children" was included in CDA I is §551, the part of the statute which dealt with the V-chip. In instituting a rating system, Congress found a "compelling governmental interest in empowering parents to limit the negative influences of video programming that is harmful to children."

19. On Feb. 1, 1999, the US District Court for the Eastern District of Pennsylvania issued a preliminary injunction barring enforcement of COPA. See *ACLU v. Reno*, 31 F. Supp. 2d 473, (E.D. Pa. 1999), affirmed, ACLU v. Reno, 217 F.3d 163 (3d Cir. 2000), vacated and remanded 122 S. Ct. 1700 (2002).

20. The opposition came from public interest groups linked both to liberal and conservative causes. Andrea Sheldon, executive director of the Traditional Values Coalition, testifying

before the Senate Commerce, Science and Transportation Committee on the initial television ratings system in February 1997, complained that TV-PG shows had nearly as many obscenities as TV-14. "Receiving the TV-PG rating were Wings, Friends, Beverly Hills 90210, and Savannah all featuring pre-marital sex, sex with various partners and sex with no commitment. In addition, all of this took place during the 'family hour.' I doubt that many parents would consider these situations acceptable for a 14-year-old. . . . Obviously, we need a rating system that is content-specific. Television viewers have a right to know what is coming into their homes. And parents should know this in advance."

Mark Honig, of the Parents Television Council in Los Angeles stated, "If we're going to have a rating system, it has to be content based. We did a ratings study. We looked at the first two weeks of the rating system, and we found that more than three-fifths of prime time programming is thrown into this black hole that they call TV-PG. Well, that's included stuff from *Promise Land*, one of the most family friendly shows on television that had no sexual dialogue, no violence of any extreme nature, and no vulgar language. That got a PG.

"You tune in a hour and a half later to an ABC show called *Spin City*, where you heard the A word twice, you heard the B word once, and you had dialogue centering on men downloading naked pictures of Amish women on the Internet. That got the same rating. That's too confusing to parents. They don't know from one show to another what to expect." *CNN Talkback Live*, Feb. 27, 1997, Transcript 97022700V14.

During its testimony before Congress on the initial network ratings system, in February 1997, Joan Dykstra, National PTA President, representing the PTA made the following recommendations: "(1) A V-chip band that is broad enough to allow parents to receive more than one rating system. (2) A rating icon on the screen that is larger, more prominently placed on the screen, and appears more frequently during the course of the program. (3) A rating board that is independent of the industry and the FCC, and . . . include[s] parents. Currently, the industry rates itself, which is a conflict of interest. The producers could hardly be an impartial audience, or capable of providing consistent and impartial information. (4) Lastly, . . . the National PTA recommends that the industry work with parents and advocacy organizations to fund an independent research study comparing their age-based system with a content-based system, such as HBO's, to determine which better meets the needs of parents. After the study is conducted, the various stakeholders in this issue should convene to review the study and make final recommendations to the FCC based on the study results."

21. As the notion of filtering and labeling caught the imagination of the politician, and all those who wish to consider new ways to alter bargaining over imagery in society, the very idea of the chip or its equivalent moved back across technologies and forms of information. In the United States, the Federal Communications Commission came to require the installation of a V-chip or its equivalent in computers that are capable of receiving broadcast transmissions, depending on screen size, with implications for Internet screening and labeling. See "FCC ruling gives go-ahead to Tri-Vision's V-Chip," *Financial Post*, Mar. 13, 1998, p. 3.

22. See Mark Steyn, "TV cynics zap Clinton's cure-all: The V-chip, the in-home censor, is coming soon to small screens in the US," *Sunday Telegraph*, Mar. 3, 1996, p. 24; "Meeting the new chip on the block: And imagine the joy of watching television without the dross," *The Guardian*, Mar. 19, 1996, p. 16.

23. A survey of research relating to the television viewing habits of children and parental preferences with respect to content screening can be found at Joanne Cantor, "Children and television: Ratings for program content; The role of research findings," *557 Annals* (1998): 54. Major research in this area has tended to focus on areas such as the viewing habits of juvenile offenders in the United Kingdom or patterns of television ownership in the United States. See James Ferman, "Do you care what your children watch on video?" *Mail on Sunday* (London), Mar. 28, 1993, p. 20; Kathy Boccella, "Armed with their own TV sets, kids log more TV time," *Arizona Republic*, Feb. 8, 1998, p. A21.

24. According to Rosalyn Weinman, head of Standards and Practices at the network, NBC decided not to add content-based labels because "we do not believe that they add any level of information to parents when they want to make decisions for their children. We believe quite the contrary that the content labels add nothing other than misconceptions and confusion to a system that was working and working well."

25. See, for example, *Turner Broad. Sys., Inc. v. FCC*, 117 S. Ct. 1174 (1997).

26. See Jack M. Balkin, "Media filters, the V-Chip, and the foundations of broadcast regulation," *Duke Law Journal* 45 (1996): 1131.

27. See *Erznoznik v. City of Jacksonville*, 422 US 205 (1975) (overturning a city ordinance regulating nudity on drive-in screens).

28. Walter Minkel, "Zapped by ads," *School Library Journal Online* (Aug. 1, 2000). Minkel describes a company named Zapme that provides computer labs to computer-needy schools but then barrages the users with ads specific to each student through the practice of giving students a user ID and password and collecting information on Web pages that each student visits. Schools are a controversial site for advertisements though they are being approached more and more often. See "Testimony of Ralph Nader before the United States Senate Committee on Health, Education, Labor and Pensions" (May 20, 1999). Online [Jan. 12, 2001], available: *http://www.essential.org/alert/channel_one/nader.html*.

29. *Denver Area Educ. Telecomms. Consortium v. FCC*, 116 S. Ct. 2374, 2392 (1996).

30. See Programme on Comparative Media Law and Policy, University of Oxford, Parental Control of Television Broadcasting. Online [Jul. 2001], available: *http://europa.eu.int/comm/dg10/avpolicy/key_doc/parental_control/index.html*. Monroe E. Price and Stefaan Verhulst, eds., *Parental Control of Television Broadcasting* (Mahwah, NJ: Lawrence Erlbaum, 2001).

31. Monroe E. Price, "Free expression and digital dreams: The open and closed terrain of speech," *Critical Inquiry* 22 (1995): 64.

32. See, for example, Martin H. Redish, "Tobacco advertising and the First Amendment," *Iowa Law Review* 81 (1996): 589; Halberg, Note and comment, "Butt Out: An analysis of the FDA's proposed restrictions on cigarette advertising under the commercial-speech doctrine," *Loyola of Los Angeles Law Review* 29 (1996): 1219; Rachel N. Pine, "Abortion counseling and the First Amendment: Open questions after Webster," *American Journal of Law and Medicine* 15 (1989): 189; Kenneth L. Polin, "Argument for the ban of tobacco advertising: A First Amendment analysis," *Hofstra Law Review* 17 (1988): 99.

33. See Television without Frontiers, Council Directive 97/36, 1997 O.J. (L 202). Article 22 provides, in part, that "Member States shall take appropriate measures to ensure that tele-

vision broadcasts by broadcasters under their jurisdiction do not include any programmes which might seriously impair the physical, mental or moral development of minors, in particular programmes that involve pornography or gratuitous violence."

34. See, for example, Marci A. Hamilton, "Reconceptualizing ratings: From censorship to marketplace," *Cardozo Arts and Entertainment Law Journal* 15 (1997): 403; Matthew L. Spitzer, "An introduction to the law and economics of the V-Chip," *Cardozo Arts and Entertainment Law Journal* 15 (1997): 429; Howard M. Wasserman, Comment, "Second-best solution: The First Amendment, broadcast indecency, and the V-Chip," *Northwestern University Law Review* 91 (1997) 1190; Jack M. Balkin, "Media filters, the V-Chip, and the foundation of broadcast regulation," *Duke Law Journal* 45 (1996): 1131; Steven D. Feldman, Note, "The V-Chip: Protecting children from violence or doing violence to the Constitution?" *Howard Law Journal* 39 (1996): 587; David V. Scott, "The V-Chip debate: Blocking television, sex, violence, and the First Amendment," *Loyola of Los Angeles Law Review* 16 (1996): 741.

35. In February 1997, when opposition to the networks initial ratings submission was accelerating, Senators Hollings and Dorgan introduced legislation that would impose a "safe harbor" limit on TV violence limiting such programming to specific late night hours. The suggestion was implicit that such legislation might be enacted if the rating system was not amended to reflect content concerns.

36. In a letter to NBC head Bob Wright, after NBC refused to be part of the industry compromise, Senator John McCain promised to use law and regulation to pressure NBC into adopting the new ratings system. As Jeffrey Greenfield said on ABC's *Nightline*, putting a question to Senator McCain, "I can't think of a more direct use of government power than the chairman of the Commerce Committee telling prospective FCC commissioners he wants NBC's licenses looked at very carefully because they won't adopt this ratings system. How in heaven's name is that voluntary?" Senator McCain answered as follows: "Because when the affiliates sign voluntarily a piece of paper that they will act in the public interest, that's what has motivated the FCC to force them to show children's educational programming and other kinds of programming and if they're not acting in the public interest, then it's the FCC's obligation, not right, but obligation to determine that. And I believe that by refusing to provide parents with the information that they need, then they may not be acting in the public interest." When Greenfield asked "Can we not concede or agree that that is at least a very powerful use of a high government official's power?" McCain responded "I think it's a use of my obligation to see that the broadcasters live up to their obligation, which they freely entered into when they said they would act in the public interest in return for obtaining billions of dollars of taxpayer owned assets." *ABC Nightline*, Oct. 17, 1997, Transcript 97101701-j07.

37. For a survey of patterns of usage of the V-chip, suggesting low levels of usage, see Kaiser Family Foundation, *Parents and the V-Chip 2001*. Online [Jul. 2001], available: *http://www.kff.org/content/2001/3158/*.

38. In an interview with ABC, producer Dick Wolf of *Law and Order* gave this example: "It can get really crazy. We had one show where the opening was a woman who was found naked in a 60-story office building elevator vent. The standards called and said it's not acceptable. I said but she's face down in the elevator. Well, you see too much of her breast. And I

said well how could I prevent something like this happening in the future? She said, choose smaller breasted actresses." In the same program, Roland McFarland, head of the Standards and Practices Department at Fox Network said: "I suppose the question would be . . . , so I've got four damns and a hell, you know, is that the tilt factor as far as language is concerned? A kiss wouldn't necessarily, we wouldn't consider that as, a take down on a couch, not necessarily so. If there's a bed scene and a slip dropped, maybe." *ABC Nightline*, Oct. 17, 1997, Transcript # 97101701-j07.

39. Studies within any industry that try to codify accumulated practices would do well to emulate Karl N. Llewellyn and E. Adamson Hoebel, *Cheyenne Way* (Norman: University of Oklahoma Press, 1983).

40. See David Yassky, "Eras of the First Amendment," *Columbia Law Review* 91 (1991): 1699.

41. Monroe E. Price, "The market for loyalties: Electronic media and the global competition for allegiances," *Yale Law Journal* 104 (1995): 667, 685.

42. See the Indian Supreme Court Case, *Secretary, Ministry of Info. and Broad. v. Cricket Ass'n of Bengal* (1995) 2 S.C.C. 161.

43. The British Board of Film Classification, for example, codified in 1998 its procedures and guidelines into a comprehensive set of Classification Guidelines. Online [Jul. 2001], available: *http://www.bbfc.co.uk*. The Board followed a policy of periodically seeking comments on these guidelines in public meetings throughout the United Kingdom.

Chapter 6

1. Thomas Hardy, *Under the Greenwood Tree,* Tim Dolin, ed. (New York: Penguin Putnam, 1999).

2. See Susan J. Douglas, "Amateur operators and American broadcasting: Shaping the future of radio," Joseph J. Corn, ed., *Imagining Tomorrow: History, Technology, and the American Future* (Cambridge: MIT Press, 1986), p. 35.

3. Quoted in ibid., p. 39.

4. Jonathan Wallace and Michael Green, "Bridging the analogy gap: The Internet, the printing press and freedom of speech," *Seattle University Law Review* 20 (1997): 711; Hauben, Michael, "The expanding commonwealth of learning: Printing and the net," in Michael Hauben and Ronda Hauben, *Netizens: On the History and Impact of Usenet and the Internet* (Netbook: 1994). Online [Jan. 15, 2001], available: *http://www.columbia.edu/~rh120/ch106.x16*.

5. See *President's Commission on Critical Infrastructure Protection, Critical Foundations: Protecting America's Infrastructure* (1997) and Critical Infrastructure Assurance Office, Department of Justice, *White Paper: The Clinton Administration's Policy on Critical Infrastructure Protection: Presidential Decision Directive 63* (1998). The Commission's Web site may be found at *http://www.pccip.ncr.gov*.

6. President's Working Group on Unlawful Conduct on the Internet, *The Electronic Frontier: The Challenge of Unlawful Conduct Involving Use of the Internet* (Washington: GPO, 2000).

7. See Electronic Privacy Information Center, *Critical Infrastructure Protection and the Endangerment of Civil Liberties: An Assessment of the President's Commission on Critical Infrastructure Protection (PCCIP)* (1998). Online [Jan. 15, 2001], available: *http://www.epic.org/security/infowar/cip.pdf*.

8. Charles Firestone, "Digital culture and civil society: A new role for intermediaries?" *Intermedia* 22 (Dec.–Jan. 1994–95): 6. See also Symposium, "Financial services: Security, privacy, and encryption," *Boston University Journal of Science and Technology* 3 (1997): 4.

9. Kathleen M. Sullivan, "First Amendment intermediaries in the age of cyberspace," *UCLA Law Review* 45 (1998): 1653.

10. See James Boyle, "Foucault in cyberspace: Surveillance, sovereignty and hardwired censors," *University of Cincinnati Law Review* 66 (1997): 177.

11. Jack L. Goldsmith, "Against cyberanarchy," *University of Chicago Law Review* 65 (1998): 1199, 1200–1201.

12. *Janet Reno, Attorney General of the United States, et al., appellants v. American Civil Liberties Union et al.* 521 US 844 (1997). Other related cases include: *Denver Area Educ. Telecomm. Consortium, Inc. v. FCC*, 518 US 727 (1996); and *United States v. Playboy Entertainment Group*, 529 US 830 (2000).

13. 141 Cong. Rec. S1953 (daily ed. Feb. 1, 1995) (statement of Senator James Exon).

14. For an excellent discussion of questions concerning the constitutionality of regulations protecting children, as discussed in *Reno v. ACLU* see Eugene Volokh, "Freedom of speech, shielding children and transcending balancing," *Supreme Court Review* (1997): 141, 197.

15. The account is superbly described in Jonathan Weinberg, "Broadcasting and speech," *California Law Review* 81 (1993): 1103.

16. See, for example, Glen O. Robinson, "The electronic First Amendment: An essay for the new age," *Duke Law Journal* 47 (1998): 899.

17. As it happens, the post-1996 technology meant that many individuals would view the Internet on their television screen, but as received through their cable modem.

18. *Reno v. ACLU* 521 US 844, 859

19. *Reno v. ACLU* 521 US 844, 879.

20. Lawrence Lessig, "The path of cyberlaw," *Yale Law Journal* 104 (1995): 1743 [hereinafter *Cyberlaw*]; Lawrence Lessig, "Reading the Constitution in Cyberspace," *Emory Law Journal* 45 (1996): 869 [hereinafter *Constitution in Cyberspace*].

21. *Denver Area Educational Telecommunications Consortium, Inc. v. FCC*, 518 US 727, (Justice Souter concurring and quoting Lessig, *Cyberlaw, supra* note 19, p. 1745).

22. This idea is a source for Justice O'Connor in *Reno v. ACLU*, 521 US 844 (1997) citing Lessig, *Constitution in Cyberspace, supra* 19 at p. 886.

23. Lessig, *Constitution in Cyberspace*, pp. 902–903. ("We come from a tradition of translation in constitutional interpretation; in a wide range of cases, the aim has been to preserve founding values as interpretive contexts have changed. . . . But translations in cyberspace will not always be clear.")

24. Lessig, *Cyberlaw,* p. 1754. Lessig states, "Cyberspace is elsewhere, and before carving the First Amendment into its silicon, we should give the culture a chance to understand it. . . . If there is sanction to intervene, then it is simply to assure that the revolution continue, not to assure that every step conforms with the First Amendment as now understood."

25. *Denver Area Educational Telecommunications Consortium, Inc. v. FCC,* 518 US at 787 (Justice Kennedy concurring in part and dissenting in part).

26. *Pennsylvania v. Casey,* 117 S. Ct. 2258, 2260 (1997).

27. Lessig, *Cyberlaw*, p. 1753. ("[N]o court should purport to decide these questions finally or even firmly. Here especially should be the beginning of a dialogue, which perhaps more than others is meant to construct its subject more than reflect it.")

28. Lessig, *Constitution in Cyberspace*, pp. 886–95.

29. *Reno v. ACLU,* 117 S. Ct. at 2353.

30. See Lessig, *Constitution in Cyberspace*, pp. 885–88.

31. *Reno v. ACLU,* 117 S. Ct., p. 2354.

32. *Reno v. ACLU,* 117 S. Ct., p. 2353.

33. Monroe E. Price, "The market for loyalties: Electronic media and the global competition for allegiances," *Yale Law Journal* 104 (1994): 667.

34. A discussion of these questions is in Electronic Privacy Information Center, *Filters and Freedom 2.0* (Washington: 2001). Geoffrey Nunberg, "The Internet filter farce," *American Prospect*, Jan. 1–15, 2001, p. 12.

35. The solution for the Internet was quite different from the V-chip solution, discussed in the last chapter, legislated for television.

36. For a review of these issues in advance of the Supreme Court's decision in 2000 *in United States v. Playboy Entertainment Group*, 529 US 803 (2000); see the perceptive student Note by Barton Beebe, "Parental initiative in the age of signal bleed," *Yale Law Journal* 109 (1997): 627.

37. *Reno v. ACLU,* 117 S. Ct., p. 2336.

38. Ibid., p. 2336, relying on finding 72, *Reno v. ACLU,* 929 F. Supp. 824, 842 (E.D.Pa.1996). For those with a technical interest in the progress of video content analysis or "object-based video coding," see Andrew W. Appel and Edward W. Felten, "Viewpoint: Technological access control interferes with non-infringing scholarship," *Communications of the ACM*, Sept. 2000, p. 21.

39. *Reno v. ACLU,* 117 S. Ct., p. 2336.

40. The Court also made much of the fact that existing technology did not "include any effective method for a sender to prevent minors from obtaining access to its communications on the Internet without also denying access to adults." In contrast, "despite its limitations, currently available *user-based* software suggests that a reasonably effective method by which *parents* can prevent their children from accessing sexually explicit and other material which parents may believe is inappropriate for their children will soon be widely available." *Reno v. ACLU,* 929 F. Supp. at 842, finding 73. Emphasis added by the Court.

41. Lawrence Lessig, "What things regulate speech: CDA 2.0 vs. filtering," *Jurimetrics: The Journal of Law, Science, and Technology* 38 (1998): 629, 632.

42. See Volokh, "Freedom of speech, shielding children, and transcending balancing," pp. 148–57.

43. *Reno v. ACLU*, 117 S. Ct., p. 2332.

44. Volokh, "Freedom of speech, shielding children, and transcending balancing," pp. 148–57.

45. *Reno v. ACLU*, 117 S. Ct., p. 2348. A dispute, really a skirmish, within this discussion is whether or not "minor" should include individuals under 18 or under 17.

46. See *Reno v. ACLU*, 117 S. Ct., p. 2348. In dealing with this question, Justice O'Connor concluded that the record did not show that "many E-mail transmissions from an adult to a minor are conversations between family members"; but more important, she finds "no support for the legal proposition that such speech is absolutely immune from regulation." Perhaps both the Court and Justice O'Connor agree that such speech is not "absolutely immune," since the Court holds that such speech might be regulable if Congress were to meet an especially heavy burden. *Reno v. ACLU*, 117 S. Ct., pp. 2356–57.

47. *Prince v. Massachusetts*, 321 US 158, 166 (1943) (statute barring the teaching of German language in public schools constitutional).

48. But see, Justice O'Connor's dissent, *Reno v. ACLU*, 117 S. Ct., p. 2348.

49. Ibid., p. 2348.

50. Ibid., p. 2348.

51. Respondent's Brief at 37, *Denver Area Educ. Telecomms. Consortium v. FCC*, 518 US 727 (1996) (nos. 95-124, 95-227).

52. Implicit is the problem, addressed in *Butler,* of assuring sufficient adult access to speech while also protecting children. How does one tell what the profile of impact is of a congressional proscription—whether it depletes speech available to adults while protecting children. Of course, every congressional proscription or even channeling must have that impact; what constitutes too much, what constitutes adequate alternative availability of information is a matter that has never been adequately addressed by the Court, nor has it been clear what factual bases should underlie a conclusion. *Butler v. Michigan*, 352 US 380 (1957).

53. *Reno v. ACLU*, 117 S. Ct., p. 2348, n. 45.

54. See, for example, David R. Johnson and David Post, "Law and borders: The rise of law in cyberspace," *Stanford Law Review* 48 (1996): 1367, 1367. ("While these electronic communications play havoc with geographic boundaries, a new boundary, made up of the screens and passwords that separate the virtual world from the 'real world' of atoms, emerges. This new boundary defines a distinct Cyberspace that needs and can create its own law and legal institutions. Territorially based lawmakers and law-enforcers find this new environment deeply threatening.")

55. Even the term "overseas" has a certain charm as an anachronistic way of conceiving the relationship between space and jurisdiction.

56. See, generally, Henry H. Perritt Jr., "Jurisdiction in cyberspace," *Villanova Law Review* 41 (1996): 1.

57. In an important early case dealing with online censorship in the context of public library access, *Mainstream Loudon v. Board of Trustees of the Loudon County Library*, 24 F. Supp. 2d 552 (E. D. Va. 1998), a public library was forced to discontinue its use of restrictive Internet screening software. In another closely watched case, *Kathleen R. v. City of Livermore*, CV-015266-4 (Ca. Super. Ct., Alameda Country) (1998), a state court refused to force a public library to abandon its open access policy regarding Internet use. See, generally, Mark Nadel "The First Amendment's limitations on the use of Internet filtering in public and school libraries: What content can librarians exclude?" *Texas Law Review* 78 (2000): 1117; Julia M. Tedjeske, "Mainstream Loudon and access to Internet resources in public libraries," *University of Pittsburgh Law Review* 60 (1999): 1265.

58. See, generally, Gary W. Glisson, "A practitioner's defense of the White Paper," *Oregon Law Review* 75 (1996): 277; see also Vikas Arora, Note, "The Communications Decency Act: Congressional repudiation of the right stuff," *Harvard Journal on Legislation* 34 (1997): 473.

58 *Reno v. ACLU*, 117 S. Ct., p. 2336.

59. Does it mean, for example, that even though transmission or display of "obscene" material might ordinarily be prosecuted under the CDA, even after the Court's decision, the necessarily discriminatory aspect of such a prosecution (given the putative invulnerability of massive foreign purveyors) would be a defense? Compare Lawrence Lessig, "Zones of cyberspace," *Stanford Law Review* 48 (May 1996): 1405–12. Invoking Coase, Lessig argues, "[A] regulation need not be absolutely effective to be sufficiently effective. It need not raise the cost of the prohibited activity to infinity in order to reduce the level of that activity quite substantially."

60. *Red Lion Broadcasting Co. v. FCC*, 369 US 367 (1969). For a thorough and useful history and discussion of *Red Lion*, see Cass R. Sunstein, *Democracy and the Problem of Free Speech* (London: Free Press, 1993), p. 49. (arguing that the scarcity rationale in *Red Lion* is based on the need to ensure "broad diversity of views").

61. *Turner Broadcasting, Inc. v. FCC*, 512 US 622 (1994) (*Turner I*). The citation of *Turner I* is unusual. *Turner I*, after all, recites the history of regulatory distinctions only to hold that hierarchies of constitutional concern do not mutually encompass broadcasting and cable television. *Turner I* was primarily about the weaknesses of congressional law making; *Turner II*, 520 US 180 (1997), specifically rejected *Red Lion's* application of spectrum-scarcity as a ground for regulation in favor of some new "bottleneck" theory of regulation.

62. *Sable Communications of Cal., Inc. v. FCC*, 492 US 115 (1989) (prohibited provider of sexually oriented prerecorded telephone messages from participating in obscene interstate telephone communications for commercial purposes but enjoined statutory enforcement applying to indecent messages).

63. Monroe E. Price and John F. Duffy, "Technological change and doctrinal persistence: Telecommunications reform in Congress and the Court," *Columbia Law Review* 97 (1997); see also Thomas W. Hazlett, "Physical scarcity, rent seeking, and the First Amendment," *Columbia Law Review* 97 (1997): 905.

64. *Reno v. ACLU*, 117 S. Ct., p. 2343.

65. Ibid.

66. True, it was ARPANET, not the vast democratic fora of the Internet that was so regulated, but in some respects it is the same medium. Compare Hazlett, "Physical scarcity, rent seeking, and the First Amendment," *Columbia Law Review* 97 (1997): 905, 908.

67. There is something here of Bollinger's interesting, but never fully embraced theory that it was possible to regulate some parts of the media so long as there was at least one unregulated one, like newspapers or the Internet. See Lee C. Bollinger Jr., "Freedom of the press and public access: Toward a theory of partial regulation of the mass media," *Michigan Law Review* 75 (1976): 1.

68. *Reno v. ACLU,* 117 S. Ct. p. 2342.

69. *See* Henry P. Monaghan, "Constitutional fact review," *Columbia Law Review* 85 (1985): 229; Martin B. Louis, "Allocating adjudicative decision-making authority between the trial and appellate levels: A unified view of the scope of review, the judge/jury question, and procedural discretion," *North Carolina Law Review* 64 (1986): 993.

70. Based on finding 89 of the District Court decision. *Reno v. ACLU*, 929 F. Suppl., p. 845.

71. For an early First Amendment analysis of this model, see Jerry Berman and Daniel J. Weitzner, "Abundance and user control: Renewing the democratic heart of the First Amendment in the age of interactive media," *Yale Law Journal* 104 (1995): 1619.

72. In Denver Area, Justice Breyer relied on only a few books and articles to conclude that cable television was invasive in the *Pacifica* sense. Denver Area Educational Telecommunications Consortium, Inc., 518 US 727. Compare the role of the District Court's fact-findings in *Reno. Reno v. ACLU*, 117 S. Ct., p. 2329.

73. *Reno v. ACLU*, 117 S. Ct., p. 2343.

74. Ibid, p. 2344.

75. Ibid, p. 2344.

76. This is interesting because of the history of the "scarcity" rationale and its tie to limitations on spectrum. Scarcity was thought to be a physical limitation, as compared to shortages of printing presses, or limitations on the number of newspaper dailies in a market that could survive, both of which were considered economic. By shifting the phrase from spectrum scarcity to scarcity of an expressive commodity, Justice Stevens might have been opening the way for a reconsideration of this long-held distinction.

77. *Turner Broad. Sys., Inc. v. FCC (Turner II)*, 117 S. Ct. 1174 (1997).

78. See Jack M. Balkin, "Media filters, the V-Chip, and the foundations of broadcast regulation," *Duke Law Journal* 45 (1996): 1131.

79. Other comparative analysts of media law and policy have challenged the idea that scarcity no longer exists because of the Internet and various other technologies of abundance. See Stefaan Verhulst, "About scarcities and intermediaries: The regulatory paradigm shift of digital content reviewed," in Leah Lievrouw and Sonia Livingstone, eds., *Handbook of New Media* (London: Sage, 2002). Verhulst proposes that the very abundance of content has caused a need for new intermediaries that can navigate, contextualize, filter, decode, customize, and authenticate the information and its source for the user. He states, a "phenomenon of re-intermediation is emerging, [that] in many ways it creates new (artificial) scarcities." See also Monroe E. Price, "Hooks and ladders," in Charles Firestone

and Amy Korzick Garmer, eds., *Digital Broadcasting in the Public Interest* (Washington: Aspen Institute, 1998) and Monroe E. Price, "Red Lion and the constitutionality of regulation: A conversation among the Justices," in ibid.

80. Carolyn Marvin, *When Old Technologies Were New* (New York: Oxford University Press, 1988), p. 1; see also Brian Winston, *Media, Technology and Society, A History from the Telegraph to the Internet* (London: Routledge, 1998); Maxine Berg and Kristine Bruland, *Technological Revolutions in Europe* (Cheltenham, UK: Edward Elgar, 1997).

81. Xinhua General News Service, Jul. 19, 2001.

82. See, for example, George Gilder, *Telecosm: How Infinite Bandwidth Will Revolutionize Our World* (London: Free Press, 2000); Joel Kotkin, *The New Geography: How the Digital Revolution Is Reshaping the American Landscape* (New York: Random House, 2000).

83. For a study of the scope of newness of the printing press, see Elizabeth Eisenstein, *The Printing Revolution in Early Modern Europe* (Cambridge: Cambridge University Press, 1993). The Rand Corporation established a project, partly based on Eisenstein's model of change, to look at parallels between the coming of the Internet and the coming of the press. See *www.rand.org/parallels/* (Oct. 2000).

84. See M. Ethan Katsh, "Cybertime, cyberspace, and cyberlaw," *Journal of Online Law* (1995) art. 1. Online [Jan. 15, 2001], available: *http://warthog.cc.wm.edu/law/publications/jol/Katsh.html*.

Chapter 7

1. See, for instance, John Tomlinson, *Cultural Imperialism: A Critical Introduction* (Baltimore: Johns Hopkins University Press, 1991); Herbert Schiller, *Information Inequality: The Deepening Social Crisis in America* (New York: Routledge, 1996); George Gerbner, Hamid Mowlana, and Herbert I. Schiller, eds., *Invisible Crises: What Conglomerate Control of Media Means for America and the World* (Boulder, CO: Westview Press, 1996). It would be ostrich-like not to recognize the role of the United States as superpower and as the home of major exporters of entertainment programming and corporate distributors of imagery. Much global redefinition and reaction is by states vis à vis the United States (or the idea of the United States) and much, as well, is about United States policy with respect to the rest of the world.

2. Edward Herman and Noam Chomsky have written about US mass media coverage and its relationship to foreign policy. Edward S. Herman and Noam Chomsky, *Manufacturing Consent: The Political Economy of the Mass Media* (New York: Pantheon, 1988).

3. See, for example, Hamid Mowlana, *Global Information and World Communication: New Frontiers in International Relations* (London: Sage, 1997); R. Fortner, *International Communication: History, Conflict and Control of the Global Metropolis* (Belmont, CA: Wadsworth, 1993); Anthony Appadurai, *Modernity at Large: Cultural Dimensions of Globalization* (Minneapolis: University of Minnesota Press, 1996).

4. Jamie Frederic Metzl, "Popular Diplomacy," *Daedalus* 128, no. 2 (spring 1999): 187.

5. One could tie aspects of Metzl's strategy to Gramscian notions, namely that "military force was not necessarily the best instrument to retain power for the ruling classes,

but that a more effective way of wielding power was to build a consent by ideological control of cultural production and distribution." Thussu, *International Communication*, p. 68

6. Metzl, "Popular Democracy," p. 187.

7. Ibid., p. 178.

8. Ibid., p. 186.

9. Joel Bleifuss, "The first stone," *In These Times*, Mar. 20, 2000, p. 2.

10. Ibid.

11. Ibid.

12. Metzl, "Popular diplomacy," p. 182.

13. Ibid, p. 192.

14. Jamie F. Metzl, "Information intervention: When switching channels isn't enough," *Foreign Affairs* (Nov.–Dec. 1997): 15.

15. Jamie F. Metzl, "Rwandan genocide and the international law of radio jamming," *American Journal of International Law* 91, no. 4 (Oct. 1997), p. 1, cited in Alison des Forges, "Silencing the voices of hate in Rwanda," in Monroe E. Price and Mark Thompson, *Forging Peace: Intervention, Human Rights, and the Management of Media Space* (Edinburgh: Edinburgh University Press, 2002).

16. Alison des Forges, *Leave None to Tell the Story: Genocide in Rwanda* (New York: Human Rights Watch, 1998).

17. Frank G. Wisner, Memorandum for Deputy Assistant to the President for National Security Affairs, National Security Council, May 5, 1994. See also, "Intelligence briefing memo" from INR/AA—Janean Mann to AF—Ms. Render, of May 3, 1994, and Chas. W. Freeman Jr., "Memorandum for Director Joint Staff," May 3, 1994; cited in Aes Forges, op.cit., note 15 *supra*.

18. The quotes are from his article in *Foreign Affairs*. Metzl has also contributed his views in the *Human Rights Quarterly*. See Jamie Frederic Metzl, "Metzl response to Ball, Girouard, and Chapman," *Human Rights Quarterly* 19 (1997): 4; Jamie Frederic Metzl, "Information Technology and Human Rights," *Human Rights Quarterly* 18 (1996): 4; Mark Thompson, "Defining information intervention: An interview with Jamie Metzl" in Price and Thompson, eds., *Forging Peace: Intervention, Human Rights, and the Management of Media Space* (Edinburgh: Edinburgh University Press, 2002).

19. *Department of State Bulletin* 39: 337–42 at p. 339. 1958 Statement to the UN, August 1958.

20. For media participation in US overseas interventions, see the following writing on the Gulf War: W. Lance Bennett and David L. Paletz, eds., *Taken by Storm: The Media, Public Opinion, and United States Foreign Policy in the Gulf War* (Chicago: University of Chicago Press, 1994); Philip M. Taylor, *War and the Media: Propaganda and Persuasion in the Gulf War* (Manchester: Manchester University Press, 1998). For the related subject of cyberwar, see John Arquilla and David Ronfeldt, "Cyberwar and netwar: New modes, old concepts of conflict," *Rand Research Review*, fall 1995.

21. For a fuller account, see Mark Thompson and Daniel De Luce, "Escalating to success? The media intervention in Bosnia and Herzegovina," in Price and Thompson, eds., *Forging Peace*. A more extensive discussion of the issues raised in the text can be found at Monroe E. Price, "Information intervention: Bosnia, the Dayton Accords, and the seizure of broadcasting transmitters," *Cornell International Law Journal* 33 (2000): 67.

22. See "Political declaration from ministerial meeting of the steering board of the Peace Implementation Council Sintra, 30 May, 1997." Online [Nov. 27, 2000], available: *http://www.hrt.hr/arhiv/dokumenti/dok/sintra_eng.html*.

23. Memorandum of Agreement for Release of Udrigovo Tower (CQ334489), Sept. 2, 1997 (hereinafter Udrigovo Agreement). Online [Jul. 2001], available: *http://www.ohr.int/ press/p970902a.htm*. See also NATO/Sfor Briefing, Sept. 3, 1997. Online [Apr. 26, 2001], available: *http://www.nato.int/Sfor/trans/1997/t970903a.htm*. A summary of the Agreement is presented at 59 Bulletin, Office of the High Representative, Sept. 5, 1997. Online [Jul. 2001], available: *http://www.ohr.int/bulletins/b970905.htm#5*.

The Agreement was formally signed by Commander of Multinational Division (North) Major-General David Grange, the SRT editor-in-chief, Drago Vukovic, and the Deputy Minister of Interior (and chairman of the board for SRT), General Karisik.

24. "Serb broadcasts resume in North after Sfor handover," BBCSWB, Sept. 5, 1997, available in LEXIS, News Library [Bosnian Serb Radio, Pale, in Serbo-Croat, Sept. 1, 1997].

25. See Udrigovo Agreement, 59 Bulletin, Office of the High Representative, Sept. 5, 1997. Online [Jan. 17, 2001] available: *http://www.ohr.int/bulletins/b970905.htm#5*.

26. "Bosnian Serbs reject demands on SRT," BBC Summary of World Broadcasts, Oct. 17, 1997. World Broadcast Information; Bosnia-Herzegovina; WBI/0042/WB. Source: Beta News Agency, Belgrade, in Serbo-Croat (Oct. 10, 1997).

27. "SRT editor rejects attempts to set up 'protectorate,'" BBC Summary of World Broadcasts (Oct. 17, 1997). World Broadcast Information; Bosnia-Herzegovina; WBI/0042/WB. Source: Beta news agency, Belgrade, in Serbo-Croat (10 Oct. 97).

28. Ever resourceful, Karadzic's faction in Pale figured out yet another way to continue broadcasting. On November 4, they set up an "electronic media" center in eastern Bosnia-Hercegovina, this time in Foca. This "technical and information center" had the capability of broadcasting SRT Pale programs to a significant portion of eastern Bosnia-Hercegovina. This time, because the action did not interfere with the transmission of Banja Luka television, NATO and the OHR did not take action.

29. See Krug and Price, "A module for media intervention: Content regulation in post-conflict zones," in *Forging Peace*; Barry E. Carter and Phillip R. Trimble, eds., *International Law*, 2nd ed. (Boston: Little Brown, 1995), p. 1381.

30. See generally Eyal Benvenisti, *The International Law of Occupation* (Princeton: Princeton University Press, 1993).

31. See, for example, Indar Rikye et al., *The Thin Blue Line: International Peace Keeping and Its Future* (New Haven: Yale University Press, 1974): pp. 24–30.

32. Compare Sharon Korman, *The Right of Conquest* 177 (Oxford: Clarendon Press, 1996), with Benvenisti, *The International Law of Occupation*, pp. 91–93.

33. Donna E. Arzt, "Nuremberg, denazification and democracy: The hate speech problem at the international military tribunal," *New York Law School Journal of Human Rights* 12 (1995): 689, 727; Benvenisti, *The International Law of Occupation*, p. 91.

34. Arzt, "Nuremberg, Denazification and Democracy."

35. William J. Sebald and C. Nelson Spinks, *Japan: Prospects, Options, and Opportunities* (Washington: American Enterprise Institute for Public Policy Research, 1967), p. 17.

36. See, Berlin (Potsdam) Conference, chapter II, sub. A. pt. 10 (1945), reprinted in "The Department of State, Germany 1947–1949, the story in documents" 49 (1950).

37. See, for example, Regulations Respecting the Laws and Customs of War on Land (annexed to 1907 Hague Convention IV), (Oct. 18, 1907), art. 42, 36 Stat. at 2306 [hereinafter Hague Regulations]. There has been debate about the use of the term "occupation" to describe activities of the international community in Bosnia-Hercegovina and debate, as well, over use of the power of the occupier to justify media and information intervention.

38. Hague Regulations, art. 43. The article in its entirety states: "The authority of the legitimate power having in fact passed into the hands of the occupant, the latter shall take all the measures in his power to restore and ensure, as far as possible, public order and [civic life], while respecting, unless absolutely prevented, the laws in force in the country." Ibid.

39. See S.C. Res. 713, U.N. SCOR (1991); S.C. Res. 743, U.C. SCOR (1992); S.C. Res. 770, U.N. SCOR (1992); S.C. Res. 816, U.N. SCOR (1993); S.C. Res. 1031, U.N. SCOR (1995); Dayton Accords, art. IX.

40. See ibid. Annex III. Mary Fulbrook, *The Divided Nation: A History of Germany*, 1918–1990 (Oxford: Oxford University Press, 1992); See also Nigel Foster, *German Law and Legal System* (London: Blackstone Press, 1993).

41. For a valuable review, see "Media and democratization in Bosnia and Herzegovina," *www.imcbih.org;* and International Crisis Group, "Media in Bosnia and Herzegovina: How international support can be more effective," *www.crisisweb.org.*

42. General Accounting Office, "Bosnia peace operation: Mission, structure, and transition strategy of NATO's Stabilization Force" (Letter Report, 10/08/98, GAO/NSIAD-99-19), Online [January 2002] available: *http://www.fas.org/man/gao/nsiad-99-019.htm.*

43. "Serbs and Sfor agree to return transmitters," BBCSWB (Apr. 17, 1998), available in LEXIS, News Library [Radio St. John, Pale, in Serbo-Croat, Apr. 14, 1998].

44. Brian Loader, ed., *The Governance of Cyberspace: Politics, Technology and Global Restructuring* (London: Routledge, 1997).

45. See Thomas Friedman, "Digital defense," *New York Times*, Jul. 27, 2001. ("Bush missile defense plan is geared to defending the country from a rogue who might fire a missile over our walls. But the more likely threat is from a cyberterrorist who tries to sabotage our webs. The more tightly we get woven together, the more we become dependent on networks, the more a single act of terrorism can unleash serious chaos.") See also Mark T. Pasko, "Re-defining national security in the technology age: The encryption export debate," *Journal of Legislation* 26 (2000): 337.

46. Mark G. Tratos, "Symposium: Gaming on the Internet" *Stanford Journal of Law, Business, and Finance* 3 (1997): 101.

47. See, for example, Jessica Litman, *Digital Copyright: Protecting Intellectual Property on the Internet* (Buffalo, NY: Prometheus Books, 2001); Susan Mort, "The WTO, WIPO and the Internet: Confounding the borders of copyright and neighboring rights," *Fordham Intellectual Property, Media and Entertainment Law Journal* 8: (1997): 173.

48. See, as an example of this literature, Stephan Haggard and Robert R. Kaufman, *The Political Economy of Democratic Transitions* (Princeton: Princeton University Press, 1995).

49. Brian Atwood, "Midwife to democracy: The not-so-ugly American," *New Perspectives Quarterly* 13 (1996): 20. "We promote democracy because it is the right thing to do and because it enhances global stability and economic growth. A stable, growing world economy creates American jobs, keeps America out of war." Atwood was the administrator of the US Agency for International Development.

50. NAFTA followed the earlier United States–Canada Free Trade Agreement, Jan. 2, 1988, *International Law Materials* 27 (1988): 281, at art. 2005, in not covering trade in cultural products. North American Free Trade Agreement, Dec. 17, 1992, *International Law Materials* 32 (1993): 289, p. 2106, annex 2106.

51. The US position has a long history. From about 1975 to 1983, a highly emotional dispute between the United States and many developing nations burst forth over the distribution of information from the North to the South. A New World Information and Communication Order, inscribed in the MacBride Report, became an object of US scorn, and ultimately led to US abandoning the United Nations Educational Social and Cultural Organization (UNESCO) which had sponsored and promoted the MacBride Report. See Colleen Roach, "American textbooks v NWICO History," in George Gerbner, ed., *The Global Media Debate: Its Rise, Fall, and Renewal*, (Westport, CT: Ablex Publishing, 1993), pp. 35, 43–46.

52. See M. E. Footer and C. B. Graber, "Trade liberalisation and cultural policy," *Journal of International Economic Law* 3 (2000): 115–44; P. Schlesinger, "From cultural defence to political culture: Media, politics and collective identity in the European Union," *Media, Culture and Society* 19 (1997): 360–91.

53. Thomas M. Murray, "The United States dispute over GATT treatment of audiovisual products and the limits of public choice theory," *Maryland Journal of International Law and Trade* 21 (1997): 203, at n. 13. Steven S. Wildman and Stephen E. Siwek, *International Trade in Films and Television Programs* 1 (Washington: American Enterprise Institute, 1988).

54. An important round resulted in a World Trade Organization panel and appellate board decision holding that Canadian laws protecting its magazine industry violate older provisions of GATT, a legal attack adopted by the United States after Canada had carefully assured that its policy would not be covered by NAFTA. World Trade Organization Report of the Appellate Body, *Canada Certain Measures Concerning Periodicals*, Jun. 30, 1997, available in 1997 WL 398913.

55. See C. Edwin Baker, *Media, Markets, and Democracy* (Cambridge: Cambridge University Press 2001). See, for example, Robin L. Van Harpen, Note, "Mamas, don't let your babies grow up to be cowboys: Reconciling trade and cultural independence," *Minnesota Journal of Global Trade* 4 (1995): 165, 187–89; Fred H. Cate, "The First Amendment and the international free flow of information," *Virginia Journal of International Law* 30 (1990): 371, 407. Examining the rhetoric of the debate, Baker notes, "Interestingly, despite the

similarity of many of the issues—that is, national attempts to assure a rich local communications order in the face of global market forces—the United States routinely invoked First Amendment values—freedom of information and freedom of the press—to attack UNESCO while changing to an economic parlance to oppose Europe and Canada in the dispute about cultural products."

56. Marc Raboy, *Communication and Globalization—A Challenge for Public Policy* (Toronto: University of Toronto Press, forthcoming).

57. See Oliver Boyd-Barrett, "Media imperialism: Towards an international framework for the analysis of media systems," in J. Curran, M. Gurevitch, and J. Woollacott, eds, *Mass Communications and Society* (London: Edward Arnold, 1997) p. 117. (Calling media imperialism, "the process whereby the ownership, structure, distribution or content of the media in any one country are singly or together subject to substantial external pressures from the media interests of any other country or countries, without proportionate reciprocation of influence by the country so affected.")

58. According to the World Trade Organization, TRIPs is "to date the most comprehensive multilateral agreement on intellectual property." It covers: "copyright and related rights (i.e., the rights of performers, producers of sound recordings and broadcasting organizations); trademarks including service marks; geographical indications including appellations of origin; industrial designs; patents including the protection of new varieties of plants; the layout-designs of integrated circuits; and undisclosed information including trade secrets and test data." Its activities lie in setting standards, enforcement, and settling disputes. See *http://www.wto.org/english/tratop_e/trips_e/trips_e.htm* for more information. See the World Intellectual Property Organization (WIPO) Web site for information on numerous international treaties governing IPR, *http://www.wipo.int/about-wipo/en/index.html? wipo_content_frame=http://www.wipo.int/about-wipo/en/gib.htm*. John H. Barton, "Economics of TRIPs: International trade in information-intensive products," *George Washington International Law Review* 33 (2001): 473.

59. Neil Weinstock Netanel, "Asserting copyright's democratic principles in the global arena," *Vanderbilt Law Review* 51 (Mar. 1998): 217; see also Marci A. Hamilton, "The TRIPs agreement: Imperialistic, outdated, and overprotective," *Vanderbilt Journal of Transnational Law* 29 (1996): 613, 620–33.

60. Netanel contends that "the notion that upward harmonization under TRIPs will contribute to global democracy is seriously misguided. Copyright's constitutive value for democratic development depends heavily on local circumstances. Indeed, copyright may sometimes impede democratisation unless substantial limits are placed on copyright holder rights."

61. Bruce Lehman, Testimony at Hearing of the International Economic Policy and Trade Committee of the House International Relations Committee, May 21, 1998.

62. J. H. Reichman and David Lange, "Bargaining around the TRIPs agreement: The case for ongoing public-private initiatives to facilitate worldwide intellectual property transactions," *Duke Journal of Comparative and International Law* 9 (1998): 11.

63. There are solutions, consistent with copyright protection, for encouraging programming in such contexts. These include benign neglect of copyright violations or subsidy.

64. The literature on transitions and assistance is vast. See, for example, Geoffrey Pridham, ed., *Transitions to Democracy: Comparative Perspectives from Southern Europe, Latin America and Eastern Europe* (Aldershot, UK: Dartmouth, 1995); Adam Przeworski, *Sustainable Democracy* (Cambridge: Cambridge University Press, 1995); Juan J. Linz and Alfred C. Stepan, *Problems of Democratic Transition and Consolidation: Southern Europe, South America, and Post-Communist Europe* (Baltimore: Johns Hopkins University Press, 1996). A trenchant review of the critical literature is contained in Amy L. Chua, "Markets, democracy, and ethnicity: Toward a new paradigm of law and development," *Yale Law Journal* 108 (1998): 1.

65. See Ann Hudock, *The Role of Media in Democracy: A Strategic Approach* (Washington: USAID Center for Democracy and Governance, 1999).

66. "Independent media development," USAID, Bureau for Europe and Eurasia, Office of Democracy and Governance (Oct. 4, 2000).

67. The listing was made before the death of Croatian President Franjo Tudjman and the fall of former Serbian President, Slobodan Milosevic.

68. See Monroe E. Price and Peter Krug, *The Enabling Environment for Free and Independent Media* (Washington: US Agency for International Development, Office of Democracy and Governance, 2002). Online [January 2002] available: *http://www.usaid.gov/democracy/pdfs/pnacm006.pdf*.

69. The study was done together with the author of this book. See Price, Rozumilowicz, and Verhulst, *Media Reform*.

70. Richard Falk, "The nuclear weapons advisory opinion and the new jurisprudence of global civil society," *Transnational Law and Contemporary Problems* 7 (1997): 333, 335.

71. See Julie Mertus, "From legal transplants to transformative justice: Human rights and the promise of transnational civil society," *American University International Law Review* 14 (1999): 1342.

72. See Benedict Kingsbury, "The concept of compliance as a function of competing conceptions of international law," *Michigan Journal of International Law* 19 (1994): 345, 357. (discussing new "liberal" theories of international law). Mertus, "From legal transplants to transformative justice," pp. 1347–48.

73. A much-cited, strongly opinionated study is Janine Wedel, *Collision and Collusion: The Strange Case of Western Aid to Eastern Europe 1989–1998*, (New York: St. Martins, 1998); see also Frances H. Foster, "Information and the problem of democracy: The Russian experience," *American Journal of Comparative Law* 44 (1996): 243.

74. See, for example, Marina Ottoway and Thomas Carothers, eds., *Funding Virtue: Civil Society Aid and Democracy Promotion* (Washington: Carnegie Endowment for International Peace, 2000).

Chapter 8

1. For treatments of legal questions raised by aspects of international broadcasting, see Leo Gross, "Some international law aspects of the freedom of information and the right to communicate," in Kaarle Nordenstreng and Herbert I. Schiller, eds., *National Sovereignty and*

International Communication, (Norwood, NJ: Ablex, 1979), 208–209. See Bhagevatula Satyanarayana Murty, *Propaganda and World Public Order: The Legal Regulation of the Ideological Instrument of Coercion* (New Haven: Yale University Press, 1968; reissued as *The International Law of Propaganda*, 1989); David Marks, "Broadcasting across the wall: The free flow of information between East and West Germany," *Journal of Communication* 33 (1983). See also John L. Martin, *International Propaganda: Its Legal and Diplomatic Control* (Minneapolis: University of Minnesota Press, 1958; reprint, 1969). Much of this material is cited in Stephen D. Krasner, "Global communications and national power: Life on the Pareto frontier," *World Politics* 43, no. 3 (1991): 336–466, 344, to support his argument that the few international agreements that deal with international broadcasting "are filled with the kind of confusing and contradictory language that betrays underlying disagreements about principles and norms." Legal issues are also canvassed in Jamie Frederic Metzl, "Rwandan genocide and the international law of radio jamming," *American Journal of International Law* 91 (1997): 628.

2. Gary Rawnsley has made this distinction: "Public diplomacy and media diplomacy are frequently used as interchangeable terms. [But] public diplomacy is specifically targeted at a mass audience, based on the supposition that public opinion can exert considerable influence on their governments and political systems. . . . Media diplomacy is much more selective and aims to address a particular government or regime directly with a view to persuading it to modify its diplomatic position or behavior." Rawnsley uses the following example: "BBC broadcasts in English targeted at the Soviet Union during the Cold War were never 'jammed'. . . . This suggests that the Kremlin, complete with its own monitoring organization, depended upon the BBC as a reliable source of diplomatic news, information and intelligence and, of course, as a means by which the Soviets could learn how they and their policies were being presented and received in the West." Gary Rawnsley, *Media Diplomacy: Monitored Broadcasts and Foreign Policy* 4 (Leicester, UK: Centre for the Study of Diplomacy, University of Leicester 1996). One example of a study of this process, marked by its reliance on the work of Herbert Schiller, is Fred Fejes, *Imperialism, Media and the Good Neighbor: New Deal Foreign Policy and United States Shortwave Broadcasting to Latin America* (Norwood, NJ: Ablex Publishing, 1984).

3. Martin, *International Propaganda*.

4. See Fouad Ajami, "What the Muslim world is watching," *New York Times Magazine*, Nov. 18, 2001, p. 48.

5. These questions of style touch on ways the American approach to international broadcasting is different, for example, from that of the United Kingdom. US international broadcasting, as the chapter later probes, was evolving into a cluster of aggressive broadcasters with specific sectoral managements. There are those who favored a television broadcasting system that emulates the BBC World Service as a unified source of reliable, factual, and dispassionate information over this cluster approach. Also, under its latest reorganization, the VOA, together with the external radios, are subject to the Broadcasting Board of Governors, as indicated, many of whom are political appointees. Many of the members in the 1990s were advocates of the ethos of surrogacy and policy-driven radio on the VOA. One member was appointed to protect Radio and TV Marti in order to ensure that the Cuban exile community was served.

The advocates of a unified "objective" broadcaster also consider that the pressure to transform into the surrogate function and to have a specific national political objective is destructive to the ability of the VOA to perform its functions. They consider that the proliferation of Radios leads to the gratuitous duplication of resources and the use of those resources in ways that compromise the "objectivity" of the US international broadcasters.

6. See Elzbieta Olechowska and Howard Aster, *Challenges for International Broadcasting V* (Oakville, CA: Mosaic, 1998); David M. Abshire, *International Broadcasting: A New Dimension Of Western Diplomacy* (Beverly Hills, CA: Sage, 1976); Philo C. Wasburn, *Broadcasting Propaganda: International Radio Broadcasting and the Construction of Political Reality* (Westport, CT: Praeger, 1992). There are many other books that deal with these questions. See, for example, Michael Nelson, *War of the Black Heavens: The Battles of Western Broadcasting in the Cold War* (Syracuse, NY: Syracuse University Press, 1997); Philip M. Taylor, *War and the Media: Propaganda and Persuasion in the Gulf War* (Manchester: Manchester University Press, 1992); W. Lance Bennett and David L. Paletz, *Taken by Storm: The Media, Public Opinion and US Foreign Policy* (Chicago: Chicago University Press, 1994); Yoel Cohen, *Media Diplomacy: The Foreign Office in the Mass Communication Age* (London: Frank Cass, 1986); James O. H. Nason, "International Broadcasting as an Instrument of Foreign Policy," *Millennium* 6 (1977); Olive Renier and Vladimir Rubinstein, *Assigned to Listen: The Evesham Experience 1939–1943* (London: BBC External Services, 1986).

7. See Mark Hopkins, "A babel of broadcasts," *Columbia Journalism Review* (Jul. 1999): 44.

8. Michael Nelson, *War of the Black Heavens.*

9. Mark Hopkins, "A babel of broadcasts."

10. Harold D. Lasswell, *Propaganda Technique in the World War* 14 (New York: Knopf, 1927).

11. "China accuses BBC of launching 'invasion'" BBC Worldwide Monitoring, Aug. 5, 1999; Source: *Zhongliu*', Beijing, in Chinese, Jun. 12, 1999.

12. "China accuses BBC of launching 'invasion'"

13. Jon T. Powell, "Towards a negotiable definition of propaganda for international agreements related to direct broadcast satellites," *Law and Contemporary Problems* 45 (1982): 3, 25–26.

14. John B. Whitton and Arthur D. Larson, *Propaganda towards Disarmament in the War of Words* (Dobbs Ferry, NY: World Rule of Law Center, Duke University, 1964), 210.

15. Martin, *International Propaganda* 87, p. 223.

16. Bruce Kessler, "Politics among the airwaves: An analysis of Soviet and Western perspectives on international broadcasting and the right to exchange ideas and information regardless of frontiers," *Houston Journal of International Law* 7 (1985): 237, 248.

17. Stephen D. Bayer, "The legal aspects of TV Marti in relation to the law of direct broadcasting satellites," *Emory Law Journal* 41 (1992): 541; see also Omar Javier Arcia, "War over the airwaves: A comparative analysis of US and Cuban views on international law and policy governing transnational broadcasts," *Journal of Transnational Law and Policy* 5 (1996): 199; L. Alexandre, "Television Marti: 'Open skies' over the South," in K.

Nordenstreng and Herber Schiller, eds., *Beyond National Sovereignty*, (Norwood, NJ: Ablex Publishing 1993).

18. US House Committee on Foreign Affairs, Department of State Under Secretary for Security Assistance, Science and Technology James L. Buckley's testimony, *Region 2 Administrative Radio Conference on Medium Wave Frequency (MF) Broadcasting: Hearings before the Subcommittee on International Operations of the House Committee on Foreign Affairs*, 97th Cong., 4th sess., 1981.

19. Radio Broadcasting to Cuba Act sec. 2, 3(b), H. 7677.

20. "New operator of Aussie TV to be decided soon," *Jakarta Post*, Apr. 9, 2001.

21. To maintain and reinforce its service, the management at Radio Canada International made a conscious decision to be part of "Team Canada." These are assortments of business and industrial leaders sent to various countries to promote goods and services. RCI determined that Team Canada activities, "rather than just being a news story, were an integral part of reflecting what's happening in Canada." "Radio Canada International plans for 1999," BBC Summary of World Broadcasts, Jan. 1, 1999, World Broadcast Information, China, WBI/0001/WB; Source: Voice of America, 19 December 1998.

22. "DW services and staff cuts outlined," BBC Summary of World Broadcasts, Oct. 15, 1999, World Broadcast Information, WBI/0042/WB; Source: Deutsche Welle press release, Cologne, in German, Oct. 7, 1999.

23. John Tusa, "Media: Britannia rules the airwaves," *The Independent*, Dec. 9, 1992, p. 19.

24. Peter Popham, "The empire talks back," *Independent Magazine*, Jan. 17 1996, 2.

25. CNN broadcasts largely in English, though that was changing. British and US international broadcasters broadcast in more than 65 languages and reach mass audiences (more than 200 million readers/listeners/viewers a week), not just the affluent that can afford television. See Don M. Flournoy and Robert K. Stewart, *CNN: Making News in the Global Market* (Luton: University of Luton Press, 1997).

26. United States International Broadcasting Act, Pub. L. No. 103–236, title. III.

27. VOA has been broadcasting to Iraq in Arabic for more than half a century and to Iran in a restored Farsi service since 1979.

28. "Details of new radio democracy for Africa," Voice of America broadcast, April 11, 1998; reprinted in World Broadcast Information, Apr. 17, 1998, Lexis News Library, BBCSWB file.

29. United States Code, title 22, sec. 6211.

30. This section is based on research done by Dr. Michael Likosky during graduate work at the Centre for Socio-Legal Studies, University of Oxford.

31. As a historic matter, a surrogate service directed at China had previously existed from 1951 to 1953. "Radio Free Asia, an allegedly public-supported (but in reality, CIA-financed) international broadcasting station operated out of San Francisco, but transmitting from Manila, was founded. Its dual mission was to strengthen resistance within China to the new communist government plus prevent overseas China in Asia from 'falling victim to

communist Chinese propaganda.'" John A. Lent, ed., *Broadcasting in Asia and the Pacific: A Continental Survey of Radio and Television* (Philadelphia: Temple University Press, 1978). The creation of RFA was once again debated during the Vietnam War. CRS Report for Congress, *Radio Free Asia*, Jan. 2, 1997.

32. James Rosenau, ed., *Domestic Sources of Foreign Policy* (New York: Free Press, 1967).

33. US Advisory Commission on Public Diplomacy, *Diplomacy in the Information Age*, (Washington: GPO, 1993), p. 15.

34. *Diplomacy in the Information Age*, p. 30.

35. *Diplomacy in the Information Age*, p. 26.

36. *Diplomacy in the Information Age*. The Commission established by President Bush summarized the argument as follows: "China's growing participation in the global economy's already having the effect of opening its society to outside influences, with inevitable demands for increased democracy. We encourage these trends but the creation of a new and separate "surrogate" broadcasting system—which would be seen as a hostile American act—is not an effective means of accomplishing that objective."

37. *Diplomacy in the Information Age*, p. 26.

38. *Diplomacy in the Information Age*.

39. US Senate, Senator Biden of Delaware, 103rd Cong., 2nd sess., *Congressional Record*, vol. 140, S4819-02, S2420.

40. US House of Representatives, Congressman Porter of Illinois, 103rd Cong., 2nd sess., *Congressional Record*, vol. 140, 5113-04, H5125. Congressman Smith argued for the primacy of ideas as follows: "Just let me say that throughout human history, the most important battles have not been those whose object was to control territory. The battles that really matter have always been about values and ideas. When the history of our century is written it will be large part the story of a long struggle for the soul of the world, the struggle between the values of the free world on the one hand and those of communism, fascism, and other forms of totalitarianism on the other. Throughout most of the world, the values of the free world have been victorious, not only because we had better values but also because we were not afraid to stand up for them." US House of Representatives, Congressman Smith of New Jersey, 104th Cong., 2nd sess., *Congressional Record*, vol. 142, H8215-03, H8228 (1994).

41. US House of Representatives, Congressman Bentley of Michigan, 103rd Congr., 2nd sess., *Congressional Record*, vol. 140, H5125.

42. Ibid. See also Porter, *Congressional Record*, vol. 140, H5131. Such a strategic stance was discussed in particular countries contexts; for instance, Cambodia, Vietnam, and North Korea, as articulated by Bentley, H5125–H5126: "In Cambodia, 15 months after historic elections were held, the Chinese-backed Khmer Rouge were again on the offensive—waging war over the airwaves as inflammatory news broadcasts by Pol Pot's forces need only refer to the Foreign Broadcast Information Service reports that many of our offices receive on a daily basis. The growing political chaos, fueled by Khmer Rouge broadcasts, should be of serious concern to all who remember what happened inside Cambodia from 1975–1978. Radio Free Asia can play a positive role in helping Cambodia consolidate its tentative move toward democracy that is in danger of being suppressed again by the murderous Khmer Rouge.

"In Vietnam, a country of 70 million people, the VOA broadcasts 2½ hours a day—certainly not enough for a country of such pivotal regional importance. In Vietnam, economic liberalization has not necessarily been followed by political liberalization. Yet, although the Vietnamese Government continues to prohibit free expression, there has been a range of nascent, democratic activities that must be nourished through access to a Radio Free Asia. Although the Congress has lifted economic sanctions, we must not falsely assume that trade, by itself, will foster democracy. While the VOA gives these countries a window to world events, a Radio Free Asia will address a full and fair colloquy of events of the day within each country and culture.

"Then, there is the case of North Korea, a closed, militaristic society that has the potential to foment major instability throughout the region. In a closed society such as North Korea, international radio broadcasting is extremely important for another key reason—communication with the ruling elite. Contrary to the belief that North Korean leaders are of only one mind, we know from past events that there are moderate as well as hard-line factions. Make no mistake about it, members of the ruling elite can and do listen to international radio broadcasts—perhaps behind closed doors—but listening nonetheless. Kim Il-song will not live forever, and the succession is not clear. Through Radio Free Asia, we can implant the notion that a peaceful future is possible, with as much as the North Korean elite as can be reached. Must we wait for the outbreak of a second war on the Korean Peninsula before recognizing the need for a Radio Free Asia?"

43. Congressman Hughes of New Jersey, *Congressional Record*, vol. 140.

44. Ibid. And Congressman Smith of New Jersey, *Congressional Record*, vol. 142, H5113-04 and H5125.

45. *United States International Broadcasting Act of 1994*, US Code Annotated, title 22, sec. 6201 et seq. (1994).

46. *United States International Broadcasting Act of 1994*, US Code Annotated, title 22, sec. 6201 et seq. (1994).

47. Ibid., sec. 6208, para. (a)1. In order to receive a grant, the Congress required that the Board submit "to Congress a detailed plan for the establishment and operation of Radio Free Asia." Ibid., sec. 6208, para. (c)1. This plan must include how RFA will meet its funding limitations, the number and qualifications of its employees, and how it will meet its technical capabilities. Ibid., sec. 6208, para. (c)1(A), (B) and (C).

48. Ibid. Sec. 6208, para. (b)1 and (b)2.

49. President, Executive Order 12850, "Conditions for renewal of Most-Favored-Nation Status for the People's Republic of China in 1994," *Federal Register* 58, no. 31327 (May 28, 1993), Code of Federal Regulations, title 3, 606–607, sec. 1(b).

50. President's Letter to Congressional Leaders on Most-Favored Nation Trade Status for China, *Weekly Compilation of Presidential Documents* 20 (June 2, 1994): 1203.

51. The authorizing law stated: "such broadcast service shall be referred to as Radio Free Asia." CRS Report, 5.

52. The first RFA broadcast took place on September 29, 1996, broadcasting into China in Mandarin. The initial broadcasts of one hour at 7:00 a.m. and one hour at 11:00 p.m.

included regional news and feature stories. The 7:00 a.m. broadcasts consisted of a half-hour program that is repeated at 7:30 a.m., 11:00 p.m., and 11:30 p.m., with updated news added to each half hour. Broadcasting into China was expected to double by the end of the 1996 calendar year. CRS Report, 3.

53. US Code, title 22, sec. 6201, para. 1.

54. "Hanoi accuses RFA of 'cultural colonialism,'" Voice of Vietnam External Service broadcast, Oct. 4, 1996; reprinted in *World Broadcast Information*, Oct. 11, 1996; Lexis News Library, BBCSWB file.

55. Mure Disckie, "China media lambast US over propaganda politics," *Reuters World Service*, Nov. 1, 1996.

56. "China accuses BBC of launching 'invasion,'" BBC Worldwide Monitouing, Aug. 5, 1999. Source: *Zhongliu', Beijing*, in Chinese, Jun. 12, 1999.

57. "Foreign ministry spokesman berates plan for Radio Free Asia," Central Broadcasting Station broadcast, Feb. 1, 1994; reprinted in *World Broadcast Information*, Feb. 2, 1994, Lexis News Library, BBCSWB file.

58. "Radio condemns US plan to set up Radio Free Asia," broadcast from Central Broadcasting Station, Oct. 11, 1996, reprinted in *World Broadcast Information*, Oct. 25, 1996, available in Lexis News Library, BBCSWB file.

59. "Vietnamese newspaper raps US Radio," *Xinhua News Agency*, Dec. 7, 1996.

60. "Radio says revival of Radio Free Asia violates international law," Voice of Vietnam broadcast, Dec. 4, 1996; reprinted in *World Broadcast Information*, Dec. 7, 1996, Lexis News Library, BBCSWB file.

61. "Cold war remembered as Hanoi blasts US radio," *Reuters World Service*, Dec. 10, 1996.

62. See Metzl, "Rwandan genocide."

63. "Government plans to ban US-funded RFA criticized," *Samleng Yuveakchon Khmer*, Apr. 8, 1999; reprinted in *World Broadcast Information*, Apr. 23, 1999, Lexis News Library, BBCSWB file.

64. "Government plans to ban US-funded RFA criticized."

65. See Linda Kirschke, "Organization, broadcasting genocide: Censorship, propaganda and state sponsored violence in Rwanda 1990–1994" (London: Article 19/International Center against Censorship, 1996).

66. "BBC on FM in Navroli," BBC World Service Press Release, Mar. 24, 1998.

67. Sufficiently similar to be cited here was the decision of Israel to destroy the building of the Palestinian Broadcasting Corporation in January 2002. Palestinian leaders and international media watchdogs condemned the Israeli attack on the Ramallah headquarters. Israel had contended that Palestinian radio and television incited violence. The destruction of the Palestinian broadcasting headquarters renewed a debate on the propriety of attacking civilian-operated media outlets. "Analysis: Israel destroys Palestinian broadcasting HQ in West Bank," BBC Summary of World Broadcasts (Jan. 24, 2002): BBC Monitoring Research.

68. Of course, this was during an armed intervention. See "Eutelsat decision 'culmination of hypocrisy'," *Tanjug News Agency*, May 27, 1999; reprinted in *World Broadcast Information*, Jun. 4, 1999, Lexis News Library, BBCSWB file.

69. "USA 'embittered' by RTS broadcasts on Israeli satellite," BBC Summary of World Broadcasts, Nov. 12, 1999: *World Broadcast Information*; Yugoslavia/Israel/USA; WBI/0046/WB. Source: Monitoring research (Nov. 4, 99).

70. "USA 'embittered' by RTS broadcasts."

71. See Olechowska and Aster, *Challenges for International Broadcasting V*, pp. 214–57.

72. Hopkins, "A babel of broadcasts."

73. Several hundred thousand homes in Yugoslavia were equipped with satellite dishes capable of receiving international TV signals independently of local cable or terrestrial channels controlled by the government.

74. "Information Minister defends relay ban," Tanjug News Agency, Oct. 10, 1998; reprinted in *World Broadcast Information*, Oct. 16, 1998, Lexis News Library, BBCSWB file.

75. "US to surround Serbia with FM transmitters," Voice of America broadcast, Apr. 10, 1999; reprinted in *World Broadcast Information*, Apr. 16, 1999, Lexis News Library, BBCSWB file.

76. "BBC World Service to cut back broadcasts," *Daily Telegraph*, May 26, 2001.

77. On the military side, an RMA occurred when there was a fundamental shift in the nature of warfare brought about by a radical change in technologies accompanied by a change in military doctrine and organizational and operational concepts. See MacGregor Knox and Williamson Murray, *The Dynamics of Military Revolution: 1300–2050* (Cambridge: Cambridge University Press, 2001); James Der Derian, *Virtuous War: Mapping the Military–Industrial–Media–Entertainment Network* (Boulder, CO: Westview Press, 2001).

78. Public Law 94–350, Jul. 12, 1976.

79. The other two principles were as follows: (2) VOA will represent America, not any single segment of American society, and will therefore present a balanced and comprehensive projection of significant American thought and institutions, and (3) VOA will present the policies of the United States clearly and effectively, and will also present responsible discussions and opinion on these policies. Note the innate conflict between the third principle and the first.

80. William Safire, "Equal time for Hitler," *The New York Times*, Sept. 20, 2001, p. 31.

81. An account of the event was presented by the VOA itself: "VOA originally planned to air the [Mullah Omar] report on September 21. The State Department typically does not see VOA reports in advance of their broadcast. Somehow State Department officials found out about this story and objected vehemently to some members of the Broadcasting Board of Governors, which oversees all US government international broadcasting. VOA senior management decided to hold the story pending an interview with the former Afghan king and other experts. Most VOA employees learned about this incident last Sunday, September 23, when they read about it in the *Washington Post*. This past week, over 200 VOA journalists and broadcasters signed a petition which began with a statement made on VOA's first day of broadcasting, February 24, 1942, during World War II. 'Daily at the time, we shall speak to you about America and the war—the news may be good or bad—we shall tell you the truth.' The petition concluded: 'This censorship sets a most unfortunate precedent and damages our credibility with our worldwide audience.'" Voice of America, "USA/ Afghanistan: State Department's 'regret' at VOA's Taleban interview," BBC Monitoring World Media, Oct. 1.

82. Congressman Ed Royce, Press Release, Nov. 7, 2001.

83. "US dials up radio network to reach young Muslims," *Wall Street Journal*, Nov. 27, 2001, p. A24.

84. Statement of Norman J. Pattiz, "Rethinking US public diplomacy," Committee on International Relations, United States Congress, Nov. 14, 2001. All quotes by Mr. Pattiz in this section are from this Statement.

85. "Moscow's music radio glasnost," *Music and Media*, Aug. 25, 2001, p. 7.

86. Letter from Graham Spry, 1931, quoted in Robert M. McChesney, "Graham Spry and the future of public broadcasting," *Canadian Journal of Communications* 24 (1999).

Chapter 9

1. For an excellent inquiry into the resilient powers of authoritarian states, see Shanthi Kalathil and Taylor C. Boas, *The Internet and State Control in Authoritarian Regimes: China, Cuba and the Counterrevolution*, Working Papers (Washington: Carnegie Endowment for International Peace 2001).

2. Quoted in John B. Whitton, *American Journal of International Law* 52 (1958); 739, 741 "Radio propaganda—A modest proposal," also U. N. Doc. E/CN.4.Sub. 1/105 p. 29.

3. *Annals of the Organization of American States* 1 (1949): 77; *American Journal of International Law* Supp 46 (1952).

4. Just a few of the resources for this subject include: National Research Council (US), Committee on Intellectual Property Rights and the Emerging Information Infrastructure, *The Digital Dilemma: Intellectual Property in the Information Age* (Washington: National Academy Press, 2000); M. Ethan Katsh, *Law in a Digital World* (Oxford: Oxford University Press, 1995); Mike Godwin, *Cyber Rights: Defending Free Speech in the Digital Age* (New York: Times Books, 1998); Curtis E. A. Karnow, *Future Codes: Essays in Advanced Computer Technology and the Law* (Boston: Artech House, 1997); Eric Handelman, "Comment: Obscenity and the Internet: Does the current obscenity standard provide individuals with the proper constitutional safeguards?" *Albany Law Review* 59 (1995): 709; "The state of the First Amendment at the approach of the millennium: Symposium: Rationales and rationalizations." *The Catholic University of America Commlaw Conspectus* 5 (Summer 1997); Bruce W. Sanford and Michael J. Lorenger, "Symposium: Teaching an old dog new tricks: The First Amendment in an online world," *Connecticut Law Review* *Connecticut Law Review* 28 (Summer 1996): 1137.

5. The President's Commission on Critical Infrastructure Protection was established in July 1996 by Presidential Executive Order 13010. It was "tasked to formulate a comprehensive national strategy for protecting the infrastructures we all depend on from physical and cyber threats." Infrastructures addressed by the commission include: telecommunications, electrical power systems, gas and oil, banking and finance, transportation, water supply systems, government services and emergency services. See: *http://www.info-sec.com/pccip/web*.

6. An example of concern about the meaning of stated reasons is the resolution of an Article 19 meeting in November, 1999 in London, involving three international governmental offi-

cials with the kind of brief that is more common now. They were Santiago Canton, OAS special rapporteur on freedom of expression; Freimut Duve, OSCE representative on freedom of the media; Abid Hussain, UN special rapporteur on freedom of opinion and expression. Among the conclusions of the meeting were the following:

Restrictions on freedom of expression in the name of public order and national security should be imposed only where there is a real risk of harm to a legitimate interest. Restrictions purporting to serve public order and national security interests are often excessively broad and vague. To ensure that such restrictions do not exert an excessive chilling effect on freedom of expression, they should not be imposed unless they meet the conditions set out in the Johannesburg Principles on National Security, Freedom of Expression and Access to Information, including the following: there is a significant risk of imminent harm; the risk is of serious harm, that is to say violence or other unlawful action; there is a close causal link between the risk of harm and the expression; the expression was made with the intention of causing the harm.

7. See, for example, the incorporation of these standards into the normative base of the Dayton Accords and reliance upon them by the temporary media commissioner and the media appeals board in Kosovo. Peter Krug and Monroe Price, "A module for media intervention: Content regulation in post-conflict zones," in Monroe E. Price and Mark Thompson, eds., *Forging Peace.*

8. Lee C. Bollinger, *Images of a Free Press* (Chicago: University of Chicago Press, 1991); Lee C. Bollinger, "Freedom of the press and public access: Toward a theory of partial regulation of the mass media," *Michigan Law Review* 75 (1976): 1.

9. In the case of *FCC v. Pacifica* five members of the Supreme Court upheld the FCC's decision to prohibit a broadcast with inappropriate language during the hours when children could be listening. Justice Stevens stated in his plurality opinion that "among the reasons for specially treating indecent broadcasting is the uniquely pervasive presence that medium of expression occupies in the lives of our people. . . . Broadcasting, moreover, is uniquely accessible to children." See *Federal Communications Commission v. Pacifica Foundation et al*, 438 US 726 (1978).

10. In 1995, after a cricket league attempted to give broadcasting rights to its events to the broadcaster of its choice, the Indian Supreme Court ruled that broadcasting airwaves were the property of the people and should not be governed by any sort of monopoly, state, individual, or organization. The Court held that, "The Central Government shall take immediate steps to establish an independent autonomous public authority representative of all sections and interests in the society to control and regulate the use of the airwaves." *Secretary, Ministry of Info. and Broad. v. Cricket Ass'n of Bengal* (1995) 2 S.C.C. 161.

11. Peter Krug and Monroe E. Price, "A module for media intervention: Content regulation in post-conflict zones" in *Forging Peace.*

12. See, for example, Lawrence Lessig, *Code and Other Laws of Cyberspace* (New York: Basic Books, 1999); Helen Nissenbaum, "How computer systems embody values," *Computer* 34 (2001): 120; L. Introna and H. Nissenbaum, "Shaping the Web: Why the politics of search engines matters," *Information Society* 16 no. 3 (2000): 1–17.

13. For more about cyberwar, see John Arquilla and David Ronfeldt, "Cyberwar and netwar: New modes, old concepts of conflict," *Rand Research Review*, fall 1995.

14. US Department of the Army, Field Manual 33-1, *Psychological Operations* (Washington: GPO, 1992), p. 12.

15. See Julian Borger, "Cyberwar could spare bombs; Nato commander Wesley Clark boosts the case for telecom assaults with a vision of how they might have been used in Kosovo," *The Guardian*, Nov. 5, 1999, p. 17.

16. See Stephen D. Krasner, "Global communications and national power: Life on the Pareto frontier," *World Politics* 43, no. 3 (Apr. 1991): 336–66 at pp. 336–37. "The level of conflict has varied according to whether states were dealing with pure co-ordination problems or with co-ordination problems that had distributional consequences. The resolution of the former has caused little conflict because the purpose of the regime has been to avoid mutually undesirable outcomes." Ibid.

17. Indrajit Banerjee, "Broadcasting, convergence and cultural policy: Critical issues and implications in Malaysia and Singapore," *Culturelink Review* (Spring 2001): 73.

18. Tim Golden, "Crisis deepens impact of Arab TV news," *The New York Times*, Apr. 16, 2002, p. 16.

Index